A Writer's Reader

A WRITER'S READER

FIFTH EDITION

Donald Hall

D. L. Emblen
Santa Rosa Junior College

SCOTT, FORESMAN/LITTLE, BROWN COLLEGE DIVISION
SCOTT, FORESMAN AND COMPANY
Glenview, Illinois   Boston   London

1988

Library of Congress Cataloging-in-Publication Data

A Writer's reader / [edited] by D.L. Emblen, Donald Hall. — 5th ed.
     p. cm.
   Includes indexes.
   ISBN 0-673-39724-6
   1. College readers.   2. English language—Rhetoric.   I. Emblen,
D. L. (Donald Lewis), 1918– .   II. Hall, Donald, 1928– .
PE1417.W67 1988
808'.0427—dc19   87-22741
                                                                                                   CIP

1 2 3 4 5 6 7 8 9 10 — MPC — 93 92 91 90 89 88 87

Printed in the United States of America

Cover art: "Spring Point," 1977 by Elizabeth Murray. Collection of Susan and Lewis Manilow. Photograph courtesy, Paula Cooper Gallery, New York.

For William R. Booth

Preface

Reading well precedes writing well. Of all the ancestors claimed by a fine piece of prose, the most important is the prose from which the writer learned his craft. Writers learn craft, not by memorizing rules about restrictive clauses, but by striving to equal a standard formed from reading.

A composition course, then, must be two courses: one in reading, another in writing. If students lack practice in writing, they are usually unpracticed readers as well. Most students lack quality of reading as well as quantity; and if we assert that good models help us, we admit that bad models hurt us. People who read bad prose twelve hours a week—newspapers, popular fiction, textbooks—are as illserved as people who read nothing at all. Surely most textbooks, from freshman handbooks through the text for Psych 101, encourage the illusion that words merely stand in for ideas, or carry information on their backs—that words exist for the convenience of thinking much as turnpikes exist for the sake of automobiles.

This barbarism underlies the vogue of speed reading, which urges us to scan lines for comprehension, ignoring syntax and metaphor, ignoring image and feeling and sound. If we are to grow and to learn—and surely if we are to write well—we must learn to read slowly and intimately, and to read good writing. We must learn to read actively, even aggressively, without the passivity derived from watching television. The active reader questions as he reads, subjects each author's ideas to skeptical scrutiny, and engages the writer in dialogue as part of the reading process.

For language embodies the human psyche. Learning to read—that privilege so recently extended to the ancestors of most of us—allows us to enter human history. In books we perceive the gesture, the pulse, the heartbeat, the pallor, the eye movement, the pitch, and the tone of people who lived before us, or who live now in other places, in other skins, in other habits, customs, beliefs, and ideas.

Language *embodies* the human psyche, which includes ideas and the feelings that properly accompany ideas. There is no sleight-of-mind by which the idea may be separated from its body and remain alive. The body of good writing is rhythm and image, metaphor and syntax, order of phrase and order of paragraph.

A NOTE TO LATER EDITIONS

Many teachers helped us prepare the second edition of *A Writer's Reader*—in letters, in conversations at colleges all over the country, in responses to a Little, Brown survey of users. We thank more people than we can list.

We have added considerable material, and we are pleased with the result. We believe that we have made a representative sampling of good prose. We like some pieces more than others, heaven knows, but we believe that all of them provide something to learn from. We have included a wide variety of American prose, not only contemporary but historical, with high points of our history represented in their own style and syntax. We hope that young Americans will attach themselves to the body of their history by immersion in its significant utterances.

We have numbered paragraphs for ease of reference. Although *A Writer's Reader* is a collection of essays, we have again violated coherence by including fiction, feeling that the contrast afforded by a few short stories among the essays was useful and refreshing. For this edition, we have gone further afield and included several poems, for the same reason. Perhaps we should make an argument for including poems—but let us just say that we enjoy them, and we hope you do too. To satisfy students' curiosity, we have included headnotes to the poems; but we have stopped short of suggesting questions after them, lest we seem to surround a landscape garden with a hundred-foot-high concrete wall.

We have chosen to arrange our essays, stories, and poems alphabetically by author. This arrangement makes for random juxtaposition, irrational sequence, and no sense at all—which is why we chose it. We expect no one to teach these pieces in alphabetical order. (We expect teachers to find their own order—which they would do whatever order we attempted to impose.) In our first edition we struggled to make a stylistic organization, listing some essays as examples of "Sentences," others as examples of "Paragraphs." For the editors themselves, a year after deciding on our organization, it was no longer clear why essay X was to be studied for its sentences, essay Y for its paragraphs. With a rhetorical organization, one runs into another sort of problem. Although an essay may contain Division, or Process Analysis, or an example of Example, the same essay is likely to use three or four other patterns as well. No piece of real prose is ever so pure as our systems of classification. Thematic organizations, which have their attractions, have similar flaws; is E. B. White's theme, in "Once More to the Lake," Mortality? Aging? Youth and Age? or, How I Spent My Summer Vacation?

Our arrangement is more arbitrary than an arrangement by style or rhetoric or theme, and presents itself only to be ignored. At the same time, there are dozens of ways in which these essays (and poems and stories) can be used together. Our Instructor's Manual suggests several combinations. Our Rhetorical Index, printed as an appendix to the text itself, lists single-paragraph examples of rhetorical patterns as well as longer units. We hope that students will find the Rhetorical Index useful. Freshmen who return to their rooms from class, set to write a paper using Comparison and Contrast, sometimes find themselves in need of a concrete example of the assigned pattern to imitate.

Thus, we have tried to supply some useful maps to go with our arbitrary arrangement. We have also added a Thematic Index. Following suggestions from several teachers, we have chosen to represent a few authors by small clusters of their work. We have expanded our representation of writing by scientists. In response to many suggestions, we have looked for short, complete essays in exposition and argument on a variety of topics.

If we have omitted essays or authors you miss, please let us know. If there are authors we overlook, whom you would recommend, we solicit your help. Although we intend to remain alert, to good prose and to the needs of the classroom, we need help from the outside.

ACKNOWLEDGMENTS

We thank the following users of the first, second, third, and fourth editions for their helpful comments: Louise Ackley, Maureen Andrews, Tony Ardizzone, Jo Ann Asbury, Ann Avery, Conrad S. Bayley, Jane Berk, Meredith Berman, Dennis Berthold, Barbara Blaha, C. Bogarad, Charles E. Bolton, Charles Bressler, Patrick Broderick, Otis Bronson, Laurel Broughton, Ingrid Brunner, Ed Buckley, Sandra Burns, Jon Burton, Ann

Cameron, Suzanne Carlson, Marti Carpenter, Richard Cloyed, Edythe Colello, Randy Conine, Steven Connelly, Roger Conner, Rebecca Coogan, Charles L. Cornwell, Valecia Crisafulli, Garber Davidson, Virginia de Araujo, Loretta Denner, Salli and Robert Duxbury, Ida Egli, Lee Engdahl, Elizabeth Failla, Ralph Farve, Gala Fitzgerald, Frances B. Foreman, Susan Forrest, David S. Gadziola, Peggy Gledhill, Ronald Gurney, Barbara Hamilton, Bill Harby, Walter Harrison, Carol T. Hayes, Peter Heitkamp, Allan Hirsh, Samuel G. Hornsby, Jr., Nancy Hunt, John Huntington, C. S. Joyce, Donald Kansch, Gregory Keeler, Jeff Kluewer, Deborah Lambert, John Larner, Karen LeFerre, Kennedy P. Leisch, Richard H. Lerner, Opal A. Lovett, Neillie McCrory, Sherry McGuire, Andrew Makarushka, Steven J. Masello, Richard Maxwell, Deanne Milan, Molly Moore-Kehler, Harriet Napierkowski, Wayne Neel, Jean O'Donnell, Barbara Olive, Stephen O'Neil, Patrick Pacheco, Beverly Palmer, John V. Pastoor, Ray Peterson, Muriel Rada, Martha Rainbolt, Shari Rambo, Dennison G. Rice, James Rosen, Harriet Susskind Rosenblum, Robert Schwegler, Terry Shelton, Marvin and Helen Sherak, James Shokoff, Donald K. Skiles, Thomas Skmetzo, Marilyn Smith, Arnold Solkov, Andrew Solomon, Richard Speakes, David A. Spurr, Helen Stauffer, Art Suchoki, Bernard Sugarman, Kathleen Sullivan, Jane Bamblin Thomas, E. Guy Turcotte, Darlene Unrue, Peter Valenti, Sara Varhus, Craig Watson, Richard Webster, Joyce Welch, Dorothy Wells, Joseph F. Whelan, Roberta White, Shirley and Russell White, Edith Wiard, Richard A. Widmayer, Gary Williams, Suzanne Wilson, George Wymer, B. Yu, and Robert Lee Zimmerman. We thank Amy Johnson, Joe Opiela, Nan Upin, and Billie Ingram at Little, Brown, for their efforts on the book's behalf.

Contents

Edward Abbey (b. 1927) grew up in the East and has become the voice of the natural Southwest, Henry David Thoreau of a desert Walden. He lives in Oracle, Arizona, where he writes essays and novels, including The Monkey Wrench Game. *His non-fiction, which he calls "personal history," includes* Abbey's Road, Desert Solitaire, *and* Down the River. *In 1984 Abbey published a reader of his work, both essays and fiction, called* Slumgullion Stew. *He glossed the title as "a dish popular among hobos and other knights of the open road. Into a big pot over an open fire each man throws whatever he has to contribute—a stolen chicken, a hambone, a can of beans, a jar of salsa, an old shoe—anything edible. Like any serious stew, like human society itself, slumgullion should be stirred up frequently. . ."*

In this essay, which presumably would not please Stephen Jay Gould or Lewis Thomas, Abbey tries stirring us up on the subject of science.

1

EDWARD ABBEY
Science with a Human Face

Science with a human face—is such a thing possible anymore? We   1
live in a time when technology and technologists seem determined to
make the earth unfit to live upon. According to C. P. Snow, scientists
are happy in their work, especially when contrasted with poets,
novelists, artists, philosophers, all those customarily lumped together
in the category of the "humanities." The humanitarians? The term con-
notes self-mocking futility, reflecting accurately the trend and tempo

of the age. But I want to ask Mr. Snow this question: "Sir Charles, sir, if the scientists, technicians, researchers, whatever you wish to call them, are so happy in their work and so pleased with the world they are creating, why are they also and at the same time so earnestly devising ever more efficient ways to blow it all to hell?"

2   The mad scientist, once only a comic figure in a specialized branch of fiction, has now come luridly to life in a hundred thousand forms. Together with his co-workers in big government, big industry, and the military, he dominates our lives. United, they will tyrannize the planet. H. G. Wells, prophet and visionary, described the type exactly when he wrote: "Intelligences vast and cool and unsympathetic watched our world with envious eyes . . . and made their plans."

3   Wells called them Martians; we know today they are our own, sons of our fathers, the busy men with white smocks and clipboards who are planning our future. *For* us. "The World of Tomorrow—and You." And *you*, of course, are never consulted on the matter. Like the imaginary Martians in Wells's novel, the engineers and technicians have no interest in our personal preferences except as data to be tabulated and attitudes to be manipulated. They love us no more than we love them; and they certainly have no love for the earth. What is perhaps most sinister of all is the fact that in this worldwide drive to reduce life, human and otherwise, to the limits of a technetronic system, there is not even a mind at work. Many brains, but no mind. Nor heart nor soul. There is no intelligence directing this enormous and enormously complex process; merely the cumulative efforts of thousands of specialists, experts, each sequestered in his tiny niche in the technological apparatus, each unaware of or indifferent to the investigation of all but his closest colleagues, each man in his way an innocent. How can we think of a man who spends years studying the behavior of hamsters in an electrified maze as anything but a harmless idiot? Yet the results of his study, combined with the studies of many other similar harmless idiots, may result in knowledge useful, let us say, to a central police agency concerned with the problem of controlling an urban populace in revolt.

4   And in the evening, after a good day in the nausea-gas lab, the innocent scientist goes home to the arms of his wife and children and after supper plays with his model railroad in the rumpus room. As Hannah Arendt has pointed out, the most destructive men of our time are distinguished chiefly by the banality of their characters and private lives. Harry S. Truman liked to boast that he had never lost a night's sleep over Hiroshima and Nagasaki; Lyndon Johnson and General Westmoreland, with the blood of hundreds of thousands of Vietnamese

peasants and American adolescents on their hands, were perfectly
capable of getting down on their knees every Sunday morning and praying to what they guilelessly believed is the God of Love. And Adolf
Eichmann, as he correctly pointed out, was only following orders, as
millions of other men have done for their respective "authorities"; the
Nazi leaders were punished because they had the misfortune of ending
up on the losing side. Political and military leaders win the publicity,
but the fantastic crimes they have committed against humanity in this
century were made possible for them by the achievements of our scientists and technologists.

What I have written so far will seem to sober-minded professors   5
of the scientific method (the type I remember from my own student
days) as an irrational and hysterical outburst of misapplied indignation.
They will scarcely credit my insistence now that I am, despite the horrors of the twentieth century, fully in sympathy with the basic and traditional aim of science, which I define as the pursuit of knowledge.
Knowledge—not power. That I think of men like Democritus, Galileo,
Copernicus, Kepler, Newton, Lyell, Darwin, and Einstein as liberators
of the human consciousness, intellectual workers whose insight and
intelligence have expanded our awareness of existence infinitely more
than all the pronouncements of all the shamans, gurus, seers, and
mystics of the earth, East and West, combined. The simple telescope,
for instance, has given us visions of a world far greater, lovelier, more
awesome and full of wonder than that contained in an entire shipload
of magic mushrooms, LSD capsules, and yoga textbooks.

But having made this disclaimer, I can only repeat the charge, itself   6
a banality but no less true for being so, that science in our time is the
whore of industry and the slut of war, and that scientific technology
has become the instrument of a potential planetary slavery, the most
powerful weapon ever placed in the hands of despots. Nothing new in
this discovery, of course; the poets, with their fine sensitivity to changes
in the human weather, have been aware of the danger from the outset,
for 200 years. It may even be the case that the situation has so far
deteriorated that the only appropriate question now is whether or not
technology will succeed in totally enslaving mankind before it succeeds
in its corollary aim of destroying life.

In this general condemnation of the prostitution of science we must   7
allow exceptions. Many will assert that science, *true* science, cannot
be held responsible for the aberrations of uncontrolled technology.
Others will point out that some men of science, such as Linus Pauling,
Leo Szilard, Karl Morgan, Otto Hahn, Norbert Wiener, and many of their
younger students in the universities have been among the first to at-

tempt to organize resistance to the technological culture, both in America and in the Soviet Union. The latter statement is unquestionably true but, so to speak, not true enough; the defenders of freedom and sanity among professional scientists have been far outnumbered by the Herman Kahns, Glenn Seaborgs, Hans Bethes, Edward Tellers, and Dr. Barnards ("the operation was a success although—sorry—the patient died") of the scientific world.

8   Is science responsible for the perversions of technology? To what extent can science and technology be separated and distinguished from one another? Can either exist independently of the other? These are intricate questions of history, method, and practice that I am not competent to answer with more than this diffident opinion, humbly offered: Pure science is a myth; both mathematical theoreticians like Albert Einstein and practical crackpots like Henry Ford dealt with different aspects of the same world; theory and practice, invention and speculation, calculus and metallurgy have always functioned closely together, feeding upon and reinforcing each other; the only difference between the scientist and the lab technician is one of degree (or degrees)—neither has contributed much to our understanding of life on earth except knowledge of the means to destroy both. Einstein is reputed to have said, near the end of his career, that he would rather have been a good shoemaker than what he was, a great mathematician. We may take this statement as his confession of participatory guilt in the making of the modern nightmare.

9   The denunciation of science-technology that I have outlined here, simple-minded and oversimplified though it may undoubtedly be, should be taken seriously at least as an expression of the fear millions now feel for the plastic-aluminum-electronic-computerized technocracy forming around us, constricting our lives to the dimensions of the machine, divorcing our bodies and souls from the earth, harassing us constantly with its petty and haywire demands. What most humans really desire is something quite different: liberty, community, spontaneity, nakedness, mystery, wildness, and wilderness.

10   In such a climate of thought and emotion it is not surprising that a large-scale revolt against not only science but even reason itself is under way in Europe and the United States. Because of the filth, ugliness, slavery, and mass murder it has engendered, the scientific-technological establishment faces a deep-seated reaction against the whole Western tradition of rational thought which is (or was) the foundation of science. The addicts of the occult and the Eastern religions have always been among us, but probably never before have so many abandoned realism and naturalism and rushed to embrace the fantasies of spiritualism, the

life weariness of Buddhism, the world negation of Hinduism, the doper's heaven of institutional Christianity. As an antidote to a poisonous overdose of technology and crazy rationality I can understand why so many of the spiritually sick have switched to Zen, *om*, I Ching, and tarot. As an approach to effective resistance against the on-coming tyranny of the machine, however, these worn-out doctrines and obscure little magics will prove as futile as the machine can prove fatal. In fact, there is no reason why psychedelics and occultists, for example, and the most sophisticated technetronic system cannot comfortably coexist—the former inside the latter. They do; and they will. I find it ironic to see the enthusiasm with which hairy little gurus from the sickliest nation on earth (India) are welcomed by the technological idiots of all-electric California. Computerology, futurology, "high" technology and astrology—basic superstitions of our time—are comfortably compatible.

In this embrace of easily reconcilable opposites I wish to stand apart, alone if need be, and hold up the ragged flag of reason. Reason with a capital *R*—Sweet Reason, the newest and rarest thing in human life, the most delicate child of human history. Reason without technology, if that seems best; reason without science, if that seems necessary. By "reason" I mean intelligence informed by sympathy, knowledge in the arms of love. (For knowledge without conscience is the ruin of the soul, sayeth the Proverb—and the oldest wisdom is usually most reliable.) By "reason" I mean fidelity to what alone we really know and really must love—this one life, this one earth on which we live. I find myself equally opposed to the technological mania of the West and the occult morbidity of the East: Both are the enemies of reason, and of life, and of the earth.

The orthodox scientific view reduces the world to measurable and predictable units, to that which can be charted, graphed, statistically analyzed; the traditional religious or mystical view reduces the world to a reflection of human, anthropomorphic desires and intuitions. Both have in common the psychological compulsion to scale the world down to humanly comprehensible limits, and both have in common, also, at their most profound level, the tendency to think of the world as essentially (and only) a *process* that lies beyond direct sensory perception. At this point the Yogi and the physicist come close together, and both, I would like to suggest, are mistaken, guilty of the most obvious reductionism, insofar as either insists on the fallacy that existence, nature, the world, is *nothing but* the flow of process, and that the beings of this life whom we know and love—a woman, a child, a place, a tree, a rock, a cloud, a bird, the great sun itself—are mere ephemera, illusory shadows, nothing.

13   They are wrong. Even a rock is a being, a thing with character and a kind of spirit, an existence worthy of our love. To disparage the world we know for the sake of grand abstractions, whether they are called mesons and electrons or the vibrations of an endlessly slumbering and reawakening Brahma, is to be false to the mother who sustains us. The highest treason, the meanest treason, is to disavow and deny this lone but gracious planet on which we voyage through the cold void of space. Only a fool, milking his cow, denies the cow's reality. Be true to the earth, said Nietzsche.

14   For what do we really know? I think of a lightning-blasted but still living shagbark hickory in the pasture back home on my father's farm in Pennsylvania; I think of a twisted juniper on a ledge of sandstone at Cape Solitude, far above the Colorado River; I think of the pelicans that sail along the shores of the Sea of Cortez; I think of a thousand other places I have known and loved, east and west, in North America and Australia and Europe, and all the creatures great and small that live there—each a part of a greater whole but each an individual as well, one and unique, never to be known again, here or anywhere, each as precious as the vivid moment in which it first appeared on earth.

15   Don't talk to me about other worlds, separate realities, lost continents, or invisible realms—I know where I belong. Heaven is home. Utopia is here. Nirvana is now.

16   Walking up the trail to my lookout tower last night, I saw the new moon emerge from a shoal of clouds and hang for a time beyond the black silhouette of a shaggy, giant Douglas fir. I stopped to look. And what I saw was the moon—the moon itself, nothing else; and the tree, alive and conscious in its own spiral of time; and my hands, palms upward, raised toward the sky. We were there. We *are*. That is what we know. This is all we can know. And each such moment holds all that we could possibly need—if only we can see.

———— CONSIDERATIONS ————

1. In Paragraph 1, Abbey condemns scientists, technicians, and researchers as devoted to "devising ever more efficient ways to blow it [the world] all to hell." If you were to make the same statement, how would you support and illustrate it? How does Abbey attempt to support his argument? Is he successful? Elaborate.

2. Abbey refers in Paragraph 3 to "a technetronic system." Is this word in your dictionary? If not, try to determine its meaning by analyzing its roots and affixes. Does Abbey mean the same thing when he refers to "the technological culture" in Paragraph 7?

3. How are science and technology commonly distinguished from each other? What does Abbey say about this distinction (Paragraph 8) and how does it relate to the thesis of his essay?

4. "What most humans really desire is something quite different [from the technological culture]: liberty, community, spontaneity, nakedness, mystery, wildness, and wilderness." Does Abbey speak for your desires? For those of your family or friends? Can you find any evidence, in the mass media, for example, to support his statement?

5. What do you think of Abbey's definition of "reason" in Paragraph 11? Before you answer, consult a dictionary and/or an introductory logic text.

6. On what does Abbey finally rest his case? See especially his last three paragraphs. How does the tone of these paragraphs differ from that in the rest of the essay? Does it uphold Abbey's thesis?

7. In Paragraph 3, Abbey charges that scientists "have no love for the earth." Several scientists are represented in your text: Loren Eiseley (pages 150–152), Stephen Jay Gould (pages 191–197), James C. Rettie (pages 343–349), and Lewis Thomas (pages 409–412), among others. Would any of their essays inspire you to challenge Abbey?

Henry Adams (1838–1918) entertained notions of a political career, in keeping with family traditions, but never ran for office. For a time, he taught history at Harvard and edited the North American Review. *He wrote political journalism and essays on geology, economics and history; he wrote two novels that he published anonymously. In middle life he undertook and completed the massive* History of the United States During the Administrations of Jefferson and Madison, *recently reissued in two volumes by the Library of America. Later he wrote the books by which he is most remembered* Mont St. Michel and Chartres *(1904) and his autobiography—written in the third person and called* The Education of Henry Adams *(1907)—from which we take this fragment of reminiscence.*

Hundreds of American writers have recollected visits to grandfather's house; few were grandson to one president and great-grandson to another. Adams's contrasts of style—eighteenth century with nineteenth, Boston with the small town of Quincy, the Brooks grandfather with the Adams grandfather—culminate in an anecdote that illuminates the fundamental contrast of private and public.

2

HENRY ADAMS
Winter and Summer

Boys are wild animals, rich in the treasures of sense, but the   1
New England boy had a wider range of emotions than boys of more
equable climates. He felt his nature crudely, as it was meant. To the
boy Henry Adams, summer was drunken. Among senses, smell was the
strongest—smell of hot pine-woods and sweet-fern in the scorching summer noon; of new-mown hay; of ploughed earth; of box hedges; of
peaches, lilacs, syringas; of stables, barns, cow-yards; of salt water and
low tide on the marshes; nothing came amiss. Next to smell came taste,
and the children knew the taste of everything they saw or touched, from
pennyroyal and flagroot to the shell of a pignut and the letters of a spelling book—the taste of A-B, AB, suddenly revived on the boy's tongue
sixty years afterwards. Light, line, and color as sensual pleasures, came
later and were as crude as the rest. The New England light is glare, and
the atmosphere harshens color. The boy was a full man before he ever
knew what was meant by atmosphere; his idea of pleasure in light was
the blaze of a New England sun. His idea of color was a peony, with
the dew of early morning on its petals. The intense blue of the sea, as
he saw it a mile or two away, from the Quincy hills; the cumuli in a
June afternoon sky; the strong reds and greens and purples of colored
prints and children's picture-books, as the American colors then ran;
these were ideals. The opposites or antipathies, were the cold grays of
November evenings, and the thick, muddy thaws of Boston winter. With
such standards, the Bostonian could not but develop a double nature.
Life was a double thing. After a January blizzard, the boy who could
look with pleasure into the violent snow-glare of the cold white sunshine, with its intense light and shade, scarcely knew what was meant
by tone. He could reach it only by education.

Winter and summer, then, were two hostile lives, and bred two   2
separate natures. Winter was always the effort to live; summer was

9

tropical license. Whether the children rolled in the grass, or waded in the brook, or swam in the salt ocean, or sailed in the bay, or fished for smelts in the creeks, or netted minnows in the salt-marshes, or took to the pine-woods and the granite quarries, or chased muskrats and hunted snapping-turtles in the swamps, or mushrooms or nuts on the autumn hills, summer and country were always sensual living, while winter was always compulsory learning. Summer was the multiplicity of nature; winter was school.

3   The bearing of the two seasons on the education of Henry Adams was no fancy; it was the most decisive force he ever knew; it ran through life, and made the division between its perplexing, warring, irreconcilable problems, irreducible opposites, with growing emphasis to the last year of study. From earliest childhood the boy was accustomed to feel that, for him, life was double. Winter and summer, town and country, law and liberty, were hostile, and the man who pretended they were not, was in his eyes a schoolmaster—that is, a man employed to tell lies to little boys. Though Quincy was but two hours' walk from Beacon Hill, it belonged in a different world. For two hundred years, every Adams, from father to son, had lived within sight of State Street, and sometimes had lived in it, yet none had ever taken kindly to the town, or been taken kindly by it. The boy inherited his double nature. He knew as yet nothing about his great-grandfather, who had died a dozen years before his own birth: he took for granted that any great-grandfather of his must have always been good, and his enemies wicked; but he divined his great-grandfather's character from his own. Never for a moment did he connect the two ideas of Boston and John Adams; they were separate and antagonistic; the idea of John Adams went with Quincy. He knew his grandfather John Quincy Adams only as an old man of seventy-five or eighty who was friendly and gentle with him, but except that he heard his grandfather always called "the President," and his grandmother "the Madam," he had no reason to suppose that his Adams grandfather differed in character from his Brooks grandfather who was equally kind and benevolent. He liked the Adams side best, but for no other reason than that it reminded him of the country, the summer, and the absence of restraint. Yet he felt also that Quincy was in a way inferior to Boston, and that socially Boston looked down on Quincy. The reason was clear enough even to a five-year-old child. Quincy had no Boston style. Little enough style had either; a simpler manner of life and thought could hardly exist, short of cave-dwelling. The flint-and-steel with which his grandfather Adams used to light his own fires in the early morning was still on the mantelpiece of his study. The idea of a livery or even

a dress for servants, or of an evening toilette, was next to blasphemy. Bathrooms, water-supplies, lighting, heating, and the whole array of domestic comforts, were unknown at Quincy. Boston had already a bathroom, a water-supply, a furnace, and gas. The superiority of Boston was evident, but a child liked it no better for that.

The magnificence of his grandfather Brooks's house in Pearl   4
Street or South Street has long ago disappeared, but perhaps his country house at Medford may still remain to show what impressed the mind of a boy in 1845 with the idea of city splendor. The President's place at Quincy was the larger and older and far the more interesting of the two; but a boy felt at once its inferiority in fashion. It showed plainly enough its want of wealth. It smacked of colonial age, but not of Boston style or plush curtains. To the end of his life he never quite overcame the prejudice thus drawn in with his childish breath. He never could compel himself to care for nineteenth-century style. He was never able to adopt it, any more than his father or grandfather or great-grandfather had done. Not that he felt it as particularly hostile, for he reconciled himself to much that was worse; but because, for some remote reason, he was born an eighteenth-century child. The old house at Quincy was eighteenth-century. What style it had was in its Queen Anne mahogany panels and its Louis Seize chairs and sofas. The panels belonged to an old colonial vassal who built the house; the furniture had been brought back from Paris in 1789 or 1801 or 1817, along with porcelain and books and much else of old diplomatic remnants: and neither of the two eighteenth-century styles—neither English Queen Anne nor French Louis Seize—was comfortable for a boy, or for any one else. The dark mahogany had been painted white to suit daily life in the winter gloom. Nothing seemed to favor, for a child's objects, the older forms. On the contrary, most boys, as well as grown-up people, preferred the new, with good reason, and the child felt himself distinctly at a disadvantage for the taste.

Nor had personal preference any share in his bias. The Brooks   5
grandfather was as amiable and as sympathetic as the Adams grandfather. Both were born in 1767, and both died in 1848. Both were kind to children, and both belonged rather to the eighteenth than to the nineteenth centuries. The child knew no difference between them except that one was associated with winter and the other with summer; one with Boston, the other with Quincy. Even with Medford, the association was hardly easier. Once as a very young boy he was taken to pass a few days with his grandfather Brooks under charge of his aunt, but became so violently homesick that within twenty-four hours he was

brought back in disgrace. Yet he could not remember ever being seriously homesick again.

6   The attachment to Quincy was not altogether sentimental or wholly sympathetic. Quincy was not a bed of thornless roses. Even there the curse of Cain set its mark. There as elsewhere a cruel universe combined to crush a child. As though three or four vigorous brothers and sisters, with the best will, were not enough to crush any child, every one else conspired towards an education which he hated. From cradle to grave this problem of running order through chaos, direction through space, discipline through freedom, unity through multiplicity, has always been, and must always be, the task of education, as it is the moral of religion, philosophy, science, art, politics, and economy: but a boy's will is his life, and he dies when it is broken, as the colt dies in harness, taking a new nature in becoming tame. Rarely has the boy felt kindly towards his tamers. Between him and his master has always been war. Henry Adams never knew a boy of his generation to like a master, and the task of remaining on friendly terms with one's own family, in such a relation, was never easy.

7   All the more singular it seemed afterwards to him that his first serious contact with the President should have been a struggle of will, in which the old man almost necessarily defeated the boy, but instead of leaving, as usual in such defeats, a lifelong sting, left rather an impression of as fair treatment as could be expected from a natural enemy. The boy met seldom with such restraint. He could not have been much more than six years old at the time—seven at the utmost—and his mother had taken him to Quincy for a long stay with the President during the summer. What became of the rest of the family he quite forgot; but he distinctly remembered standing at the house door one summer morning in a passionate outburst of rebellion against going to school. Naturally his mother was the immediate victim of his rage; that is what mothers are for, and boys also; but in this case the boy had his mother at unfair disadvantage, for she was a guest, and had no means of enforcing obedience. Henry showed a certian tactical ability by refusing to start, and he met all efforts at compulsion by successful, though too vehement protest. He was in fair way to win, and was holding his own, with sufficient energy, at the bottom of the long staircase which led up to the door of the President's library, when the door opened, and the old man slowly came down. Putting on his hat, he took the boy's hand without a word, and walked with him, paralyzed by awe, up the road to the town. After the first moments of consternation at this interference

in a domestic dispute, the boy reflected that an old gentleman close on eighty would never trouble himself to walk near a mile on a hot summer morning over a shadeless road to take a boy to school, and that it would be strange if a lad imbued with the passion of freedom could not find a corner to dodge around, somewhere before reaching the school door. Then and always, the boy insisted that this reasoning justified his apparent submission; but the old man did not stop, and the boy saw all his strategical points turned, one after another, until he found himself seated inside the school, and obviously the centre of curious if not malevolent criticism. Not till then did the President release his hand and depart.

The point was that this act, contrary to the inalienable rights of   8
boys, and nullifying the social compact, ought to have made him dislike his grandfather for life. He could not recall that it had this effect even for a moment. With a certain maturity of mind, the child must have recognized that the President, though a tool of tyranny, had done his disreputable work with a certain intelligence. He had shown no temper, no irritation, no personal feeling, and had made no display of force. Above all, he had held his tongue. During their long walk he had said nothing; he had uttered no syllable of revolting cant about the duty of obedience and the wickedness of resistance to law; he had shown no concern in the matter; hardly even a consciousness of the boy's existence. Probably his mind at that moment was actually troubling itself little about his grandson's iniquities, and much about the iniquities of President Polk, but the boy could scarcely at that age feel the whole satisfaction of thinking that President Polk was to be the vicarious victim of his own sins, and he gave his grandfather credit for intelligent silence. For this forbearance he felt instinctive respect. He admitted force as a form of right; he admitted even temper, under protest; but the seeds of moral education would at that moment have fallen on the stoniest soil in Quincy, which is, as every one knows, the stoniest glacial and tidal drift known in any Puritan land.

_____ **CONSIDERATIONS** _____

1. Earlier in his autobiography, Adams gives the reader some idea of how the young Henry, because of the peculiar nature of his family and its position, was burdened with expectations arising from the family's deep involvement in American history and politics. In this excerpt, study his vocabulary and look for words that express his constant awareness of that involvement.

2. Adams chose an unusual point of view for an autobiography—the third person. Change a given paragraph to the first person point of view to see what difference the author's decision on that technical matter can make.

3. What illustrations does Adams use to help the reader understand what is meant by "He felt his nature crudely. . . ."?

4. Adams's essay might fairly be said to be built upon a system of opposites. List several of these opposites to understand how a series of contrasts can serve as an organizing principle of an essay.

5. In Paragraph 6, Adams sets forth clearly and firmly his conviction about what education must be. Judging from your educational experience, to what extent can you agree with him?

6. What allowed the boy to respect his grandfather, even as the old man was disciplining him?

James Agee (1909–1955) was a journalist, critic, poet, and novelist. He was an early critic of film as art, and wrote the script for The African Queen, *among other movies. A heart attack killed him at forty-five, before he had finished his novel,* A Death in the Family. *Editors assembled the final manuscript and included as a prologue the essay reprinted here. The novel was awarded the Pulitzer Prize in 1958. Agee's prose evokes lost time; detail is described with intimate precision, landscape rendered exactly, with a wash of nostalgia.*

3

JAMES AGEE
Knoxville: Summer 1915

We are talking now of summer evenings in Knoxville, Tennessee in the time that I lived there so successfully disguised to myself as a child. It was a little bit mixed sort of block, fairly solidly lower middle class, with one or two juts apiece on either side of that. The houses corresponded: middle-sized gracefully fretted wood houses built in the late nineties and early nineteen hundreds, with small front and side and more spacious back yards, and trees in the yards, and porches. These were soft-wooded trees, poplars, tulip trees, cottonwoods. There were fences around one or two of the houses, but mainly the yards ran into each other with only now and then a low hedge that wasn't doing very well. There were few good friends among the grown people, and they were not poor enough for the other sort of intimate acquaintance, but everyone nodded and spoke, and even might talk short times, trivially, and at the two extremes of the general or the particular, and ordinarily nextdoor neighbors talked quite a bit when they happened to run into each other, and never paid calls. The men were mostly small businessmen, one or two very modestly executives, one or two worked with their hands, most of them clerical, and most of them between thirty and forty-five.

2   But it is of these evenings, I speak.

3   Supper was at six and was over by half past. There was still daylight, shining softly and with a tarnish, like the lining of a shell; and the carbon lamps lifted at the corners were on in the light, and the locusts were started, and the fire flies were out, and a few frogs were flopping in the dewy grass, by the time the fathers and the children came out. The children ran out first hell bent and yelling those names by which they were known; then the fathers sank out leisurely in crossed suspenders, their collars removed and their necks looking tall and shy. The mothers stayed back in the kitchen washing and drying, putting things away, recrossing their traceless footsteps like the lifetime journey of bees, measuring out the dry cocoa for breakfast. When they came out they had taken off their aprons and their skirts were dampened and they sat in rockers on their porches quietly.

4   It is not of the games children played in the evening that I want to speak now, it is of a contemporaneous atmosphere that has little to do with them: that of the fathers of families, each in his space of lawn, his shirt fishlike pale in the unnatural light and his face nearly anonymous, hosing their lawns. The hoses were attached at spigots that stood out of the brick foundations of the houses. The nozzles were variously set but usually so there was a long sweet stream of spray, the nozzle wet in the hand, the water trickling the right forearm and the peeled-back cuff, and the water whishing out a long loose and low-curved cone, and so gentle a sound. First an insane noise of violence in the nozzle, then the still irregular sound of adjustment, then the smoothing into steadiness and a pitch as accurately tuned to the size and style of stream as any violin. So many qualities of sound out of one hose: so many choral differences out of those several hoses that were in earshot. Out of any one hose, the almost dead silence of the release, and the short still arch of the separate big drops, silent as a held breath, and the only noise the flattering noise on leaves and the slapped grass at the fall of each big drop. That, and the intense hiss with the intense stream; that, and that same intensity not growing less but growing more quiet and delicate with the turn of the nozzle, up to that extreme tender whisper when the water was just a wide bell of film. Chiefly, though, the hoses

were set much alike, in a compromise between distance and tenderness of spray (and quite surely a sense of art behind this compromise, and a quiet deep joy, too real to recognize itself), and the sounds therefore were pitched much alike; pointed by the snorting start of a new hose; decorated by some man playful with the nozzle; left empty, like God by the sparrow's fall, when any single one of them desists; and all, though near alike, of various pitch; and in this unison. These sweet pale streamings in the light lift out their pallors and their voices all together, mothers hushing their children, the hushing unnaturally prolonged, the men gentle and silent and each snail-like withdrawn into the quietude of what he singly is doing, the urination of huge children stood loosely military against an invisible wall, and gentle happy and peaceful, tasting the mean goodness of their living like the last of their suppers in their mouths, while the locusts carry on this noise of hoses on their much higher and sharper key. The noise of the locust is dry, and it seems not to be rasped or vibrated but urged from him as if through a small orifice by breath that can never give out. Also there is never one locust but an illusion of at least a thousand. The noise of each locust is pitched in some classic locust range out of which none of them varies more than two full tones: and yet you seem to hear each locust discrete from all the rest, and there is a long, slow pulse in their noise, like the scarcely defined arch of a long and high set bridge. They are all around in every tree, so that the noise seems to come from nowhere and everywhere at once, from the whole shell heaven, shivering in your flesh and teasing your eardrums, the boldest of all the sounds of night. And yet it is habitual to summer nights, and is of the great order of noises, like the noises of the sea and of the blood her precocious grandchild, which you realize you are hearing only when you catch yourself listening. Meantime from low in the dark, just outside the swaying horizons of the hoses, conveying always grass in the damp of dew and its strong greenblack smear of smell, the regular yet spaced noises of the crickets, each a sweet cold silver noise threenoted, like the slipping each time of three matched links of a small chain.

But the men by now, one by one, have silenced their hoses and   5
drained and coiled them. Now only two, and now only one, is left, and you see only ghostlike shirt with the sleeve garters, and sober mystery of his mild face like the lifted face of large cattle enquiring of your presence in a pitchdark pool of meadow; and how he too is gone; and it has become that time of evening when people sit on their porches, rocking gently and talking gently and watching the street and the standing up

into their sphere of possession of the trees, of bird-hung havens, hangars. People go by; things go by. A horse, drawing a buggy, breaking his hollow iron music on the asphalt; a loud auto; a quiet auto; people in pairs, not in a hurry, scuffling, switching their weight of aestival body, talking casually, the taste hovering over them of vanilla, strawberry, pasteboard and starched milk, the image upon them of lovers and horsemen, squared with clowns in hueless amber. A street car raising its iron moan; stopping, belling and starting; stertorous; rousing and raising again its iron increasing moan and swimming its gold windows and straw seats on past and past and past, the bleak spark crackling and cursing above it like a small malignant spirit set to dog its tracks; the iron whine rises on rising speed; still risen, faints; halts, the faint stinging bell; rises again, still fainter; fainting, lifting, lifts, faints forgone: forgotten. Now is the night one blue dew.

> Now is the night one blue dew, my father has drained, he has
>   coiled the hose.
> Low on the length of lawns, a frailing of fire who breathes.
> Content, silver, like peeps of light, each cricket makes his com-
>   ment over and over in the drowned grass.
> A cold toad thumpily flounders.
> Within the edges of damp shadows of side yards are hovering
>   children nearly sick with joy of fear, who watch the unguard-
>   ing of a telephone pole.
> Around white carbon corner lamps bugs of all sizes are lifted
>   elliptic, solar systems. Big hardshells bruise themselves,
>   assailant: he is fallen on his back, legs squiggling.
> Parents on porches: rock and rock: From damp strings morning
>   glories: hang their ancient faces.
> The dry and exalted noise of the locusts from all the air at once
>   enchants my eardrums.

6   On the rough wet grass of the back yard my father and mother have spread quilts. We all lie there, my mother, my father, my uncle, my aunt, and I too am lying there. First we were sitting up, then one of us lay down, and then we all lay down, on our stomachs, or on our sides, or on our backs, and they have kept on talking. They are not talking much, and the talk is quiet, of nothing in particular, of nothing at all in particular, of nothing at all. The stars are wide and alive, they seem each like a smile of great sweetness, and they seem very near. All my people are larger bodies than mine, quiet, with voices gentle and meaningless like the voices of sleeping birds. One is an artist, he is living at home. One is a musician, she is living at home. One is my mother

who is good to me. One is my father who is good to me. By some chance, here they are, all on this earth; and who shall ever tell the sorrow of being on their earth, lying, on quilts, on the grass, in a summer evening, among the sounds of the night. May God bless my people, my uncle, my aunt, my mother, my good father, oh, remember them kindly in their time of trouble; and in the hour of their taking away.

After a little I am taken in and put to bed. Sleep, soft smiling, draws me unto her: and those receive me, who quietly treat me, as one familiar and well beloved in that home: but will not, oh, will not, not now, not ever; but will not ever tell me who I am.   7

_____ CONSIDERATIONS _____

1. Agee is famous for his close attention to the senses. In this piece, which one—seeing, hearing, smelling, tasting, touching—is exercised the most?

2. What do you make of Agee's paragraph sense? Compare, for example, Paragraph 2 with Paragraph 4. Would you recommend breaking the latter into smaller units? Where? Why, or why not?

3. The first sentence of Paragraph 1 offers an opportunity for experimentation. Copy it out *without* the following words or phrases: "so successfully," "disguised," and "to myself." Then replace the phrases, one at a time, considering how each addition changes the dimension, the direction, or the depth of the story. Which of the three works the greatest change? Why?

4. How does the opening sentence embody a theme important to the whole story? Where else is that theme sounded in the story?

5. Agee's evocation of a summer evening might seem strange to an apartment-dweller in Knoxville in 1987. Would it be possible to write so serenely about a summer evening in the Knoxville—or Detroit, or Minneapolis, or San Francisco—of today?

6. Agee's attempt to recapture and thus understand his childhood—or at least a moment of it—relates to the efforts of several other writers in this book. Compare and contrast "Knoxville: Summer 1915" with one of these: Henry Adams (pages 8–14); Frank Conroy (pages 119–126); Lillian Hellman (pages 198–204); Langston Hughes (pages 215–219); or E. B. White (pages 461–471).

Woody Allen (b. 1935) is a universal genius, best known for acting in, writing, and directing movies. His films range from What's New, Pussycat? *(1964) through* Love and Death *(1975) and* Annie Hall *(1977) to* Hannah and Her Sisters *(1986) and* Radio Days *(1987). He has also published short fiction in* Playboy *and* The New Yorker. *In 1978 he won an O. Henry Award for the best American short story of the previous year. His prose is collected in three volumes,* Getting Even *(1972).* Without Feathers *(1975), and* Side Effects *(1980).*

Allen began his career as a comedy writer for television shows, then became a comedian himself. His first great successes were Broadway plays. Don't Drink the Water *(1966) and* Play It Again, Sam *(1969). This playlet comes from* Getting Even.

4

WOODY ALLEN
Death Knocks

1   *(The play takes place in the bedroom of the Nat Ackermans' two-story house, somewhere in Kew Gardens. The carpeting is wall-to-wall. There is a big double bed and a large vanity. The room is elaborately furnished and curtained, and on the walls there are several paintings and a not really attractive barometer. Soft theme music as the curtain rises. Nat Ackerman, a bald, paunchy fifty-seven-year-old dress manufacturer, is lying on the bed finishing off tomorrow's* Daily News. *He wears a bathrobe and slippers, and reads by a bed light clipped to the white headboard of the bed. The time is near midnight. Suddenly we hear a noise, and Nat sits up and looks at the window.)*

Nat: What the hell is that?

(Climbing awkwardly through the window is a sombre, caped figure. The intruder wears a black hood and skintight black clothes. The hood covers his head but not his face, which is middle-aged and stark white. He is something like Nat in appearance. He huffs audibly and then trips over the windowsill and falls into the room.)

Death *(for it is no one else):* Jesus Christ. I nearly broke my neck.

Nat *(watching with bewilderment):* Who are you?   5

Death: Death.

Nat: Who?

Death: Death. Listen — can I sit down? I nearly broke my neck. I'm shaking like a leaf.

Nat: Who *are* you?

Death: *Death.* You got a glass of water?   10

Nat: Death? What do you mean, Death?

Death: What is wrong with you? You see the black costume and the whitened face?

Nat: Yeah.

Death: Is it Halloween?

Nat: No.   15

Death: Then I'm Death. Now can I get a glass of water — or a Fresca?

Nat: If this is some joke —

Death: What kind of joke? You're fifty-seven? Nat Ackerman? One eighteen Pacific Street? Unless I blew it — where's that call sheet? *(He fumbles through pocket, finally producing a card with an address on it. It seems to check.)*

Nat: What do you want with me?

Death: What do I want? What do you think I want?   20

Nat: You must be kidding. I'm in perfect health.

Death *(unimpressed):* Uh-huh. *(Looking around)* This is a nice place. You do it yourself?

Nat: We had a decorator, but we worked with her.

Death *(looking at the picture on the wall):* I love those kids with the big eyes.

Nat: I don't want to go yet.   25

Death: *You* don't want to go? Please don't start in. As it is, I'm nauseous from the climb.

Nat: What climb?

Death: I climbed up the drainpipe. I was trying to make a dramatic entrance. I see the big windows and you're awake reading. I figure it's worth a shot. I'll climb up and enter with a little — you know . . . *(Snaps fingers)* Meanwhile, I get my heel caught on some vines, the drainpipe breaks, and I'm hanging by a thread. Then my cape begins to tear. Look, let's just go. It's been a rough night.

Nat: You broke my drainpipe?

30   Death: Broke. It didn't break. It's a little bent. Didn't you hear anything? I slammed into the ground.

Nat: I was reading.

Death: You must have really been engrossed. *(Lifting newspaper Nat was reading)* "NAB COEDS IN POT ORGY." Can I borrow this?

Nat: I'm not finished.

Death: Er—I don't know how to put this to you, pal . . .

35   Nat: Why didn't you just ring downstairs?

Death: I'm telling you, I could have, but how does it look? This way I get a little drama going. Something. Did you read *Faust?*

Nat: What?

Death: And what if you had company? You're sitting there with important people. I'm Death—I should ring the bell and traipse right in the front? Where's your thinking?

Nat: Listen, Mister, it's very late.

40   Death: Yeah. Well, you want to go?

Nat: Go where?

Death: Death. It. The Thing. The Happy Hunting Grounds. *(Looking at his own knee)* Y'know, that's a pretty bad cut. My first job, I'm liable to get gangrene yet.

Nat: Now, wait a minute. I need time. I'm not ready to go.

Death: I'm sorry. I can't help you. I'd like to, but it's the moment.

45   Nat: How can it be the moment? I just merged with Modiste Originals.

Death: What's the difference, a couple of bucks more or less.

Nat: Sure, what do you care? You guys probably have all your expenses paid.

Death: You want to come along now?

Nat *(studying him):* I'm sorry, but I cannot believe you're Death.

50   Death: Why? What'd you expect—Rock Hudson?

Nat: No, it's not that.

Death: I'm sorry if I disappointed you.

Nat: Don't get upset. I don't know, I always thought you'd be . . . uh . . . taller.

Death: I'm five seven. It's average for my weight.

55   Nat: You look a little like me.

Death: Who should I look like? I'm your death.

Nat: Give me some time. Another day.

Death: I can't. What do you want me to say?

Nat: One more day. Twenty-four hours.

Death: What do you need it for? The radio said rain tomorrow.   60

Nat: Can't we work out something?

Death: Like what?

Nat: You play chess?

Death: No, I don't.

Nat: I once saw a picture of you playing chess.   65

Death: Couldn't be me, because I don't play chess. Gin rummy, maybe.

Nat: You play gin rummy?

Death: Do I play gin rummy? Is Paris a city?

Nat: You're good, huh?

Death: Very good.   70

Nat: I'll tell you what I'll do—

Death: Don't make any deals with me.

Nat: I'll play you gin rummy. If you win, I'll go immediately. If I win, give me some more time. A little bit—one more day.

Death: Who's got time to play gin rummy?

Nat: Come on. If you're so good.   75

Death: Although I feel like a game . . .

Nat: Come on. Be a sport. We'll shoot for a half hour.

Death: I really shouldn't.

Nat: I got the cards right here. Don't make a production.

Death: All right, come on. We'll play a little. It'll relax me.   80

Nat *(getting cards, pad, and pencil)*: You won't regret this.

Death: Don't give me a sales talk. Get the cards and give me a Fresca and put out something. For God's sake, a stranger drops in, you don't have potato chips or pretzels.

Nat: There's M&M's downstairs in a dish.

Death: M&M's. What if the President came? He'd get M&M's too?

Nat: You're not the President.   85

Death: Deal.

(Nat deals, turns up a five.)

Nat: You want to play a tenth of a cent a point to make it interesting?

Death: It's not interesting enough for you?

Nat: I play better when money's at stake.   90

Death: Whatever you say, Newt.

Nat: Nat. Nat Ackerman. You don't know my name?

Death: Newt, Nat—I got such a headache.

Nat: You want that five?

95   Death: No.

Nat: So pick.

Death *(surveying his hand as he picks):* Jesus, I got nothing here.

Nat: What's it like?

Death: What's what like?

100   *(Throughout the following, they pick and discard.)*

Nat: Death.

Death: What should it be like? You lay there.

Nat: Is there anything after?

Death: Aha, you're saving twos.

105   Nat: I'm asking. Is there anything after?

Death *(absently):* You'll see.

Nat: Oh, then I will actually see something?

Death: Well, maybe I shouldn't have put it that way. Throw.

Nat: To get an answer from you is a big deal.

110   Death: I'm playing cards.

Nat: All right, play, play.

Death: Meanwhile, I'm giving you one card after another.

Nat: Don't look through the discards.

Death: I'm not looking. I'm straightening them up. What was the knock card?

115   Nat: Four. You ready to knock already?

Death: Who said I'm ready to knock? All I asked was what was the knock card.

Nat: And all I asked was is there anything for me to look forward to.

Death: Play.

Nat: Can't you tell me anything? Where do we go?

120   Death: We? To tell you the truth, *you* fall in a crumpled heap on the floor.

Nat: Oh, I can't wait for that! Is it going to hurt?

Death: Be over in a second.

Nat: Terrific *(Sighs)* I needed this. A man merges with Modiste Originals . . .

Death: How's four points?

125   Nat: You're knocking?

Death: Four points is good?

Nat: No, I got two.

Death: You're kidding.

Nat: No, you lose.

Death: Holy Christ, and I thought you were saving sixes.   130

Nat: No. Your deal. Twenty points and two boxes. Shoot. *(Death deals.)* I must fall on the floor, eh? I can't be standing over the sofa when it happens?

Death: No. Play.

Nat: Why not?

Death: Because you fall on the floor! Leave me alone. I'm trying to concentrate.

Nat: Why must it be on the floor? That's all I'm saying! Why can't   135
the whole thing happen and I'll stand next to the sofa?

Death: I'll try my best. Now can we play?

Nat: That's all I'm saying. You remind me of Moe Lefkowitz. He's also stubborn.

Death: I remind him of Moe Lefkowitz. I'm one of the most terrifying figures you could possibly imagine, and him I remind of Moe Lefkowitz. What is he, a furrier?

Nat: You should be such a furrier. He's good for eighty thousand a year. Passementeries. He's got his own factory. Two points.

Death: What?   140

Nat: Two points. I'm knocking. What have you got?

Death: My hand is like a basketball score.

Nat: And it's spades.

Death: If you didn't talk so much.

(They redeal and play on.)   145

Nat: What'd you mean before when you said this was your first job?

Death: What does it sound like?

Nat: What are you telling me—that nobody ever went before?

Death: Sure they went. But I didn't take them.

Nat: So who did?   150

Death: Others.

Nat: There's others?

Death: Sure. Each one has his own personal way of going.

Nat: I never knew that.

Death: Why should you know? Who are you?   155

Nat: What do you mean who am I? Why—I'm nothing?

Death: Not nothing. You're a dress manufacturer. Where do you come to knowledge of the eternal mysteries?

Nat: What are you talking about? I make a beautiful dollar. I sent two kids through college. One is in advertising, the other's married. I got my own home. I drive a Chrysler. My wife has whatever she wants. Maids, mink coat, vacations. Right now she's at the Eden Roc. Fifty dollars a day because she wants to be near her sister. I'm supposed to join her next week, so what do you think I am—some guy off the street?

Death: All right. Don't be so touchy.

160   Nat: Who's touchy?

Death: How would you like it if I got insulted quickly?

Nat: Did I insult you?

Death: You didn't say you were disappointed in me?

Nat: What do you expect? You want me to throw you a block party?

165   Death: I'm not talking about that. I mean me personally. I'm too short, I'm this, I'm that.

Nat: I said you looked like me. It's a reflection.

Death: All right, deal, deal.

(They continue to play as music steals in and the lights dim until all is in total darkness. The lights slowly come up again, and now it is later and their game is over. Nat tallies.)

Nat: Sixty-eight . . . one-fifty . . . Well, you lose.

170   Death *(dejectedly looking through the deck):* I knew I shouldn't have thrown that nine. Damn it.

Nat: So I'll see you tomorrow.

Death: What do you mean you'll see me tomorrow?

Nat: I won the extra day. Leave me alone.

Death: You were serious?

175   Nat: We made a deal.

Death: Yeah, but—

Nat: Don't "but" me. I won twenty-four hours. Come back tomorrow.

Death: I didn't know we were actually playing for time.

Nat: That's too bad about you. You should pay attention.

180   Death: Where am I going to go for twenty-four hours?

Nat: What's the difference? The main thing is I won an extra day.

Death: What do you want me to do—walk the streets?

Nat: Check into a hotel and go to a movie. Take a *schvitz.* Don't make a federal case.

Death: Add the score again.

185   Nat: Plus you owe me twenty-eight dollars.

Death: *What!*

Nat: That's right, Buster. Here it is—read it.

Death *(going through pockets):* I have a few singles—not twenty-eight dollars.

Nat: I'll take a check.

190   Death: From what account?

Nat: Look who I'm dealing with.

Death: Sue me. Where do I keep my checking account?

Nat: All right, gimme what you got and we'll call it square.

Death: Listen, I need that money.

Nat: Why should you need money? 195

Death: What are you talking about? You're going to the Beyond.

Nat: So?

Death: So—you know how far that is?

Nat: So?

Death: So where's gas? Where's tolls? 200

Nat: We're going by car!

Death: You'll find out. *(Agitatedly)* Look—I'll be back tomorrow, and you'll give me a chance to win the money back. Otherwise I'm in definite trouble.

Nat: Anything you want. Double or nothing we'll play. I'm liable to win an extra week or a month. The way you play, maybe years.

Death: Meantime I'm stranded.

Nat: See you tomorrow. 205

Death: *(being edged to the doorway):* Where's a good hotel? What am I talking about hotel, I got no money. I'll go sit in Bickford's. *(He picks up the* News.*)*

Nat: Out. Out. That's my paper *(He takes it back.)*

Death *(exiting):* I couldn't just take him and go. I had to get involved in rummy.

Nat *(calling after him):* And be careful going downstairs. On one of the steps the rug is loose.

(And, on cue, we hear a terrific crash. Nat sighs, then crosses to 210 *the bedside table and makes a phone call.)*

Nat: Hello, Moe? Me. Listen, I don't know if somebody's playing a joke, or what, but Death was just here. We played a little gin . . . No, *Death.* In person. Or somebody who claims to be Death. But, Moe, he's such a *schlep!*

CURTAIN

___ **CONSIDERATIONS** _____

1. Death is a subject most people avoid discussing; instead they fall back on euphemisms. Make a list of euphemisms for death and dying and write an essay on the subject.

2. Nat is insulted by the suggestion that he doesn't know anything about death. "I make a beautiful dollar," he protests. "I sent two kids through college . . ." What do you think of the *logic* of his reply?

3. Obviously, dialogue is everything in a play. Study how some of the other writers in this book make use of dialogue in essays and stories. Try using dialogue in a forthcoming essay.

4. Nat: You want to play a tenth of a cent a point to make it interesting?
      Death: It's not interesting enough for you?
What does this exchange suggest about habitual or superficial vs. real or essential values? Are the same ideas suggested by the hackneyed expression, "The condemned man ate a hearty breakfast"?

5. The Kew Gardens mentioned in the stage-setting for "Death Knocks" is not the site of the Royal Botanical Gardens in London, but a residential section in a suburb of New York City. As you *listen* to the lines of the play, do you hear any clues that the characters are New Yorkers, not Londoners? Can you find other authors in this book who make use of voice in their work?

6. Woody Allen's playlet presents a somewhat unusual exmaple of personification. What are some more common personifications of death—in essays, stories, poems, cartoons, movies? Many other authors in this book use this literary device. Study their examples, then try your hand at personification.

Maya Angelou (b. 1928) told an interviewer, "One would say of my life—born loser—had to be; from a broken family, raped at eight, unwed mother at sixteen . . . it's a fact, but it's not the truth."

When she grew up, Maya Angelou became an actress, a singer, a dancer, a songwriter, a teacher, an editor, and a poet. She sang and danced professionally in Porgy and Bess *with a company that traveled through twenty-two countries of Europe and Asia. She wrote for the* Ghana Times *and she taught modern dance in Rome and in Tel Aviv. Her recent books are* And Still I Rise *(1978) and* The Heart of a Woman *(1981).*

In 1969 she began her autobiography, I Know Why the Caged Bird Sings, *which was an immediate success. As she says, "I speak to the black experience, but I am always talking about the human condition." The book recounts her early life, with realism and with joy. This section describes a masterful black con man, skillful at turning white bigotry into black profits.*

5

MAYA ANGELOU
Mr. Red Leg

Our house was a fourteen-room typical San Franciscan post-Earthquake affair. We had a succession of roomers, bringing and taking their different accents, and personalities and foods. Shipyard workers clanked up the stairs (we all slept on the second floor except Mother and Daddy Clidell) in their steel-tipped boots and metal hats, and gave way to much-powdered prostitutes, who giggled through their makeup and hung their wigs on the door-knobs. One couple (they were college

1

graduates) held long adult conversations with me in the big kitchen downstairs, until the husband went off to war. Then the wife who had been so charming and ready to smile changed into a silent shadow that played infrequently along the walls. An older couple lived with us for a year or so. They owned a restaurant and had no personality to enchant or interest a teenager, except that the husband was called Uncle Jim, and the wife Aunt Boy. I never figured that out.

2   The quality of strength lined with tenderness is an unbeatable combination, as are intelligence and necessity when unblunted by formal education. I was prepared to accept Daddy Clidell as one more faceless name added to Mother's roost of conquests. I had trained myself so successfully through the years to display interest, or at least attention, while my mind skipped free on other subjects that I could have lived in his house without ever seeing him and without his becoming the wiser. But his character beckoned and elicited admiration. He was a simple man who had no inferiority complex about his lack of education and, even more amazing, no superiority complex because he had succeeded despite that lack. He would say often, "I had been to school three years in my life. In Slaten, Texas, times was hard, and I had to help my daddy on the farm."

3   No recriminations lay hidden under the plain statement, nor was there boasting when he said, "If I'm living a litter better now, it's because I treats everybody right."

4   He owned apartment buildings and, later, pool halls, and was famous for being that rarity "a man of honor." He didn't suffer, as many "honest men" do, from the detestable righteousness that diminishes their virtue. He knew cards and men's hearts. So during the age when Mother was exposing us to certain facts of life, like personal hygiene, proper posture, table manners, good restaurants and tipping practices, Daddy Clidell taught me to play poker, blackjack, tonk and high, low, Jick, Jack and the Game. He wore expensive tailored suits and a large yellow diamond stickpin. Except for the jewelry, he was a conservative dresser and carried himself with the unconscious pomp of a man of secure means. Unexpectedly, I resembled him, and when he, Mother and I walked down the street his friends often said, "Clidell, that's sure your daughter. Ain't no way you can deny her."

5   Proud laughter followed those declarations, for he had never had children. Because of his late-arriving but intense paternal sense, I was introduced to the most colorful characters in the Black underground. One afternoon, I was invited into our smoke-filled dining room to make the acquaintance of Stonewall Jimmy, Just Black, Cool Clyde, Tight Coat and Red Leg. Daddy Clidell explained to me that they were the most

successful con men in the world, and they were going to tcll mc about some games so that I would never be "anybody's mark."

To begin, one man warned me, "There ain't never been a mark 6 yet that didn't want something for nothing." Then they took turns showing me their tricks, how they chose their victims (marks) from the wealthy bigoted whites and in every case how they used the victims' prejudice against them.

Some of the tales were funny, a few were pathetic, but all were 7 amusing or gratifying to me, for the Black man, the con man who could act the most stupid, won out every time over the powerful, arrogant white.

I remember Mr. Red Leg's story like a favorite melody. 8

"Anything that works against you can also work for you once you 9 understand the Principle of Reverse.

"There was a cracker in Tulsa who bilked so many Negroes he 10 could set up a Negro Bilking Company. Naturally he got to thinking, Black Skin means Damn Fool. Just Black and I went to Tulsa to check him out. Come to find out, he's a perfect mark. His momma must have been scared in an Indian massacre in Africa. He hated Negroes only a little more than he despised Indians. And he was greedy.

"Black and I studied him and decided he was worth setting up 11 against the store. That means we were ready to put out a few thousand dollars in preparation. We pulled in a white boy from New York, a good con artist, and had him open an office in Tulsa. He was supposed to be a Northern real estate agent trying to buy up valuable land in Oklahoma. We investigated a piece of land near Tulsa that had a toll bridge crossing it. It used to be part of an Indian reservation but had been taken over by the state.

"Just Black was laid out as the decoy, and I was going to be the 12 fool. After our friend from New York hired a secretary and had his cards printed, Black approached the mark with a proposition. He told him that he had heard that our mark was the only white man colored people could trust. He named some of the poor fools that had been taken by that crook. It just goes to show you how white folks can be deceived by their own deception. The mark believed Black.

"Black told him about his friend who was half Indian and half col- 13 ored and how some Northern white real estate agent had found out that he was the sole owner of a piece of valuable land and the Northerner wanted to buy it. At first the man acted like he smelled a rat, but from the way he gobbled up the proposition, turns out what he thought he smelled was some nigger money on his top lip.

"He asked the whereabouts of the land but Black put him off. He 14 told this cracker that he just wanted to make sure that he would be interested. The mark allowed how he was being interested, so Black said he would tell his friend and they'd get in touch with him. Black met the mark for about three weeks in cars and in alleys and kept putting him off until the white man was almost crazy with anxiety and greed and then accidentally it seemed Black let drop the name of the Northern real estate agent who wanted the property. From that moment on we knew we had the big fish on the line and all we had to do was to pull him in.

15   "We expected him to try to contact our store, which he did. That cracker went to our setup and counted on his whiteness to ally him with Spots, our white boy, but Spots refused to talk about the deal except to say the land had been thoroughly investigated by the biggest real estate concern in the South and that if our mark did not go around raising dust he would make sure that there would be a nice piece of money in it for him. Any obvious inquiries as to the rightful ownership of the land could alert the state and they would surely push through a law prohibiting the sale. Spots told the mark he would keep in touch with him. The mark went back to the store three or four times but to no avail, then just before we knew he would crack, Black brought me to see him. That fool was as happy as a sissy in a C.C.C. camp. You would have thought my neck was in a noose and he was about to light the fire under my feet. I never enjoyed taking anybody so much.

16   "Anyhow, I played scary at first but Just Black told me that this was one white man that our people could trust. I said I did not trust no white man because all they wanted was to get a chance to kill a Black man legally and get his wife in the bed. (I'm sorry, Clidell.) The mark assured me that he was the only white man who did not feel like that. Some of his best friends were colored people. In fact, if I didn't know it, the woman who raised him was a colored woman and he still sees her to this day. I let myself be convinced and then the mark began to drag the Northern whites. He told me that they made Negroes sleep in the street in the North and that they had to clean out toilets with their hands in the North and even things worse than that. I was shocked and said, 'Then I don't want to sell my land to that white man who offered seventy-five thousand dollars for it.' Just Black said, 'I wouldn't know what to do with that kind of money,' and I said that all I wanted was to have enough money to buy a home for my old mom, to buy a business and to make one trip to Harlem. The mark asked how much would that cost and I said I reckoned I could do it on fifty thousand dollars.

"The mark told me no Negro was safe with that kind of money.   17
That white folks would take it from him. I said I knew it but I had to
have at least forty thousand dollars. He agreed. We shook hands. I said
it would do my heart good to see the mean Yankee go down on some
of 'our land.' We met the next morning and I signed the deed in his car
and he gave me the cash.

"Black and I had kept most of our things in a hotel over in Hot   18
Springs, Arkansas. When the deal was closed we walked to our car, drove
across the state line and on to Hot Springs.

"That's all there was to it."   19

When he finished, more triumphant stories rainbowed around the   20
room riding the shoulders of laughter. By all accounts those storytellers,
born Black and male before the turn of the twentieth century, should
have been ground into useless dust. Instead they used their intelligence
to pry open the door of rejection and not only became wealthy but got
some revenge in the bargain.

It wasn't possible for me to regard them as criminals or be any-   21
thing but proud of their achievements.

The needs of a society determine its ethics, and in the Black   22
American ghettos the hero is that man who is offered only the crumbs
from his country's table but by ingenuity and courage is able to take
for himself a Lucullan feast. Hence the janitor who lives in one room
but sports a robin's-egg-blue Cadillac is not laughed at but admired, and
the domestic who buys forty-dollar shoes is not criticized but is appreciated. We know that they have put to use their full mental and
physical powers. Each single gain feeds into the gains of the body
collective.

Stories of law violations are weighed on a different set of scales   23
in the Black mind than in the white. Petty crimes embarrass the community and many people wistfully wonder why Negroes don't rob more
banks, embezzle more funds and employ graft in the unions. "We are
the victims of the world's most comprehensive robbery. Life demands
a balance. It's all right if we do a little robbing now." This belief appeals
particularly to one who is unable to compete legally with his fellow
citizens.

My education and that of my Black associates were quite differ-   24
ent from the education of our white schoolmates. In the classroom we
all learned past participles, but in the streets and in our homes the Blacks
learned to drop s's from plurals and suffixes from past-tense verbs. We
were alert to the gap separating the written word from the colloquial.
We learned to slide out of one language and into another without being

conscious of the effort. At school, in a given situation, we might respond with "That's not unusual." But in the street, meeting the same situation, we easily said, "It be's like that sometimes."

_____ CONSIDERATIONS _____

1. Most of Angelou's essay is devoted to Mr. Red Leg telling a story. Notice how close to pure narration that story is. Compare it with the selections in this book by Annie Dillard (pages 137–139), George Orwell (pages 292–319), or Richard Wright (pages 481–490), and contrast the amount of description and narration in Mr. Red Leg's story to that in one of the others.

2. Compare Angelou's essay with that of Frank Conroy (pages 119–126), who also emphasizes memorable characters. How do the two authors differ in their reasons for devoting so much space to Mr. Red Leg and to Ramos and Ricardo?

3. At the end of her essay, Angelou sets out an important linguistic principle. Paraphrase that idea and provide examples from your own experience or research.

4. "Stories of law violations are weighed on a different set of scales in the Black mind than in the white." Does a similar difference occur in the minds of two generations? Discuss relative justice versus absolute law.

5. Angelou demonstrates her versatility as a writer throughout this essay by managing two voices. Find examples and discuss.

6. From what you learn of Angelou's upbringing in the essay, compile a *negative report* by a social worker on Angelou's childhood. Are thre positive details in the essay that would allow you to refute a negative report?

Barbara Lazear Ascher (b. 1946) graduated from Bennington College in 1968 and currently lives in New York City. After marrying and having a daughter she attended law school, practiced law for two years, then gave it up to become a writer. Ascher's essays appear in the New York Times, Vogue, Redbook, McCalls, Newsday, *and* The Yale Review. *This piece comes from her collection,* Playing After Dark *(1986), essays that are personal and that work toward the universal.*

6

BARBARA LAZEAR ASCHER

On the Road
with the College Applicant

My sixteen-year-old daughter slumped against the doorway of the college admissions office. "It happened," she groaned. "I had a stress interview." 1

She exhaled as though she'd been holding her breath for the previous forty-five minutes, and sank to the ground, risking grass stains on the carefully selected, conservative interview skirt that must appear the next day on the next campus. "The minute I walked into his office," she explained, "he demanded, 'So! What can you do for this college?'" The tone she captured sounded like that of a police interrogator—"Were-you-or-were-you-not-at-the-scene-of-the-crime-the-night-of-the-crime?"— a tone that tempts one to admit guilt in order to be free of the questioning. "Then it turned into a game show. If I responded the way he wanted 2 me to, he'd say, 'Good answer! Good answer!' " She looked at me with astonishment, "And *then* he said, 'There's an invisible box on my desk with things in it that describe you. What's in the box?' "

3   "What did you say? What did you do?" I asked anxiously, the beats of my heart quickly catching up to the race of her own. Did she black out? Did she excuse herself and go to the bathroom? Was the course of her future determined by five minutes of silence?

4   "I went on automatic pilot," my daughter responded, adding, "In a stress interview, you separate your mouth from your brain and hope it works."

5   Later the adults in her life become witty, bright and piercingly intelligent over the food and wine of a family dinner. With a safe distance between ourselves and the Ivy League interrogation chamber, with a safe distance between ourselves and our own tremulous youth, we sound like Bartlett's Familiar Quotations. We are not struggling to describe ourselves with objects that could fit inside an invisible box. There are no cold sweats, stutters, blushes or stammers here.

6   Her grandfather says, "When he asked what she could do for the college, she should have said, "What can your college do for me?' " Another diner suggests, "She should have looked him in the eye and said, 'If the point of an interview is to become acquainted with the applicant, why are you determined to make me ill at ease?" A wise guy notes, "When he asked what was in the box, she should have said, 'Your head!' and walked out."

7   Easy for us to say. Smug as we are with degrees under our belts. She, on the other hand, can't afford the luxury of brashness nor the time to change the system. Chances are she'll even apply to and pray for acceptance at the source of the stress interview. It's a seller's market. College-bound high school seniors can rattle off admissions statistics the way they once might have memorized batting averages. Numbers culled from college catalogues march through their brains: "In 1984 approximately 12,636 applications were reviewed for 1,360 places in the freshman class." SAT scores, CEEB scores, AP scores and grade point averages join the parade. It keeps them up nights.

8   Lack of sleep and fear of rejection take their toll. My daughter has become crazed. Every high school senior I know has become crazed. One of them told me that she thought it was a trick question when her interviewer asked her one balmy August morning, "It's such a lovely day, would you like to meet outside?" Another became so nervous that he lost all sense of spatial relations, and after pulling up a chair across from the interviewer's desk, he promptly sat on the floor. When it was time to leave, he walked into the closet rather than out the door. My

daughter tells me that she is certain, "When the interviewer asks you where you want to sit, your choice MEANS something." Even successful interviews are belittled in the general mood of overwhelming pessimism that the students adopt, in part to protect themselves from what they perceive as inevitable disappointment.

There's perversion at work here. Applicants begin to assume that   9
the harder it is to get into a college, the better that college. And they, who happen to be at the age of least self-confidence, feel they couldn't possibly be "good" enough to be acceptable. Admissions committees aggravate this sense of insecurity by flaunting the number of applications they receive, statistics of which they are justly proud—statistics that reduce sixteen- and seventeen-year-olds to a sense of barely tolerable inadequacy.

I watched an applicant walk onto the campus of one of the "hardest   10
to get into" universities, look around at what appeared to me to be no more than the normal sampling of collegiate scruffiness, and remark fearfully, "Look at all those geniuses!"

"It's hard not to feel victimized," my daughter tells me. "Even when   11
it's not a stress interview, these are strangers probing into your life, and you didn't invite them there." Some interviewers are sensitive to the intrusive nature of their jobs and the vulnerability of their "victims." At one of the most competitive colleges an admissions officer, upon shaking my daughter's hand and finding it cold said, "Let me make some coffee to warm you up." If an applicant is in a position to decide, decisions have been based on less than that.

They're also based on the personality of the tour guide and some   12
sort of Rorschach reaction to the appearance of students and campus. While admissions officers are seated in the position of power, they are not alone in the seat of judgment. Applications come equipped with the ruthlessly critical eye of adolescence. I have heard hundreds of years of academic glory dismissed in a sentence:

College A "is full of preps."   13

College B "is like Coca-Cola, they spend more money on their im-   14
age than the product."

At College C, "The students are refugees from Westchester   15
going native in L. L. Bean boots."

College D "has gone commercial with the quota system. They   16
make certain to show you a specific number of jocks, brains, wimps and weirdos."

College E "was great! The guy who interviewed me was a Mets   17
fan."

Chance encounters also make an impression. My daughter and   18

I were having a pre-interview lunch in College F's cafeteria when a student walked in with a Steiff bunny rabbit puppet on her hand. She spoke exclusively through the rabbit. When another student asked, "How are you?" the bunny's head bobbed up and down to the lilt of a Walt Disney cartoon voice, "Just fine, thank you." I promptly addressed the tuna fish sandwich at hand, but caught a glimpse of my companion rolling her eyes.

19   It doesn't look good for College F.

20   However, in spite of the stress, the defenses, the critical eye, there are moments of love at first sight. Such events are unpredictable except that they hardly ever happen on rainy days and rarely on Saturdays when one senses the interviewer's annoyance at having to work weekends. For my own daughter, these moments occurred when an interviewer lost track of time and talked with her for two hours, when she met with a Classics professor who had the tenderness and wisdom of Catullus behind his eyes, and when she dined with a professor who shared her passion for Shelley and Keats.

21   And that is supposed to be the point of all this—passion. The goal of higher education is to seduce students into a love of learning, to nurture and encourage a lifelong love affair. The root of the word "education," comes from the Latin *educo*—to bring out or lead forth. It seems that both applicants and admissions personnel lose sight of this in a system that has become rife with stress, statistics, slick catalogues and superficial encounters, that has created a kind of painful endurance test for parents and children. I wonder if colleges are even aware that admissions procedures have placed intimidation and interviewers' invisible boxes before their gates? And that many will stumble there, many who should be brought in, in order to be "brought out."

———— CONSIDERATIONS ————————————————

1. If an interviewer in the admissions office of your school asked, "What can you do for this college?" what would you say? Is this an effective question?

2. Suppose you, as an applicant, had the chance to visit three or four colleges you had heard might be desirable choices. Ignoring the possibility of interviews for the moment, what would you look for on each campus to help you make a judgment? For that matter, why did you choose your school?

3. Ascher says that "The goal of higher education is to seduce students into a love of learning." Read Caroline Bird's "Where College Fails Us" (pages 79–89) and discuss how the two writers' ideas differ.

4. Is the attempt to select and enter a school as stressful an experience for everyone as it was for Ascher's daughter, or is that experience limited to a relatively small group? If necessary, ask several of your classmates before explaining your answer.

Margaret Atwood (b. 1939) is a Canadian novelist and poet. Born in Ottawa, she now lives in Toronto with her daughter and husband. Her novels include The Edible Woman *(1969),* Surfacing *(1972),* Lady Oracle *(1976),* Life Before Man *(1979),* Bodily Harm *(1982), and* The Handmaid's Tale *(1986). Her* Selected Poems *came out in 1976, and she has published nine other collections of poetry. In 1978 she issued a collection of short stories,* Dancing Girls, *and in 1986 she issued* Bluebeard's Egg and Other Stories. *She has written literary criticism as well as topical essays like this one.*

7

MARGARET ATWOOD
Pornography

1   When I was in Finland a few years ago for an international writers' conference, I had occasion to say a few paragraphs in public on the subject of pornography. The context was a discussion of political repression, and I was suggesting the possibility of a link between the two. The immediate result was that a male journalist took several large bites out of me. Prudery and pornography are two halves of the same coin, said he, and I was clearly a prude. What could you expect from an Anglo-Canadian? Afterward, a couple of pleasant Scandinavian men asked me what I had been so worked up about. All "pornography" means, they said, is graphic depictions of whores, and what was the harm in that?

2   Not until then did it strike me that the male journalist and I had two entirely different things in mind. By "pornography," he meant

naked bodies and sex. I, on the other hand, had recently been doing the research for my novel *Bodily Harm*, and was still in a state of shock from some of the material I had seen, including the Ontario Board of Film Censors' "outtakes." By "pornography," I meant women getting their nipples snipped off with garden shears, having meat hooks stuck into their vaginas, being disemboweled; little girls being raped; men (yes, there are some men) being smashed to a pulp and forcibly sodomized. The cutting edge of pornography, as far as I could see, was no longer simple old copulation, hanging from the chandelier or otherwise: it was death, messy, explicit and highly sadistic. I explained this to the nice Scandinavian men. "Oh, but that's just the United States," they said. "Everyone knows they're sick." In their country, they said, violent "pornography" of that kind was not permitted on television or in movies; indeed, excessive violence of any kind was not permitted. They had drawn a clear line between erotica, which earlier studies had shown did not incite men to more aggressive and brutal behavior toward women, and violence, which later studies indicated did.

Some time after that I was in Saskatchewan, where, because of 3
the scenes in *Bodily Harm*, I found myself on an open-line radio show answering questions about "pornography." Almost no one who phoned in was in favor of it, but again they weren't talking about the same stuff I was, because they hadn't seen it. Some of them were all set to stamp out bathing suits and negligees, and, if possible, any depictions of the female body whatsoever. God, it was implied, did not approve of female bodies, and sex of any kind, including that practised by bumblebees, should be shoved back into the dark, where it belonged. I had more than a suspicion that *Lady Chatterley's Lover*, Margaret Laurence's *The Diviners*, and indeed most books by most serious modern authors would have ended up as confetti if left in the hands of these callers.

For me, these two experiences illustrate the two poles of the 4
emotionally heated debate that is now thundering around this issue. They also underline the desirability and even the necessity of defining the terms. "Pornography" is now one of those catchalls, like "Marxism" and "feminism," that have become so broad they can mean almost anything, ranging from certain verses in the Bible, ads for skin lotion and sex texts for children to the contents of Penthouse, Naughty '90s postcards and films with titles containing the word *Nazi* that show vicious scenes of torture and killing. It's easy to say that sensible people can tell the difference. Unfortunately, opinions on what constitutes a sensible person vary.

But even sensible people tend to lose their cool when they 5 start talking about this subject. They soon stop talking and start yelling, and the name-calling begins. Those in favor of censorship (which may include groups not noticeably in agreement on other issues, such as some feminists and religious fundamentalists) accuse the others of exploiting women through the use of degrading images, contributing to the corruption of children, and adding to the general climate of violence and threat in which both women and children live in this society; or, though they may not give much of a hoot about actual women and children, they invoke moral standards and God's supposed aversion to "filth," "smut" and deviated *preversion*, which may mean ankles.

6   The camp in favor of total "freedom of expression" often comes out howling as loud as the Romans would have if told they could no longer have innocent fun watching the lions eat up Christians. It too may include segments of the population who are not natural bedfellows: those who proclaim their God-given right to freedom, including the freedom to tote guns, drive when drunk, drool over chicken porn and get off on videotapes of women being raped and beaten, may be waving the same anticensorship banner as responsible liberals who fear the return of Mrs. Grundy, or gay groups for whom sexual emancipation involves the concept of "sexual theatre." *Whatever turns you on* is a handy motto, as is *A man's home is his castle* (and if it includes a dungeon with beautiful maidens strung up in chains and bleeding from every pore, that's his business).

7   Meanwhile, theoreticians theorize and speculators speculate. Is today's pornography yet another indication of the hatred of the body, the deep mind-body split, which is supposed to pervade Western Christian society? Is it a backlash against the women's movement by men who are threatened by uppity female behavior in real life, so like to fantasize about women done up like outsize parcels, being turned into hamburger, kneeling at their feet in slavelike adoration or sucking off guns? Is it a sign of collective impotence, of a generation of men who can't relate to real women at all but have to make do with bits of celluloid and paper? Is the current flood just a result of smart marketing and aggressive promotion by the money men in what has now become a multibillion-dollar industry? If they were selling movies about men getting their testicles stuck full of knitting needles by women with swastikas on their sleeves, would they do as well, or is this penchant somehow peculiarly male? If so, why? Is pornography a power trip rather than a sex one? Some say that those ropes, chains, muzzles and other restraining devices are an argument for the immense power female sex-

uality still wields in the male imagination: you don't put these things on dogs unless you're afraid of them. Others, more literary, wonder about the shift from the 19th-century Magic Woman or Femme Fatale image to the lollipop-licker, airhead or turkey-carcass treatment of women in porn today. The proporners don't care much about theory: they merely demand product. The anti-porners don't care about it in the final analysis either: there's dirt on the street, and they want it cleaned up, now.

It seems to me that this conversation, with its *You're-a-prude/ You're-a-pervert* dialectic, will never get anywhere as long as we continue to think of this material as just "entertainment." Possibly we're deluded by the packaging, the format: magazine, book, movie, theatrical presentation. We're used to thinking of these things as part of the "entertainment industry," and we're used to thinking of ourselves as free adult people who ought to be able to see any kind of "entertainment" we want to. That was what the First Choice pay-TV debate was all about. After all, it's only entertainment, right? Entertainment means fun, and only a killjoy would be antifun. What's the harm? 8

This is obviously the central question: *What's the harm?* If there isn't any real harm to any real people, then the antiporners can tsk-tsk and/or throw up as much as they like, but they can't rightfully expect more legal controls or sanctions. However, the no-harm position is far from being proven. 9

(For instance, there's a clear-cut case for banning—as the federal government has proposed—movies, photos and videos that depict children engaging in sex with adults: real children are used to make the movies, and hardly anybody thinks this is ethical. The possibilities for coercion are too great.) 10

To shift the viewpoint, I'd like to suggest three other models for looking at "pornography"—and here I mean the violent kind. 11

Those who find the idea of regulating pornographic materials repugnant because they think it's Fascist or Communist or otherwise not in accordance with the principles of an open democratic society should consider that Canada has made it illegal to disseminate material that may lead to hatred toward any group because of race or religion. I suggest that if pornography of the violent kind depicted these acts being done predominantly to Chinese, to blacks, to Catholics, it would be off the market immediately, under the present laws. Why is hate literature illegal? Because whoever made the law thought that such material might incite real people to do real awful things to other real people. The human brain is to a certain extent a computer: garbage in, garbage out. We only hear about the extreme cases (like that of American 12 multimurderer Ted Bundy) in which pornography has contributed to the death and/or mutilation of women and/or men. Although pornography is not the only factor involved in the creation of such deviance, it certainly has upped the ante by suggesting both a variety of techniques and the social acceptability of such actions. Nobody knows yet what effect this stuff is having on the less psychotic.

13   Studies have shown that a large part of the market for all kinds of porn, soft and hard, is drawn from the 16-to-21-year-old population of young men. Boys used to learn about sex on the street, or (in Italy, according to Fellini movies) from friendly whores, or, in more genteel surroundings, from girls, their parents, or, once upon a time, in school, more or less. Now porn has been added, and sex education in the schools is rapidly being phased out. The buck has been passed, and boys are being taught that all women secretly like to be raped and that real men get high on scooping out women's digestive tracts.

14   Boys learn their concept of masculinity from other men: is this what most men want them to be learning? If word gets around that rapists are "normal" and even admirable men, will boys feel that in order to be normal, admirable and masculine they will have to be rapists? Human beings are enormously flexible, and how they turn out depends a lot on how they're educated, by the society in which they're immersed as well as by their teachers. In a society that advertises and glorifies rape or even implicitly condones it, more women get raped. It becomes socially acceptable. And at a time when men and the traditional male role have taken a lot of flak and men are confused and casting around for an acceptable way of being male (and, in some cases, not getting much comfort from women on that score), this must be at times a pleasing thought.

15   It would be naïve to think of violent pornography as just harmless entertainment. It's also an educational tool and a powerful propaganda device. What happens when boy educated on porn meets girl brought up on Harlequin romances? The clash of expectations can be heard around the block. She wants him to get down on his knees with a ring, he wants her to get down on all fours with a ring in her nose. Can this marriage be saved?

16   Pornography has certain things in common with such addictive substances as alcohol and drugs: for some, though by no means for all, it induces chemical changes in the body, which the user finds exciting and pleasurable. It also appears to attract a "hard core" of habitual users and a penumbra of those who use it occasionally but aren't dependent

on it in any way. There are also significant numbers of men who aren't much interested in it, not because they're undersexed but because real life is satisfying their needs, which may not require as many appliances as those of users.

For the "hard core," pornography may function as alcohol does for   17
the alcoholic: tolerance develops, and a little is no longer enough. This may account for the short viewing time and fast turnover in porn theatres. Mary Brown, chairwoman of the Ontario Board of Film Censors, estimates that for every one mainstream movie requesting entrance to Ontario, there is one porno flick. Not only the quantity consumed but the quality of explicitness must escalate, which may account for the growing violence: once the big deal was breasts, then it was genitals, then copulation, then that was no longer enough and the hard users had to have more. The ultimate kick is death, and after that, as the Marquis de Sade so boringly demonstrated, multiple death.

The existence of alcoholism has not led us to ban social drinking.   18
On the other hand, we do have laws about drinking and driving, excessive drunkenness and other abuses of alcohol that may result in injury or death to others.

This leads us back to the key question: what's the harm? No-   19
body knows, but this society should find out fast, before the saturation point is reached. The Scandinavian studies that showed a connection between depictions of sexual violence and increased impulse toward it on the part of male viewers would be a starting point, but many more questions remain to be raised as well as answered. What, for instance, is the crucial difference between men who are users and men who are not? Does using affect a man's relationship with actual women, and, if so, adversely? Is there a clear line between erotica and violent pornography, or are they on an escalating continuum? Is this a "men versus women" issue, with all men secretly siding with the proporners and all women secretly siding against? (I think not; there *are* lots of men who don't think that running their true love through the Cuisinart is the best way they can think of to spend a Saturday night, and they're just as nauseated by films of someone else doing it as women are.) Is pornography merely an expression of the sexual confusion of this age or an active contributor to it?

Nobody wants to go back to the age of official repression, when   20
even piano legs were referred to as "limbs" and had to wear pantaloons to be decent. Neither do we want to end up in George Orwell's *1984*, in which pornography is turned out by the State to keep the proles in

a state of torpor, sex itself is considered dirty and the approved practise it only for reproduction. But Rome under the emperors isn't such a good model either.

21   If all men and women respected each other, if sex were considered joyful and life-enhancing instead of a wallow in germ-filled glop, if everyone were in love all the time, if, in other words, many people's lives were more satisfactory for them than they appear to be now, pornography might just go away on its own. But since this is obviously not happening, we as a society are going to have to make some informed and responsible decisions about how to deal with it.

_____ CONSIDERATIONS _____

1. In explaining that "pornography" means different things to different people, Atwood separates "erotica" from *her* definition of "pornography." How does she make that distinction, and more important, why?

2. Paragraph 7 consists largely of questions. Are they real questions or rhetorical questions? Explain the difference.

3. According to Atwood, what is the central question in the debate about pornography?

4. What is Atwood's strategy as demonstrated in Paragraph 11? What does she hope to accomplish using it?

5. In Paragraph 6, Atwood refers to "the return of Mrs. Grundy." Who was Mrs. Grundy, and why does her name pop up in many discussions of pornography, sexual values, and the like? You will find references to Mrs. Grundy in a literary handbook (e.g., *The Reader's Encyclopedia*, edited by William Rose Benet, or *The Oxford Companion to English Literature*, edited by Margaret Drabble).

6. Why do many people, including judges and lawyers, continue to disagree on a definition of "pornography"? Think of issues that pose the same problem. Note Atwood's wisdom in clarifying early in her essay what *she* means by the word. Discuss your own views of pornography.

Francis Bacon (1561–1626), born in London and educated at Cambridge, was a baron and a viscount who became a lawyer and a member of Parliament. He served Queen Elizabeth, and after her death continued to rise in the government of James I. In 1621, however, he admitted taking bribes, was briefly imprisoned in the Tower of London, and saw his public life come to an end. By this time he had already written The Advancement of Learning *(1605). His ideas of science and of scientific method,* Novum Organum *(1620), were innovative and influential. He wrote a utopian fable called the* New Atlantis, *but it is the* Essays, *which he brought out in several editions from 1497 to 1625, that most reflect the progressive, exploratory viewpoint of the new man in a new age.*

8

FRANCIS BACON
The Sphinx

Sphinx, says the story, was a monster combining many shapes in one. She had the face and voice of a virgin, the wings of a bird, the claws of a griffin. She dwelt on the ridge of a mountain near Thebes and infested the roads, lying in ambush for travellers, whom she would suddenly attack and lay hold of; and when she had mastered them, she propounded to them certain dark and perplexing riddles, which she was thought to have obtained from the Muses. And if the wretched captives could not at once solve and interpret the same, as they stood hesitating and confused she cruelly tore them to pieces. Time bringing no abatement of the calamity, the Thebans offered to any man who should expound the Sphinx's riddles (for this was the only way to subdue her) the sovereignty of Thebes as his reward. The greatness of the prize induced Œdipus, a man of wisdom and penetration, but lame from wounds

1

in his feet, to accept the condition and make the trial: who presenting himself full of confidence and alacrity before the Sphinx, and being asked what kind of animal it was which was born four-footed, afterwards became two-footed, then three-footed, and at last four-footed again, answered readily that it was man; who at his birth and during his infancy sprawls on all fours, hardly attempting to creep; in a little while walks upright on two feet; in later years leans on a walking-stick and so goes as it were on three; and at last in extreme age and decrepitude, his sinews all failing, sinks into a quadruped again, and keeps his bed. This was the right answer and gave him the victory; whereupon he slew the Sphinx; whose body was put on the back of an ass and carried about in triumph; while himself was made according to compact King of Thebes.

2   The fable is an elegant and a wise one, invented apparently in allusion to Science; especially in its application to practical life. Science, being the wonder of the ignorant and unskilful, may be not absurdly called a monster. In figure and aspect it is represented as many-shaped, in allusion to the immense variety of matter with which it deals. It is said to have the face and voice of a woman, in respect of its beauty and facility of utterance. Wings are added because the sciences and the discoveries of science spread and fly abroad in an instant, the communication of knowledge being like that of one candle with another, which lights up at once. Claws, sharp and hooked, are ascribed to it with great elegance, because the axioms and arguments of science penetrate and hold fast the mind, so that it has no means of evasion or escape; a point which the sacred philosopher also noted: *The words of the wise are as goads, and as nails driven deep in.* Again, all knowledge may be regarded as having its station on the heights of mountains; for it is deservedly esteemed a thing sublime and lofty, which looks down upon ignorance as from an eminence, and has moreover a spacious prospect on every side, such as we find on hill-tops. It is described as infesting the roads, because at every turn in the journey or pilgrimage of human life, matter and occasion for study assails and encounters us. Again Sphinx proposes to men a variety of hard questions and riddles which she received from the Muses. In these, while they remain with the Muses, there is probably no cruelty; for so long as the object of meditation and inquiry is merely to know, the understanding is not oppressed or straitened by it, but is free to wander and expatiate, and finds in the very uncertainty of conclusion and variety of choice a certain pleasure and delight; but when they pass from the Muses to Sphinx, that is from contemplation to practice, whereby there is necessity for present ac-

tion, choice, and decision, then they begin to be painful and cruel; and unless they be solved and disposed of they strangely torment and worry the mind, pulling it first this way and then that, and fairly tearing it to pieces. Moreover the riddles of the Sphinx have always a twofold condition attached to them; distraction and laceration of mind, if you fail to solve them; if you succeed, a kingdom. For he who understands his subject is master of his end; and every workman is king over his work.

Now of the Sphinx's riddles there are in all two kinds; one concerning the nature of things, another concerning the nature of man; and in like manner there are two kinds of kingdom offered as the reward of solving them; one over nature, and the other over man. For the command over things natural,—over bodies, medicines, mechanical powers, and infinite other of the kind—is the one proper and ultimate end of true natural philosophy; however the philosophy of the School, content with what it finds, and swelling with talk, may neglect or spurn the search after realities and works. But the riddle proposed to Œdipus, by the solution of which he became King of Thebes, related to the nature of man; for whoever has a thorough insight into the nature of man may shape his fortune almost as he will, and is born for empire; as was well declared concerning the arts of the Romans,— 3

> Be thine the art,
> O Rome, with government to rule the nations,
> And to know whom to spare and whom to abate,
> And settle the condition of the world.

And therefore it fell out happily that Augustus Caesar, whether on purpose or by chance, used a Sphinx for his seal. For he certainly excelled in the art of politics if ever man did; and succeeded in the course of his life in solving most happily a great many new riddles concerning the nature of man, which if he had not dexterously and readily answered he would many times have been in imminent danger of destruction. The fable adds very prettily that when the Sphinx was subdued, her body was laid on the back of an ass: for there is nothing so subtle and abstruse, but when it is once thoroughly understood and published to the world, even a dull wit can carry it. Nor is that other point to be passed over, that the Sphinx was subdued by a lame man with club feet; for men generally proceed too fast and in too great a hurry to the solution of the Sphinx's riddles; whence it follows that the Sphinx has the better of them, and instead of obtaining the sovereignty by works and effects, they only distract and worry their minds with disputations.

___ **CONSIDERATIONS** _____

1. Why, according to Francis Bacon, did Augustus Caesar use a Sphinx for his seal?

2. The fable of the Sphinx, says Bacon in Paragraph 2, was "invented apparently in allusion to Science." Bearing in mind when Bacon wrote the essay, how did his concept of science differ from ours? Consult the unabridged *Oxford English Dictionary* for a history of the word "science."

3. How does Bacon distinguish between the questions as posed by the Muse and then by the Sphinx? Could you draw a comparison here to the difference between science and technology? See also Abbey's "Science with a Human Face" (pages 1–7) for help with this question.

4. Bacon's paragraphs are longer than those favored by most contemporary writers. Look over either Paragraph 2 or 3 and decide where you might break it into smaller units. How would you justify such changes?

5. If you are not familiar with *Œdipus Rex*, by Sophocles, a great playwrite of ancient Greece, read it now to see how Bacon's story of the Sphinx figures in that tragedy.

James Baldwin (b. 1924), son of a Harlem minister, published his first novel Go Tell It on the Mountain *when he was still in his twenties. His most recent, published in 1985, is* Evidence of Things Not Seen. *In addition, Baldwin has written other novels, a book of stories, one play, and several collections of essays. In these pages he summarizes his life to the age of thirty-one, then concentrates a life's ambition into one sentence.*

9

JAMES BALDWIN

Autobiographical Notes

I was born in Harlem thirty-one years ago. I began plotting novels   1
at about the time I learned to read. The story of my childhood is the
usual bleak fantasy, and we can dismiss it with the restrained observation that I certainly would not consider living it again. In those days
my mother was given to the exasperating and mysterious habit of having babies. As they were born, I took them over with one hand and held
a book with the other. The children probably suffered, though they have
since been kind enough to deny it, and in this way I read *Uncle Tom's
Cabin* and *A Tale of Two Cities* over and over and over again; in this
way, in fact, I read just about everything I could get my hands on—
except the Bible, probably because it was the only book I was encouraged
to read. I must also confess that I wrote—a great deal—and my first professional triumph, in any case, the first effort of mine to be seen in print,
occurred at the age of twelve or thereabouts, when a short story I had
written about the Spanish revolution won some sort of prize in an extremely short-lived church newspaper. I remember the story was cen-

sored by the lady editor, though I don't remember why, and I was outraged.

2   Also wrote plays, and songs, for one of which I received a letter of congratulations from Mayor La Guardia, and poetry, about which the less said, the better. My mother was delighted by all these goings-on, but my father wasn't, he wanted me to be a preacher. When I was fourteen I became a preacher, and when I was seventeen I stopped. Very shortly thereafter I left home. For God knows how long I struggled with the world of commerce and industry—I guess they would say they struggled with *me*—and when I was about twenty-one I had enough done of a novel to get a Saxton Fellowship. When I was twenty-two the fellowship was over, the novel turned out to be unsalable, and I started waiting on tables in a Village restaurant and writing book reviews— mostly, as it turned out, about the Negro problem, concerning which the color of my skin made me automatically an expert. Did another book, in company with photographer Theodore Pelatowski, about the store-front churches in Harlem. This book met exactly the same fate as my first—fellowship, but no sale. (It was a Rosenwald Fellowship.) By the time I was twenty-four I had decided to stop reviewing books about the Negro problem—which, by this time, was only slightly less horrible in print than it was in life—and I packed my bags and went to France, where I finished, God knows how, *Go Tell It on the Mountain*.

3   Any writer, I suppose, feels that the world into which he was born is nothing less than a conspiracy against the cultivation of his talent—which attitude certainly has a great deal to support it. On the other hand, it is only because the world looks on his talent with such a frightening indifference that the artist is compelled to make his talent important. So that any writer, looking back over even so short a span of time as I am here forced to assess, finds that the things which hurt him and the things which helped him cannot be divorced from each other; he could be helped in a certain way only because he was hurt in a certain way; and his help is simply to be enabled to move from one conundrum to the next—one is tempted to say that he moves from one disaster to the next. When one begins looking for influences one finds them by the score. I haven't thought much about my own, not enough anyway; I hazard that the King James Bible, the rhetoric of the store-front church, something ironic and violent and perpetually understated in Negro speech—and something of Dickens' love for bravura—have something to do with me today; but I wouldn't stake my life on it. Likewise, innumerable people have helped me in many ways; but finally, I suppose, the most difficult (and most rewarding) thing in my life has

been the fact that I was born a Negro and was forced, therefore, to effect some kind of truce with this reality. (Truce, by the way, is the best one can hope for.)

One of the difficulties about being a Negro writer (and this is not special pleading, since I don't mean to suggest that he has it worse than anybody else) is that the Negro problem is written about so widely. The bookshelves groan under the weight of information, and everyone therefore considers himself informed. And this information, furthermore, operates usually (generally, popularly) to reinforce traditional attitudes. Of traditional attitudes there are only two—For or Against—and I, personally, find it difficult to say which attitude has caused me the most pain. I am speaking as a writer; from a social point of view I am perfectly aware that the change from ill-will to good-will, however motivated, however imperfect, however expressed, is better than no change at all. 4

But it is part of the business of the writer—as I see it—to examine attitudes, to go beneath the surface, to tap the source. From this point of view the Negro problem is nearly inaccessible. It is not only written about so widely; it is written about so badly. It is quite possible to say that the price a Negro pays for becoming articulate is to find himself, at length, with nothing to be articulate about. ("You taught me language," says Caliban to Prospero, "and my profit on't is I know how to curse.") Consider: the tremendous social activity that this problem generates imposes on whites and Negroes alike the necessity of looking forward, of working to bring about a better day. This is fine, it keeps the waters troubled; it is all, indeed, that has made possible the Negro's progress. Nevertheless, social affairs are not generally speaking the writer's prime concern, whether they ought to be or not; it is absolutely necessary that he establish between himself and these affairs a distance which will allow, at least, for clarity, so that before he can look forward in any meaningful sense, he must first be allowed to take a long look back. In the context of the Negro problem neither whites nor blacks, for excellent reasons of their own, have the faintest desire to look back; but I think that the past is all that makes the present coherent, and further, that the past will remain horrible for exactly as long as we refuse to assess it honestly. 5

I know, in any case, that the most crucial time in my own development came when I was forced to recognize that I was a kind of bastard of the West; when I followed the line of my past I did not find myself in Europe but in Africa. And this meant that in some subtle way, in a really profound way, I brought to Shakespeare, Bach, Rembrandt, to 6 the stones of Paris, to the cathedral at Chartres and to the Empire State Building, a special attitude. These were not really my creations, they did not contain my history; I might search in them in vain forever for any reflection of myself. I was an interloper; this was not my heritage. At the same time I had no other heritage which I could possibly hope to use—I had certainly been unfitted for the jungle or the tribe. I would have to appropriate these white centuries, I would have to make them mine—I would have to accept my special attitude, my special place in this scheme—otherwise I would have no place in *any* scheme. What was the most difficult was the fact that I was forced to admit something I had always hidden from myself, which the American Negro has had to hide from himself as the price of his public progress; that I hated and feared white people. This did not mean that I loved black people; on the contrary, I despised them, possibly because they failed to produce Rembrandt. In effect, I hated and feared the world. And this meant, not only that I thus gave the world an altogether murderous power over me, but also that in such a self-destroying limbo I could never hope to write.

7   One writes out of one thing only—one's own experience. Everything depends on how relentlessly one forces from this experience the last drop, sweet or bitter, it can possibly give. This is the only real concern of the artist, to recreate out of the disorder of life that order which is art. The difficulty then, for me, of being a Negro writer was the fact that I was, in effect, prohibited from examining my own experience too closely by the tremendous demands and the very real dangers of my social situation.

8   I don't think the dilemma outlined above is uncommon. I do think, since writers work in the disastrously explicit medium of language, that it goes a little way towards explaining why, out of the enormous resources of Negro speech and life, and despite the example of Negro music, prose written by Negroes has been generally speaking so pallid and so harsh. I have not written about being a Negro at such length because I expect that to be my only subject, but only because it was the gate I had to unlock before I could hope to write about anything else. I don't think that the Negro problem in America can be even discussed coherently without bearing in mind its context; its context being the history, traditions, customs, the moral assumptions and preoccupations of the country; in short, the general social fabric. Appearances to the contrary, no one in America escapes its effects and everyone in America bears some responsibility for it. I believe this the more firmly because it is the overwhelming tendency to speak of this problem as though it were a thing apart. But in the work of Faulkner,

in the general attitude and certain specific passages in Robert Penn War-
ren, and, most significantly, in the advent of Ralph Ellison, one sees
the beginnings — at least — of a more genuinely penetrating search. Mr.
Ellison, by the way, is the first Negro novelist I have ever read to utilize
in language, and brilliantly, some of the ambiguity and irony of Negro
life.

About my interests: I don't know if I have any, unless the morbid   9
desire to own a sixteen-millimeter camera and make experimental
movies can be so classified. Otherwise, I love to eat and drink — it's my
melancholy conviction that I've scarcely ever had enough to eat (this
is because it's *impossible* to eat enough if you're worried about the next
meal) — and I love to argue with people who do not disagree with me
too profoundly, and I love to laugh. I do *not* like bohemia, or bohemians,
I do not like people whose principal aim is pleasure, and I do not like
people who are *earnest* about anything. I don't like people who like me
because I'm a Negro; neither do I like people who find in the same accident grounds for contempt. I love America more than any other country in the world, and, exactly for this reason, I insist on the right to
criticize her perpetually. I think all theories are suspect, that the finest
principles may have to be modified, or may even be pulverized by the
demands of life, and that one must find, therefore, one's own moral center and move through the world hoping that this center will guide one
aright. I consider that I have many responsibilities, but none greater than
this: to last, as Hemingway says, and get my work done.

I want to be an honest man and a good writer.   10

_____ **CONSIDERATIONS** _____

1. Why didn't the young Baldwin read the Bible? In your education, have
you ever been possessed by similar feelings?
2. Point out specific features of Baldwin's style that account for its slightly
ironic tone. What other authors in this book make use of irony? To what ends?
3. Baldwin finds it difficult, he says, to distinguish the things that helped
him as a writer from those that have hurt him. Can you draw any parallels with
your own experience?
4. Baldwin wrote this essay for a book that appeared in 1955, when he
was thirty-one years old and had already published two successful novels. How
do these facts affect your response to the last sentence in the essay?
5. Many black writers have argued that the black artist must reject all
of white culture. What is your opinion of this argument? Support your answer
with examples from Baldwin's essay or from other black writers. How does

Baldwin explain his acceptance of Shakespeare, Bach, Rembrandt, the cathedral at Chartres, and the Empire State Building?

6. Note how many years Baldwin covers in the fist half-dozen sentences of Paragraph 2. How do you explain the lack of details about those years? Is this a weakness or a strength of the essay?

John Berger (b. 1926) was born in London and has lived much of his life in France. While renowned for his Marxist art criticism, he has written with a range as large as his success. His novel G *won the prestigious Booker Prize in 1972.* Permanent Red, *his essays from the fifties, has recently been reprinted, and* The White Bird *(1985) is a collection of recent nonfiction. With Jean Mohr he wrote* A Fortunate Man, *an account of rural England which has been compared with* Let Us Now Praise Famous Men *by James Agee.*

Here Berger extends his talents into autobiography.

10

JOHN BERGER

Her Secrets

From the age of five or six I was worried about the death of my parents. The inevitability of death was one of the first things I learnt about the world on my own. Nobody else spoke of it yet the signs were so clear. 1

Every time I went to bed—and in this I am sure I was like millions of other children—the fear that one or both my parents might die in the night touched the nape of my neck with its finger. Such a fear has, I believe, little to do with a particular psychological climate and a great deal to do with nightfall. Yet since it was impossible to say: You won't die in the night, will you? (when Grandmother died, I was told she had gone to have a rest, or—this was from my Uncle who was more outspoken—that she had passed over), since I couldn't ask the real ques- 2

From *The Threepenny Review*, Summer, 1986. Reprinted by permission of the author.

tion and I sought a reassurance, I invented—like millions before me—
the euphemism: See you in the morning! To which either my father
or mother who had come to turn out the light in my bedroom, would
reply: See you in the morning, John.

3   After their footsteps had died away, I would try for as long as
possible not to lift my head from the pillow so that the last words spoken remained, trapped like fish in a rock-pool at low tide, between my
pillow and ear. The implicit promise of the words was also a protection
against the dark. The words promised that I would not (yet) be alone.

4   Now I'm no longer usually frightened by the dark and my father
died ten years ago and my mother a month ago at the age of ninety-
three. It would be a natural moment to write an autobiography. My version of my life can no longer hurt either of them. And the book, when
finished, would be there, a little like a parent. Autobiography begins
with a sense of being alone. It is an orphan form. Yet I have no wish
to do so. All that interests me about my past life are the common
moments. The moments—which if I relate them well enough—will join
countless others lived by people I do not personally know.

5   Six weeks ago my mother asked me to come and see her; it would
be the last time, she said. A few days later, on the morning of my birthday, she believed she was dying. Open the curtains, she asked my
brother, so I can see the trees. In fact, she died the following week.

6   On my birthdays as a child, it was my father rather than she
who gave me memorable presents. She was too thrifty. Her moments
of generosity were at the table, offering what she had bought and
prepared and cooked and served to whoever came into the house. Otherwise she was thrifty. Nor did she ever explain. She was secretive, she
kept things to herself. Not for her own pleasure, but because the world
would not forgive spontaneity, the world was mcan. I must make that
clearer. She didn't believe life was mean—it was generous—but she had
learnt from her own childhood that survival was hard. She was the opposite of quixotic—for she was not born a knight and her father was
a warehouse foreman in Lambeth. She pursed her lips together, knitted
her brows as she calculated and thought things out and carried on with
an unspoken determination. She never asked favors of anyone. Nothing
shocked her. From whatever she saw, she just drew the necessary conclusions so as to survive and to be dependent on nobody. If I were Aesop,
I would say that in her prudence and persistence my mother resembled
the agouti. (I once wrote about an agouti in the London zoo but I did
not then realize why the animal so touched me.) In my adult life, the

only occasions on which we shouted at each other were when she estimated I was being quixotic.

When I was in my thirties she told me for the first time that,   7
ever since I was born, she had hoped I would be a writer. The writers she admired when young were Bernard Shaw, J. M. Barrie, Compton Mackenzie, Warwick Deeping, E. M. Dell. The only painter she really admired was Turner—perhaps because of her childhood on the banks of the Thames.

Most of my books she didn't read. Either because they dealt with   8
subjects which were alien to her or because—under the protective influence of my father—she believed they might upset her. Why suffer surprise from something which, left unopened, gives you pleasure? My being a writer was unqualified for her by what I wrote. To be a writer was to be able to see to the horizon where, anyway, nothing is ever very distinct and all questions are open. Literature had little to do with the writer's vocation as she saw it. It was only a by-product. A writer was a person familiar with the secrets. Perhaps in the end she didn't read my books so that they should remain more secret.

If her hopes of my becoming a writer—and she said they began   9
on the night after I was delivered—were eventually realized, it was not because there were many books in our house (there were few) but because there was so much that was unsaid, so much that I had to discover the existence of on my own at an early age: death, poverty, pain (in others), sexuality . . .

These things were there to be discovered within the house or from   10
its windows—until I left for good, more or less prepared for the outside world, at the age of eight. My mother never spoke of these things. She didn't hide the fact that she was aware of them. For her, however, they were wrapped secrets, to be lived with, but never to be mentioned or opened. Superficially this was a question of gentility, but profoundly, of a respect, a secret loyalty to the enigmatic. My rough and ready preparation for the world did not include a single explanation—it simply consisted of the principle that events carried more weight than the self.

Thus, she taught me very little—at least in the usual sense of   11
the term: she a teacher about life, I a learner. By imitating her gestures I learnt how to roast meat in the oven, how to clean celery, how to cook rice, how to choose vegetables in a market. As a young woman she had been a vegetarian. Then she gave it up because she did not want to influence us children. Why were you a vegetarian? I once asked her, eating my Sunday roast, much later when I was first working as a journalist.

Because I'm against killing. She would say no more. Either I understood or I didn't. There was nothing more to be said.

12   In time—and I understand this only now writing these pages—I chose to visit abattoirs in different cities of the world and to become something of an expert concerning the subject. The unspoken, the unfaceable beckoned me. I followed. Into the abattoirs and, differently, into many other places and situations.

13   The last, the largest and the most personally prepared wrapped secret was her own death. Of course I was not the only witness. Of those close to her, I was maybe the most removed, the most remote. But she knew, I think, with confidence that I would pursue the matter. She knew that if anybody can be at home with what is kept a secret, it was me, because I was her son whom she hoped would become a writer.

14   The clinical history of her illness is a different story about which she herself was totally uncurious. Sufficient to say that with the help of drugs she was not in pain, and that, thanks to my brother and sister-in-law who arranged everything for her, she was not subjected to all the mechanical ingenuity of aids for the artificial prolongation of life.

15   Of how many deaths—though never till now of my own mother's—have I written? Truly we writers are the secretaries of death.

16   She lay in bed, propped up by pillows, her head fallen forward, as if asleep.

17   I shut my eyes, she said, I like to shut my eyes and think. I don't sleep though. If I slept now, I wouldn't sleep at night.

18   What do you think about?

19   She screwed up her eyes which were gimlet sharp and looked at me, twinkling, as if I'd never, not even as a small child, asked such a stupid question.

20   Are you working hard? What are you writing?

21   A play, I answered.

22   The last time I went to the theater I didn't understand a thing, she said. It's not my hearing that's bad though.

23   Perhaps the play was obscure, I suggested.

24   She opened her eyes again. The body has closed shop, she announced. Nothing, nothing at all from here down. She placed a hand on her neck. It's a good thing, make no mistake about it, John, it makes the waiting easier.

25   On her bedside table was a tin of handcream. I started to massage her left hand.

26   Do you remember a photograph I once took of your hands? Working hands, you said.

No, I don't.   27

Would you like some more photos on your table? Katya, her   28
granddaughter, asked her.

She smiled at Katya and shook her head, her voice very slightly   29
broken by a laugh. It would be *so* difficult, so difficult, wouldn't it, to
choose.

She turned towards me. What exactly are you doing?   30

I'm massaging your hand. It's meant to be pleasurable.   31

To tell you the truth, dear, it doesn't make much difference.   32
What plane are you taking back?

I mumbled, took her other hand.   33

You are all worried, she said, especially when there are sev-   34
eral of you. I'm not. Maureen asked me the other day whether I wanted
to be cremated or buried. Doesn't make one iota of difference to me.
How could it? She shut her eyes to think.

For the first time in her life and in mine, she could openly place   35
the wrapped enigma between us. She didn't watch me watching it, for
we had the habits of a lifetime. Openly she knew that at that moment
her faith in a secret was bound to be stronger than any faith of mine
in facts. With her eyes still shut, she fingered the Arab necklace I'd attached round her neck with a charm against the evil eye. I'd given her
the necklace a few hours before. Perhaps for the first time I had offered
her a secret and now her hand kept looking for it.

She opened her eyes. What time is it?   36

Quarter to four.   37

It's not very interesting talking to me, you know. I don't have   38
any ideas any more. I've had a good life. Why don't you take a walk?

Katya stayed with her.   39

When you are very old, she told Katya confidentially, there's one   40
thing that's very very difficult — it's very difficult to persuade other people that you're happy.

She let her head go back on to the pillow. As I came back in,   41
she smiled.

In her right hand she held a crumpled paper handkerchief. With   42
it she dabbed from time to time the corner of her mouth when she felt
there was the slightest excess of spittle there. The gesture was reminis-
cent of one with which, many years before, she used to wipe her mouth
after drinking Earl Grey tea and eating watercress sandwiches. Meanwhile with her left hand she fingered the necklace, cushioned on her
forgotten bosom.

Love, my mother had the habit of saying, is the only thing that   43 counts in this world. Real love, she would add, to avoid any factitious misunderstanding. But apart from that simple adjective, she never added anything more.

_____ **CONSIDERATIONS** _____

1. Explain what Berger means when, in Paragraph 2, he describes "See you in the morning" as a euphemism.

2. How is it that Berger's mother enjoyed the books he wrote without ever opening them? Compare this behavior to her avoidance of death, poverty, pain, and sexuality (see Paragraph 10).

3. What is an agouti, and how does Berger connect it with Aesop in Paragraph 6?

4. Ponder what Berger means, at the close of Paragraph 10, when he says that his preparation for the world "consisted of the principle that events carried more weight than the self." Do you find this a popular idea today? How do you think Berger's upbringing affected his choice of work?

5. Berger's mother was evidently a woman of few words (see the concluding sentences of the essay). What was it about her, then, that drew her son so close to her during her last days? Do the actions or words of this dying woman surprise you?

6. Do you have any mysteries that you would prefer not to unravel? Are you like Berger's mother?

7. What is an "abattoir," mentioned in Paragraph 16, and how is it related both to Berger the investigator, and to his mother the accepter?

Wendell Berry (b. 1934), essayist, novelist, and poet, was born and educated in Kentucky. He left home to teach in New York and California, and eventually returned to his native hill. In 1986 his collection of short stories, The Wild Birds, *was published by the North Point Press, which has also reissued his earlier novels,* A Place on Earth *and* Nathan Coulter. *Among his many volumes of poetry is* Collected Poems: 1957–1982. *His essays include* Recollected Essays, The Gift of Good Land *(both 1982), and* Standing By Words *(1984).*

Wendell Berry writes an essay—or a novel or a short story or a poem—in the same spirit with which he plows a field.

11

WENDELL BERRY
A Native Hill

I start down from one of the heights of the upland, the town of   1
Port Royal at my back. It is a winter day, overcast and still, and the
town is closed in itself, humming and muttering a little, like a winter
beehive.

The dog runs ahead, prancing and looking back, knowing the way   2
we are about to go. This is a walk well established with us—a route
in our minds as well as on the ground. There is a sort of mystery in
the establishment of these ways. Any time one crosses a given stretch
of country with some frequency, no matter how wanderingly one begins,
the tendency is always toward habit. By the third or fourth trip, without realizing it, one is following a fixed path, going the way one went
before. After that, one may still wander, but only by deliberation, and

when there is reason to hurry, or when the mind wanders rather than the feet, one returns to the old route. Familiarity has begun. One has made a relationship with the landscape, and the form and the symbol and the enactment of the relationship is the path. These paths of mine are seldom worn on the ground. They are habits of mind, directions and turns. They are as personal as old shoes. My feet are comfortable in them.

3   From the height I can see far out over the country, the long open ridges of the farmland, the wooded notches of the streams, the valley of the river opening beyond, and then more ridges and hollows of the same kind.

4   Underlying this country, nine hundred feet below the highest ridgetops, more than four hundred feet below the surface of the river, is sea level. We seldom think of it here; we are a long way from the coast and the sea is alien to us. And yet the attraction of sea level dwells in this country as an ideal dwells in a man's mind. All our rains go in search of it and, departing, they have carved the land in a shape that is fluent and falling. The streams branch like vines, and between the branches the land rises steeply and then rounds and gentles into the long narrowing fingers of ridgeland. Near the heads of the streams even the steepest land was not too long ago farmed and kept cleared. But now it has been given up and the woods is returning. The wild is flowing back like a tide. The arable ridgetops reach out above the gathered trees like headlands into the sea, bearing their human burdens of fences and houses and barns, crops and roads.

5   Looking out over the country, one gets a sense of the whole of it: the ridges and hollows, the clustered buildings of the farms, the open fields, the woods, the stock ponds set like coins into the slopes. But this is a surface sense, an exterior sense, such as you get from looking down on the roof of a house. The height is a threshold from which to step down into the wooded folds of the land, the interior, under the trees and along the branching streams.

6   I pass through a pasture gate on a deep-worn path that grows shallow a little way beyond, and then disappears altogether into the grass. The gate has gathered thousands of passings to and fro, that have divided like the slats of a fan on either side of it. It is like a fist holding together the strands of a net.

7   Beyond the gate the land leans always more steeply toward the branch. I follow it down, and then bear left along the crease at the bottom of the slope. I have entered the downflow of the land. The way I am going is the way the water goes. There is something comfortable and fit-feeling in this, something free in this yielding to gravity and tak-

ing the shortest way down. The mind moves through the watershed as
the water moves.

As the hollow deepens into the hill, before it has yet entered the   8
woods, the grassy crease becomes a raw gulley, and along the steepening slopes on either side I can see the old scars of erosion, places where
the earth is gone clear to the rock. My people's errors have become the
features of my country.

It occurs to me that it is no longer possible to imagine how this   9
country looked in the beginning, before the white people drove their
plows into it. It is not possible to know what was the shape of the land
here in this hollow when it was first cleared. Too much of it is gone,
loosened by the plows and washed away by the rain. I am walking the
route of the departure of the virgin soil of the hill. I am not looking at
the same land the first-comers saw. The original surface of the hill is
as extinct as the passenger pigeon. The pristine America that the first
white men saw is a lost continent, sunk like Atlantis in the sea. The
thought of what was here once and is gone forever will not leave me
as long as I live. It is as though I walk knee-deep in its absence.

The slopes along the hollow steepen still more and I go in under   10
the trees. I pass beneath the surface. I am enclosed, and my sense, my
interior sense, of the country becomes intricate. There is no longer the
possibility of seeing very far. The distances are closed off by the trees
and the steepening walls of the hollow. One cannot grow familiar here
by sitting and looking as one can up in the open on the ridge. Here the
eyes become dependent on the feet. To see the woods from the inside
one must look and move and look again. It is inexhaustible in its stand-
points. A lifetime will not be enough to experience it all.

Not far from the beginning of the woods, and set deep in the   11
earth in the bottom of the hollow, is a rock-walled pool not a lot bigger
than a bathtub. The wall is still nearly as straight and tight as when
it was built. It makes a neatly turned narrow horseshoe, the open end
downstream. This is a historical ruin, dug here either to catch and hold
the water of the little branch, or to collect the water of a spring whose
vein broke to the surface here — it is probably no longer possible to know
which. The pool is filled with earth now, and grass grows in it. And
the branch bends around it, cut down to the bare rock, a torrent after
heavy rain, other times bone dry. All that is certain is that when the
pool was dug and walled there was deep topsoil on the hill to gather
and hold the water. And this high up, at lest, the bottom of the hollow,
instead of the present raw notch of the streambed, wore the same mantle of soil as the slopes, and the stream was a steady seep or trickle,

running most or all of the year. This tiny pool no doubt once furnished water for a considerable number of stock through the hot summers. And now it is only a lost souvenir, archaic and useless, except for the bitter intelligence there is in it. It is one of the monuments to what is lost.

12   Like the pasture gates, the streams are great collectors of comings and goings. The streams go down, and paths always go down beside the streams. For a while I walk along an old wagon road that is buried in leaves—a fragment, beginningless and endless as the middle of a sentence on some scrap of papyrus. There is a cedar whose branches reach over this road, and under the branches I find the leavings of two kills of some bird of prey. The most recent is a pile of blue jay feathers. The other has been rained on and is not identifiable. How little we know. How little of this was intended or expected by any man. The road that has become the grave of men's passages has led to the life of the woods.

> And I say to myself: Here is your road
> without beginning or end, appearing
> out of the earth and ending in it, bearing
> no load but the hawk's kill, and the leaves
> building earth on it, something more
> to be borne. Tracks fill with earth
> and return to absence. The road was worn
> by men bearing earth along it. They have come
> to endlessness. In their passing
> they could not stay in, trees have risen
> And stand still. It is leading to the dark,
> to morning where you are not. Here
> is your road, beginningless and endless as God.

13   Now I have come down within the sound of the water. The winter has been rainy, and the hill is full of dark seeps and trickles, gathering finally, along these creases, into flowing streams. The sound of them is one of the elements, and defines a zone. When their voices return to the hill after their absence during summer and autumn, it is a better place to be. A thirst in the mind is quenched.

14   I have already passed the place where water began to flow in the little stream bed I am following. It broke into the light from beneath a rock ledge, a thin glittering stream. It lies beside me as I walk, overtaking me and going by, yet not moving, a thread of light and sound. And now from below comes the steady tumble and rush of the water of Camp Branch—whose nameless camp was it named for?—and gradually as I descend the sound of the smaller stream is lost in the sound of the larger.

The two hollows join, the line of the meeting of the two spaces   15
obscured even in winter by the trees. But the two streams meet precisely
as two roads. That is, the stream *beds* do; the one ends in the other.
As for the meeting of the waters, there is no looking at that. The one
flow does not end in the other, but continues in it, one with it, two
clarities merged without a shadow.

All waters are one. This is a reach of the sea, flung like a net over   16
the hill, and now drawn back to the sea. And as the sea is never raised
in the earthly nets of fishermen, so the hill is never caught and pulled
down by the watery net of the sea. But always a little of it is. Each of
the gathering strands of the net carries back some of the hill melted
in it. Sometimes, as now, it carries so little that the water seems to flow
clear; sometimes it carries a lot and is brown and heavy with it. Whenever greedy or thoughtless men have lived on it, the hill has literally
flowed out of their tracks into the bottom of the sea.

There appears to be a law that when creatures have reached the   17
level of consciousness, as men have, they must become conscious of
the creation; they must learn how they fit into it and what its needs
are and what it requires of them, or else pay a terrible penalty: the spirit
of the creation will go out of them, and they will become destructive.
The very earth will depart from them and go where they cannot follow.

My mind is never empty or idle at the joinings of streams. Here   18
is the work of the world going on. The creation is felt, alive and intent
on its materials, in such places. In the angle of the meeting of the two
streams stands the steep wooded point of the ridge, like the prow of
an upturned boat—finished, as it was a thousand years ago, as it will
be in a thousand years. Its becoming is only incidental to its being. It
will be because it is. It has no aim or end except to be. By being it is
growing and wearing into what it will be. The fork of the stream lies
at the foot of the slope like hammer and chisel laid down at the foot
of a finished sculpture. But the stream is no dead tool; it is alive, it is
still at its work. Put your hand to it to learn the health of this part of
the world. It is the wrist of the hill.

Perhaps it is to prepare to hear some day the music of the spheres   19
that I am always turning my ears to the music of streams. There is indeed a music in streams, but it is not for the hurried. It has to be loitered
by and imagined. Or imagined *toward,* for it is hardly for men at all.
Nature has a patient ear. To her the slowest funeral march sounds like
a jig. She is satisfied to have the notes drawn out to the lengths of days
or weeks or months. Small variations are acceptable to her, modula-
tions as leisurely as the opening of a flower.

The stream is full of stops and gates. Here it has piled up rocks in   20 its path, and pours over them into a tiny pool it has scooped at the foot of its fall. Here it has been dammed by a mat of leaves caught behind a fallen limb. Here it must force a narrow passage, here a wider one. Tomorrow the flow may increase or slacken, and the tone will shift. In an hour or a week that rock may give way, and the composition will advance by another note. Some idea of it may be got by walking slowly along and noting the changes as one passes from one little fall or rapid to another. But this is a highly simplified and diluted version of the real thing, which is too complex and widespread ever to be actually heard by us. The ear must imagine an impossible patience in order to grasp even the unimaginableness of such music.

21   But the creation is musical, and this is a part of its music, as birdsong is, or the words of poets. The music of the streams is the music of the shaping of the earth, by which the rocks are pushed and shifted downward toward the level of the sea.

22   And now I find lying in the path an empty beer can. This is the track of the ubiquitous man Friday of all our woods. In my walks I never fail to discover some sign that he has preceded me. I find his empty shotgun shells, his empty cans and bottles, his sandwich wrappings. In wooded places along roadsides one is apt to find, as well, his over-travelled bedsprings, his outcast refrigerator, and heaps of the imperishable refuse of his modern kitchen. A year ago, almost in this same place where I have found his beer can, I found a possum that he had shot dead and left lying, in celebration of his manhood. He is the true American pioneer, perfectly at rest in his assumption that he is the first and the last whose inheritance and fate this place will ever be. Going forth, as he may think, to sow, he only broadcasts his effects.

23   As I go on down the path alongside Camp Branch, I walk by the edge of croplands abandoned only within my own lifetime. On my left are south slopes where the woods are old, long undisturbed. On my right, the more fertile north slopes are covered with patches of briars and sumacs and a lot of young walnut trees. Tobacco of an extraordinary quality was once grown here, and then the soil wore thin, and these places were given up for the more accessible ridges that were not so steep, where row-cropping made better sense anyway. But now, under the thicket growth, a mat of bluegrass has grown to testify to the good nature of this ground. It was fine dirt that lay here once, and I am far from being able to say that I could have resisted the temptation to plow it. My understanding of what is best for it is the tragic understanding of hindsight, the awareness that I have been taught what was here to be lost by the loss of it.

We have lived by the assumption that what was good for us would 24 be good for the world. And this has been based on the even flimsier assumption that we could know with any certainty what was good even for us. We have fulfilled the danger of this by making our personal pride and greed the standard of our behavior toward the world—to the incalculable disadvantage of the world and every living thing in it. And now, perhaps very close to too late, our great error has become clear. It is not only our own creativity—our own capacity for life—that is stifled by our arrogant assumption; the creation itself is stifled.

We have been wrong. We must change our lives, so that it will be 25 possible to live by the contrary assumption that what is good for the world will be good for us. And that requires that we make the effort to *know* the world and to learn what is good for it. We must learn to cooperate in its processes, and to yield to its limits. But even more important, we must learn to acknowledge that the creation is full of mystery; we will never entirely understand it. We must abandon arrogance and stand in awe. We must recover the sense of the majesty of creation, and the ability to be worshipful in its presence. For I do not doubt that it is only on the condition of humility and reverence before the world that our species will be able to remain in it.

Standing in the presence of these worn and abandoned fields, 26 where the creation has begun its healing without the hindrance or the help of man, with the voice of the stream in the air and the woods standing in silence on all the slopes around me, I am deep in the interior not only of my place in the world, but of my own life, its sources and searches and concerns. I first came into these places following the men to work when I was a child. I knew the men who took their lives from such fields as these, and their lives to a considerable extent made my life what it is. In what came to me from them there was both wealth and poverty, and I have been a long time discovering which was which.

It was in the woods here along Camp Branch that Bill White, my 27 grandfather's hired hand, taught me to hunt squirrels. Bill lived in a little tin-roofed house on up nearer the head of the hollow. And this was, I suppose more than any other place, his hunting ground. It was the place of his freedom, where he could move without subservience, without considering who he was or who anybody else was. On late summer mornings, when it was too wet to work, I would follow him into the woods. As soon as we stepped in under the trees he would become silent, and absolutely attentive to the life of the place. He was a good teacher and an exacting one. The rule seemed to be that if I wanted to stay with him, I had to make it possible for him to forget I was there. I was to

make no noise. If I did he would look back and make a downward em-
phatic gesture with his hand, as explicit as writing: Be quiet, or go home.
He would see a squirrel crouched in a fork or lying along the top of a
branch, and indicate with a grin and a small jerk of his head where I
should look; and then wait, while I, conscious of being watched and
demanded upon, searched it out for myself. He taught me to look and
to listen and to be quiet. I wonder if he knew the value of such teaching
or the rarity of such a teacher.

28   In the years that followed I hunted often here alone. And later in
these same woods I experienced my first obscure dissatisfactions with
hunting. Though I could not have put it into words then, the sense had
come to me that hunting as I knew it—the eagerness to kill something
I did not need to eat—was an artificial relation to the place, when what
I was beginning to need, just as inarticulately then, was a relation that
would be deeply natural and meaningful. That was a time of great
uneasiness and restlessness for me. It would be the fall of the year, the
leaves would be turning, and ahead of me would be another year of
school. There would be confusions about girls and ambitions, the
wordless hurried feeling that time and events and my own nature were
pushing me toward what I was going to be—and I had no notion what
it was, or how to prepare.

29   And then there were years when I did not come here at all—
when these places and their history were in my mind, and part of me,
in places thousands of miles away. And now I am here again, changed
from what I was, and still changing. The future is no more certain to
me now than it ever was, though its risks are clearer, and so are my
own desires. I am the father of two young children whose lives are
hostages given to the future. Because of them and because of events in
the world, life seems more fearful and difficult to me now than ever
before; but it is also more inviting, and I am constantly aware of its
nearness to joy. Much of the interest and excitement that I have in my
life now has come from the deepening, in the years since my return here,
of my relation to this countryside that is my native place. For in spite
of all that has happened to me in other places, the great change and the
great possibility of change in my life has been in my sense of this place.
The major difference is perhaps only that I have grown able to be
wholeheartedly present here. I am able to sit and be quiet at the foot
of some tree here in this woods along Camp Branch, and feel a deep
peace, both in the place and in my awareness of it, that not too long
ago I was not conscious of the possibility of. This peace is partly in being free of the suspicion that pursued me for most of my life, no matter

where I was, that there was perhaps another place I *should* be, or would be happier or better in; it is partly in the increasingly articulate consciousness of being here, and of the significance and importance of being here.

After more than thirty years I have at last arrived at the candor   30
necessary to stand on this part of the earth that is so full of my own history and so much damaged by it, and ask: What *is* this place? What is in it? What is its nature? How should men live in it? What must I do?

I have not found the answers, though I believe that in partial and   31
fragmentary ways they have begun to come to me. But the questions are more important than their answers. In the final sense they *have* no answers. They are like the questions—they are perhaps the same questions—that were the discipline of Job. They are part of the necessary enactment of humility, teaching a man what his importance is, what his responsibility is, and what his place is, both on the earth and in the order of things. And though the answers must always come obscurely and in fragments, the questions must be persistently asked. They are fertile questions. In their implications and effects, they are moral and esthetic and, in the best and fullest sense, practical. They promise a relationship to the world that is decent and preserving.

They are also, both in origin and effect, religious. I am uneasy   32
with the term, for such religion as has been openly practiced in this part of the world has promoted and fed upon a destructive schism between body and soul, heaven and earth. It has encouraged people to believe that the world is of no importance, and that their only obligation in it is to submit to certain churchly formulas in order to get to heaven. And so the people who might have been expected to care most selflessly for the world have had their minds turned elsewhere—to a pursuit of "salvation" that was really only another form of gluttony and self-love, the desire to perpetuate their own small lives beyond the life of the world. The heaven-bent have abused the earth thoughtlessly, by inattention, and their negligence has permitted and encouraged others to abuse it deliberately. Once the creator was removed from the creation, divinity became only a remote abstraction, a social weapon in the hands of the religious institutions. This split in public values produced or was accompanied by, as it was bound to be, an equally artificial and ugly division in people's lives, so that a man, while pursuing heaven with the sublime appetite he thought of as his soul, could turn his heart against his neighbors and his hands against the world. For these reasons, though I know that my questions *are* religious, I dislike having to *say* that they are.

33   But when I ask them my aim is not primarily to get to heaven. Though heaven is certainly more important than the earth if all they say about it is true, it is still morally incidental to it and dependent on it, and I can only imagine it and desire it in terms of which I know of the earth. And so my questions do not aspire beyond the earth. They aspire *toward* it and *into* it. Perhaps they aspire *through* it. They are religious because they are asked at the limit of what I know; they acknowledge mystery and honor its presence in the creation; they are spoken in reverence for the order and grace that I see, and that I trust beyond my power to see.

34   The stream has led me down to an old barn built deep in the hollow to house the tobacco once grown on those abandoned fields. Now it is surrounded by the trees that have come back on every side — a relic, a fragment of another time, strayed out of its meaning. This is the last of my historical landmarks. To here, my walk has had insistent over-tones of memory and history. It has been a movement of consciousness through knowledge, eroding and shaping, adding and wearing away. I have descended like the water of the stream through what I know of myself, and now that I have there is a little more to know. But here at the barn, the old roads and the cow paths — the formal connections with civilization — come to an end.

35   I stoop between the strands of a barbed wire fence, and in that movement I go out of time into timelessness. I come into a wild place. I walk along the foot of a slope that was once cut bare of trees, like all the slopes of this part of the country — but long ago; and now the woods is established again, the ground healed, the trees grown big, their trunks rising clean, free of undergrowth. The place has a serenity and dignity that one feels immediately; the creation is whole in it and unobstructed. It is free of the strivings and dissatisfactions, the partialities and im-perfections of places under the mechanical dominance of men. Here, what to a housekeeper's eye might seem disorderly is nonetheless or-derly and within order; what might seem arbitrary or accidental is in-cluded in the design of the whole as if by intention; what might seem evil or violent is a comfortable member of the household. Where the creation is whole nothing is extraneous. The presence of the creation here makes this a holy place, and it is as a pilgrim that I have come — to give the homage of awe and love, to submit to mystification. It is the creation that has attracted me, its perfect interfusion of life and design. I have made myself its follower and its apprentice.

36   One early morning last spring, I came and found the woods floor strewn with bluebells. In the cool sunlight and the lacy shadows of the

spring woods the blueness of those flowers, their elegant shape, their delicate fresh scent kept me standing and looking. I found a rich delight in them that I cannot describe and that I will never forget. Though I had been familiar for years with most of the spring woods flowers, I had never seen these and had not known they grew here. Looking at them, I felt a strange feeling of loss and sorrow that I had never seen them before. But I was also exultant that I saw them now—that they were here.

For me, in the thought of them will always be the sense of the joyful surprise with which I found them—the sense that came suddenly to me then that the world is blessed beyond my understanding, more abundantly than I will ever know. What lives are still ahead of me here to be discovered and exulted in, tomorrow, or in twenty years? What wonder will be found here on the morning after my death? Though as a man I inherit great evils and the possibility of great loss and suffering, I know that my life is blessed and graced by the yearly flowering of the bluebells. How perfect they are! In their presence I am humble and joyful. If I were given all the learning and all the methods of my race I could not make one of them, or even imagine one. Solomon in all his glory was not arrayed like one of these. It is the privilege and the labor of the apprentice of creation to come with his imagination into the unimaginable, and with his speech into the unspeakable. 37

_____ CONSIDERATIONS _____

1. To think of habits as paths worn in the mind is no very original metaphor. How does Berry distinguish this image as he works it into the essay?

2. Berry's essay, like the walk he is reporting, is a leisurely experience that should be taken in an unhurried manner. Much of this easy pace is due to his style: he makes an observation, then pauses to reflect on it and related things, then moves along to another observation, and another reflective pause, and so on. The result is a pleasing, thoughtful mix of the factual and the insightful. Try writing a short, descriptive essay in this style.

3. "Nature has a patient ear," writes Berry in Paragraph 19, using a figure of speech called personification. Look for examples in other writers, or make up several yourself (e.g., "the blindness of the night," "the laughter of the wind," "the soul of the abandoned house"). Then explain the meaning of personification and its value to a writer like Berry.

4. Assuming Paragraph 30 is an explicit pronouncement of his thesis, what varied means does Berry use to embody these ideas?

5. On his walk, Berry follows the downward course of streams and slopes and gulleys. In what way does his essay also follow downward, converging courses to lead you to his conclusion?

6. Throughout his essay, Berry works to evoke a sense of place—that hill where he grew up and to which he now returns. Yet he also thinks on a wider scale—the state of the nation, and even the world. Is he successful in fusing the various planes? If so, how does he manage it? If not, why not?

Ambrose Bierce (1842–1914?) was born in a log cabin on Horse Cave Creek in Ohio. He educated himself by reading the books in his father's small library, and as a young man served in the army during the Civil War. Starting as a journalist in California, he made himself an elegant writer of short stories, which were often supernatural or macabre in theme. Because he was writing in the primitive West, in a country still generally primitive, his serious work went largely unrecognized. Melancholy deepened into misanthropy. The definitions in The Devil's Dictionary *(1906) are funny indeed—but the humor is serious, and the wit is bitter.*

In 1913, Bierce put his affairs in order and went to Mexico, which was in the midst of a civil war. He wrote a friend as he left, ". . . if you hear of my being stood up against a Mexican stone wall and shot to rags please know that I think it a pretty good way to depart this life. It beats old age, disease, or falling down a flight of stairs." He was never heard from again.

12

AMBROSE BIERCE
Some Devil's Definitions

Belladonna, n. In Italian a beautiful lady; in English a deadly poison. A striking example of the essential identity of the two tongues.   1

Bigot, n. One who is obstinately and zealously attached to an opinion that you do not entertain.   2

Bore, n. A person who talks when you wish him to listen.   3

Brute, n. See HUSBAND.   4

Cabbage, n. A familiar kitchen-garden vegetable about as large and wise as a man's head.   5

6   *Calamity, n.* A more than commonly plain and unmistakable reminder that the affairs of this life are not of our own ordering. Calamities are of two kinds: misfortune to ourselves, and good fortune to others.

7   *Cannibal, n.* A gastronome of the old school who preserves the simple tastes and adheres to the natural diet of the pre-pork period.

8   *Cannon, n.* An instrument employed in the rectification of national boundaries.

9   *Cat, n.* A soft, indestructible automaton provided by nature to be kicked when things go wrong in the domestic circle.

10   *Christian, n.* One who believes that the New Testament is a divinely inspired book admirably suited to the spiritual needs of his neighbor. One who follows the teachings of Christ in so far as they are not inconsistent with a life of sin.

11   *Clairvoyant, n.* A person, commonly a woman, who has the power of seeing that which is invisible to her patron—namely, that he is a blockhead.

12   *Commerce, n.* A kind of transaction in which A plunders from B the goods of C, and for compensation B picks the pocket of D of money belonging to E.

13   *Compromise, n.* Such an adjustment of conflicting interests as gives each adversary the satisfaction of thinking he has got what he ought not to have, and is deprived of nothing except what was justly his due.

14   *Compulsion, n.* The eloquence of power.

15   *Congratulation, n.* The civilty of envy.

16   *Conservative, n.* A statesman who is enamored of existing evils, as distinguished from the Liberal, who wishes to replace them with others.

17   *Consul, n.* In American politics, a person who having failed to secure an office from the people is given one by the Administration on condition that he leave the country.

18   *Consult, v. t.* To seek another's approval of a course already decided on.

19   *Corsair, n.* A politician of the seas.

20   *Coward, n.* One who in a perilous emergency thinks with his legs.

21   *Curiosity, n.* An objectionable quality of the female mind. The desire to know whether or not a woman is cursed with curiosity is one of the most active and insatiable passions of the masculine soul.

22   · *Cynic, n.* A blackguard whose faulty vision sees things as they

are, not as they ought to be. Hence the custom among the Scythians of plucking out a cynic's eyes to improve his vision.

Dance, v. i. To leap about to the sound of tittering music, preferably with arms about your neighbor's wife or daughter. There are many kinds of dances, but all those requiring the participation of the two sexes have two characteristics in common: they are conspicuously innocent, and warmly loved by the vicious.   23

Debauchee, n. One who has so earnestly pursued pleasure that he has had the misfortune to overtake it.   24

Decalogue, n. A series of commandments, ten in number—just enough to permit an intelligent selection for observance, but not enough to embarrass the choice.   25

Defame, v. t. To lie about another. To tell the truth about another.   26

Dentist, n. A prestidigitator who, putting metal in your mouth, pulls coins out of your pocket.   27

Die, n. The singular of "dice." We seldom hear the word, because there is a prohibitory proverb, "Never say die."   28

Discussion, n. A method of confirming others in their errors.   29

Distance, n. The only thing that the rich are willing for the poor to call theirs, and keep.   30

Duel, n. A formal ceremony preliminary to the reconciliation of two enemies. Great skill is necessary to its satisfactory observance; if awkwardly performed the most unexpected and deplorable consequences sometimes ensue. A long time ago a man lost his life in a duel.   31

Eccentricity, n. A method of distinction so cheap that fools employ it to accentuate their incapacity.   32

Edible, adj. Good to eat, and wholesome to digest, as a worm to a toad, a toad to a snake, a snake to a pig, a pig to a man, and a man to a worm.   33

Education, n. That which discloses to the wise and disguises from the foolish their lack of understanding.   34

Effect, n. The second of two phenomena which always occur together in the same order. The first, called a Cause, is said to generate the other—which is no more sensible than it would be for one who has never seen a dog except in pursuit of a rabbit to declare the rabbit the cause of the dog.   35

Egotist, n. A person of low taste, more interested in himself than in me.   36

37   *Erudition, n.* Dust shaken out of a book into an empty skull.

38   *Eulogy, n.* Praise of a person who has either the advantages of wealth and power, or the consideration to be dead.

39   *Female, n.* One of the opposing, or unfair, sex.

40   *Fib, n.* A lie that has not cut its teeth. An habitual liar's nearest approach to truth: the perigee of his eccentric orbit.

41   *Fiddle, n.* An instrument to tickle human ears by friction of a horse's tail on the entrails of a cat.

42   *Friendship, n.* A ship big enough to carry two in fair weather, but only one in foul.

43   *Garter, n.* An elastic band intended to keep a woman from coming out of her stockings and desolating the country.

44   *Ghost, n.* The outward and visible sign of an inward fear.

45   *Glutton, n.* A person who escapes the evils of moderation by committing dyspepsia.

46   *Gout, n.* A physician's name for the rheumatism of a rich patient.

47   *Grammar, n.* A system of pitfalls thoughtfully prepared for the feet of the self-made man, along the path by which he advances to distinction.

48   *Guillotine, n.* A machine which makes a Frenchman shrug his shoulders with good reason.

——— CONSIDERATIONS ———————————

1. To appreciate the humor in some of Bierce's definitions, you may have to look up in your dictionary some of his words, such as "gastronome," "zealously," "adversary," "civility," "insatiable," "prestidigitator," "perigee," "dyspepsia." How do you add words to your working vocabulary?

2. *The Devil's Dictionary* was first published in 1906. Judging from the definitions here, would you say that Bierce's book is dated? Which items strike you as most relevant to our times? Which are least relevant? Why?

3. Do you find a consistent tone or attitude in Bierce's dictionary? Explain and provide ample evidence.

4. George Orwell, in "Politics and the English Language" (pages 292–305), is critical of euphemisms. Would Bierce agree with Orwell?

5. Who among these authors would most appreciate Bierce's brand of humor: Annie Dillard ("Strangers to Darkness"), Frederick Douglass ("Plantation Life"), Flannery O'Connor ("A Good Man Is Hard to Find"), or George Orwell ("A Hanging")? Explain, making comparisons.

6. Compose a page of definitions for your own Devil's Dictionary, perhaps concentrating on words currently popular.

Caroline Bird (b. 1915) was born in New York City, taught at Vassar, and now divides her time between Manhattan and Poughkeepsie. She has been an editor and a teacher, as well as the author of Born Female *(1968),* The Case against College *(1975),* What Women Want *(1979),* The Two Paycheck Marriage *(1982), and* The Good Years: Your Life in the 21st Century *(1983). Here she argues the case against college with a clear vigor, a committed pugnacity; only a skilled debater with a good college education could dispute her.*

13

CAROLINE BIRD
Where College Fails Us

The case *for* college has been accepted without question for more than a generation. All high school graduates ought to go, says Conventional Wisdom and statistical evidence, because college will help them earn more money, become "better" people, and learn to be more responsible citizens than those who don't go. 1

But college has never been able to work its magic for everyone. And now that close to half our high school graduates are attending, those who don't fit the pattern are becoming more numerous, and more obvious. College graduates are selling shoes and driving taxis; college students sabotage each other's experiments and forge letters of recommendation in the intense competition for admission to graduate school. 2

Others find no stimulation in their studies, and drop out—often encouraged by college administrators.

3   Some observers say the fault is with the young people themselves —they are spoiled, stoned, overindulged, and expecting too much. But that's mass character assassination, and doesn't explain all campus unhappiness. Others blame the state of the world, and they are partly right. We've been told that young people have to go to college because our economy can't absorb an army of untrained eighteen-year-olds. But disillusioned graduates are learning that it can no longer absorb an army of trained twenty-two-year-olds, either.

4   Some adventuresome educators and campus watchers have openly begun to suggest that college may not be the best, the proper, the only place for every young person after the completion of high school. We may have been looking at all those surveys and statistics upside down, it seems, and through the rosy glow of our own remembered college experiences. Perhaps college doesn't make people intelligent, ambitious, happy, liberal, or quick to learn new things— maybe it's just the other way around, and intelligent, ambitious, happy, liberal, and quick-learning people are merely the ones who have been attracted to college in the first place. And perhaps all those successful college graduates would have been successful whether they had gone to college or not. This is heresy to those of us who have been brought up to believe that if a little schooling is good, more has to be much better. But contrary evidence is beginning to mount up.

5   The unhappiness and discontent of young people is nothing new, and problems of adolescence are always painfully intense. But while traveling around the country, speaking at colleges, and interviewing students at all kinds of schools—large and small, public and private—I was overwhelmed by the prevailing sadness. It was as visible on campuses in California as in Nebraska and Massachusetts. Too many young people are in college reluctantly, because everyone told them they ought to go, and there didn't seem to be anything better to do. Their elders sell them college because it's good for them. Some never learn to like it, and talk about their time in school as if it were a sentence to be served.

6   Students tell us the same thing college counselors tell us—they go because of pressure from parents and teachers, and stay because it seems to be an alternative to a far worse fate. It's "better" than the Army or a dead-end job, and it has to be pretty bad before it's any worse than staying at home.

7   College graduates say that they don't want to work "just" for the

money: They want work that matters. They want to help people and save the world. But the numbers are stacked against them. Not only are there not enough jobs in world-saving fields, but in the current slowdown it has become evident that there never were, and probably never will be, enough jobs requiring higher education to go around.[1]

Students who tell their advisers they want to help people, for example, are often directed to psychology. This year the Department of Labor estimates that there will be 4,300 new jobs for psychologists, while colleges will award 58,430 bachelor's degrees in psychology.[2]   8

Sociology has become a favorite major on socially conscious campuses, but graduates find that social reform is hardly a paying occupation. Male sociologists from the University of Wisconsin reported as gainfully employed a year after graduation included a legal assistant, sports editor, truck unloader, Peace Corps worker, publications director, and a stockboy—but no sociologist per se. The highest paid worked for the post office.   9

Publishing, writing, and journalism are presumably the vocational goal of a large proportion of the 104,000 majors in Communications and Letters expected to graduate in 1975.[3] The outlook for them is grim. All of the daily newspapers in the country combined are expected to hire a total of 2,600 reporters this year. Radio and television stations may hire a total of 500 announcers, most of them in local radio stations.[4] Nonpublishing organizations will need 1,100 technical writers, and public-relations activities another 4,400.[5] Even if new graduates could get all these jobs (they can't, of course), over 90,000 of them will have to find something less glamorous to do.   10

---

[1][Editors' Note: Ms. Bird's article appeared in 1975.] According to the Department of Labor Bureau of Statistics, 20.8 million college graduates will enter the work force from 1982 to 1995; the bureau predicts only 16.9 million job openings in traditional jobs for college graduates during that period.

[2]Through 1955: approximately 2100 new jobs each year for psychologists; an average of 41,000 bachelor's degrees in psychology granted yearly.

[3]Through 1955: 74,900 graduates each year in Communications and Letters.

[4]The Department of Labor Bureau of Statistics no longer calculates total yearly job openings in each field. Instead, it projects only the number of new jobs created in a field over a 13-year period. (New job openings account for only 10–20% of all job openings, with the other 80–90% resulting from workers vacating already established positions.) All figures quoted in the footnotes represent an estimated annual average based on this projection. For the period 1982–1995, the bureau projects 1153 new jobs in reporting and 1153 new jobs in radio and television announcing each year.

[5]Statistics for technical writers and public relations personnel are not available.

11   Other fields most popular with college graduates are also pathetically small. Only 1,900 foresters a year will be needed during this decade, although schools of forestry are expected to continue graduating twice that many.[6] Some will get sub-professional jobs as forestry aides. Schools of architecture are expected to turn out twice as many as will be needed,[7] and while all sorts of people want to design things, the Department of Labor forecasts that there will be jobs for only 400 new industrial designers[8] a year. As for anthropologists, only 400 will be needed every year in the 1970s[9] to take care of all the college courses, public-health research, community surveys, museums, and all the archaeological digs on every continent. (For these jobs graduate work in anthropology is required.)

12   Many popular occupations may seem to be growing fast without necessarily offering employment to very many. "Recreation work" is always cited as an expanding field, but it will need relatively few workers who require more special training than life guards. "Urban planning" has exploded in the media, so the U.S. Department of Labor doubled its estimate of the number of jobs to be filled every year in the 1970s—to a big, fat 800.[10] A mere 200 oceanographers[11] a year will be able to do all the exploring of "inner space"—and all that exciting underwater diving you see demonstrated on television—for the entire decade of the 1970s.

13   Whatever college graduates *want* to do, most of them are going to wind up doing what *there is* to do. During the next few years, according to the Labor Department, the biggest demand will be for stenographers and secretaries, followed by retail-trade salesworkers, hospital attendants, bookkeepers, building custodians, registered nurses, foremen, kindergarten and elementary-school teachers, receptionists, cooks, cosmetologists, private-household workers, manufacturing inspectors, and industrial machinery repairmen.[12] These are the jobs which

[6]Projected figures through the 1990s indicate there will be a need for an average of 1400 new foresters each year, while schools of forestry are expected to grant an average of 3000 bachelor's degrees each year.

[7]An average of 9700 students graduate each year with BAs in architecture, while there were an estimated 2600 new job openings in the field that year.

[8]Current projections indicate 550 new job openings for industrial designers each year through the 1990s.

[9]Through the 1990s, approximately 350 anthropologists will be needed each year.

[10]This figure remains the same through the 1990s.

[11]Only 150 through the 1990s.

will eventually absorb the surplus archaeologists, urban planners, oceanographers, sociologists, editors, and college professors.

Vocationalism is the new look on campus because of the discour- 14
aging job market faced by the generalists. Students have been opting for medicine and law in droves. If all those who check "doctor" as their career goal succeed in getting their MDs, we'll immediately have ten times the target ratio of doctors for the population of the United States. Law schools are already graduating twice as many new lawyers every year as the Department of Labor thinks we will need, and the oversupply grows annually.[13]

Specialists often find themselves at the mercy of shifts in de- 15
mand, and the narrower the vocational training, the more risky the long-term prospects. Engineers are the classic example of the "Yo-Yo" effect in supply and demand. Today's shortage is apt to produce a big crop of engineering graduates after the need has crested, and teachers face the same squeeze.

Worse than that, when the specialists turn up for work, they 16
often find that they have learned a lot of things in classrooms that they will never use, that they will have to learn a lot of things on the job that they were never taught, and that most of what they have learned is less likely to "come in handy later" than to fade from memory. One disillusioned architecture student, who had already designed and built houses, said, "It's the degree you need, not everything you learn getting it."

A diploma saves the employer the cost of screening candidates 17
and gives him a predictable product: He can assume that those who have survived the four-year ordeal have learned how to manage themselves. They have learned how to budget their time, meet deadlines, set priorities, cope with impersonal authority, follow instructions, and stick with a task that may be tiresome without direct supervision.

The employer is also betting that it will be cheaper and easier to 18

---

[12]This year, according to the Labor Department, the fastest-growing professions, in terms of new jobs created, are: building custodians, cashiers, secretaries, general office clerks, retail sales workers, registered nurses, waiters and waitresses, kindergarten and elementary school teachers, truck drivers, nursing aides and orderlies, technical sales representatives, automobile mechanics, supervisors of blue collar workers, kitchen helpers, guards and doorkeepers, fast food preparers, and service personnel, store managers, and electric and electronic technicians.

[13]These figures are similar through the 1990s.

train the college graduate because he has demonstrated his ability to learn. But if the diploma serves only to identify those who are talented in the art of schoolwork, it becomes, in the words of Harvard's Christopher Jencks, "a hell of an expensive aptitude test." It is unfair to the candidates because they themselves must bear the cost of the screening—the cost of college. Candidates without the funds, the academic temperament, or the patience for the four-year obstacle race are ruled out, no matter how well they may perform on the job. But if "everyone" has a diploma, employers will have to find another way to choose employees, and it will become an empty credential.

19   (Screening by diploma may in fact already be illegal. The 1971 ruling of the Supreme Court in *Griggs* v. *Duke Power Co.* contended that an employer cannot demand a qualification which systematically excludes an entire class of applicants, unless that qualification reliably predicts success on the job. The requiring of a high school diploma was outlawed in the *Griggs* case, and this could extend to a college diploma.)

20   The bill for four years at an Ivy League college is currently climbing toward $70,000; at a state university, a degree will cost the student and his family about $10,000 (with taxpayers making up the difference.)[14]

21   Not many families can afford these sums, and when they look for financial aid, they discover that someone else will decide how much they will actually have to pay. The College Scholarship Service, which establishes a family's degree of need for most colleges, is guided by noble principles: uniformity of sacrifice, need rather than merit. But families vary in their willingness to "sacrifice" as much as the bureaucracy of the CSS thinks they ought to. This is particularly true of middle-income parents, whose children account for the bulk of the country's college students. Some have begun to rebel against this attempt to enforce the same values and priorities on all. "In some families, a college education competes with a second car, a color television, or a trip to Europe—and it's possible that college may lose," one financial-aid officer recently told me.

22   Quite so. College is worth more to some middle-income families than to others. It is chilling to consider the undercurrent of resentment that families who "give up everything" must feel toward their college-

---

[14][Editor's Note: the following figures have been updated for 1986–87] According to the National Center for Educational Statistics, the cost of four years at the average private university is now approaching $50,000; the average cost of four years at a public institution is approximately $17,500. Ivy League universities report their current tuition, including room and board, at approximately $68,000 for four years.

age children, or the burden of guilt children must bear every time they goof off or receive less than top grades in their courses.

The decline in return for a college degree within the last genera-   23
tion has been substantial. In the 1950s, a Princeton student could pay his expenses for the school year—eating club and all—on less than $3,000. When he graduated, he entered a job market which provided a comfortable margin over the earnings of his agemates who had not been to college. To be precise, a freshman entering Princeton in 1956, the earliest year for which the Census has attempted to project lifetime earnings, could expect to realize a 12.5 percent return on his investment. A freshman entering in 1972, with the cost nearing $6,000 annually, could expect to realize only 9.3 percent, less than might be available in the money market. This calculation was made with the help of a banker and his computer, comparing college as an investment in future earnings with other investments available in the booming money market of 1974, and concluded that in strictly financial terms, college is not always the best investment a young person can make.

I postulated a young man in 1974 (the figures are different with a   24
young woman, but the principle is the same) whose rich uncle would give him, in cash, the total cost of four years at Princeton—$34,181.[15] (The total includes what the young man would earn if he went to work instead of to college right after high school.) If he did not spend the money on Princeton, but put it in the savings bank at 7.5 percent interest compounded daily, he would have, at retirement age sixty-four, more than five times as much as the $199,000 extra he could expect to earn between twenty-two and sixty as a college man rather than a mere high school graduate. And with all that money accumulating in the bank, he could invest in something with a higher return than a diploma. At age twenty-eight, when his nest egg had reached $73,113, he could buy a liquor store, which would return him well over 20 percent on his investment, as long as he was willing to mind the store. He might get a bit fidgety sitting there, but he'd have to be dim-witted to lose money on a liquor store, and right now we're talking only about dollars.

If the young man went to a public college rather than Princeton,   25
the investment would be lower, and the payoff higher, of course, because other people—the taxpayers—put up part of the capital for him. But the difference in return between an investment in public and private colleges is minimized because the biggest part of the investment in either case is the money a student might earn if he went to work, not to

---

[15][Editor's Note: 1987 figures] Students in the class of 1991 will pay $67,392 for four years at Princeton.

college—in economic terms, his "foregone income." That he bears himself.

26   Rates of return and dollar signs on education are a fascinating brain teaser, and, obviously, there is a certain unreality to the game. But the same unreality extends to the traditional calculations that have always been used to convince taxpayers that college is a worthwhile investment.

27   The ultimate defense of college has always been that while it may not teach you anything vocationally useful, it will somehow make you a better person, able to do anything better, and those who make it through the process are initiated into the "fellowship of educated men and women." In a study intended to probe what graduates seven years out of college thought their colleges should have done for them, the Carnegie Commission found that most alumni expected the "development of my abilities to think and express myself." But if such respected educational psychologists as Bruner and Piaget are right, specific learning skills have to be acquired very early in life, perhaps even before formal schooling begins.

28   So, when pressed, liberal-arts defenders speak instead about something more encompassing, and more elusive. "College changed me inside," one graduate told us fervently. The authors of a Carnegie Commission report, who obviously struggled for a definition, concluded that one of the common threads in the perceptions of a liberal education is that it provides "an integrated view of the world which can serve as an inner guide." More simply, alumni say that college should have "helped me to formulate the values and goals of my life."

29   In theory, a student is taught to develop these values and goals himself, but in practice, it doesn't work quite that way. All but the wayward and the saintly take their sense of the good, the true, and the beautiful from the people around them. When we speak of students acquiring "values" in college, we often mean that they will acquire the values—and sometimes that means only the tastes—of their professors. The values of professors may be "higher" than many students will encounter elsewhere, but they may not be relevant to situations in which students find themselves in college and later.

30   Of all the forms in which ideas are disseminated, the college professor lecturing a class is the slowest and most expensive. You don't have to go to college to read the great books or learn about the great ideas of Western Man. Today you can find them everywhere—in paperbacks, in the public libraries, in museums, in public lectures, in adult-

education courses, in abridged, summarized, or adapted form in magazines, films, and television. The problem is no longer one of access to broadening ideas; the problem is the other way around: how to choose among the many courses of action proposed to us, how to edit the stimulations that pour into our eyes and ears every waking hour. A college experience that piles option on option and stimulation on stimulation merely adds to the contemporary nightmare.

What students and graduates say that they did learn on campus 31 comes under the heading of personal, rather than intellectual, development. Again and again I was told that the real value of college is learning to get along with others, to practice social skills, to "sort out my head," and these have nothing to do with curriculum.

For whatever impact the academic experience used to have on 32 college students, the sheer size of many undergraduate classes in the 1970s dilutes faculty-student dialogue, and, more often than not, they are taught by teachers who were hired when colleges were faced with a shortage of qualified instructors, during their years of expansion and when the big rise in academic pay attracted the mediocre and the less than dedicated.

On the social side, colleges are withdrawing from responsibility 33 for feeding, housing, policing, and protecting students at a time when the environment of college may be the most important service it could render. College officials are reluctant to "intervene" in the personal lives of the students. They no longer expect to take over from parents, but often insist that students—who have, most often, never lived away from home before—take full adult responsibility for their plans, achievements, and behavior.

Most college students do not live in the plush, comfortable coun- 34 try-clublike surroundings their parents envisage, or, in some cases, remember. Open dorms, particularly when they are coeducational, are noisy, usually overcrowded, and often messy. Some students desert the institutional "zoos" (their own word for dorms) and move into run-down, overpriced apartments. Bulletin boards in student centers are littered with notices of apartments to share and the drift of conversation suggests that a lot of money is dissipated in scrounging for food and shelter.

Taxpayers now provide more than half of the astronomical sums 35 that are spent on higher education. But less than half of today's high school graduates go on, raising a new question of equity: Is it fair to make all the taxpayers pay for the minority who actually go to college? We decided long ago that it is fair for childless adults to pay school taxes because everyone, parents and nonparents alike, profits by a literate population. Does the same reasoning hold true for state-supported higher education? There is no conclusive evidence on either side.

36   Young people cannot be expected to go to college for the general good of mankind. They may be more altruistic than their elders, but no great numbers are going to spend four years at hard intellectual labor, let alone tens of thousands of family dollars, for "the advancement of human capability in society at large," one of the many purposes invoked by the Carnegie Commission report. Nor do any considerable number of them want to go to college to beat the Russians to Jupiter, improve the national defense, increase the Gross National Product, lower the crime rate, improve automobile safety, or create a market for the arts—all of which have been suggested at one time or other as benefiits taxpayers get for supporting higher education.

37   One sociologist said that you don't have to have a reason for going to college because it's an institution. His definition of an institution is something everyone subscribes to without question. The burden of proof is not on why you should go to college, but why anyone thinks there might be a reason for not going. The implication—and some educators express it quite frankly—is that an eighteen-year-old high school graduate is still too young and confused to know what he wants to do, let alone what is good for him.

38   Mother knows best, in other words.

39   It had always been comfortable for students to believe that authorities, like Mother, or outside specialists, like educators, could determine what was best for them. However, specialists and authorities no longer enjoy the credibility former generations accorded them. Patients talk back to doctors and are not struck suddenly dead. Clients question the lawyer's bills and sometimes get them reduced. It is no longer self-evident that all adolescents must study a fixed curriculum that was constructed at a time when all educated men could agree on precisely what it was that made them educated.

40   The same with college. If high school graduates don't want to continue their education, or don't want to continue it right away, they may perceive more clearly than their elders that college is not for them.

41   College is an ideal place for those young adults who love learning for its own sake, who would rather read than eat, and who like nothing better than writing research papers. But they are a minority, even at the prestigious colleges, which recruit and attract the intellectually oriented.

The rest of our high school graduates need to look at college more   42
closely and critically, to examine it as a consumer product, and decide
if the cost in dollars, in time, in continued dependency, and in future
returns, is worth the very large investment each student—and his family
must make.

_____ CONSIDERATIONS _____

1. To what extent is Bird's essay an attack on the conviction that universal education is the surest way to cure the ills and injustices of the world?

2. In her first paragraph, the author states three popular justifications for
a college education. Examine her essay to see how closely it is organized around
those three reasons.

3. In her final paragraph, Bird urges high school graduates to examine college "as a consumer product." Is this possible? Explain. Read about Richard
Wright's struggle to educate himself ("The Library Card," pages 481–490) and
try to imagine him examining that experience as "a consumer product."

4. Bird makes extensive use of statistics to prove her first proposition:
that college is a poor investment. Does she cite the sources of her figures? Does
she use the figures fairly? How can you tell?

5. How many of your college friends have clear ideas of their vocational
or educational goals? Do you? What about friends who are not in college?

6. Bird points out, rightly enough, that "you don't have to go to college
to read the great books or learn about the great ideas of Western Man." Judging
from your experience with self-directed reading programs, how effective is Bird's
statement as an argument?

7. What would Barbara Lazear Ascher (pages 35–39) and Lynne V. Cheney
(pages 105–108) think of Bird's emphasis on college as a vocational prep school?

Roy Blount, Jr., (b. 1941) was born in Georgia and currently lives in Massachusetts. His work appears frequently in The Atlantic, Sports Illustrated, *and* Esquire. *He also has written and performed for the popular radio program, "A Prairie Home Companion." Among Blount's earlier books is a meditation on the Pittsburgh Steelers called* Three Bricks Shy of a Load *(1981). His essay collections include* What Men Don't Tell Women *(1984) and* One Fell Swoop *(1982), as well as* Not Exactly What I Had in Mind *(1985), from which we take this account of the making of a football player.*

14

ROY BLOUNT, JR.

How to Raise Your Boy to Play Pro Ball

1   Since I have done a good deal of work in the sportswriting field, people ask me, "Where did you get that unusual tan?" (I go to a nearby tannery every spring, lay out twenty-eight dollars and a little something for the attendant, and have myself dipped.) "What is the right grip for squash?" (Grasp the squash firmly by the neck with your left hand, then take a knife with the right hand and bring it down in short, crisp strokes on the part of the squash not covered by the left hand.) But most of all they ask me, "How do I raise my boy to be a professional football player?" This last question I answer by saying, "Set an example. Lay and finish nine sets of steps in one day."

And then I speak of concrete grit, pride of workmanship, and what   2
Ray Mansfield's father, the man who laid the steps, called "that preservation meanness."

Mansfield still sells his millions of insurance in Pittsburgh, but   3
he has finished out his career on the gridiron, where, he once told me,
he felt like a knight in armor. For over a decade, through 1976, he was
the Steeler's starting center, emergency placekicker, and stalwart of beer
and stories. The Old Ranger, they called him. Still call him, actually.
His father, Owen Mansfield, was proof that you can be legendary in your
work even if your work isn't something glamorous like bowling people
over so that somebody can run a leather-covered bladder past them.

In '75 I went with Ray to visit Owen in Kennewick, Washington.   4
Owen was a tall, well-preserved-looking man of sixty-five who had
finally given up heavy labor because of his heart. He puttered around
his small house, picked and sang Jimmie Rodgers songs, and reminisced
about working and fighting.

Owen grew up on an Arkansas farm. When he was no more than   5
a sprout himself, he was "putting sprouts in the new ground. Start plowing and the plow would hit me in the stomach. Plow'd run into a root
right under the ground, the mules would stop, the end of the plow would
come around and hit me in the shin." But he had the example of *his*
father before him. "My dad. That was the workingest old man you ever
saw. And he was a Christian, believed in living right. I remember one
day my dad was getting the best of Uncle Port, and Uncle Port's dog
run up and bit him. He turned around and held Uncle Port and hollered,
'Somebody kill that god-d . . . that dog.' He thought better of himself,
you see. Uncle Port was the meanest man that ever hit that country
down there."

Since he couldn't be the meanest or the most industrious man in   6
Arkansas, in the late twenties Owen rode the rails west. He'd stop off
and scratch around for work or live off the land. "I remember if somebody
had eaten a lot of bananas, I'd pick up them banana peelings and eat
'em. They was good. I could eat a tree, I believe." He dodged the railroad
cops. "Texas Slim. He lined up forty of us one time and said, 'All right.
First one that catches the train, I'm going to shoot him.' He wore a nice
suit, a big white hat, two guns. He was a *nice*-looking guy. But a *mean*
son of a gun. I just patted my hands when I heard he was killed. I wish
I'd a been a fast draw, *I*'d a killed him.

"I was 'Slim,' too, all my life nearly, working. Had the longest neck   7
of anybody in the country."

8   His first job as a married man was splitting logs for rails. He and Mrs. Mansfield eventually had nine kids. When Ray was born, the family was living in a tent in a farm labor camp outside Bakersfield, California, and Owen was in the hospital with a rattlesnake bite. "They gave me a shot of some stuff and I started trembling all over, got quivery all through my body. I said, 'Dag burn it, I guess I'm going to die in this little old place.'

9   "Then, when I got well, our first daughter, Merelene, got pneumonia. They took Merelene to the same room I'd been in. Wasn't long till she died. I tell you, it was hard times. She was seven and a half. Merelene. A name I studied out myself, to get something there wasn't anything like."

10   "We all took Merelene back to Missouri," Ray says. "Like the marines never leave their dead behind, my parents didn't want to leave their child out there in California on the road. This was in 'forty-one. Dad put Merelene and all the rest of us except Gene, my oldest brother, on the train, and then he put a mattress on the back seat of the car and put Gene on it and just took off. I don't know whether he got to Missouri before the train or just after it. Driving a broken-down 1929 Chevy. Mother said she saw my dad the whole day, off and on, when the road came close to the tracks."

11   Owen told me, "The car broke down once and I was fixing it and that train passed. Made me so lonesome I couldn't sit still."

12   When they got Merelene buried back home, they headed back out looking for a place to settle. A few years later, living in Arizona, Owen flipped a coin to decide whether to go just to Joplin, Missouri, or all the way to the state of Washington. And Washington won. That's where Ray grew up, in Kennewick, where Owen got into concrete. "One of the hardest jobs in America," Ray says.

13   "Dad was always top hand on the job," says Ray's younger brother Bill, who played football at Washington State and now is back in Kennewick, in concrete himself. "It's a good thing he's not working today. It'd kill him to see the way people work these days. He wasn't any college professor, but he was as good as there was at what he did. Guys like him are gone forever. We'd lay a floor, I'd think it was finished—it would be, today—and he'd say, 'Son, we can't leave until you can dance on it.'

14   "You talk to Dad's old foreman and he says, 'That Owen was the finest-working man I ever knew.' When we'd work with him, he'd grab a shovel and all you'd see was sand. A forty-eight-year-old man outworking our ass. When he was fifty-nine years old, he was going full speed. My brother Gene kept saying, 'Dad, cool it a little bit.' He'd say, 'Ah,

let's get the job done.' Now it's: make money and get by if you can. He never learned. . . ."

Ray says, "We grew up expecting to work. It came with breathing   15
air. He hired us out when I was in the second or third grade. Me and my sister and older brother, we'd be out at four in the morning cutting asparagus until eight, go right from work to school.

"When I got older, I'd sell papers on the streets. I just loved being   16
on the streets. Even though there wasn't but one main street in Kennewick. I was afraid I would miss something.

"I worked all one morning to get fifteen cents to go to the movie.   17
I ran all the way to the movie and found out it was twenty cents. I ran all the way home, pissed off, kicking things. I told my father what was wrong. (He was home in between his work in concrete. He had to lay it in the morning, wait for it to set, and then go back late to finish it up.) He reached in his pocket, pulled out a handful of sand, and came up with a nickel. His fingers all dry and split open from the concrete. He gave me the nickel. It was probably the only nickel in the house. I ran all the way back to the movie: James Mason as Rommel in *The Desert Fox.*

"When I came home, my father was back at work. I lay awake   18
until one in the morning, when he came home. I sneaked downstairs and watched him get undressed and go to bed. I never thanked him. I just wanted to look at him and think what kind of dad I had.

"There was so much warmth around the house," Ray says. "We   19
didn't have any mean kids in our family. Everybody was loving of each other and tolerant of other people. I got into a lot of fights, but I didn't like it especially. If you ever want to get a Mansfield mad, pick on another Mansfield. We've got almost too much family pride. I remember there was a big kid around Campbell's Cabins, where we lived for a while. I did everything I could to avoid him. But he picked on my little brother Odie, and I went after him and nearly coldcocked him. I had no fear when one of my brothers was being picked on. But even after I whipped that big kid, I was still scared of him."

Bill tells an old family story: "This guy, thirty-five, got into an alter-   20
cation with our grandfather, Pa, when Pa was sixty-five years old. Our Uncle Granville was seventeen, and he goes flying through the air, kicks the guy's ass through the dusty streets till the guy whimpers like a dog and gets out of there. My dad's eyes gleam when he tells about it. That's why it was good having Moynihan in the U.N. You can't take too much shit."

Ray and Bill Mansfield and I were drinking and getting profound   21 in this place in Kennewick, and Bill said to Ray, "Remember when we were working out—I was just getting ready to go to Washington State—and you said, 'Bill, don't ever, ever accept getting beat. Don't ever let a guy beat you and walk away and say, "Well, he beat me." You have to fight and scratch and bite. If you're bleeding and crying and scratching and shitting, keep on fighting and that guy will quit. As long as *you* don't.' "

22   Not many occupations today bring together fighting and working the way football does. But working was a kind of fighting for Owen. And both working and fighting were kinds of sports. "I'd get a kick out of troweling cement with other trowers," he said. "Out of staying about the length of this table ahead of the other fella. That would tickle me to death." The story about their father that made Ray's and Bill's eyes light up the brightest—Bill almost boiled up out of his chair telling it—was the one about the steps.

23   "He laid and finished *nine sets of steps in one day*. Did a Cool Hand Luke shot. Then two thousand, three thousand square feet of concrete. It was superhuman. How it happened: It was a Monday, and the man told him it had to be done by Wednesday. My dad said, 'Don't worry.' The man said, 'Well, you better get it done.'

24   "That made my dad mad. So he said, 'I'll show you.' And he did it all in eight hours. Edged it, everything. He was running the whole time, and he was forty-five. When he finished, there was smoke coming off his body, but there were the nine sets of steps. All those assholes were scratching their heads and saying, How did he do it? It's still a legend around here."

25   Right after Ray's last season, Owen was talking to Gene and Odie, and they told him he'd better do something about his hair—he'd let it grow awfully long. "I'm not going to get a haircut," Owen said. "I'm going to go buy a dress." And he rocked back laughing and suddenly died.

26   Afterward, Ray's brother told him Owen had been glad that Ray was retiring from football. Owen had said he'd always thought of Ray as a boy, of course, but that Ray was getting too old to play a kid's game.

_____ CONSIDERATIONS _____

1. One of the attractive features of Blount's essay is the way he captures the voice of Owen Mansfield. Make a small collection of words and phrases that distinguish his voice, and compare it with Studs Terkel's rendering of "Phil Stallings, Spot Welder," (pages 403–408), or with the voices of characters in short stories.

2. How did the father's hard-working life spill over into the son's, and what does that have to do with how to raise your boy to be a professional football player?

3. Is there anything negative about the competitiveness that kept Owen Mansfield ahead of other concrete workers?

4. Was the father's "preservation meanness" tempered by a sense of humor? Is humor at work in the closing sentence of the essay, or is it simply an expression of the man's values? Find support for your answer elsewhere in the essay.

5. There is a gap between Paragraphs 20 and 21. What is the function of that extra space?

Jimmy Breslin (b. 1929) was born in New York City, where he has remained a fixture ever since. Today, he writes a newspaper column for the New York Daily News. *His lively, wisecracking newspaper style never conceals the depth of his concern for his city. Breslin's short-lived attempt at late-night television also made the news in 1986; he claimed to fire the network before the network fired him. He has written several novels, beginning in 1969 with* The Gang That Couldn't Shoot Straight. *"Dies the Victim, Dies the City" first appeared in his* Daily News *column.*

15

JIMMY BRESLIN
Dies the Victim, Dies the City

1   They were walking along in the empty gray afternoon, three of them, Allen Burnett, Aaron Freeman, and Billy Mabry, Burnett the eldest at seventeen, walking up Bedford Avenue in Brooklyn and singing out Muhammad Ali rhymes into the chill air. As they reached the corner of Kosciusko Street, it was Allen Burnett's turn to give his Ali rhyme: "AJB is the latest. And he is the greatest."

2   "Who AJB?" one of them said.

3   "Allen J. Burnett."

4   They were laughing at this as they turned the corner onto Kosciusko Street. The three wore coats against the cold. Burnett was in a brown trench coat; Freeman, a three-quarter burgundy leather; and Mabry, a three-quarter beige corduroy with a fox collar. A white paint

stain was on the bottom at the tack of Mabry's coat. Mabry, walking on the outside, suddenly was shoved forward.

"Keep on walking straight," somebody behind him said.   5

Billy Mabry turned his head. Behind him was this little guy of   6 maybe eighteen, wearing a red sweater, dark pants, and black gun. Aaron Freeman, walking next to Mabry, says he saw two others besides the gunman. The three boys kept walking, although Mabry thought the guy in the red sweater had a play gun.

"Give me the money."   7

"I don't have any money," Allen Burnett said.   8

The guy with the gun shot Allen Burnett in the back of the head.   9 Burnett pitched into the wall of an apartment house and went down on his back, dead.

The gunman stood with Allen Burnett's body at his feet and said   10 that now he wanted coats. Billy Mabry handed back the corduroy with the paint stain. Freeman took off his burgundy leather. The gunman told the two boys to start running. "You don't look back!" Billy Mabry and Aaron Freeman ran up Kosciusko Street, past charred buildings with tin nailed over the windows, expecting to be shot in the back. People came onto the street and the guy in the red sweater waved his gun at them. The people dived into doorways. He stuffed the gun into his belt and ran up Bedford Avenue, ran away with his new coats. Some saw one other young guy with him. Others saw two.

It was another of last week's murders that went almost unnoticed.   11 Allen Burnett was young. People in the city were concentrating all week on the murders of elderly people. Next week you can dwell on murders of the young, and then the killing of the old won't seem as important.

Allen Burnett's murder went into the hands of the Thirteenth   12 Homicide Squad, situated on the second floor of a new police building on Utica Avenue. The outdoor pay phone in front of the precinct house has been ripped out. The luncheonette across the street is empty and fire-blackened. At first, a detective upstairs thought the interest was in a man who had just beaten his twenty-two-month-old child to death with a riding crop. That was unusual. Allen Burnett was just another homicide. Assured that Burnett was the subject, the detective pointed to Harold Ruger, who sat at a desk going through a new manila folder with Burnett's name on it. Ruger is a blue-eyed man with wavy dark-brown hair that is white at the temples. The twenty-four years he has spent on the job have left him with a melancholy face and a soft voice underlined with pleasant sarcasm: "They got two coats. Helluva way to go shopping. Looks like there was three of them. That leaves one guy out there without a coat. I'll look now for somebody who gets taken off for a coat tonight, tomorrow night, the next few days."

13   In a city that seems virtually ungoverned, Harold Ruger forms the only municipal presence with any relationship to what is happening on the streets where the people live. Politicians attend dinners at hotels with contractors. Bankers discuss interest rates at lunch. Harold Ruger goes into a manila folder on his desk and takes out a picture of Allen Burnett, a young face covered with blood staring from a morgue table. In Allen Burnett's hand there is a piece of the veins of the city of New York.

14   Dies the victim, dies the city. Nobody flees New York because of accounting malpractice. People run from murder and fire. Those who remain express their fear in words of anger.

15   "Kill him for nothing, that's life — that's what it is today," his sister Sadie was saying. The large, impressive family had gathered in the neat frame house at 30 Van Buren Street. "He was going into the army in January and they kill him for nothing. That's the leniency of the law. Without capital punishment they do what they want. There's no respect for human life."

16   Horace Jones, an uncle, said, "The bleeding hearts years ago cut out the electric chair. When the only way to stop all this is by havin' the electric chair."

17   "We look at mug shots all last night," Sadie said. "None of them was under sixteen. If the boy who shot Allen is under sixteen, there won't be any picture of him. How do you find him if he's under sixteen? Minors should get treated the same as everybody else. Equal treatment."

18   "Electric chair for anybody who kills, don't talk to me about ages," Horace Jones said.

19   The dead boy's mother, Lillian Burnett, sat with her head down and her hands folded in her lap.

20   "Do you think there should be an electric chair?" she was asked.

21   "I sure do," she said, eyes closed, head nodding. "Won't bring back my son, but I sure do want it. They tied up three old women and killed them. If they had the electric chair I believe they would rob the three women, but I don't believe they'd kill them."

22   The funeral was held two days later, at the Brown Memorial Baptist Church, on Washington Avenue. A crowd of three hundred of Allen Burnett's family and friends walked two by two into church. Walked erectly, solemnly, with the special dignity of those to whom suffering is a bitter familiarity. Seeing them, workmen in the street shut off pneumatic drills. Inside the church, the light coming through the door-

way gleamed on the dark, polished wood of the benches. The casket was brought in by men walking soundlessly on the carpeted floor. The doors were closed, an organ sounded, and the people faced the brutality of a funeral service; a baby cried, a woman rocked and screamed, a boy sobbed, a woman fainted, heads were cradled in arms. The mother screamed through a black veil, "My baby's gone!"

An aunt, Mabel Mabry, walked out of the church with lips trembl-   23
ing and arms hugging her shaking body. "My little nephew's dead," she said loudly. "They find the ones who killed him. I'm tellin' you, they got to kill them too, for my nephew."

The city government, Harold Ruger, just wants to find the killer.   24
Ruger was not at the funeral. "I got stuck in an eighty-floor elevator," he said when he came to work yesterday. "I was going around seeing people. We leave the number, maybe they'll call us. That's how it happens a lot. They call." He nodded toward a younger detective at the next desk. "He had one, an old man killed by a kid. Information came on a phone call, isn't that right, Al?"

"Stabbed eight times, skull fractured," the younger detective said.   25

Harold Ruger said, "What does it look like you have? Nothing. And   26
he gets a phone call, see what I mean? The answer is out there and it will come." His finger tapped the file he was keeping on the murder of Allen Burnett.

_____ CONSIDERATIONS _____

1. In a piece notable for its plain, terse, unhesitating style, Breslin uses a chilling metaphor in Paragraph 13. How effective is that device in this place? Can you connect it with the title of the essay?

2. How, in this straightforward account, does the reporter Breslin express his own opinions and feelings?

3. Some of the reaction to the murder of Allen Burnett focused on age: the age of the victim, the age of the killer. How does age figure in your thoughts about such an event and its implications?

4. What descriptive details of the environment does Breslin work into his account of the murder and its aftermath? In what way do those details contribute to his central point?

5. Could Breslin's piece be called an argument for capital punishment? Explain. What are your views on capital punishment?

6. Compare and contrast Breslin's report with Martin Gansberg's in "38 Who Saw Murder Didn't Call the Police," (pages 187–190).

Bruce Catton (1899–1978) became a historian while working as a newspaper reporter and magazine editor. His books, many on the Civil War, include Mr. Lincoln's Army *(1951) and* A Stillness at Appomattox *(1953). Catton received both the Pulitzer Prize and the National Book Award.*

16

BRUCE CATTON

Grant and Lee: A Study in Contrasts

1   When Ulysses S. Grant and Robert E. Lee met in the parlor of a modest house at Appomattox Court House, Virginia, on April 9, 1865, to work out the terms for the surrender of Lee's Army of Northern Virginia, a great chapter in American life came to a close, and a great new chapter began.

2   These men were bringing the Civil War to its virtual finish. To be sure, other armies had yet to surrender, and for a few days the fugitive Confederate government would struggle desperately and vainly, trying to find some way to go on living now that its chief support was gone. But in effect it was all over when Grant and Lee signed the papers. And the little room where they wrote out the terms was the scene of one of the poignant, dramatic contrasts in American history.

3   They were two strong men, these oddly different generals, and they represented the strengths of two conflicting currents that, through them, had come into final collision.

Back of Robert E. Lee was the notion that the old aristocratic 4
concept might somehow survive and be dominant in American life.

Lee was tidewater Virginia, and in his background were family 5
culture, and tradition . . . the age of chivalry transplanted to a New
World which was making its own legends and its own myths. He embodied a way of life that had come down through the age of knighthood
and the English country squire. America was a land that was beginning
all over again, dedicated to nothing much more complicated than the
rather hazy belief that all men had equal rights and should have an equal
chance in the world. In such a land Lee stood for the feeling that it was
somehow of advantage to human society to have a pronounced ine-
quality in the social structure. There should be a leisure class, backed
by ownership of land; in turn, society itself should be keyed to the land
as the chief source of wealth and influence. It would bring forth (according to this ideal) a class of men with a strong sense of obligation
to the community; men who lived not to gain advantage for themselves,
but to meet the solemn obligations which had been laid on them by
the very fact that they were privileged. From them the country would
get its leadership; to them it could look for the higher values—of
thought, of conduct, of personal deportment—to give it strength and
virtue.

Lee embodied the noblest elements of this aristocratic ideal. 6
Through him, the landed nobility justified itself. For four years, the
Southern states had fought a desperate war to uphold the ideals for which
Lee stood. In the end, it almost seemed as if the Confederacy fought
for Lee; as if he himself was the Confederacy . . . the best thing that the
way of life for which the Confederacy stood could ever have to offer.
He had passed into legend before Appomattox. Thousands of tired,
underfed, poorly clothed Confederate soldiers, long since past the simple enthusiasm of the early days of the struggle, somehow considered
Lee the symbol of everything for which they had been willing to die.
But they could not quite put this feeling into words. If the Lost Cause,
sanctified by so much heroism and so many deaths, had a living justification, its justification was General Lee.

Grant, the son of a tanner on the Western frontier, was everything 7
Lee was not. He had come up the hard way and embodied nothing in
particular except the eternal toughness and sinewy fiber of the men who
grew up beyond the mountains. He was one of a body of men who owed
reverence and obeisance to no one, who were self-reliant to a fault, who
cared hardly anything for the past but who had a sharp eye for the future.

8   These frontier men were the precise opposites of the tidewater aristocrats. Back of them, in the great surge that had taken people over the Alleghenies and into the opening Western country, there was a deep, implicit dissatisfaction with a past that had settled into grooves. They stood for democracy, not from any reasoned conclusion about the proper ordering of human society, but simply because they had grown up in the middle of democracy and knew how it worked. Their society might have privileges, but they would be privileges each man had won for himself. Forms and patterns meant nothing. No man was born to anything except perhaps to a chance to show how far he could rise. Life was competition.

9   Yet along with this feeling had come a deep sense of belonging to a national community. The Westerner, who developed a farm, opened a shop, or set up in business as a trader, could hope to prosper only as his own community prospered—and his community ran from the Atlantic to the Pacific and from Canada down to Mexico. If the land was settled, with towns and highways and accessible markets, he could better himself. He saw his fate in terms of the nation's own destiny. As its horizons expanded so did his. He had, in other words, an acute dollars-and-cents stake in the continued growth and development of his country.

10   And that, perhaps, is where the contrast between Grant and Lee becomes most striking. The Virginia aristocrat, inevitably, saw himself in relation to his own region. He lived in a static society which could endure almost anything except change. Instinctively, his first loyalty would go to the locality in which that society existed. He would fight to the limit of endurance to defend it, because in defending it he was defending everything that gave his own life its deepest meaning.

11   The Westerner, on the other hand, would fight with an equal tenacity for the broader concept of society. He fought so because everything he lived by was tied to growth, expansion, and a constantly widening horizon. What he lived by would survive or fall with the nation itself. He could not possibly stand by unmoved in the face of an attempt to destroy the Union. He would combat it with everything he had, because he could only see it as an effort to cut the ground out from under his feet.

12   So Grant and Lee were in complete contrast, representing two diametrically opposed elements in American life. Grant was the modern man emerging; beyond him, ready to come on the stage, was the great age of steel and machinery, of crowded cities and a restless burgeoning vitality. Lee might have ridden down from the old age of chivalry, lance in hand, silken banner fluttering over his head. Each man was the

perfect champion of his cause, drawing both his strengths and his weaknesses from the people he led.

Yet it was not all contrast, after all. Different as they were — in background, in personality, in underlying aspriation — these two great soldiers had much in common. Under everything else, they were marvelous fighters. Furthermore, their fighting qualities were really very much alike.   13

Each man had, to begin with, the great virtue of utter tenacity and fidelity. Grant fought his way down the Mississippi Valley in spite of acute personal discouragement and profound military handicaps. Lee hung on in the trenches at Petersburg after hope itself had died. In each man there was an indomitable quality . . . the born fighter's refusal to give up as long as he can still remain on his feet and lift his two fists.   14

Daring and resourcefulness they had, too; the ability to think faster and move faster than the enemy. These were the qualities which gave Lee the dazzling campaigns of Second Manassas and Chancellorsville and won Vicksburg for Grant.   15

Lastly, and perhaps greatest of all, there was the ability, at the end, to turn quickly from war to peace once the fighting was over. Out of the way these two men behaved at Appomattox came the possibility of a peace of reconciliation. It was a possibility not wholly realized, in the years to come, but which did, in the end, help the two sections to become one nation again . . . after a war whose bitterness might have seemed to make such a reunion wholly impossible. No part of either man's life became him more than the part he played in their brief meeting in the McLean house at Appomattox. Their behavior there put all succeeding generations of Americans in their debt. Two great Americans, Grant and Lee — very different, yet under everything very much alike. Their encounter at Appomattox was one of the great moments of American history.   16

———— CONSIDERATIONS ————

1. Bruce Catton's "Grant and Lee" is a classic example of the comparison-contrast essay, both in subject matter and organization. Select equally different figures of your own time and write about them, following Catton's organizational method.

2. After studying the contrast Catton offers in Paragraphs 10 and 11, consider an essay on similar trends in modern American life — adherents of no-growth against those who argue for expansion.

3. "Two great Americans, Grant and Lee," writes Catton in his last paragraph. Do you find evidence that Catton favored either?

4. In Paragraph 6, Catton describes Lee as a "symbol." A symbol of what? How can you recognize a symbol when you see one? Why would anyone fight for a symbol?

5. Nowhere in his essay does Catton describe physical appearances. A half hour's research in your college library should give you enough description to add at least a paragraph to Catton's essay. Where in the essay would you insert such an addition? Would physical description contribute to or confuse Catton's character study?

6. Judging by the proportions of this essay, decide whether Catton found the differences between the two men more interesting than their similarities.

Lynne V. Cheney (b. 1941) was appointed Chairman of the National Endowment for the Humanities in Washington by President Reagan in 1986. She has published two novels and (with her husband, Republican Representative Richard Cheney of Wyoming) written a history of the House of Representatives called Kings of the Hill. *She took her Bachelor's Degree with highest honors from Colorado College, followed by a Master's Degree from the University of Colorado and a Ph.D. in Nineteenth-Century British Literature from the University of Wisconsin.*

This brief essay appeared in the Newsweek, *column "My Turn."*

17

LYNNE V. CHENEY
Students of Success

Not long ago, my college-age daughter read about a software 1
genius who became a multimillionaire before he was 30. "That does it,"
she said, "I'm going into computers."

This daughter, who has never met a political-science course she 2
didn't like, was only joking. But a study conducted by the Carnegie Foundation shows that many young people do think seriously along these lines. Instead of choosing college majors—and careers—according to their interests, they are channeling themselves into fields that promise to be profitable: business, engineering, computer science, allied health programs.

3   Given the high cost of a college education, this trend is not surprising. A bachelor's degree now costs $40,000 at an average independent college. Can we expect students to major in the liberal arts when their starting salaries will be significantly lower than they are for business and professional majors? Shouldn't they get the best possible return on their investment?

4   They should, but I would suggest that there are better ways to calculate profit and loss than by looking at starting salaries. Consider, first of all, that very few people stay in the same line of work over a lifetime. They switch jobs, even change professions, and what is crucial for advancement is not specialized training but the ability to think critically and judge wisely. Given the difficulty of predicting which skills will be in demand even five years from now, let alone over a lifetime, a student's best career preparation is one that emphasizes general understanding and intellectual curiosity: a knowledge of how to learn and the desire to do it. Literature, history, philosophy and the social sciences — majors that students avoid today — are the ones traditionally believed to develop such habits of mind.

5   I recently conducted an informal survey of successful Americans, and while several dozen phone calls aren't proof of the value of a liberal-arts major, the results are suggestive. The communications world, for example, is dominated by liberal-arts majors. Thomas H. Wyman, chairman of CBS, majored in English, as did Cathleen Black, publisher of USA Today. Washington Post columnist William Raspberry studied history; NBC News anchorman Tom Brokaw, political science.

6   In public life, too, leaders more often than not were students of the liberal arts. They form a majority in the president's cabinet. Secretary of State George Shultz and Secretary of Energy John Herrington majored in economics. Interior Secretary Donald Hodel majored in government, and Transportation Secretary Elizabeth Dole, political science. Secretary of the Treasury James Baker read history with a minor in classics; Secretary of Education William Bennett studied philosophy.

7   The president himself majored in economics and sociology. His communications director, Pat Buchanan, majored in English and philosophy. White House chief of staff (and former treasury secretary) Donald Regan was an English major and before he came to government had a remarkably successful business career as the head of Merrill Lynch. Secretary of Commerce Malcolm Baldrige headed Scovill Manufacturing, and now the former English major is leading a campaign for clear writing in government.

Executives like Regan and Baldrige are not unusual. According 8
to a recent report in Fortune magazine, 38 percent of today's CEO's majored in the liberal arts, and a close reading of The New York Times
shows that 9 of the top 13 executives at IBM are liberal-arts majors. At
AT&T, a study showed social-science and humanities graduates moving into middle management faster than engineers and doing at least
as well as their business and engineering counterparts in reaching top
management levels.

For several years now, corporate executives have extolled the 9
wide range of knowledge and interests that a study of the liberal arts
encourages. And now under Tom Wyman's direction, CBS has funded
an organization that investigates exactly why it is that liberal-arts training is valuable to the American corporation. "In an increasingly competitive, internationally oriented and technologically innovative
society," Wyman recently wrote, "successful executives will be those
who can understand—and interpret—complex relationships and who
are capable of continually reconsidering assumptions underlying old
operating practices."

In the past, such top-level views did not always filter down to 10
where entry-level hiring is done. But reports from that front are en-
couraging. A study by Northwestern University shows that many major companies plan to increase their hiring of liberal-arts graduates by
some 20 percent in 1986. Or as one employer recently told "Today" show
viewers, "Those that are involved in recruiting people to the company
are looking for . . . broader skills . . . Then we will worry about teaching
them terminology, specifics of the jobs."

I don't mean to argue that liberal arts is the only road to success. 11
The average starting salary for engineers remains impressively high, almost $30,000 compared to $21,000 for a liberal-arts graduate. In fact,
my informal survey also shows that engineers are doing well in a variety of fields. Chrysler chairman Lee Iacocca was an engineering major,
as was former Delaware Gov. Pete du Pont. My point is that there are
many paths to success and students shouldn't force themselves down
any single one if their true interests lie elsewhere. College should be
a time for intellectual enthusiasm, for trying to read one's way through
the library, for heated debate with those who see the world differently.
College should be a time for learning to enjoy the life of the mind rather
than for learning to tolerate what one doesn't find interesting.

Students who follow their hearts in choosing majors will most 12
likely end up laboring at what they love. They're the ones who will put

in the long hours and intense effort that achievement requires. And they're the ones who will find the sense of purpose that underlies most human happiness.

_____ CONSIDERATIONS _____

1. "College should be a time for learning to enjoy the life of the mind rather than for learning to tolerate what one doesn't find interesting," writes Lynne Cheney, deploring the tendency of many students to think of college as vocational training. Read Caroline Bird's "Where College Fails Us," (pages 79–89) for a different view, and decide where you stand.

2. Cheney's essay questions trends of thought she sees in today's college students, but she uses as the opening of her piece a joking decision made by her daughter. How could you employ a similar device to begin an essay on a serious topic like crime, the threat of the nuclear arms race, or the destruction of the natural environment?

3. Cheney made a telephone survey to test her own convictions. She points out that such a survey may not provide realistic results. Does it have any value? Consider taking a similar survey among your friends as a way of testing your views on a topic you intend to write about.

4. Think of an older teacher, employer, or relative whom Cheney might have used as an illustration of her closing paragraph. Write a realistic interview with that person.

Evan Connell, Jr., (b. 1924) grew up in Kansas City and went to Dartmouth College. He served as an aviator in the Navy, and has lived in California for many years. His novels Mrs. Bridge *(1959) and* Mr. Bridge *(1969) have been reprinted by the North Point Press, which has also published other Connell books, notably his recent best-seller about General Custer and Little Big Horn,* Son of the Morning Star. *Connell also has published two long poems and a collection of short stories.*

This essay, with its irrepressible leaping about, first appeared in Esquire *in 1965.*

18

EVAN CONNELL, JR.

A Brief Essay on the Subject of Celebrity with Numerous Digressions and Particular Attention to the Actress, Rita Hayworth

West of Albuquerque a hundred miles or so there is a national 1 monument that nobody visits. It is maintained by the Department of the Interior, but except for a picnic area there are no accommodations, and it is considerably off the highway. The road is passable, the monument is not difficult to reach, but when you arrive you find only a small government station with an American flag snapping in the windy silence, juniper and prickly pear, and a gigantic sandstone bluff standing like a memorial tablet on the valley floor. Few birds are visible, no people, no animals, only an occasional glossy black beetle struggling with mindless determination through the crumbled rock at the base of the enormous cliff. Tourists do not come here: Paradise lies at the end of Route 66; immortality waits in Beverly Hills. A monument such as this can be overlooked; it is academic—one brief paragraph in a guidebook, a red star on a road map—surely nothing speaks from this dead land of Zuñi Indians, from the shadows of the Seven Cities of Cíbola. There would be only broken walls, pictographs, shards of coarse white pottery a thousand years old, and inscriptions left by early travelers who paused for a little while. So it is.

> *Paso por aquí adelanto*
> *Don Juan de Oñate*
> *del descubrimiento de la mar del sur*
> *a 16 de Abril de 1605.*

2   Oñate, who rode through this valley before the pilgrims arrived at Plymouth Rock, took thirty men along with two priests to the Gulf of California and stopped on his return to set down the fact that he had discovered the sea of the south. Nearby another inscription, partly hidden by a yucca plant, is carved in Spanish on the cliff:

> *By here passed the Ensign Don Joséph*
> *de Payba Basconzelos*
> *the year he brought the cabildo of the realm*
> *at his own expense*
> *the 18th of February, of the year 1726.*

The meaning of this man's text is muddled, but what is unmistakable is that here was another who set down his deed, his name, and the date, in order that he should not be forgotten.

> *The 28th day of September 1737,*
> *arrived here the illustrious Señor*
> *Don Martin de Elizacochea, Bishop of Durango,*
> *and the day following, went on to Zuñi.*

> *By here passed Pedro Romero*
> *on the 22nd of August, year of 1751.*

I am of the hand of Felipe de Arellano
on the 16th of September, soldier.

Then the Spaniards were gone, leaving records only a little more   3
complex than those of the primitive Zuñi; and the first Americans arrived, rested, watered their horses, wrote, and went away. Lt. J. H. Simpson. E. Pen Long of Baltimore. Mr. P. Gilmer Breckenridge. Mr. Engle.
Mr. Byrn.

Today around this cliff the wind boils through ponderosa pines   4
and acorns drop from scrub oaks on the mesa. Beetles clamber insistently
toward an incomprehensible goal while the wispy trail of an Air Force
jet miles above fades into cirrus clouds. Inscription Rock no longer is
a crossroads; it is now meaningless, except as evidence of the human
wish to be remembered, for indeed there are not more than two things
that we want: the first being our fair share of corporeal bliss, generally
consisting of food, warmth, and sex; the second being that after we have
been tucked away we shall be remembered. Little else concerns us. Symbols of affluence, say, are merely to remind the neighbors that we are
of some consequence and will not easily be forgotten. Exploration and
conquest, works of art, singing, dancing, humors of every sort—modesty,
lust, wrath—all may exist to perpetuate our name just as children do,
notifying the future that we are worth at least a minor celebration.

Now, if you keep traveling west from Inscription Rock, you come   5
ultimately to California on whose golden shore all promises must be
honored. Let this be noted. Without knowing why, we do believe that
in California we shall discover what we started toward so long ago. Yes,
we say in our hearts, when we have reached California our value cannot go unrecognized. There, in consequence, we shall be happy. We will
be fulfilled. Our needs will be ministered. Afternoon shall find us loitering beside a private pool in the shade of imported palms, while a vulgar
public clusters outside the gate. This is the promise that somewhere,
once upon a time, was made to us, and we do not doubt it.

Mirabile visu! The promise is kept, usually. Just once in a while,   6
to one or two or three of us, does it seem that the salty smell of fraud
has mingled with the orange blossoms.

Taking this example. A few weeks ago about five o'clock one pleas-   7
ant evening in Los Angeles when Wilshire Boulevard was populated with
the homeward-bound after another day when the contract had not quite
been honored, there came one woman steadily marching up the boulevard with a businesslike expression, a woman so average in each detail
that she became formidable. She neither spoke to nor looked at anyone.

Perhaps she was reflecting on the inequities of life. Who can be sure? She wore a pair of ballet slippers but nothing else, because forty years had come and gone and as yet nobody cared. The magic words had not been spoken. So much time had elapsed and nobody had told her how valuable she was, how significant, how inestimable and precious. Not one man, woman, or child thus far had stepped aside or bowed when she went by, because she was as unremarkable as Felipe de Arellano, who could put after his name only the one word: Soldier. So she had grown tired of waiting and thought that she would cause the world to take some notice. It did, of course. To be sensational is not particularly difficult. For five full minutes, there was no one more famous. The crowd did open as obediently as though she were the wife of Caesar.

8   However, to carve one's name on a cliff or to take a spectacular stroll along Wilshire Boulevard are more less identical, being surrogates of fame. If there is some genuine talent or resource, a strangeness of proportion to the body or to the mind that elevates a person so that he or she exists in the sight of millions, there is no more need to walk blindly naked through a crowd than to carve private data on a rock. Such secretarial work may then be left to others, the amanuenses: they shall set down that someone of consequence passed by this place, giving the style and nature of the accomplishment.

9   To these few, the authentically famous, we are attracted. We follow them and we speculate. We wonder in what respect they are different from ourselves. Is it circumstance? Or has a genie chosen them?

10   Let us consider. Let us say that there is a ballplayer seven feet tall, which there is, whose name is known to a certain part of the population. In his way he is talented, he is muscular, and energetic; but suppose that he were six feet tall, who would ever have heard of him? Is this not, therefore, the purest kind of circumstantial celebrity? A game exists for which a uniquely suitable body was born. Whistles blow, drums beat. Had such a man been twelve inches shorter than he is, his name would be recorded only with a crayon on the bricks of a tenement, scratched with the tip of a switchblade knife on a lavatory partition, and the date he was there.

11   Or is this true? Possibly we still would know of him. He might have become the warehouseman who one afternoon for no evident reason opens fire with a rifle from a window of his apartment, the epilogue as follows:

> *Tell us, Bud, why did you shoot those people?*
> *I dunno, man, I dunno. I felt like it, that's all.*

If such is the case, circumstance becomes peripheral and we must conclude that within certain individuals a genie resides, directing them to eminence of one sort or another, however commendable or bizarre. Then we wish to descry this genie, to find where he or it lives, and fathom its nature; knowing that if we too possessed the demon we would not go unrecorded. The Earth's bright doors should swing open for us as well.

So we look after the celebrities of the world, whether they are 12 statesmen, actors, athletes or murderers, wondering at their essence. Hopefully, wistfully, we send them gifts and write to them; we seek to make friends with them in order that we may divine their secret and appropriate this to our own purpose.

But the secret is hidden, ordinarily. We look and wait and listen, 13 but divine nothing. The genie is not visible, not audible. Only once in a while can we perceive him.

For example, in San Francisco are thousands of middle-aged Italian 14 gentlemen playing boccie on the public greens, solemnly sitting in hotel lobbies, shuffling along the narrow streets of North Beach, and they are very nearly as indistinguishable from each other, unless you happen to be acquainted with them, as twenty thousand herring. They mind small shops, they work around Fisherman's Wharf, and each one is attached to a baggy suit and a stout wife and a clutch of children and grandchildren and more relatives than there are mushrooms in Tuscany. Because their differences are negligible you cannot tell them apart, just as you cannot identify particular fish, bowling balls, or women at market. However, some evening, perhaps browsing through a bookstore, you may encounter one of these greying little Italian men and pay him no attention unless you meet his gaze. Then, after he is gone, you follow him with your eyes, troubled by an obscure sense of respect and inquire:

Who was that?

The sculptor, Bufano. Gandhi was a friend of his, and Roosevelt. . . .

A year goes by but you do not forget that cold electric-blue gaze. 15 You pass him on the street, watch him on a scaffold—apparently a laborer cleaning St. Francis—and there is nothing to tell you that he is who he is, nothing unless you look into his eyes. Then you know, instantly, beyond every doubt. Sometimes, as it is with Bufano, the mystery is visible to those who look closely, even to those who do not see what is in front of them; but more often the spirit is bottled, the radiance concealed, the mask set, a curtain drawn, so that you spend hours, days, or weeks in the presence of some exceptional person without detecting much. That is how it is with the supreme Aphrodite of a splintered age, Rita Hayworth, singularly American, who offers acquaintances a mild and friendly brown eye, nothing more.

16   There is the Hollywood mansion, yes, and the blue-painted swimming pool, the palm trees tilting against the Pacific sky like totem poles, or, more properly, like symbols of national insanity. Nor can there be the least doubt that the United States of America is mad. Symptoms are too numerous to catalog. Let us take one, possibly two: Respectable citizens seated on the pavement outside their homes because there are neither public benches for loitering nor sidewalk cafés. Why are there none? Because it is believed in the United States that there is something depraved and subversive about those who are not occupied, something scurrilous, ominous. If you go for a stroll through Beverly Hills the police will stop and question you. It is quicker to get wherever you are going by automobile, therefore if you are walking you must be bent on evil.

17   Or say that you draw pictures of a man and a woman fulfilling the promise of love; you will be positively arrested, you will be imprisoned. You may represent hate in the most egregious fashion, you may picture all conceivable butcheries, that is permissible, but love is more alarming. However, that is a third instance. There are thousands. It is futile to itemize them; better to content yourself with abstruse knowledge.

18   So there are the palms, the painted pool, and the rest. Everything, close to your eyes. Visualize the scene. Whatever you imagine is valid. The long drive winding away from the street, high guardian hedges, a maid in a black uniform to answer the bell. You are ushered in, instructed almost crisply to choose a seat.

19   A few minutes later, after you have had time to wait, because that is the way it is done, Rita Hayworth enters—swiftly, rather silently. The delayed entrance is the only sign of artifice. She would open the door herself, except that she was long ago taught otherwise and now thinks no more about it. That is the way things are.

20   Presently she is seated, not quite at ease on the sofa, fingering her necklace, occasionally tugging at the hem of an Irish green dress. She no more displays the imperial mannerisms of a Love Goddess than does Mamie Eisenhower. There she sits, Rita Hayworth, the subject of poems, colored reams, threats, grotesque fantasies, memories and speculation, the warm brown eyes telling much of what she is not— mendacious, spiteful, conniving, treacherous—but little of what she is. She inquires if you would care for sugar in your tea.

21   *Would you care for sugar in your tea?*
22   *Thank you, no, this is fine.*

That is the memorable conversation. What is significant is the   23
omission.

Would you care for sugar in your tea?   24

The mundane query lodges in the mind like a bug sealed im-   25
mutably in amber. Because these are the words of Aphrodite, because
they are natural, inevitable, and unexpected, because she fails to say
what you half-anticipate, gradually you recall other omissions: the
publicity agent, Rick Ingersoll, in a booth at the Brown Derby who
carefully answered all questions and brought out of his briefcase a five-
page resumé.

"Few stars in the history of Hollywood have captured the   26
public's imagination with the magnetic impact of Rita Hayworth. Internationally renowned as the 'Love Goddess,' Miss Hayworth casts an
aura of glamour wherever she appears. One of movieland's all-time
greats . . . was born Margarita Carmen Cansino . . . curvaceous, exotic
star . . . turned down numerous offers . . . returned to dramatic
parts . . . created memorable characterizations . . . presently lives in
Beverly Hills. . . ."

It is complete, but of course it tells nothing. Ingersoll is a hand-   27
some, affable young man who zips through the pink stucco majesty of
Beverly Hills in a Volks as black as a Zuñi beetle. Assiduously he is
polishing the Image; perhaps he is not unlike Bufano tending St. Francis.
It is not his job to promote iconoclasm, but to make certain that the
idol remains on the pedestal. It is not his fault if he presents a five-page
summary of nothing. He is doing his appointed job, he is paid for this,
he has a family. It is easy to be critical or cynical. Most of us are obliged
to work for a living, which necessitates some adjustment.

All the same, it isn't there. The truth has been circumnavigated.   28
Not deliberately, not even consciously, perhaps, but effectually.

The actor Mark Roberts, who years ago played in one of Rita   29
Hayworth's films, thinks back and at last observes in his leisurely voice
that she was a sweet, likable girl. She could dance, says he, just a little
bit better than I could. But then, he adds reflectively, her old man taught
dancing so she'd been practicing.

Well, yes, but is that all? Did she make no deeper imprint? She   30
casts an aura of glamour wherever she appears. She is internationally
renowned as the Love Goddess. Surely you must have been excited?

Roberts leans back, tries to remember. He is from Kansas City;   31
he is as substantial as a Missouri farmer. He is not going to be rushed.
He thinks. He scratches his jaw. I haven't seen her in fifteen years, he
says finally. She was always sweet and worked hard. . . .

Nor is it found in the movie magazines nor in the yellow   32 journals, not that it could be there. But most of all it is absent in the presence of the woman herself. The difference is that she knows it is absent; the others do not. Somerset Maugham points out in *The Summing Up* that the celebrated develop a technique to deal with the persons they come across. They show the world a mask, often an impressive one, says Maugham, but take care to conceal their real selves. They play the part that is expected from them and with practice learn to play it very well, but you are stupid if you think that this public performance corresponds with the person within.

33   Immaculately she has prepared herself; she knows that she is not going to say anything. That is as it should be. All the chic lady journalists, all the inquisitive males, with pad and pencil, with photographic mind—they have trooped in and out of London suites, premieres, banquets, et cetera, et cetera, and they have asked and they have asked. Tell us the truth about Orson Welles! About Aly Khan! She has answered. It was not obligatory, but she has answered because she is polite, and each time has said nothing. It is splendid to have such dignity. Nor does she smile unnecessarily. That, too, is a relief and a pleasure, for there is nothing so tiresome as a decided smile. One may draw sustenance from a woman's somber face.

34   Half-hidden among the records beside her phonograph is an album of Haydn. Ingersoll, omnipresent if not omniscient, is quick to point out the record of *Pal Joey*. But that is his job; she was in *Pal Joey*.

35   Just visible in the hall stands an archaic stone figure. Near it hangs a painting by Derain. On a corner table repose *House Beautiful* and *Harper's Bazaar*, two sleek and wealthy sisters eternally congratulating one another. There also is the seventy millionth copy of a vapid little book of cartoons; Ingersoll, slightly abashed, mentions that this is not indicative of the star's taste in reading. All right, there is nothing criminal about owning a book as ephemeral as a moth.

36   On the coffee table in the center of the room lies an old first edition of a drama by Edna Millay. Its very existence seems a reproach to the commercial pap. Like Derain, like the sculpture, or Joseph Haydn, the presence of Millay could be calculated, might be there to suggest Culture, but that is not so; the volume lies on the coffee table because it is being read. Rita Hayworth explains this almost apologetically; she is unmistakably American.

37   Rick Ingersoll will inform you that she was born in New York, but it doesn't matter, it could as easily have been Des Moines, and even now she is not far from home. After the soirees and the safaris she speaks one language, English, like all reasonable Americans. She shoots a good

game of golf, drives the ball 175 yards. She doesn't go to the movies much. One day in Ireland she saw a leprechaun. There again, as with Millay, she becomes a bit apologetic, explains that on closer inspection the leprechaun was a tree stump. It requires an American, a Puritan down to the marrow of one's bones, to say such a thing.

She has traveled four directions, married herself to baroque and talented men. She has lived the life of a celebrity for thirty years, yet has failed to acquire the sheen of a sixth-rank European countess. It is not plausible. Indeed, it is altogether impossible. You conclude that she must be somebody else. She isn't Rita Hayworth after all, she's Ike's niece in disguise.   38

How many weeks were you in Germany entertaining the troops, Rita? inquires Ingersoll, who already knows. Dutifully she answers, revealing nothing.   39

Would you care for . . . ?   40

So the shadows of the wild palms turn across the fabled swimming pool, whose waters are rocked by nothing. Evening comes, wan and feckless, to Beverly Hills. Tourists ride past the mansion, stare at the protective hedge, wondering. There is the gate to Paradise, is it not? It is so, according to our map, which cost a dollar. Yes, there it is, the home of Love. We have come so far to see it and we are very near. Only guess what pleasures we would find if we could enter. Tomorrow, perhaps, we will be invited.   41

Illusion is our price and purchase. Love and Fame, both are adulation. Various warmths encourage us to the end of each desperate centennial. If the reign of a singular goddess is too soon ended, as it soon ends for the warehouseman with his rifle, for the Spanish foot soldier plodding through the dust of savage lands toward some far blue ocean, an ocean bluer than a dream, for Mr. P. Gilmer Breckenridge and Lt. Simpson—if it is quickly ended, still each has contrived to make himself remembered. It seems necessary. Even the Zuñi pictograph says that I was here, this is from my hand. I have watched two animals by a pool of water, yes, and a strange woman. It was I who saw these things. I was here. Behold me.   42

———— **CONSIDERATIONS** ————————————————————————

1. On first reading, Connell's essay seems to wander. How does he take the reader from Inscription Rock to the Beverly Hills home of Rita Hayworth? And why does he impose that journey on the reader?

2. In addition to research on Inscription Rock, what other material did Connell collect for his essay?

3. Explain the irony, the humor, and the point of Connell's closing sentence, "Behold me." You will need to think about the whole varied journey.

4. The final quarter of Connell's essay is the product of an interview with the movie star. Compare Connell's interview with Roy Blount's encounter in "How to Raise Your Boys to Play Pro Ball," (pages 90–95), Stud Terkel's "Phil Stallings, Spot Welder," (pages 403–408), or Lynne V. Cheney's "Students of Success," (pages 105–108).

5. Who were Mr. P. Gilmer Breckenridge and Lt. Simpson and how do they figure in Connell's closing paragraph? What valuable technique for a writer do they point up?

6. Explain why Connell insists that "to carve one's name on a cliff and to take a spectacular stroll along Wilshire Boulevard are more or less identical."

*Frank Conroy (b. 1936) grew up in various towns along the
eastern seaboard, and attended Haverford College in Pennsylvania. He plays jazz piano, was director of the literature program at the National Endowment for the Arts from 1982 to
January of 1987, and now directs the writing program at the
University of Iowa. He writes about his early life in Stop-Time,
from which we take this episode. His prose possesses the
qualities that make the best reminiscence: details feel exact
and bright, though miniature with distance, like the landscape
crafted for background to model trains. In 1985 he published a
collection of short stories called Midair.*

19

FRANK CONROY
A Yo-Yo Going Down

The common yo-yo is crudely made, with a thick shank between 1
two widely spaced wooden disks. The string is knotted or stapled to
the shank. With such an instrument nothing can be done except the
simple up-down movement. My yo-yo, on the other hand, was a perfectly
balanced construction of hard wood, slightly weighted, flat, with only
a sixteenth of an inch between the halves. The string was not attached
to the shank, but looped over it in such a way as to allow the wooden
part to spin freely on its own axis. The gyroscopic effect thus created
kept the yo-yo stable in all attitudes.

I started at the beginning of the book and quickly mastered the 2
novice, intermediate, and advanced stages, practicing all day every day
in the woods across the street from my house. Hour after hour of practice, never moving to the next trick until the one at hand was mastered.

3   The string was tied to my middle finger, just behind the nail. As I threw—with your palm up, make a fist; throw down your hand, fingers unfolding, as if you were casting grain—a short bit of string would tighten across the sensitive pad of flesh at the tip of my finger. That was the critical area. After a number of weeks I could interpret the condition of the string, the presence of any imperfections on the shank, but most importantly the exact amount of spin or inertial energy left in the yo-yo at any given moment—all from that bit of string on my fingertip. As the throwing motion became more and more natural I found I could make the yo-yo "sleep" for an astonishing length of time—fourteen or fifteen seconds—and still have enough spin left to bring it back to my hand. Gradually the basic moves became reflexes. Sleeping, twirling, swinging, and precise aim. Without thinking, without even looking, I could run through trick after trick involving various combinations of the elemental skills, switching from one to the other in a smooth continuous flow. On particularly good days I would hum a tune under my breath and do it all in time to the music.

4   Flicking the yo-yo expressed something. The sudden, potentially comic extension of one's arm to twice its length. The precise neatness of it, intrinsically soothing, as if relieving an inner tension too slight to be noticeable, the way a man might hitch up his pants simply to enact a reassuring gesture. It felt good. The comfortable weight in one's hand, the smooth, rapid-descent down the string, ending with a barely audible snap as the yo-yo hung balanced, spinning, pregnant with force and the slave of one's fingertip. That it was vaguely masturbatory seems inescapable. I doubt that half the pubescent boys in America could have been captured by any other means, as, in the heat of the fad, half of them were. A single Loop-the-Loop might represent, in some mysterious way, the act of masturbation, but to break down the entire repertoire into the three stages of throw, trick, and return representing erection, climax, and detumescence seems immoderate.

5   The greatest pleasure in yo-yoing was an abstract pleasure—watching the dramatization of simple physical laws, and realizing they would never fail if a trick was done correctly. The geometric purity of it! The string wasn't just a string, it was a tool in the enactment of theorems. It was a line, an idea. And the top was an entirely different sort of idea, a gyroscope, capable of storing energy and of interacting with the line. I remember the first time I did a particularly lovely trick, one in which the sleeping yo-yo is swung from right to left while the string is interrupted by an extended index finger. Momentum carries the yo-yo in a circular path around the finger, but instead of completing

the arc the yo-yo falls on the taut string between the performer's hands, where it continues to spin in an upright position. My pleasure at that moment was as much from the beauty of the experiment as from pride. Snapping apart my hands I sent the yo-yo into the air above my head, bouncing it off nothing, back into my palm.

I practiced the yo-yo because it pleased me to do so, without the slightest application of will power. It wasn't ambition that drove me, but the nature of yo-yoing. The yo-yo represented my first organized attempt to control the outside world. It fascinated me because I could see my progress in clearly defined stages, and because the intimacy of it, the almost spooky closeness I began to feel with the instrument in my hand, seemed to ensure that nothing irrelevant would interfere. I was, in the language of jazz, "up tight" with my yo-yo, and finally free, in one small area at least, of the paralyzing sloppiness of life in general. 6

The first significant problem arose in the attempt to do fifty consecutive Loop-the-Loops. After ten or fifteen the yo-yo invariably started to lean and the throws became less clean, resulting in loss of control. I almost skipped the whole thing because fifty seemed excessive. Ten made the point. But there it was, written out in the book. To qualify as an expert you had to do fifty, so fifty I would do. 7

It took me two days, and I wouldn't have spent a moment more. All those Loop-the-Loops were hard on the strings. Time after time the shank cut them and the yo-yo went sailing off into the air. It was irritating, not only because of the expense (strings were a nickel each, and fabricating your own was unsatisfactory), but because a random element had been introduced. About the only unforeseeable disaster in yo-yoing was to have your string break, and here was a trick designed to do exactly that. Twenty-five would have been enough. If you could do twenty-five clean Loop-the-Loops you could do fifty or a hundred. I supposed they were simply trying to sell strings and went back to the more interesting tricks. 8

The witty nonsense of Eating Spaghetti, the surprise of The Twirl, the complex neatness of Cannonball, Backwards Round the World, or Halfway Round the World—I could do them all, without false starts or sloppy endings. I could do every trick in the book. Perfectly. 9

The day was marked on the kitchen calendar (God Gave Us Bluebell Natural Bottled Gas). I got on my bike and rode into town. Pedaling along the highway I worked out with the yo-yo to break in a new string. The twins were appearing at the dime store. 10

I could hear the crowd before I turned the corner. Kids were 11 coming on bikes and on foot from every corner of town, rushing down the streets like madmen. Three or four policemen were busy keeping the street clear directly in front of the store, and in a small open space around the doors some of the more adept kids were running through their tricks, showing off to the general audience or stopping to compare notes with their peers. Standing at the edge with my yo-yo safe in my pocket, it didn't take me long to see I had them all covered. A boy in a sailor hat could do some of the harder tricks, but he missed too often to be a serious threat. I went inside.

12   As Ramos and Ricardo performed I watched their hands carefully, noticing little differences in style, and technique. Ricardo was a shade classier, I thought, although Ramos held an edge in the showy two-handed stuff. When they were through we went outside for the contest.

13   "Everybody in the alley!" Ramos shouted, his head bobbing an inch or two above the others. "Contest starting now in the alley!" A hundred excited children followed the twins into an alley beside the dime store and lined up against the wall.

14   "Attention all kids!" Ramos yelled, facing us from the middle of the street like a drill sergeant. "To qualify for contest you got to Rock the Cradle. You got to rock yo-yo in cradle four time. Four time! Okay? Three time no good. Okay. Everybody happy?" There were murmurs of disappointment and some of the kids stepped out of line. The rest of us closed ranks. Yo-yos flicked nervously as we waited. "Winner receive grand prize. Special Black Beauty Prize Yo-Yo with Diamonds," said Ramos, gesturing to his brother who smiled and held up the prize, turning it in the air so we could see the four stones set on each side. ("The crowd gasped . . . " I want to write. Of course they didn't. They didn't make a sound, but the impact of the diamond yo-yo was obvious.) We'd never seen anything like it. One imagined how the stones would gleam as it revolved, and how much prettier the tricks would be. The ultimate yo-yo! The only one in town! Who knew what feats were possible with such an instrument? All around me a fierce, nervous resolve was settling into the contestants, suddenly skittish as racehorses.

15   "Ricardo will show trick with Grand Prize Yo-Yo. Rock the Cradle four time!"

16   "One!" cried Ramos.

17   "Two!" the kids joined in.

18   "Three!" It was really beautiful. He did it so slowly you would have thought he had all the time in the world. I counted seconds under my breath to see how long he made it sleep.

"Four!" said the crowd.   19

"Thirteen" I said to myself as the yo-yo snapped back into his hand.   20
Thirteen seconds. Excellent time for that particular trick.

"Attention all kids!" Ramos announced. "Contest start now at   21
head of line."

The first boy did a sloppy job of gathering his string but managed   22
to rock the cradle quickly four times.

"Okay." Ramos tapped him on the shoulder and moved to the   23
next boy, who fumbled. "Out." Ricardo followed, doing an occasional
Loop-the-Loop with the diamond yo-yo. "Out . . . out . . . okay," said
Ramos as he worked down the line.

There was something about the man's inexorable advance that   24
unnerved me. His decisions were fast, and there was no appeal. To my
surprise I felt my palms begin to sweat. Closer and closer he came, his
voice growing louder, and then suddenly he was standing in front of
me. Amazed, I stared at him. It was as if he'd appeared out of thin air.

"What happen boy, you swarrow bubble gum?"   25

The laughter jolted me out of it. Blushing, I threw down my yo-   26
yo and executed a slow Rock the Cradle, counting the four passes and
hesitating a moment at the end so as not to appear rushed.

"Okay." He tapped my shoulder. "Good."   27

I wiped my hands on my blue jeans and watched him move down   28
the line. "Out . . . out . . . out." He had a large mole on the back of his
neck.

Seven boys qualified. Coming back, Ramos called out, "Next   29
trick Backward Round the World! Okay? Go!"

The first two boys missed, but the third was the kid in the sailor   30
hat. Glancing quickly to see that no one was behind him, he hunched
up his shoulder, threw, and just barely made the catch. There was some
loose string in his hand, but not enough to disqualify him.

Number four missed, as did number five, and it was my turn. I   31
stepped forward, threw the yo-yo almost straight up over my head, and
as it began to fall pulled very gentle to add some speed. It zipped neatly
behind my legs and there was nothing more to do. My head turned to
one side, I stood absolutely still and watched the yo-yo come in over
my shoulder and slap into my hand. I added a Loop-the-Loop just to show
the tightness of the string.

"Did you see that?" I heard someone say.   32

Number seven missed, so it was between myself and the boy in   33
the sailor hat. His hair was bleached by the sun and combed up over

his forehead in a pompadour, held from behind by the white hat. He was a year or two older than me. Blinking his blue eyes nervously, he adjusted the tension of his string.

34   "Next trick Cannonball! Cannonball! You go first this time," Ramos said to me.

35   Kids had gathered in a circle around us, those in front quiet and attentive, those in back jumping up and down to get a view. "Move back for room," Ricardo said, pushing them back. "More room, please."

36   I stepped into the center and paused, looking down at the ground. It was a difficult trick. The yo-yo had to land exactly on the string and there was a chance I'd miss the first time. I knew I wouldn't miss twice. "Can I have one practice?"

37   Ramos and Ricardo consulted in their mother tongue, and then Ramos held up his hands. "Attention all kids! Each boy have one practice before trick."

38   The crowd was then silent, watching me. I took a deep breath and threw, following the fall of the yo-yo with my eyes, turning slightly, matador-fashion, as it passed me. My finger caught the string, the yo-yo came up and over, and missed. Without pausing I threw again. "Second time," I yelled, so there would be no misunderstanding. The circle had been too big. This time I made it small, sacrificing beauty for security. The yo-yo fell where it belonged and spun for a moment. (A moment I don't rush, my arms widespread, my eyes locked on the spinning toy. The Trick! There it is, brief and magic right before your eyes! My hands are frozen in the middle of a deaf-and-dumb sentence, holding the whole airy, tenuous statement aloft for everyone to see.) With a quick snap I broke up the trick and made my catch.

39   Ramos nodded. "Okay. Very good. Now next boy."

40   Sailor-hat stepped forward, wiping his nose with the back of his hand. He threw once to clear the string.

41   "One practice," said Ramos.

42   He nodded.

43   "C'mon Bobby," someone said. "You can do it."

44   Bobby threw the yo-yo out to the side, made his move, and missed. "Damn," he whispered. (He said "dahyum.") The second time he got halfway through the trick before his yo-yo ran out of gas and fell impotently off the string. He picked it up and walked away, winding slowly.

45   Ramos came over and held my hand in the air. "The winner!" he yelled. "Grand prize Black Beauty Diamond Yo-Yo will now be awarded."

46   Ricardo stood in front of me. "Take off old yo-yo." I loosened the knot and slipped it off. "Put out hand." I held out my hand and he looped

the new string on my finger, just behind the nail, where the mark was. "You like Black Beauty," he said, smiling as he stepped back. "Diamond make pretty colors in the sun."

"Thank you," I said.   47

"Very good with yo-yo. Later we have contest for whole town.   48
Winner go to Miami for State Championship. Maybe you win. Okay?"

"Okay." I nodded. "Thank you."   49

A few kids came up to look at Black Beauty. I threw it once or   50
twice to get the feel. It seemed a bit heavier than my old one. Ramos
and Ricardo were surrounded as the kids called out their favorite tricks.

"Do Pickpocket! Pickpocket!"   51

"Do the Double Cannonball!"   52

"Ramos! Ramos! Do the Turkish Army!"   53

Smiling, waving their hands to ward off the barrage of requests,   54
the twins worked their way through the crowd toward the mouth of
the alley. I watched them moving away and was immediately struck
by a wave of fierce and irrational panic. "Wait," I yelled, pushing through
after them. "Wait!"

I caught them on the street.   55

"No more today," Ricardo said, and then paused when he saw it   56
was me. "Okay. The champ. What's wrong? Yo-yo no good?"

"No. It's fine."   57

"Good. You take care of it."   58

"I wanted to ask when the contest is. The one where you get to   59
go to Miami."

"Later. After school begins." They began to move away. "We   60
have to go home now."

"Just one more thing," I said, walking after them. "What is the   61
hardest trick you know?"

Ricardo laughed. "Hardest trick is killing flies in air."   62

"No, no. I mean a real trick."   63

They stopped and looked at me. "There is a very hard trick,"   64
Ricardo said. "I don't do it, but Ramos does. Because you won the contest he will show you. But only once, so watch carefully."

We stepped into the lobby of the Sunset Theater. Ramos cleared   65
his string. "Watch," he said, and threw. The trick started out like a
Cannonball, and then unexpectedly folded up, opened again, and as I
watched breathlessly the entire complex web spun around in the air,
propelled by Ramos' two hands making slow circles like a swimmer.
The end was like the end of a Cannonball.

"That's beautiful," I said, genuinely awed. "What's it called?"   66

"The Universe."   67

68   "The Universe," I repeated.

69   "Because it goes around and around," said Ramos, "like the planets."

_____ **CONSIDERATIONS** _____

1. List the ways in which Conroy says one can get pleasure from the yo-yo.

2. How much of performance is play? Would you use the word performance for the work of a painter, an opera singer, a tennis star, a poet? Are professional athletes paid to play? What is the difference between work and play?

3. One respected writer says that "play is the direct opposite of seriousness," yet writers like Conroy are serious in recalling their childhood play. Can you resolve this apparent contradiction?

4. Conroy's essay might be divided into two major sections. Where would you draw the dividing line? Describe the two sections in terms of the author's intention. In the second section, the author makes constant use of dialogue; in the first, there is none. Why?

5. "I practiced the yo-yo because it pleased me to do so, without the slightest application of will power." Consider the relevance or irrelevance of will power to pleasure. Are they mutually exclusive?

6. In Paragraph 14, Conroy interrupts his narrative with a parenthetical remark about himself as the writer: "(' The crowd gasped . . .' I want to write. Of course they didn't. They didn't make a sound, but the impact of the diamond yo-yo was obvious.)" Are such glimpses of the writer useful or merely distracting? Discuss.

Emily Dickinson (1830–1886) was little known as a poet in her lifetime, but now is acknowledged as among the greatest American poets. She lived her entire life in Amherst, Massachusetts, and spent her later years as a virtual recluse in the Dickinsons' brick homestead on Main Street. She always remained close to her family, and kept contact with the outside world through a vast correspondence.

She published little poetry in her lifetime; after her death more than a thousand poems were discovered neatly arranged in the bureau of the upstairs bedroom where she wrote. In 1955, a definitive edition of The Poems of Emily Dickinson *was published, containing 1,775 poems and fragments.*

20

EMILY DICKINSON
There's a certain Slant of light

There's a certain Slant of light,   1
Winter Afternoons—
That oppresses, like the Heft
Of Cathedral Tunes—

Heavenly Hurt, it gives us—   5
We can find no scar,
But internal difference,
Where the Meanings, are—

None may teach it—Any—
10 ' Tis the Seal Despair—
An imperial affliction
Sent us of the Air—

When it comes, the Landscape listens—
Shadows—hold their breath—
15 When it goes, ' tis like the Distance
On the look of Death—

21

JOAN DIDION
On Keeping a Notebook

" ' That woman Estelle,' " the note reads, " ' is partly the reason why   1
George Sharp and I are separated today.' *Dirty crepe-de-Chine wrapper, hotel bar, Wilmington RR, 9:45* A.M. August Monday morning."

Since the note is in my notebook, it presumably has some mean-   2
ing to me. I study it for a long while. At first I have only the most general notion of what I was doing on an August Monday morning in the bar of the hotel across from the Pennsylvania Railroad station in Wil-mington, Delaware (waiting for a train? missing one? 1960? 1961? why Wilmington?), but I do remember being there. The woman in the dirty crepe-de-Chine wrapper had come down from her room for a beer, and

the bartender had heard before the reason why George Sharp and she were separated today. "Sure," he said, and went on mopping the floor. "You told me." At the other end of the bar is a girl. She is talking, pointedly, not to the man beside her but to a cat lying in the triangle of sunlight cast through the open door. She is wearing a plaid silk dress from Peck & Peck, and the hem is coming down.

3   Here is what it is: the girl has been on the Eastern Shore, and now she is going back to the city, leaving the man beside her, and all she can see ahead are the viscous summer sidewalks and the 3 A.M. long-distance calls that will make her lie awake and then sleep drugged through all the steaming mornings left in August (1960? 1961?). Because she must go directly from the train to lunch in New York, she wishes that she had a safety pin for the hem of the plaid silk dress, and she also wishes that she could forget about the hem and the lunch and stay in the cool bar that smells of disinfectant and malt and make friends with the woman in the crepe-de-Chine wrapper. She is afflicted by a little self-pity, and she wants to compare Estelles. That is what that was all about.

4   Why did I write it down? In order to remember, of course, but exactly what was it I wanted to remember? How much of it actually happened? Did any of it? Why do I keep a notebook at all? It is easy to deceive oneself on all those scores. The impulse to write things down is a peculiarly compulsive one, inexplicable to those who do not share it, useful only accidentally, only secondarily, in the way that any compulsion tries to justify itself. I suppose that it begins or does not begin in the cradle. Although I have felt compelled to write things down since I was five years old, I doubt that my daughter ever will, for she is a singularly blessed and accepting child, delighted with life exactly as life presents itself to her, unafraid to go to sleep and unafraid to wake up. Keepers of private notebooks are a different breed altogether, lonely and resistant rearrangers of things, anxious malcontents, children afflicted apparently at birth with some presentiment of loss.

5   My first notebook was a Big Five tablet, given to me by my mother with the sensible suggestion that I stop whining and learn to amuse myself by writing down my thoughts. She returned the tablet to me a few years ago; the first entry is an account of a woman who believed herself to be freezing to death in the Arctic night, only to find, when day broke, that she had stumbled onto the Sahara Desert, where she would die of the heat before lunch. I have no idea what turn of a five-year-old's mind could have prompted so insistently "ironic" and exotic a story, but it does reveal a certail predilection for the extreme which

has dogged me into adult life; perhaps if I were analytically inclined I would find it a truer story than any I might have told about Donald Johnson's birthday party or the day my cousin Brenda put Kitty Litter in the aquarium.

So the point of my keeping a notebook has never been, nor is it 6 now, to have an accurate factual record of what I have been doing or thinking. That would be a different impulse entirely, an instinct for reality which I sometimes envy but do not possess. At no point have I ever been able successfully to keep a diary; my approach to daily life ranges from the grossly negligent to the merely absent, and on those few occasions when I have tried dutifully to record a day's events, boredom has so overcome me that the results are mysterious at best. What is this business about "shopping, typing piece, dinner with E, depressed"? Shopping for what? Typing what piece? Who is E? Was this "E" depressed, or was I depressed? Who cares?

In fact I have abandoned altogether that kind of pointless entry; 7 instead I tell what some would call lies. "That's simply not true," the members of my family frequently tell me when they come up against my memory of a shared event. "The party was *not* for you, the spider was *not* a black widow, *it wasn't that way at all.*" Very likely they are right, for not only have I always had trouble distinguishing between what happened and what merely might have happened, but I remain unconvinced that the distinction, for my purposes, matters. The cracked crab that I recall having for lunch the day my father came home from Detroit in 1945 must certainly be embroidery, worked into the day's pattern to lend verisimilitude; I was ten years old and would not now remember the cracked crab. The day's events did not turn on cracked crab. And yet it is precisely that fictitious crab that makes me see the afternoon all over again, a home movie run all too often, the father bearing gifts, the child weeping, an exercise in family love and guilt. Or that is what it was to me. Similarly, perhaps it never did snow that August in Vermont; perhaps there never were fluries in the night wind, and maybe no one else felt the ground hardening and summer already dead even as we pretended to bask in it, but that was how it felt to me, and it might as well have snowed, could have snowed, did snow.

How it felt to me: that is getting closer to the truth about a 8 notebook. I sometimes delude myself about why I keep a notebook, imagine that some thrifty virtue derives from preserving everything observed. See enough and write it down, I tell myself, and then some morning when the world seems drained of wonder, some day when I am only going through the motions of doing what I am supposed to do, which is write—on that bankrupt morning I will simply open my notebook and there it will all be, a forgotten account with accumulated interest, paid passage back to the world out there: dialogue overheard in hotels and elevators and at the hat-check counter in Pavillon (one middle-aged man shows his hat check to another and says, "That's my old football number"); impressions of Bettina Aptheker and Benjamin Sonnenberg and Teddy ("Mr. Acapulco") Stauffer; careful *aperçus* about tennis bums and failed fashion models and Greek shipping heiresses, one of whom taught me a significant lesson (a lesson I could have learned from F. Scott Fitzgerald, but perhaps we must meet the very rich for ourselves) by asking, when I arrived to interview her in her orchid-filled sitting room on the second day of a paralyzing New York blizzard, whether it was snowing outside.

9   I imagine, in other words, that the notebook is about other people. But of course it is not. I have no real business with what one stranger said to another at the hat-check counter in Pavillon; in fact I suspect that the line "That's my old football number" touched not my own imagination at all, but merely some memory of something once read, probably "The Eighty-Yard Run." Nor is my concern with a woman in a dirty crepe-de-Chine wrapper in a Wilmington bar. My stake is always, of course, in the unmentioned girl in the plaid silk dress. *Remember what it was to be me:* that is always the point.

10   It is a difficult point to admit. We are brought up in the ethic that others, any others, all others, are by definition more interesting than ourselves; taught to be diffident, just this side of self-effacing. ("You're the least important person in the room and don't forget it," Jessica Mitford's governess would hiss in her ear on the advent of any social occasion; I copied that into my notebook because it is only recently that I have been able to enter a room without hearing some such phrase in my inner ear.) Only the very young and the very old may recount their dreams at breakfast, dwell upon self, interrupt with memories of beach picnics and favorite Liberty lawn dresses and the rainbow trout in a creek near Colorado Springs. The rest of us are expected, rightly, to affect absorption in other people's favorite dresses, other people's trout.

11   And so we do. But our notebooks give us away, for however dutifully we record what we see around us, the common denominator of all we see is always, transparently, shamelessly, the implacable "I." We are not talking here about the kind of notebook that is patently for public consumption, a structural conceit for binding together a series of graceful *pensées:* we are talking about something private, about bits

of the mind's string too short to use, an indiscriminate and erratic assemblage with meaning only for its maker.

And sometimes even the maker has difficulty with the meaning. 12 There does not seem to be, for example, any point in my knowing for the rest of my life that, during 1964, 720 tons of soot fell on every square mile of New York City, yet there it is in my notebook, labeled "FACT." Nor do I really need to remember that Ambrose Bierce liked to spell Leland Stanford's[1] name "£eland $tanford" or that "smart women almost always wear black in Cuba," a fashion hint without much potential for practical application. And does not the relevance of these notes seem marginal at best?:

> In the basement museum of the Inyo County Courthouse in Independence, California, sign pinned to a mandarin coat: "This MANDARIN COAT was often worn by Mrs. Minnie S. Brooks when giving lectures on her TEAPOT COLLECTION."

> Redhead getting out of car in front of Beverly Wilshire Hotel, chinchilla stole, Vuitton bags with tags reading:
> MRS LOU FOX
> HOTEL SAHARA
> VEGAS

Well perhaps not entirely marginal. As a matter of fact, Mrs. 13 Minnie S. Brooks and her MANDARIN COAT pull me back into my own childhood, for although I never knew Mrs. Brooks and did not visit Inyo County until I was thirty, I grew up in just such a world, in houses cluttered with Indian relics and bits of gold ore and ambergris and the souvenirs my Aunt Mercy Farnsworth brought back from the Orient. It is a long way from that world to Mrs. Lou Fox's world, where we all live now, and it is not just as well to remember that? Might not Mrs. Minnie S. Brooks help me to remember what I am? Might not Mrs. Lou Fox help me to remember what I am not?

But sometimes the point is harder to discern. What exactly did I 14 have in mind when I noted down that it cost the father of someone I know $650 a month to light the place on the Hudson in which he lived before the Crash? What use was I planning to make of this line by Jimmy Hoffa: "I may have my faults, but being wrong ain't one of them"? And although I think it interesting to know where the girls who travel with the Syndicate have their hair done when they find themselves on the West Coast, will I ever make suitable use of it? Might I not be better

---

[1]Railroad magnate (1834–1893) who founded the university. —ED.

off just passing it on to John O'Hara? What is a recipe for sauerkraut doing in my notebook? What kind of magpie keeps this notebook? *"He was born the night the Titanic went down."* That seems a nice enough line, and I even recall who said it, but is it not really a better line in life than it could ever be in fiction?

15   But of course that is exactly it: not that I should ever use the line, but that I should remember the woman who said it and the afternoon I heard it. We were on her terrace by the sea, and we were finishing the wine left from lunch, trying to get what sun there was, a California winter sun. The woman whose husband was born the night the *Titanic* went down wanted to rent her house, wanted to go back to her children in Paris. I remember wishing that I could afford the house, which cost $1,000 a month. "Someday you will," she said lazily. "Someday it all comes." There in the sun on her terrace it seemed easy to believe in someday, but later I had a low-grade afternoon hangover and ran over a black snake on the way to the supermarket and was flooded with inexplicable fear when I heard the checkout clerk explaining to the man ahead of me why she was finally divorcing her husband. "He left me no choice," she said over and over as she punched the register. "He has a little seven-month-old baby by her, he left me no choice." I would like to believe that my dread then was for the human condition, but of course it was for me, because I wanted a baby and did not then have one and because I wanted to own the house that cost $1,000 a month to rent and because I had a hangover.

16   It all comes back. Perhaps it is difficult to see the value in having one's self back in that kind of mood, but I do see it; I think we are well advised to keep on nodding terms with the people we used to be, whether we find them attractive company or not. Otherwise they turn up unannounced and surprise us, come hammering on the mind's door at 4 A.M. of a bad night and demand to know who deserted them, who betrayed them, who is going to make amends. We forget all too soon the things we thought we could never forget. We forget the loves and the betrayals alike, forget what we whispered and what we screamed, forget who we were. I have already lost touch with a couple of people I used to be; one of them, a seventeen-year-old, presents little threat, although it would be of some interest to me to know again what it feels like to sit on a river levee drinking vodka-and-orange-juice and listening to Les Paul and Mary Ford and their echoes sing "How High the Moon" on the car radio. (You see I still have the scenes, but I no longer perceive myself among those present, no longer could even improvise the dialogue.) The other one, a twenty-three-year-old, bothers me more. She was always a good deal of trouble, and I suspect she will reappear when I least want to see

her, skirts too long, shy to the point of aggravation, always the injured party, full of recriminations and little hurts and stories I do not want to hear again, at once saddening me and angering me with her vulnerability and ignorance, an apparition all the more insistent for being so long banished.

It is a good idea, then, to keep in touch, and I suppose that keeping in touch is what notebooks are all about. And we are all on our own when it comes to keeping those lines open to ourselves: your notebook will never help me, nor mine you. *"So what's new in the whiskey business?"* What could that possibly mean to you? To me it means a blonde in a Pucci bathing suit sitting with a couple of fat men by the pool at the Beverly Hills Hotel. Another man approaches, and they all regard one another in silence for a while. "So what's new in the whiskey business?" one of the fat men finally says by way of welcome, and the blonde stands up, arches one foot and dips it in the pool, looking all the while at the cabaña where Baby Pignatari is talking on the telephone. That is all there is to that, except that several years later I saw the blonde coming out of Saks Fifth Avenue in New York with her California complexion and a voluminous mink coat. In the harsh wind that day she looked old and irrevocably tired to me, and even the skins in the mink coat were not worked the way they were doing them that year, not the way she would have wanted them done, and there is the point of the story. For a while after that I did not like to look in the mirror, and my eyes would skim the newspapers and pick out only the deaths, the cancer victims, the premature coronaries, the suicides, and I stopped riding the Lexington Avenue IRT because I noticed for the first time that all the strangers I had seen for years—the man with the seeing-eye dog, the spinster who read the classified pages every day, the fat girl who always got off with me at Grand Central—looked older than they once had. 17

It all comes back. Even that recipe for sauerkraut: even that brings it back. I was on Fire Island when I first made that sauerkraut, and it was raining, and we drank a lot of bourbon and ate the sauerkraut and went to bed at ten, and I listened to the rain and the Atlantic and felt safe. I made the sauerkraut again last night and it did not make me feel any safer, but that is, as they say, another story. 18

CONSIDERATIONS

1. What is the difference between the selection by Didion and those by Henry David Thoreau (pages 413–423) and Sylvia Plath (pages 326–333)?

2. How far must you read in Didion's piece before you know her real reason for keeping a journal? Why does she delay that announcement so long? Might such a delay work well in one of your essays?

3. "You're the least important person in the room and don't forget it" is a line from Didion's journal. Does she believe that statement? If not, why does she include it in her essay?

4. Didion discusses the randomness of a notebook. How does she use this randomness, or lack of order or purpose, to bring order and purpose to her essay? Take Paragraphs 14 and 15 and study the method she derives from her seeming madness.

5. In Paragraph 16, Didion says she has already "lost touch with a couple of people I used to be." How does this awareness relate to the last line of James Agee's "Knoxville: Summer 1915" (pages 15–19)? Have you ever had similar feelings about some of the people you used to be? What significant details in your memory come to mind?

6. Using a periodical index in your college library, see how quickly you can locate one of Didion's many journalistic essays.

Annie Dillard (b. 1945) was born in Pittsburgh, went to Hollins College, and lived for a while in Virginia in the Roanoke Valley—the area she describes so beautifully in her writing. She currently lives in Connecticut. In 1974, she published her first book of poems. Tickets for a Prayer Wheel, *and her first book of prose,* Pilgrim at Tinker Creek, *which won a Pulitzer Prize. In 1977 she published* Holy the Firm, *and in 1982* Living by Fiction.

This passage of description comes from Pilgrim at Tinker Creek. *A walk in failing light, with the eyes of the body wide open, takes on the fears of nightmare.*

22

ANNIE DILLARD

Strangers to Darkness

Where Tinker Creek flows under the sycamore log bridge to the tear-shaped island, it is slow and shallow, fringed thinly in cattail marsh. At this spot an astonishing bloom of life supports vast breeding populations of insects, fish, reptiles, birds, and mammals. On windless summer evenings I stalk along the creek bank or straddle the sycamore log in absolute stillness, watching for muskrats. The night I stayed too late I was hunched on the log staring spellbound at spreading, reflected stains of lilac on the water. A cloud in the sky suddenly lighted as if turned on by a switch; its reflection just as suddenly materialized on the water upstream, flat and floating, so that I couldn't see the creek bottom, or life in the water under the cloud. Downstream, away from the cloud on the water, water turtles smooth as beans were gliding down with the current in a series of easy, weightless push-offs, as men bound on the moon. I didn't know whether to trace the progress of one turtle I was sure of, risking sticking my face in one of the bridge's spider webs made invisible by the gathering dark, or take a chance on seeing the carp, or scan the mudbank in hope of seeing a muskrat, or follow the last of the swallows who caught at my heart and trailed it after them like streamers as they appeared from directly below, under the log, flying upstream with their tails forked, so fast.

2   But shadows spread and deepened and stayed. After thousands of years we're still strangers to darkness, fearful aliens in an enemy camp with our arms crossed over our chests. I stirred. A land turtle on the bank, startled, hissed the air from its lungs and withdrew to its shell. An uneasy pink here, an unfathomable blue there, gave great suggestion of lurking beings. Things were going on. I couldn't see whether that rustle I heard was a distant rattlesnake, slit-eyed, or a nearby sparrow kicking in the dry flood debris slung at the foot of a willow. Tremendous action roiled the water everywhere I looked, big action, inexplicable. A tremor welled up beside a gaping muskrat burrow in the bank and I caught my breath, but no muskrat appeared. The ripples continued to fan upstream with a steady, powerful thrust. Night was knitting an eyeless mask over my face, and I still sat transfixed. A distant airplane, a delta wing out of nightmare, made a gliding shadow on the creek's bottom that looked like a stingray cruising upstream. At once a black fin slit the pink cloud on the water, shearing it in two. The two halves merged together and seemed to dissolve before my eyes. Darkness pooled in the cleft of the creek and rose, as water collects in a well. Untamed, dreaming lights flickered over the sky. I saw hints of hulking underwater shadows, two pale splashes out of the water, and round ripples rolling close together from a blackened center.

3   At last I stared upstream where only the deepest violet remained of the cloud, a cloud so high its underbelly still glowed, its feeble color reflected from a hidden sky lighted in turn by a sun halfway to China. And out of that violet, a sudden enormous black body arced over the water. Head and tail, if there was a head and tail, were both submerged in cloud. I saw only one ebony fling, a headlong dive to darkness; then the water closed, and the lights went out.

4   I walked home in a shivering daze, up hill and down. Later I lay openmouthed in bed, my arms flung wide at my sides so steady the whirling darkness. At this latitude I'm spinning 836 miles an hour round the earth's axis; I feel my sweeping fall as a breakneck arc like the dive

of dolphins, and the hollow rushing of wind raises the hairs on my neck and the side of my face. In orbit around the sun I'm moving 64,800 miles an hour. The solar system as a whole, like a merry-go-round unhinged, spins, bobs, and blinks at the speed of 43,200 miles an hour along a course set east of Hercules. Someone has piped, and we are dancing a tarantella until the sweat pours. I open my eyes and I see dark, muscled forms curl out of water, with flapping gills and flattened eyes. I close my eyes and I see stars, deep stars giving way to deeper stars, deeper stars bowing to deepest stars at the crown of an infinite cone.

_____ CONSIDERATIONS _____

1. Like exposition and argument, description and narration are encountered together more often than they are encountered separately. Still, there are real differences between describing something and following a sequence of actions. To see this difference, compare and contrast Dillard's descriptive writing with a clearly narrative selection in this book: Jimmy Breslin, Martin Gansberg, Lillian Hellman, Langston Hughes ("Salvation"), Beryl Markham, George Orwell ("Shooting an Elephant"), James C. Rettie, or Eudora Welty ("A Worn Path").

2. Telling what she saw that night along Tinker Creek, Dillard uses many literal and figurative images; list them and discuss their differences. In your own essays, do you use phrases that appeal to the senses?

3. Toward the end of this short selection, Dillard suddenly injects facts—the speed of the earth's rotation, for instance. How does this information contribute to her attempt to evoke wonder in us?

4. "Night was knitting an eyeless mask over my face. . . ." Many might describe such language as fancy, flowery, or indirect, and protest that the writer should "just come out and say what she means." Discuss these complaints, in light of what Dillard intends to accomplish.

5. Dillard describes the effects of one evening on one small creek in one rural neighborhood. Why, then, does she refer to China and the solar system?

Teaching a Stone to Talk (1982) gathers Annie Dillard's miscellaneous essays from periodicals. Book reviewers often condescend to such collections; in her introduction to the work Annie Dillard wants to be certain that readers understand and tells us ". . . this is my real work." Indeed, the brief essay is her literary form, and she masters it as Chekhov mastered the short story.

23

ANNIE DILLARD
Sojourner

1   If survival is an art, then mangroves are artists of the beautiful: not only that they exist at all — smooth-barked, glossy-leaved, thickets of lapped mystery — but that they can and do exist as floating islands, as trees upright and loose, alive and homeless on the water.

2   I have seen mangroves, always on tropical ocean shores, in Florida and in the Galápagos. There is the red mangrove, the yellow, the button, and the black. They are all short, messy trees, waxy-leaved, laced all over with aerial roots, woody arching buttresses, and weird leathery berry pods. All this tangles from a black muck soil, a black muck matted like a mud-sopped rag, a muck without any other plants, shaded, cold to the touch, tracked at the water's edge by herons and nosed by sharks.

3   It is these shoreline trees which, by a fairly common accident, can become floating islands. A hurricane flood or a riptide can wrest a tree from the shore, or from the mouth of a tidal river, and hurl it into the ocean. It floats. It is a mangrove island, blown.

There are floating islands on the planet; it amazes me. Credulous   4
Pliny described some islands thought to be mangrove islands floating
on a river. The people called these river islands *the dancers*, "because
in any consort of musicians singing, they stir and move at the stroke
of the feet, keeping time and measure."

Trees floating on rivers are less amazing than trees floating on   5
the poisonous sea. A tree cannot live in salt. Mangrove trees exude salt
from their leaves; you can see it, even on shoreline black mangroves,
as a thin white crust. Lick a leaf and your tongue curls and coils; your
mouth's a heap of salt.

Nor can a tree live without soil. A hurricane-born mangrove   6
island may bring its own soil to the sea. But other mangrove trees make
their own soil—and their own islands—from scratch. These are the ones
which interest me. The seeds germinate in the fruit on the tree. The
germinated embryo can drop anywhere—say, onto a dab of floating
muck. The heavy root end sinks; a leafy plumule unfurls. The tiny seed-
ling, afloat, is on its way. Soon aerial roots shooting out in all directions trap debris. The sapling's networks twine, the interstices narrow,
and water calms in the lee. Bacteria thrive on organic broth; amphipods
swarm. These creatures grow and die at the trees' wet feet. The soil
thickens, accumulating rainwater, leaf rot, seashells, and guano; the
island spreads.

More seeds and more muck yield more trees on the new island.   7
A society grows, interlocked in a tangle of dependencies. The island
rocks less in the swells. Fish throng to the backwaters stilled in snarled
roots. Soon, Asian mudskippers—little four-inch fish—clamber up the
mangrove roots into the air and peer about from periscope eyes on stalks,
like snails. Oysters clamp to submersed roots, as do starfish, dog whelk,
and the creatures that live among tangled kelp. Shrimp seek shelter
there, limpets a holdfast, pelagic birds a rest.

And the mangrove island wanders on, afloat and adrift. It walks   8
teetering and wanton before the wind. Its fate and direction are random.
It may bob across an ocean and catch on another mainland's shores. It
may starve or dry while it is still a sapling. It may topple in a storm,
or pitchpole. By the rarest of chances, it may stave into another
mangrove island in a crash of clacking roots, and mesh. What it is most
likely to do is drift anywhere in the alien ocean, feeding on death and
growing, netting a makeshift soil as it goes, shrimp in its toes and terns
in its hair.

We could do worse.   9

10   I alternate between thinking of the planet as home — dear and familiar stone hearth and garden — and as a hard land of exiled in which we are all sojourners. Today I favor the latter view. The word "sojourner" occurs often in the English Old Testament. It invokes a nomadic people's sense of vagrancy, a praying people's knowledge of estrangement, a thinking people's intuition of sharp loss: "For we are strangers before thee, and sojourners, as were all our fathers: our days on the earth are as a shadow, and there is none abiding."

11   We don't know where we belong, but in times of sorrow it doesn't seem to be here, here with these silly pansies and witless mountains, here with sponges and hard-eyed birds. In times of sorrow the innocence of the other creatures — from whom and with whom we evolved — seems a mockery. Their ways are not our ways. We seem set among them as among lifelike props for a tragedy — or a broad lampoon — on a thrust rock stage.

12   It doesn't seem to be here that we belong, here where space is curved, the earth is round, we're all going to die, and it seems as wise to stay in bed as budge. It is strange here, not quite warm enough, or too warm, too leafy, or inedible, or windy, or dead. It is not, frankly, the sort of home for people one would have thought of — although I lack the fancy to imagine another.

13   The planet itself is a sojourner in airless space, a wet ball flung across nowhere. The few objects in the universe scatter. The coherence of matter dwindles and crumbles toward stillness. I have read, and repeated, that our solar system as a whole is careering through space toward a point east of Hercules. Now I wonder: what could that possibly mean, east of Hercules? Isn't space curved? When we get "there," how will our course change, and why? Will we slide down the universe's inside arc like mud slung at a wall? Or what sort of welcoming shore is this east of Hercules? Surely we don't anchor there, and disembark, and sweep into dinner with our host. Does someone cry, "Last stop, last stop"? At any rate, east of Hercules, like east of Eden, isn't a place to call home. It is a course without direction; it is "out." And we are cast.

14   These are enervating thoughts, the thoughts of despair. They crowd back, unbidden, when human life as it unrolls goes ill, when we lose control of our lives or the illusion of control, and it seems that we are not moving toward any end but merely blown. Our life seems cursed to be a wiggle merely, and a wandering without end. Even nature is hostile and poisonous, as though it were impossible for our vulnerability to survive on these acrid stones.

Whether these thoughts are true or not I find less interesting than 15
the possibilities for beauty they may hold. We are down here in time,
where beauty grows. Even if things are as bad as they could possibly
be, and as meaningless, then matters of truth are themselves indifferent;
we may as well please our sensibilities and, with as much spirit as we
can muster, go out with a buck and wing.

The planet is less like an enclosed spaceship—spaceship earth 16
—than it is like an exposed mangrove island beautiful and loose. We
the people started small and have since accumulated a great and solac-
ing muck of soil, of human culture. We are rooted in it; we are bearing
it with us across nowhere. The word "nowhere" is our cue: the consort
of musicians strikes up, and we in the chorus stir and move and start
twirling our hats. A mangrove island turns drift to dance. It creates its
own soil as it goes, rocking over the salt sea at random, rocking day
and night and round the sun, rocking round the sun and out toward east
of Hercules.

____ CONSIDERATIONS _____

1. In many passages, Annie Dillard's prose verges on poetry, particularly
in her high degree of compression in alluding to persons ("Pliny," Paragraph 4),
places ("Galápagos," Paragraph 2; "east of Hercules," Paragraph 13), and sources
(see Psalms 39 for the quotation in Paragraph 10) that may not be immediately
recognizable to the hurried reader. You will enjoy her essay more and appreciate
her skill if you take the time to determine the significance of these allusions.

2. One of the hallmarks of an accomplished writer like Dillard is the
ability to integrate the various materials of an essay. As one example, study
her closing paragraph to see how tightly she brings together elements she has
introduced earlier.

3. Explain why a reader would be foolish to conclude that Dillard's essay
is simply a study of the mangrove islands, of interest only to students of natural history. What elements of the essay might account for such a conclusion?

4. Dillard's diction (choice of words) mixes vocabularies. Find a few other
contrasts, such as the scientific ("plumule," "amphipods," "pelagic") vs. the imaginative ("matted like a mud-sopped rag," or "shrimp in its toes and terns in
its hair") vs. the nautical ("pitchpole," "stave," "lee") and discuss the delights and
difficulties for a reader encountering such diversity.

5. Does Dillard offer any consolation for the sense of despairing
rootlessness she expresses in Paragraph 13? Explain in a short essay based on
your own ideas about the destiny or purpose of humankind's presence on the
planet.

Frederick Douglass (1817–1895) was born a slave in Maryland, and escaped to Massachusetts in 1838, and lectured against slavery and wrote of his experience. "Plantation Life" comes from A Narrative of the Life of Frederick Douglass, an American Slave, Written by Himself *(1845). During the Civil War he organized two regiments of black troops in Massachusetts; in the Reconstruction period he worked for the government.*

24

FREDERICK DOUGLASS
Plantation Life

1   My master's family consisted of two sons, Andrew and Richard; one daughter, Lucretia, and her husband, Captain Thomas Auld. They lived in one house, upon the home plantation of Colonel Edward Lloyd. My master was Colonel Lloyd's clerk and superintendent. He was what might be called the overseer of the overseers. I spent two years of childhood on this plantation in my old master's family. . . . As I received my first impressions of slavery on this plantation, I will give some description of it, and of slavery as it there existed. The plantation is about twelve miles north of Easton, in Talbot county, and is situated on the border of Miles River. The principal products raised upon it were tobacco, corn, and wheat. These were raised in great abundance; so that, with the products of this and the other farms belonging to him, he was able to keep in almost constant employment a large sloop, in carrying them to market at Baltimore. This sloop was named Sally Lloyd, in honor of one of the colonel's daughters. My master's son-in-law, Captain Auld, was master of the vessel; she was otherwise manned by the colonel's own slaves. Their names were Peter, Isaac, Rich, and Jake. These were esteemed very highly by the other slaves, and looked upon

as the privileged ones of the plantation; for it was no small affair, in the eyes of the slaves, to be allowed to see Baltimore.

Colonel Lloyd kept from three to four hundred slaves on his home plantation, and owned a large number more on the neighboring farms belonging to him. The names of the farms nearest to the home plantation were Wye Town and New Design. "Wye Town" was under the overseership of a man named Noah Willis. New Design was under the overseership of a Mr. Townsend. The overseers of these, and all the rest of the farms, numbering over twenty, received advice and direction from the managers of the home plantation. This was the great business place. It was the seat of government for the whole twenty farms. All disputes among the overseers were settled here. If a slave was convicted of any high misdemeanor, became unmanageable, or evinced a determination to run away, he was brought immediately here, severely whipped, put on board the sloop, carried to Baltimore, and sold to Austin Woolfolk, or some other slave-trader, as a warning to the slaves remaining.

Here, too, the slaves of all the other farms received their monthly allowance of food, and their yearly clothing. The men and women slaves received, as their monthly allowance of food, eight pounds of pork, or its equivalent in fish, and one bushel of corn meal. Their yearly clothing consisted of two coarse linen shirts, one pair of linen trousers, like the shirts, one jacket, one pair of trousers for winter, made of coarse negro cloth, one pair of stockings, and one pair of shoes; the whole of which could not have cost more than seven dollars. The allowance of the slave children was given to their mothers, or the old women having the care of them. The children unable to work in the field had neither shoes, stockings, jackets, nor trousers, given to them; their clothing consisted of two coarse linen shirts per year. When these failed them, they went naked until the next allowance-day. Children from seven to ten years old, of both sexes, almost naked, might be seen at all seasons of the year.

There were no beds given the slaves, unless one coarse blanket be considered such, and none but the men and women had these. This, however, is not considered a very great privation. They find less difficulty from the want of beds, than from the want of time to sleep; for when their day's work in the field is done, the most of them having their washing, mending, and cooking to do, and having few or none of the ordinary facilities for doing either of these, very many of their sleeping hours are consumed in preparing for the field the coming day; and when this is done, old and young, male and female, married and single, drop down side by side, on one common bed,—the cold, damp floor,—

2

3

4

each covering himself or herself with their miserable blankets; and here they sleep till they are summoned to the field by the driver's horn. At the sound of this, all must rise, and be off to the field. There must be no halting; every one must be at his or her post; and woe betides them who hear not this morning summons to the field; for if they are not awakened by the sense of hearing, they are by the sense of feeling: no age nor sex finds any favor. Mr. Severe, the overseer, used to stand by the door of the quarter, armed with a large hickory stick and heavy cowskin, ready to whip any one who was so unfortunate as not to hear, or, from any other cause, was prevented from being ready to start for the field at the sound of the horn.

5   Mr. Severe was rightly named: he was a cruel man. I have seen him whip a woman, causing the blood to run half an hour at the time; and this, too, in the midst of her crying children, pleading for their mother's release. He seemed to take pleasure in manifesting his fiend-ish barbarity. Added to his cruelty, he was a profane swearer. It was enough to chill the blood and stiffen the hair of an ordinary man to hear him talk. Scarce a sentence escaped him but that was commenced or concluded by some horrid oath. The field was the place to witness his cruelty and profanity. His presence made it both the field of blood and of blasphemy. From the rising till the going down of the sun, he was cursing, raving, cutting, and slashing among the slaves of the field, in the most frightful manner. His career was short. He died very soon after I went to Colonel Lloyd's; and he died as he lived, uttering, with his dying groans, bitter curses and horrid oaths. His death was regarded by the slaves as the result of a merciful providence.

6   Mr. Severe's place was filled by a Mr. Hopkins. He was a very different man. He was less cruel, less profane, and made less noise, than Mr. Severe. His course was characterized by no extraordinary demonstra-tions of cruelty. He whipped, but seemed to take no pleasure in it. He was called by the slaves a good overseer.

7   The home plantation of Colonel Lloyd wore the appearance of a country village. All the mechanical operations for all the farms were performed here. The shoemaking and mending, the blacksmithing, cart-wrighting, coopering, weaving, and grain-grinding, were all performed by the slaves on the home plantation. The whole place wore a business-like aspect very unlike the neighboring farms. The number of houses, too, conspired to give it advantage over the neighboring farms. It was called by the slaves the *Great House Farm.* Few privileges were esteemed higher, by the slaves of the out-farms, than that of being selected to do errands at the Great House Farm. It was associated in their minds with

greatness. A representative could not be prouder of his election to a seat in the American Congress, than a slave on one of the out-farms would be of his election to do errands at the Great House Farm. They regarded it as evidence of great confidence reposed in them by their overseers; and it was on this account, as well as a constant desire to be out of the field from under the driver's lash, that they esteemed it a high privilege, one worth careful living for. He was called the smartest and most trusty fellow, who had this honor conferred upon him the most frequently. The competitors for this office sought as diligently to please their overseers, as the office-seekers in the political parties seek to please and deceive the people. The same traits of character might be seen in Colonel Lloyd's slaves, as are seen in the slaves of the political parties.

The slaves selected to go to the Great House Farm, for the monthly   8 allowance for themselves and their fellow-slaves, were peculiarly enthusiastic. While on their way, they would make the dense old woods, for miles around, reverberate with their wild songs, revealing at once the highest joy and the deepest sadness. They would compose and sing as they went along, consulting neither time nor tune. The thought that came up, came out — if not in the word, in the sound; — and as frequently in the one as in the other. They would sometimes sing the most pathetic sentiment in the most rapturous tone, and the most rapturous sentiment in the most pathetic tone. Into all of their songs they would manage to weave something of the Great House Farm. Especially would they do this, when leaving home. They would then sing most exultingly the following words: —

> I am going away to the Great House Farm!
> A, yea! O, yea! O!

This they would sing, as a chorus, to words which to many would seem unmeaning jargon, but which, nevertheless, were full of meaning to themselves. I have sometimes thought that the mere hearing of those songs would do more to impress some minds with the horrible character of slavery, than the reading of whole volumes of philosophy on the subject could do.

I did not, when a slave, understand the deep meaning of those   9 rude and apparently incoherent songs. I was myself within the circle; so that I neither saw nor heard as those without might see and hear. They told a tale of woe which was then altogether beyond my feeble comprehension; they were tones loud, long, and deep; they breathed the prayer and complaint of souls boiling over with the bitterest anguish. Every tone was a testimony against slavery, and a prayer to God for deliverance from chains. The hearing of those wild notes always depressed my spirit, and filled me with ineffable sadness. I have frequently found myself in tears while hearing them. The mere recurrence of those songs, even now, afflicts me; and while I am writing these lines, an expression of feeling has already found its way down my cheek. To those songs I trace my first glimmering conception of the dehumanizing character of slavery. I can never get rid of that conception. Those songs still follow me, to deepen my hatred of slavery, and quicken my sympathies for my brethren in bonds. If any one wishes to be impressed with the soul-killing effects of slavery, let him go to Colonel Lloyd's plantation, and, on allowance-day, place himself in the deep pine woods, and there let him, in silence, analyze the sounds that shall pass through the chambers of his soul, — and if he is not thus impressed, it will only be because "there is no flesh in his obdurate heart."

10   I have often been utterly astonished, since I came to the north, to find persons who could speak of the singing, among slaves, as evidence of their contentment and happiness. It is impossible to conceive of a greater mistake. Slaves sing most when they are most unhappy. The songs of the slave represent the sorrows of his heart; and he is relieved by them, only as an aching heart is relieved by its tears. At least, such is my experience. I have often sung to drown my sorrow, but seldom to express my happiness. Crying for joy, and singing for joy, were alike uncommon to me while in the jaws of slavery. The singing of a man cast away upon a desolate island might be as appropriately considered as evidence of contentment and happiness, as the singing of a slave; the songs of the one and of the other are prompted by the same emotion.

_____ CONSIDERATIONS _____

1. Is there anything to suggest, at the end of Paragraph 7, that Douglass had a talent for satire?

2. In Paragraphs 2 and 7, Douglass sketches the operations of the home plantation and its relationship to the outlying farms owned by the same man. Does the arrangement sound feudal? How did the plantation system differ from feudalism?

3. "I was myself within the circle; so that I neither saw nor heard as those without might see and hear," writes Douglass in Paragraph 9. Is a fish aware that its medium is water? Are you, as a student, always conscious of the knowledge you acquire?

4. What single phenomenon, according to Douglass, taught him the most moving and enduring lesson about the dehumanizing character of slavery? In what way did that lesson surprise those who had not had Douglass's experience?

5. Paragraph 5 offers a good example of Douglass's typical sentence structure: a linear series of independent clauses, with little or no subordination, all of which produces a blunt, stop-and-go effect. Without losing any of the information provided, rewrite the paragraph, reducing the number of sentences from twelve to six. Do this by converting some of the sentences to phrases, modifying clauses, or, in some cases, single-word modifiers.

Loren Eiseley (1907–1977) was an anthropologist who taught at the University of Pennsylvania, and a writer of unusual ability. He wrote two books of poems and numerous collections of prose, including The Night Country *(1971) and* All the Strange Hours *(1975). Eiseley was a scientist-poet, a human brooder over the natural world, determined never to distort the real world by his brooding dream, an objective anthropologist with a talent for subjective response.*

Imagination and chemistry equally inform "More Thoughts on Wilderness." When Eiseley writes about an experience in the badlands of Nebraska and South Dakota, he combines not only imagination and chemistry, not only archaeology and imagery, but religious feeling and scientific thought.

25

LOREN EISELEY
More Thoughts on Wilderness

1   On the maps of the old voyageurs it is called *Mauvaises Terres,* the evil lands, and, slurred a little with the passage through many minds, it has come down to us anglicized as the badlands. The soft shuffle of moccasins has passed through its canyons on the grim business of war and flight, but the last of those slight disturbances of immemorial silences died out almost a century ago. The land, if one can call it a land, is a waste as lifeless as that valley in which lie the kings of Egypt. Like the Valley of the Kings, it is a mausoleum, a place of dry bones in what once was a place of life. Now it has silences as deep as those in the moon's airless chasms.

Nothing grows among its pinnacles; there is no shade except   2
under great toadstools of sandstone whose bases have been eaten to the
shape of wine glasses by the wind. Everything is flaking, cracking,
disintegrating, wearing away in the long, imperceptible weather of time.
The ash of ancient volcanic outbursts still sterilizes its soil, and its colors
in that waste are the colors that flame in the lonely sunsets on dead
planets. Men come there but rarely, and for one purpose only, the collection of bones.

It was a late hour on a cold, wind-bitten autumn day when I   3
climbed a great hill spined like a dinosaur's back and tried to take my
bearings. The tumbled waste fell away in waves in all directions. Blue
air was darkening into purple along the bases of the hills. I shifted my
knapsack, heavy with the petrified bones of long-vanished creatures, and
studied my compass. I wanted to be out of there by nightfall, and already
the sun was going sullenly down in the west.

It was then that I saw the flight coming on. It was moving like a   4
little close-knit body of black specks that danced and darted and closed
again. It was pouring from the north and heading toward me with the
undeviating relentlessness of a compass needle. It streamed through the
shadows rising out of monstrous gorges. It rushed over towering pinnacles in the red light of the sun or momentarily sank from sight within
their shade. Across that desert of eroding clay and windworn stone they
came with a faint wild twittering that filled all the air about me as those
tiny living bullets hurtled past into the night.

It may not strike you as a marvel. It would not, perhaps, unless   5
you stood in the middle of a dead world at sunset, but that was where
I stood. Fifty million years lay under my feet, fifty million years of
bellowing monsters moving in a green world now gone so utterly that
its very light was traveling on the farther edge of space. The chemicals
of all that vanished age lay about me in the ground. Around me still
lay the shearing molars of dead titanotheres, the delicate sabers of soft-
stepping cats, the hollow sockets that had held the eyes of many a
strange, outmoded beast. Those eyes had looked out upon a world as
real as ours: dark, savage brains had roamed and roared their challenges
into the steaming night.

Now they were still here, or, put it as you will, the chemicals   6
that made them were here about me in the ground. The carbon that
had driven them ran blackly in the eroding stone. The stain of iron was
in the clays. The iron did not remember the blood it had once moved
within, the phosphorus had forgot the savage brain. The little individual
moment had ebbed from all those strange combinations of chemicals

as it would ebb from our living bodies into the sinks and runnels of on-coming time.

7   I had lifted up a fistful of that ground. I held it while that wild flight of south-bound warblers hurtled over me into the oncoming dark. There went phosphorus, there went iron, there went carbon, there beat the calcium in those hurrying wings. Alone on a dead planet I watched that incredible miracle speeding past. It ran by some true compass over field and waste land. It cried its individual ecstasies into the air until the gullies rang. It swerved like a single body, it knew itself, and, lonely, it bunched close in the racing darkness, its individual entities feeling about them the rising night. And so, crying to each other their identity, they passed away out of my view.

8   I dropped my fistful of earth. I heard it roll inanimate back into the gully at the base of the hill: iron, carbon, the chemicals of life. Like men from those wild tribes who had haunted these hills before me seek-ing visions. I made my sign to the great darkness. It was not a mocking sign, and I was not mocked. As I walked into my camp late that night, one man, rousing from his blankets beside the fire, asked sleepily, "What did you see?"

9   "I think, a miracle," I said softly, but I said it to myself. Behind me that vast waste began to glow under the rising moon.

_____ **CONSIDERATIONS** _____

1. Eiseley draws the reader by enlivening his expository prose with figures of speech. Write a brief study of his figurative writing, beginning with the half-dozen examples presented in Paragraphs 2 and 3.

2. As a professional anthropologist and archaeologist, Eiseley had many occasions to write the "process essay," a step-by-step explanation of a particular process. To what extent could "More Thoughts on Wilderness' be called a pro-cess essay? Why would that term be unsatisfactory as a complete description of the piece?

3. Eiseley's reflections take him to the chemical elements of life — carbon, iron, phosphorus. How does he escape the sterile kind of analysis and categoriza-tion that Henry David Thoreau criticizes in his "Journal entry for October 12, 1857" (pages 419–420)?

4. What prompts Eiseley to conclude that he has seen a miracle? Explain.

5. Using the passage of long periods of time, as Eiseley does, write a short, descriptive essay reflecting on a landscape you know well.

Ralph Ellison (b. 1914) born in Oklahoma, won the National Book Award in 1953 for his novel The Invisible Man. *His essays are collected in* Shadow and Act *(1964). For thirty years, Ellison has lectured and written on literature and race.*

26

RALPH ELLISON
On Becoming a Writer

In the beginning writing was far from a serious matter; it was a reflex of reading, an extension of a source of pleasure, escape, and instruction. In fact, I had become curious about writing by way of seeking to understand the aesthetic nature of literary power, the devices through which literature could command my mind and emotions. It was not, then, the *process* of writing which initially claimed my attention, but the finished creations, the artifacts, poems, plays, novels. The act of learning writing technique was, therefore, an amusing investigation of what seemed at best a secondary talent, an exploration, like dabbling in sculpture, of one's potentialities as a "Renaissance Man." This, surely, would seem a most unlikely and even comic concept to introduce here; and yet, it is precisely because I come from where I do (the Oklahoma of the years between World War I and the Great Depression) that I must introduce it, and with a straight face.

Anything and everything was to be found in the chaos of Oklahoma; thus the concept of the Renaissance Man has lurked long within the shadow of my past, and I shared it with at least a half dozen of my Negro friends. How we actually acquired it I have never learned, and since there is no true sociology of the dispersion of ideas within the

1

2

153

American democracy, I doubt if I ever shall. Perhaps we breathed it in with the air of the Negro community of Oklahoma City, the capital of that state whose Negroes were often charged by exasperated white Texans with not knowing their "place." Perhaps we took it defiantly from one of them. Or perhaps I myself picked it up from some transplanted New Englander whose shoes I had shined of a Saturday afternoon. After all, the most meaningful tips do not always come in the form of money, nor are they intentionally extended. Most likely, however, my friends and I acquired the idea from some book or some idealistic Negro teacher, some dreamer seeking to function responsibly in an environment which at its most normal took on some of the mixed character of nightmare and of dream.

3   One thing is certain, ours was a chaotic community, still characterized by frontier attitudes and by that strange mixture of the naive and sophisticated, the benign and malignant, which makes the American past so puzzling and its present so confusing; that mixture which often affords the minds of the young who grow up in the far provinces such wide and unstructured latitude, and which encourages the individual's imagination—up to the moment "reality" closes in upon him—to range widely and, sometimes, even to soar.

4   We hear the effects of this in the Southwestern jazz of the 30's, that joint creation of artistically free and exuberantly creative adventurers, of artists who had stumbled upon the freedom lying within the restrictions of their musical tradition as within the limitations of their social background, and who in their own unconscious way have set an example for any Americans, Negro or white, who would find themselves in the arts. They accepted themselves and the complexity of life as they knew it, they loved their art and through it they celebrated American experience definitively in sound. Whatever others thought or felt, this was their own powerful statement, and only non-musical assaults upon their artistic integrity—mainly economically inspired changes of fashion—were able to compromise their vision.

5   Much of so-called Kansas City jazz was actually brought to perfection in Oklahoma by Oklahomans. It is an important circumstance for me as a writer to remember, because while these musicians and their fellows were busy creating out of tradition, imagination, and the sounds and emotions around them, a freer, more complex, and driving form of jazz, my friends and I were exploring an idea of human versatility and possibility which went against the barbs or over the palings of almost every fence which those who controlled social and political power had erected to restrict our roles in the life of the country. Looking back,

one might say that the jazzmen, some of whom we idolized, were in their own way better examples for youth to follow than were most judges and ministers, legislators and governors (we were stuck with the notorious Alfalfa Bill Murray). For as we viewed these pillars of society from the confines of our segregated community we almost always saw crooks, clowns, or hypocrites. Even the best were revealed by their attitudes toward us as lacking the respectable qualities to which they pretended and for which they were accepted outside by others, while despite the outlaw nature of their art, the jazzmen were less torn and damaged by the moral compromises and insincerities which have so sickened the life of our country.

Be that as it may, our youthful sense of life, like that of many 6
Negro children (though no one bothers to note it—especially the specialists and "friends of the Negro" who view our Negro-American life as essentially non-human) was very much like that of Huckleberry Finn, who is universally so praised and enjoyed for the clarity and courage of his moral vision. Like Huck, we observed, we judged, we imitated and evaded as we could the dullness, corruption, and blindness of "civilization." We were undoubtedly comic because, as the saying goes, we weren't supposed to know what it was all about. But to ourselves we were "boys," members of a wild, free, outlaw tribe which transcended the category of race. Rather we were Americans born into the forty-sixth state, and thus, into the context of Negro-American post-Civil War history, "frontiersmen." And isn't one of the implicit functions of the American frontier to encourage the individual to a kind of dreamy wakefulness, a state in which he makes—in all ignorance of the accepted limitations of the possible—rash efforts, quixotic gestures, hopeful testings of the complexity of the known and the given?

Spurring us on in our controlled and benign madness was the 7
voracious reading of which most of us were guilty and the vicarious identification and empathetic adventuring which it encouraged. This was due, in part, perhaps to the fact that some of us were fatherless—my own father had died when I was three—but most likely it was because boys are natural romantics. We were seeking examples, patterns to live by, out of a freedom which for all its being ignored by the sociologists and subtle thinkers, was implicit in the Negro situation. Father and mother substitutes also have a role to play in aiding the child to help create himself. Thus we fabricated our own heroes and ideals catch-as-catch-can; and with an outrageous and irreverent sense of freedom. Yes, and in complete disregard of ideas of respectability or the surreal incongruity of some of our projections. Gamblers and scholars, jazz musi-

cians and scientists, Negro cowboys and soldiers from the Spanish-American and First World Wars, movie stars and stunt men, figures from the Italian Renaissance and literature, both classical and popular, were combined with the special virtues of some local bootlegger, the eloquence of some Negro preacher, the strength and grace of some local athlete, the ruthlessness of some businessman-physician, the elegance in dress and manners of some head-waiter or hotel doorman.

8   Looking back through the shadows upon this absurd activity, I realize now that we were projecting archetypes, recreating folk figures, legendary heroes, monsters even, most of which violated all ideas of social hierarchy and order and all accepted conceptions of the hero handed down by cultural, religious, and racist tradition. But we remember, were under the intense spell of the early movies, the silents as well as the talkies; and in our community, life was not so tightly structured as it would have been in the traditional South—or even in deceptively *"free"* Harlem. And our imaginations processed reality and dream, natural man and traditional hero, literature and folklore, like maniacal editors turned loose in some frantic film-cutting room. Remember, too, that being boys, yet in the play-stage of our development, we were dream-serious in our efforts. But serious nevertheless, for *culturally* play is a preparation, and we felt that somehow the human ideal lay in the vague and constantly shifting figures—sometimes comic but always versatile, picaresque, and self-effacingly heroic—which evolved from our wildly improvisatory projections: figures neither white nor black, Christian nor Jewish, but representative of certain desirable essences, of skills and powers, physical, aesthetic, and moral.

9   The proper response to these figures was, we felt, to develop ourselves for the performance of many and diverse roles, and the fact that certain definite limitations had been imposed upon our freedom did not lessen our sense of obligation. Not only were we to prepare but we were to perform—not with mere competence but with an almost reckless verve; with, may we say (without evoking the quaint and questionable notion of *négritude*) Negro-American style? Behind each artist there stands a traditional sense of style, a sense of the felt tension indicative of expressive completeness; a mode of humanizing reality and of evoking a feeling of being at home in the world. It is something which the artist shares with the group, and part of our boyish activity expressed a yearning to make any and everything of quality *Negro-American*; to appropriate it, possess it, recreate it in our own group and individual images.

10   And we recognized and were proud of our group's own style wherever we discerned it, in jazzmen and prize-fighters, ballplayers, and

tap dancers; in gesture, inflection, intonation, timbre, and phrasing. Indeed, in all those nuances of expression and attitude which reveal a
culture. We did not fully understand the cost of that style, but we
recognized within it an affirmation of life beyond all question of our
difficulties as Negroes.

Contrary to the notion currently projected by certain specialists   11
in the "Negro problem" which characterizes the Negro American as self-
hating and defensive, we did not so regard ourselves. We felt, among
ourselves at least, that we were supposed to be whoever we would and
could be and do anything and everything which other boys did, and do
it better. Not defensively, because we were ordered to do so; nor because
it was held in the society at large that we were naturally, as Negroes,
limited—but because we demanded it of ourselves. Because to measure
up to our own standards was the only way of affirming our notion of
manhood.

Hence it was no more incongruous, as seen from our own partic-   12
ular perspective in this land of incongruities, for young Negro
Oklahomans to project themselves as Renaissance men than for white
Mississippians to see themselves as ancient Greeks or noblemen out
of Sir Walter Scott. Surely our fantasies have caused far less damage
to the nation's sense of reality, if for no other reason than that ours were
expressive of a more democratic ideal. Remember, too, as William
Faulkner made us so vividly aware, that the slaves often took the essence
of the aristocratic ideal (as they took Christianity) with far more
seriousness than their masters, and that we, thanks to the tight telescop-
ing of American history, were but two generations from that previous
condition. Renaissance men, indeed!

I managed, by keeping quiet about it, to cling to our boyish ideal   13
during three years in Alabama, and I brought it with me to New York,
where it not only gave silent support to my explorations of what was
then an unknown territory, but served to mock and caution me when
I became interested in the Communist ideal. And when it was suggested
that I try my hand at writing it was still with me.

The act of writing requires a constant plunging back into the   14
shadow of the past where time hovers ghostlike. When I began writing
in earnest I was forced, thus, to relate myself consciously and imaginatively to my mixed background as American, as Negro-American,
and as a Negro from what in its own belated way was a pioneer
background. More important, and inseparable from this particular effort,
was the necessity of determining my true relationship to that body of
American literature to which I was most attracted and through which,

aided by what I could learn from the literatures of Europe, I would find my own voice and to which I was challenged, by way of achieving myself, to make some small contribution, and to whose composite picture of reality I was obligated to offer some necessary modifications.

15   This was no matter of sudden insight but of slow and blundering discovery, of a struggle to stare down the deadly and hypnotic temptation to interpret the world and all its devices in terms of race. To avoid this was very important to me, and in light of my background far from simple. Indeed, it was quite complex, involving as it did, a ceaseless questioning of all those formulas which historians, politicians, sociologists, and an older generation of Negro leaders and writers—those of the so-called "Negro Renaissance"—had evolved to describe my group's identity, its predicament, its fate, and its relation to the larger society and the culture which we share.

16   Here the question of reality and personal identity merge. Yes, and the question of the nature of the reality which underlies American fiction and thus the human truth which gives fiction viability. In this quest, for such it soon became, I learned that nothing could go unchallenged; especially that feverish industry dedicated to telling Negroes who and what they are, and which can usually be counted upon to deprive both humanity and culture of their complexity. I had undergone, not too many months before taking the path which led to writing, the humiliation of being taught in a class in sociology at a Negro college (from Park and Burgess, the leading textbook in the field) that Negroes represented the "lady of the races." This contention the Negro instructor passed blandly along to us without even bothering to wash his hands, much less his teeth. Well, I had no intention of being bound by any such humiliating definition of my relationship to American literature. Not even to those works which depicted Negroes negatively. Negro Americans have a highly developed ability to abstract desirable qualities from those around them, even from their enemies, and my sense of reality could reject bias while appreciating the truth revealed by achieved art. The pleasure which I derived from reading had long been a necessity, and in the *act* of reading, that marvelous collaboration between the writer's artful vision and the reader's sense of life, I had become acquainted with other possible selves; freer, more courageous and ingenuous and, during the course of the narrative at least, even wise.

17   At the time I was under the influence of Ernest Hemingway, and his description, in *Death in the Afternoon,* of his thinking when he first went to Spain became very important as translated in my own naïve fashion. He was trying to write, he tells us,

and I found the greatest difficulty aside from knowing truly what you really felt, rather than what you were supposed to feel, and had been taught to feel, was to put down what really happened in action; what the actual things were which produced the emotion that you experienced. . . .

His statement of moral and aesthetic purpose which followed 18 focused my own search to relate myself to American life through literature. For I found the greatest difficulty for a Negro writer was the problem of revealing what he truly felt, rather than serving up what Negroes were supposed to feel, and were encouraged to feel. And linked to this was the difficulty, based upon our long habit of deception and evasion, of depicting what really happened within our areas of American life, and putting down with honesty and without bowing to ideological expediencies the attitudes and values which give Negro-American life, its sense of wholeness and which render it bearable and human and, when measured by our own terms, desirable.

I was forced to this awareness through my struggles with the 19 craft of fiction; yes, and by my attraction (soon rejected) to Marxist political theory, which was my response to the inferior status which society sought to impose upon me (I did not then, now, or ever *consider* myself inferior).

I did not know my true relationship to America—what citizen 20 of the U.S. really does?—but I did know and accept how I felt inside. And I also knew, thanks to the old Renaissance Man, what I expected of myself in the matter of personal discipline and creative quality. Since by the grace of the past and the examples of manhood picked willy-nilly from the continuing-present of my background, I rejected all negative definitions imposed upon me by others, there was nothing to do but search for those relationships which were fundamental.

In this sense fiction became the agency of my efforts to answer 21 the questions, Who am I, what am I, how did I come to be? What shall I make of the life around me, what celebrate, what reject, how confront the snarl of good and evil which is inevitable? What does American society *mean* when regarded out of my *own* eyes, when informed by my *own* sense of the past and viewed by my *own* complex sense of the present? How, in other words, should I think of myself and my pluralistic sense of the world, how express my vision of the human predicament, without reducing it to a point which would render it sterile before that necessary and tragic—through enhancing—reduction which must occur before the fictive vision can come alive? It is quite possible that much potential fiction by Negro Americans fails precisely at this point: through the writers' refusal (often through provincialism or lack of courage or through opportunism) to achieve a vision of life and a resourcefulness of craft commensurate with the complexity of their actual situation. Too often they fear to leave the uneasy sanctuary of race to take their chances in the world of art.

_____ CONSIDERATIONS _____

1. Ellison's opening statement that writing was "a reflex of reading" points to the experience of many other students and writers (see Richard Wright's "The Library Card," pages 481–490) and implies an important relationship between the two activities. Are reading and writing two sides of the same coin?

2. Look in a good dictionary for a definition of "Renaissance man" and explain why this concept is central to an understanding of Ellison's essay.

3. How, in Paragraph 7, does Ellison specify, and thus clarify, what he means by "ours was a chaotic community" in Paragraph 3?

4. At several points in his essay, Ellison is critical of "specialists and 'friends of the Negro.'" What is his primary criticism of their efforts?

5. Does Ellison's remark "boys are natural romantics" in Paragraph 7 help explain his first sentence in Paragraph 8? Do you think that sentence is limited to the boys of one race or class? Use your own experience to write an essay on the subject.

6. Would Eiseley's short essay "More Thoughts on Wilderness" (pages 150–152) be an example of what Ellison expresses in the first sentence of his Paragraph 14?

Nora Ephron (b. 1941), daughter of two screen writers, grew up in Hollywood wanting to move to New York and become a writer. She did. She began by working for Newsweek, *and soon was contributing articles to* The New Yorker *and a monthly column to* Esquire. *Most of her writing is about women, and manages to be at once funny and serious, profound and irreverent—and on occasion outrageous. In 1983 she published a novel entitled* Heartburn *which, in 1986, was made into a film. Her essays are collected in* Wallflower at the Orgy *(1970) and* Crazy Salad *(1975), from which we take this essay on growing up flat-chested.*

27

NORA EPHRON

A Few Words about Breasts: Shaping Up Absurd

I have to begin with a few words about androgyny. In grammar   1
school, in the fifth and sixth grades, we were all tyrannized by a rigid set of rules that supposedly determined whether we were boys or girls. The episode in *Huckleberry Finn* where Huck is disguised as a girl and gives himself away by the way he threads a needle and catches a ball — that kind of thing. We learned that the way you sat, crossed your legs, held a cigarette and looked at your nails, your wristwatch, the way you did these things instinctively was absolute proof of your sex. Now obviously most children did not take this literally, but I did. I thought that just one slip, just one incorrect cross of my legs or flick of an imaginary

cigarette ash would turn me from whatever I was into the other thing; that would be all it took, really. Even though I was outwardly a girl and had many of the trappings generally associated with the field of girldom—a girl's name, for example, and dresses, my own telephone, an autograph book—I spent the early years of my adolescence absolutely certain that I might at any point gum it up. I did not feel at all like a girl. I was boyish. I was athletic, ambitious, outspoken, competitive, noisy, rambunctious. I had scabs on my knees and my socks slid into my loafers and I could throw a football. I wanted desperately not to be that way, not to be a mixture of both things but instead just one, a girl, a definite indisputable girl. As soft and as pink as a nursery. And nothing would do that for me, I felt, but breasts.

2   I was about six months younger than everyone in my class, and so for about six months after it began, for six months after my friends had begun to develop—that was the word we used, develop—I was not particularly worried. I would sit in the bathtub and look down at my breasts and know that any day now, any second now, they would start growing like everyone else's. They didn't. "I want to buy a bra," I said to my mother one night. "What for?" she said. My mother was really hateful about bras, and by the time my third sister had gotten to the point where she was ready to want one, my mother had worked the whole business into a comedy routine. "Why not use a Band-Aid instead?" she would say. It was a source of great pride to my mother that she had never even had to wear a brassiere until she had her fourth child, and then only because her gynecologist made her. It was incomprehensible to me that anyone would ever be proud of something like that. It was the 1950's, for God's sake. Jane Russell. Cashmere sweaters. Couldn't my mother see that? *"I am too old to wear an undershirt."* Screaming. Weeping. Shouting. "Then don't wear an undershirt," said my mother. "But I want to buy a bra," "What for?"

3   I suppose that for most girls, breasts, brassieres, that entire thing, has more trauma, more to do with the coming of adolescence, of becoming a woman, than anything else. Certainly more than getting your period, although that too was traumatic, symbolic. But you could *see* breasts; they were there; they were visible. Whereas a girl could claim to have her period for months before she actually got it and nobody would ever know the difference. Which is exactly what I did. All you had to do was make a great fuss over having enough nickels for the Kotex machine and walk around clutching your stomach and moaning for three to five days a month about The Curse and you could convince anybody. There is a school of thought somewhere in the women's lib/women's

mag/gynecology establishment that claims that menstrual cramps are purely psychological, and I lean toward it. Not that I didn't have them finally. Agonizing cramps, heating-pad cramps, go-down-to-the-school-nurse-and-lie-on-the-cot cramps. But unlike any pain I have ever suffered, I adored the pain of cramps, welcomed it, wallowed in it, bragged about it. "I can't go. I have cramps." "I can't do that. I have cramps." And most of all, gigglingly, blushingly: "I can't swim. I have cramps." Nobody ever used the hard-core word. Menstruation. God, what an awful word. Never that. "I have cramps."

The morning I first got my period, I went into my mother's bedroom to tell her. And my mother, my utterly-hateful-about-bras mother, burst into tears. It was really a lovely moment, and I remember it so clearly not just because it was one of the two times I ever saw my mother cry on my account (the other was when I was caught being a six-year-old kleptomaniac), but also because the incident did not mean to me what it meant to her. Her little girl, her firstborn, had finally become a woman. That was what she was crying about. My reaction to the event, however, was that I might well be a woman in some scientific, textbook sense (and could at least stop faking every month and stop wasting all those nickels). But in another sense—in a visible sense—I was an androgynous and as liable to tip over into boyhood as ever. 4

I started with a 28AA bra. I don't think they made them any smaller in those days, although I gather that now you can buy bras for five year olds that don't have any cups whatsoever in them; trainer bras they are called. My first brassiere came from Robinson's Department Store in Beverly Hills. I went there alone, shaking, positive they would look me over and smile and tell me to come back next year. An actual fitter took me into the dressing room and stood over me while I took off my blouse and tried the first one on. The little puffs stood out on my chest. "Lean over," said the fitter (to this day I am not sure what fitters in bra departments do except to tell you to lean over). I leaned over, with the fleeing hope that my breasts would miraculously fall out of my body and into the puffs. Nothing. 5

"Don't worry about it," said my friend Libby some months later, when things had not improved. "You'll get them after you're married." 6

"What are you talking about?" I said. 7

"When you get married," Libby explained, "your husband will touch your breasts and rub them and kiss them and they'll grow." 8

That was the killer. Necking I could deal with. Intercourse I could deal with. But it had never crossed my mind that a man was go- 9 ing to touch my breasts, that breasts had something to do with all that, petting, my God they never mentioned petting in my little sex manual about the fertilization of the ovum. I became dizzy. For I knew instantly—as naïve as I had been only a moment before—that only part of what she was saying was true: the touching, rubbing, kissing part, not the growing part. And I knew that no one would ever want to marry me. I had no breasts. I would never have breasts.

10   My best friend in school was Diana Raskob. She lived a block from me in a house full of wonders. English muffins, for instance. The Raskobs were the first people in Beverly Hills to have English muffins for breakfast. They also had an apricot tree in the back, and a badminton court, and a subscription to *Seventeen* magazine, and hundreds of games like Sorry and Parcheesi and Treasure Hunt and Anagrams. Diana and I spent three or four afternoons a week in their den reading and playing and eating. Diana's mother's kitchen was full of the most colossal assortment of junk food I have ever been exposed to. My house was full of apples and peaches and milk and homemade chocolate-chip cookies— which were nice, and good for you, but-not-right-before-dinner-or-you'll-spoil-your-appetite. Diana's house had nothing in it that was good for you, and what's more, you could stuff it in right up until dinner and nobody cared. Bar-B-Q potato chips (they were the first in them, too), giant bottles of ginger ale, fresh popcorn with melted butter, hot fudge sauce on Baskin-Robbins jamoca ice cream, powdered-sugar doughnuts from Van de Kamps. Diana and I had been best friends since we were seven; we were about equally popular in school (which is to say, not particularly), we had about the same success with boys (extremely intermittent) and we looked much the same. Dark. Tall. Gangly.

11   It is September, just before school begins. I am eleven years old, about to enter the seventh grade, and Diana and I have not seen each other all summer. I have been to camp and she has been somewhere like Banff with her parents. We are meeting, as we often do, on the street midway between our two houses and we will walk back to Diana's and eat junk and talk about what has happened to each of us that summer. I am walking down Walden Drive in my jeans and my father's shirt hanging out and my old red loafers with the socks falling into them and coming toward me is . . . I take a deep breath . . . a young woman. Diana. Her hair is curled and she has a waist and hips and a bust and she is wearing a straight skirt, an article of clothing I have been repeatedly told I will be unable to wear until I have the hips to hold it up. My jaw drops, and suddenly I am crying, crying hysterically, can't catch my

breath sobbing. My best friend has betrayed me. She has gone ahead without me and done it. She has shaped up.

Here are some things I did to help: 12
Bought a Mark Eden Bust Developer. 13
Slept on my back for four years. 14
Splashed cold water on them every night because some French 15
actress said in *Life* magazine that that was what *she* did for her perfect bustline.

Ultimately, I resigned myself to a bad toss and began to wear 16
padded bras. I think about them now, think about all those years in high school I went around in them, my three padded bras, every single one of them with different sized breasts. Each time I changed bras I changed sizes: one week nice perky but not too obtrusive breasts, the next medium-sized slightly pointed onces, the next week knockers, true knockers; all the time, whatever size I was, carrying around this rubberized appendage on my chest that occasionally crashed into a wall and was poked inward and had to be poked outward—I think about all that and wonder how anyone kept a straight face through it. My parents, who normally had no restraints about needling me—why did they say nothing as they watched my chest go up and down? My friends, who would periodically inspect my breasts for signs of growth and reassure me—why didn't they at least counsel consistency?

And the bathing suits. I die when I think about the bathing suits. 17
That was the era when you could lay an uninhabited bathing suit on the beach and someone would make a pass at it. I would put one on, an absurd swimsuit with its enormous bust built into it, the bones from the suit stabbing me in the rib cage and leaving little red welts on my body, and there I would be, my chest plunging straight downward absolutely vertically from my collarbone to the top of my suit and then suddenly, wham, out came all that padding and material and wiring absolutely horizontally.

Buster Klepper was the first boy who ever touched them. He was 18
my boyfriend my senior year of high school. There is a picture of him in my high-school yearbook that makes him look quite attractive in a Jewish, horn-rimmed glasses sort of way, but the picture does not show the pimples, which were air-brushed out, or the dumbness. Well, that isn't really fair. He wasn't dumb. He just wasn't terribly bright. His mother refused to accept it, refused to accept the relentlessly average report cards, refused to deal with her son's inevitable destiny in some

junior college or other. "He was tested," she would say to me, apropos of nothing, "and it came out 145. That's near-genius." Had the word underachiever been coincd, she probably would have lobbed that one at me, too. Anyway, Buster was really very sweet—which is, I know, damning with faint praise, but there it is. I was the editor of the front page of the high-school newspaper and he was editor of the back page; we had to work together, side by side, in the print shop, and that was how it started. On our first date, we went to see *April Love* starring Pat Boone. Then we started going together. Buster had a green coupe, a 1950 Ford with an engine he had handchromed until it shone, dazzled, reflected the image of anyone who looked into it, anyone usually being Buster polishing it or the gas-station attendants he constantly asked to check the oil in order for them to be overwhelmed by the sparkle on the valves. The car also had a boot stretched over the back seat for reasons I never understood; hanging from the rearview mirror, as was the custom, was a pair of angora dice. A previous girl friend named Solange who was famous throughout Beverly Hills High School for having no pigment in her right eyebrow had knitted them for him. Buster and I would ride around town, the two of us seated to the left of the steering wheel. I would shift gears. It was nice.

19   There was necking. Terrific necking. First in the car, overlooking Los Angeles from what is now the Trousdale Estates. Then on the bed of his parents' cabana at Ocean House. Incredibly wonderful, frustrating necking, I loved it, really, but no further than necking, please don't, please, because there I was absolutely terrified of the general implications of going-a-step-further with a near-dummy and also terrified of his finding out there was next to nothing there (which he knew, of course; he wasn't that dumb).

20   I broke up with him at one point. I think we were apart for about two weeks. At the end of that time I drove down to see a friend at a boarding school in Palos Verdes Estates and a disc jockey played *April Love* on the radio four times during the trip. I took it as a sign. I drove straight back to Griffith Park to a golf tournament Buster was playing in (he was the sixth-seeded teen-age golf player in Southern California) and presented myself back to him on the green of the 18th hole. It was all very dramatic. That night we went to a drive-in and I let him get his hand under my protuberances and onto my breasts. He really didn't seem to mind at all.

21   *"Do you want to marry my son?" the woman asked me.*
22   *"Yes," I said.*

I was nineteen years old, a virgin, going with this woman's son,   23
this big strange woman who was married to a Lutheran minister in
New Hampshire and pretended she was Gentile and had this son, by
her first husband, this total fool of a son who ran the hero-sandwich
concession at Harvard Business School and whom for one moment one
December in New Hampshire I said—as much out of politeness as
anything else—that I wanted to marry.

"Fine," she said. "Now, here's what you do. Always make sure   24
you're on top of him so you won't seem so small. My bust is very large,
you see, so I always lie on my back to make it look smaller, but you'll
have to be on top most of the time."

I nodded. "Thank you," I said.   25

"I have a book for you to read," she went on. "Take it with you   26
when you leave. Keep it." She went to the bookshelf, found it, and gave
it to me. It was a book on frigidity.

"Thank you," I said.   27

That is a true story. Everything in this article is a true story, but   28
I feel I have to point out that that story in particular is true. It happened
on December 30, 1960. I think about it often. When it first happened,
I naturally assumed that the woman's son, my boyfriend, was responsible. I invented a scenario where he had had a little heart-to-heart with
his mother and had confessed that his only objection to me was that
my breasts were small; his mother then took it upon herself to help
out. Now I think I was wrong about the incident. The mother was acting on her own, I think: that was her way of being cruel and competitive
under the guise of being helpful and maternal. You have small breasts,
she was saying; therefore you will never make him as happy as I have.
Or you have small breasts; therefore you will doubtless have sexual problems. Or you have small breasts; therefore you are less woman than
I am. She was, as it happens, only the first of what seems to me to be
a never-ending string of women who have made competitive remarks
to me about breast size. "I would love to wear a dress like that," my
friend Emily says to me, "but my bust is too big." Like that. Why do
women say these things to me? Do I attract these remarks the way other
women attract married men or alcoholics or homosexuals? This summer, for example. I am at a party in East Hampton and I am introduced
to a woman from Washington. She is a minor celebrity, very pretty and
Southern and blonde and outspoken and I am flattered because she has
read something I have written. We are talking animatedly, we have been
talking no more than five minutes, when a man comes up to join us.
"Look at the two of us," the woman says to the man, indicating me and

her. "The two of us together couldn't fill an A cup." Why does she say that? It isn't even true, dammit, so why? Is she even more addled than I am on this subject? Does she honestly believe there is something wrong with her size breasts, which, it seems to me, now that I look hard at them, are just right. Do I unconsciously bring out competitiveness in women? In that form? What did I do to deserve it?

29   As for men.

30   There were men who minded and let me know they minded. There were men who did not mind. In any case, I always minded.

31   And even now, now that I have been countlessly reassured that my figure is a good one, now that I am grown up enough to understand that most of my feelings have very little to do with the reality of my shape, I am nonetheless obsessed by breasts. I cannot help it. I grew up in the terrible Fifties—with rigid stereotypical sex roles, the insistence that men be men and dress like men and women be women and dress like women, the intolerance of androgyny—and I cannot shake it, cannot shake my feelings of inadequacy. Well, that time is gone, right? All those exaggerated examples of breast worship are gone, right? Those women were freaks, right? I know all that. And yet, here I am, stuck with the psychological remains of it all, stuck with my own peculiar version of breast worship. You probably think I am crazy to go on like this: here I have set out to write a confession that is meant to hit you with the shock of recognition and instead you are sitting there thinking I am thoroughly warped. Well, what can I tell you? If I had had them, I would have been a completely different person. I honestly believe that.

32   After I went into therapy, a process that made it possible for me to tell total strangers at cocktail parties that breasts were the hang-up of my life, I was often told that I was insane to have been bothered by my condition. I was also frequently told, by close friends, that I was extremely boring on the subject. And my girl friends, the ones with nice big breasts, would go on endlessly about how their lives had been far more miserable than mine. Their bra straps were snapped in class. They couldn't sleep on their stomachs. They were stared at whenever the word "mountain" cropped up in geography. And *Evangeline*, good God what they went through every time someone had to stand up and recite the Prologue to Longfellow's *Evangeline:* "*. . . stand like druids of eld . . . / With beards that rest on their bosoms.*" It was much worse for them, they tell me. They had a terrible time of it, they assure me. I don't know how lucky I was, they say.

33   I have thought about their remarks, tried to put myself in their place, considered their point of view. I think they are full of shit.

_____ CONSIDERATIONS _____

1. Nora Ephron's account offends some readers and attracts others for the same reason—the frank and casual exploration of a subject that generations have believed unmentionable. This problem is worth investigating: Are there, in fact, subjects that should not be discussed in the popular press? Are there words a writer must not use? Why? And who should make the list of things not to be talked about?

2. Imagine an argument about Ephron's article between a feminist and an antifeminist. What ammunition could each find in the article? Write the dialogue as you hear it.

3. Ephron reports that from a very early age she worried that she might not be "a girl, a definite indisputable girl." Is this anxiety as uncommon as she thought it was? Is worry about one's sex an exclusively female problem?

4. Are our ideas about masculinity and femininity changing? How are such ideas determined? How important are they in shaping personality and in channeling thoughts?

5. Ephron's article is a good example of the very informal essay. What does she do that makes it so informal? Consider both diction and sentence structure.

6. How can one smile at others' problems—or at one's own disappointments, for that matter? How can Ephron see humor now in what she thought of as tragic then? Provide an example from your own experience.

28

WILLIAM FAULKNER
A Rose for Emily

I

1   When Miss Emily Grierson died, our whole town went to her funeral: the men through a sort of respectful affection for a fallen monument, the women mostly out of curiosity to see the inside of her house, which no one save an old manservant—a combined gardener and cook— had seen in at least ten years.

2   It was a big, squarish frame house that had once been white, decorated with cupolas and spires and scrolled balconies in the heavily lightsome style of the seventies, set on what had once been our most select street. But garages and cotton gins had encroached and obliterated even the august names of that neighborhood; only Miss Emily's house was left, lifting its stubborn and coquettish decay above the cotton wagons and the gasoline pumps—an eyesore among eyesores. And now Miss Emily had gone to join the representatives of those august names

where they lay in the cedar-bemused cemetery among the ranked and anonymous graves of Union and Confederate soldiers who fell at the battle of Jefferson.

Alive, Miss Emily had been a tradition, a duty, and a care; a sort 3 of hereditary obligation upon the town, dating from that day in 1894 when Colonel Sartoris, the mayor—he who fathered the edict that no Negro woman should appear on the streets without an apron—remitted her taxes, the dispensation dating from the death of her father on into perpetuity. Not that Miss Emily would have accepted charity. Colonel Sartoris invented an involved tale to the effect that Miss Emily's father had loaned money to the town, which the town, as a matter of business, preferred this way of repaying. Only a man of Colonel Sartoris' generation and thought could have invented it, and only a woman could have believed it.

When the next generation, with its more modern ideas, became 4 mayors and aldermen, this arrangement created some little dissatisfaction. On the first of the year they mailed her a tax notice. February came, and there was no reply. They wrote her a formal letter, asking her to call at the sheriff's office at her convenience. A week later the mayor wrote her himself, offering to call or to send his car for her, and received in reply a note on paper of an archaic shape, in a thin, flowing calligraphy in faded ink, to the effect that she no longer went out at all. The tax notice was also enclosed, without comment.

They called a special meeting of the Board of Aldermen. A depu- 5 tation waited upon her, knocked at the door through which no visitor had passed since she ceased giving china-painting lessons eight or ten years earlier. They were admitted by the old Negro into a dim hall from which a staircase mounted into still more shadow. It smelled of dust and disuse—a close, dank smell. The Negro led them into the parlor. It was furnished in heavy, leather-covered furniture. When the Negro opened the blinds of one window, a faint dust rose sluggishly about their thighs, spinning with slow motes in the single sun-ray. On a tarnished gilt easel before the fireplace stood a crayon portrait of Miss Emily's father.

They rose when she entered—a small, fat woman in black, with 6 a thin gold chain descending to her waist and vanishing into her belt, leaning on an ebony cane with a tarnished gold head. Her skeleton was small and spare; perhaps that was why what would have been merely plumpness in another was obesity in her. She looked bloated, like a body long submerged in motionless water, and of that pallid hue. Her eyes, lost in the fatty ridges of her face, looked like two small pieces of coal pressed into a lump of dough as they moved from one face to another while the visitors stated their errand.

7   She did not ask them to sit. She just stood in the door and listened quietly until the spokesman came to a stumbling halt. Then they could hear the invisible watch ticking at the end of the gold chain.

8   Her voice was dry and cold. "I have no taxes in Jefferson. Colonel Sartoris explained it to me. Perhaps one of you can gain access to the city records and satisfy yourselves."

9   "But we have. We are the city authorities, Miss Emily. Didn't you get a notice from the sheriff, signed by him?"

10   "I received a paper, yes," Miss Emily said. "Perhaps he considers himself the sheriff. . . . I have no taxes in Jefferson."

11   "But there is nothing on the books to show that, you see. We must go by the—"

12   "See Colonel Sartoris. I have no taxes in Jefferson."

13   "But, Miss Emily—"

14   "See Colonel Sartoris." (Colonel Sartoris had been dead almost ten years.) "I have no taxes in Jefferson. Tobe!" The Negro appeared. "Show these gentlemen out."

II

15   So she vanquished them, horse and foot, just as she had vanquished their fathers thirty years before about the smell. That was two years after her father's death and a short time after her sweetheart—the one we believed would marry her—had deserted her. After her father's death she went out very little; after her sweetheart went away, people hardly saw her at all. A few of the ladies had the temerity to call, but were not received, and the only sign of life about the place was the Negro man—a young man then—going in and out with a market basket.

16   "Just as if a man—any man—could keep a kitchen properly," the ladies said; so they were not surprised when the smell developed. It was another link between the gross, teeming world and the high and mighty Griersons.

17   A neighbor, a woman, complained to the mayor, Judge Stevens, eighty years old.

18   "But what will you have me do about it, madam?" he said.

19   "Why, send her word to stop it," the woman said. "Isn't there a law?"

20   "I'm sure that won't be necessary," Judge Stevens said. "It's probably just a snake or a rat that nigger of hers killed in the yard. I'll speak to him about it."

The next day he received two more complaints, one from a man 21
who came in diffident deprecation. "We really must do something about
it, Judge. I'd be the last one in the world to bother Miss Emily, but we've
got to do something." That night the Board of Aldermen met—three gray-
beards and one younger man, a member of the rising generation.

"It's simple enough," he said. "Send her word to have her place 22
cleaned up. Give her a certain time to do it in, and if she don't . . ."

"Dammit, sir," Judge Stevens said, "will you accuse a lady to her 23
face of smelling bad?"

So the next night, after midnight, four men crossed Miss Emily's 24
lawn and slunk about the house like burglars, sniffing along the base
of the brickwork and at the cellar openings while one of them performed
a regular sowing motion with his hand out of a sack slung from his
shoulder. They broke open the cellar door and sprinkled lime there, and
in all the out-buildings. As they recrossed the lawn, a window that had
been dark was lighted and Miss Emily sat in it, the light behind her,
and her upright torso motionless as that of an idol. They crept quietly
across the lawn and into the shadow of the locusts that lined the street.
After a week or two the smell went away.

That was when people had begun to feel really sorry for her. Peo- 25
ple in our town remembering how old lady Wyatt, her great-aunt, had
gone completely crazy at last, believed that the Griersons held
themselves a little too high for what they really were. None of the young
men were quite good enough for Miss Emily and such. We had long
thought of them as a tableau: Miss Emily a slender figure in white in
the background, her father a spraddled silhouette in the foreground, his
back to her and clutching a horsewhip, the two of them framed by the
back-flung front door. So when she got to be thirty and was still single,
we were not pleased exactly, but vindicated; even with insanity in the
family she wouldn't have turned down all of her chances if they had
really materialized.

When her father died, it got about that the house was all that was 26
left to her; and in a way, people were glad. At last they could pity Miss
Emily. Being left alone, and a pauper, she had become humanized. Now
she too would know the old thrill and the old despair of a penny more
or less.

The day after his death all the ladies prepared to call at the house 27
and offer condolence and aid, as is our custom. Miss Emily met them
at the door, dressed as usual and with no trace of grief on her face. She
told them that her father was not dead. She did that for three days, with
the ministers calling on her, and the doctors trying to persuade her to

let them dispose of the body. Just as they were about to resort to law and force, she broke down, and they buried her father quickly.

28   We did not say she was crazy then. We believed she had to do that. We remembered all the young men her father had driven away, and we knew that with nothing left, she would have to cling to that which had robbed her, as people will.

III

29   She was sick for a long time. When we saw her again, her hair was cut short, making her look like a girl, with a vague resemblance to those angels in colored church windows — sort of tragic and serene.

30   The town had just let the contracts for paving the sidewalks, and in the summer after her father's death they began to work. The construction company came with niggers and mules and machinery, and a foreman named Homer Barron, a Yankee — a big, dark, ready man, with a big voice and eyes lighter than his face. The little boys would follow in groups to hear him cuss the niggers, and the niggers singing in time to the rise and fall of picks. Pretty soon he knew everybody in town. Whenever you heard a lot of laughing anywhere about the square, Homer Barron would be in the center of the group. Presently we began to see him and Miss Emily on Sunday afternoons driving in the yellow-wheeled buggy and the matched team of bays from the livery stable.

31   At first we were glad that Miss Emily would have an interest, because the ladies all said, "Of course a Grierson would not think seriously of a Northener, a day laborer." But there were still others, older people, who said that even grief could not cause a real lady to forget *noblesse oblige* — without calling it *noblesse oblige.* They just said, "Poor Emily. Her kinsfolk should come to her." She had some kin in Alabama; but years ago her father had fallen out with them over the estate of old lady Wyatt, the crazy woman, and there was no communication between the two families. They had not even been represented at the funeral.

32   And as soon as the old people said, "Poor Emily," the whispering began. "Do you suppose it's really so?" they said to one another. "Of course it is. What else could . . ." This behind their hands; rustling of craned silk and satin behind jalousies closed upon the sun of Sunday afternoon as the thin, swift clop-clop-clop of the matched team passed: "Poor Emily."

33   She carried her head high enough — even when we believed that she was fallen. It was as if she demanded more than ever the recogni-

tion of her dignity as the last Grierson; as if it had wanted that touch of earthliness to reaffirm her imperviousness. Like when she bought the rat poison, the arsenic. That was over a year after they had begun to say "Poor Emily," and while the two female cousins were visiting her.

"I want some poison," she said to the druggist. She was over thirty   34
then, still a slight woman, though thinner than usual, with cold, haughty black eyes in a face the flesh of which was strained across the temples and about the eyesockets as you imagine a lighthouse-keeper's face ought to look. "I want some poison," she said.

"Yes, Miss Emily. What kind? For rats and such? I'd recom —"   35
"I want the best you have. I don't care what kind."   36
The druggist named several. "They'll kill anything up to an ele-   37
phant. But what you want is —"
"Arsenic," Miss Emily said. "Is that a good one?"   38
"Is . . . arsenic? Yes ma'am. But what you want —"   39
"I want arsenic."   40
The druggist looked down at her. She looked back at him, erect,   41
her face like a strained flag. "Why, of course," the druggist said. "If that's what you want. But the law requires you to tell what you are going to use it for."

Miss Emily just stared at him, her head tilted back in order to look   42
him eye for eye, until he looked away and went and got the arsenic and wrapped it up. The Negro delivery boy brought her the package; the druggist didn't come back. When she opened the package at home there was written on the box, under the skull and bones: "For rats."

IV

So the next day we all said, "She will kill herself"; and we said it   43
would be the best thing. When she had first begun to be seen with Homer Barron, we had said, "She will marry him." Then we said, "She will persuade him yet," because Homer himself had remarked — he liked men, and it was known that he drank with the younger men in the Elk's Club — that he was not a marrying man. Later we said, "Poor Emily," behind the jalousies as they passed on Sunday afternoon in the glittering buggy, Miss Emily with her head high and Homer Barron with his hat cocked and a cigar in his teeth, reins and whip in a yellow glove.

Then some of the ladies began to say that it was a disgrace to the   44
town and a bad example to the young people. The men did not want to interfere, but at last the ladies forced the Baptist minister — Miss Emily's people were Episcopal — to call upon her. He would never di-

vulge what happened during that interview, but he refused to go back again. The next Sunday they again drove about the streets and the following day the minister's wife wrote to Miss Emily's relations in Alabama.

45   So she had blood-kin under her roof again and we sat back to watch developments. At first nothing happened. Then we were sure that they had to be married. We learned that Miss Emily had been to the jeweler's and ordered a man's toilet set in silver, with the letters H.B. on each piece. Two days later we learned that she had bought a complete outfit of men's clothing, including a nightshirt, and we said "They are married." We were really glad. We were glad because the two female cousins were even more Grierson than Miss Emily had ever been.

46   So we were surprised when Homer Barron — the streets had been finished some time since — was gone. We were a little disappointed that there was not a public blowing-off, but we believed that he had gone on to prepare for Miss Emily's coming, or to give a chance to get rid of the cousins. (By that time it was a cabal, and we were all Miss Emily's allies to help circumvent the cousins.) Sure enough, after another week they departed. And, as we had expected all along, within three days Homer Barron was back in town. A neighbor saw the Negro man admit him at the kitchen door at dusk one evening.

47   And that was the last we saw of Homer Barron. And of Miss Emily for some time. The Negro man went in and out with the market basket, but the front door remained closed. Now and then we would see her at a window for a moment, as the men did that night when they sprinkled the lime, but for almost six months she did not appear on the streets. Then we knew that this was to be expected too; as if that quality of her father which had thwarted her woman's life so many times had been too virulent and too furious to die.

48   When we next saw Miss Emily, she had grown fat and her hair was turning gray. During the next few years it grew grayer and grayer until it attained an even pepper-and-salt iron-gray, when it ceased turning. Up to the day of her death at seventy-four it was still that vigorous iron-gray, like the hair of an active man.

49   From that time on her front door remained closed, save for a period of six or seven years, when she was about forty, during which she gave lessons in china-painting. She fitted up a studio in one of the downstairs rooms, where the daughters and granddaughters of Colonel Sartoris' contemporaries were sent to her with the same regularity and in the same spirit that they were sent on Sundays with a twenty-five cent piece for the collection plate. Meanwhile her taxes had been remitted.

Then the newer generation became the backbone and the spirit 50
of the town, and the painting pupils grew up and fell away and did not
send their children to her with boxes of color and tedious brushes and
pictures cut from the ladies' magazines. The front door closed upon the
last one and remained closed for good. When the town got free postal
delivery Miss Emily alone refused to let them fasten the metal numbers
above her door and attach a mailbox to it. She would not listen to them.

Daily, monthly, yearly we watched the Negro grow grayer and 51
more stooped, going in and out with the market basket. Each December
we sent her a tax notice, which would be returned by the post office
a week later, unclaimed. Now and then we would see her in one of the
downstairs windows — she had evidently shut up the top floor of the
house — like the carven torso of an idol in a niche, looking or not looking at us, we could never tell which. Thus she passed from generation
to generation — dear, inescapable, impervious, tranquil, and perverse.

And so she died. Fell ill in the house filled with dust and shadows, 52
with only a doddering Negro man to wait on her. We did not even know
she was sick; we had long since given up trying to get any information
from the Negro. He talked to no one, probably not even to her, for his
voice had grown harsh and rusty, as if from disuse.

She died in one of the downstairs rooms, in a heavy walnut bed 53
with a curtain, her gray head propped on a pillow yellow and moldy
with age and lack of sunlight.

V

The Negro met the first of the ladies at the front door and let them 54
in, with their hushed, sibilant voices and their quick, curious glances,
and then he disappeared. He walked right through the house and out
the back and was not seen again.

The two female cousins came at once. They held the funeral on 55
the second day, with the town coming to look at Miss Emily beneath
a mass of bought flowers, with the crayon face of her father musing profoundly above the bier and the ladies sibilant and macabre; and the very
old men — some in their brushed Confederate uniforms — on the porch
and the lawn, talking of Miss Emily as if she had been a contemporary
of theirs, believing that they had danced with her and courted her perhaps, confusing time with its mathematical progression, as the old do,
to whom all the past is not a diminishing road, but, instead, a huge
meadow which no winter ever quite touches, divided from them now
by the narrow bottleneck of the most recent decade of years.

56   Already we knew that there was one room in the region above the stairs which no one had seen in forty years, and which would have to be forced. They waited until Miss Emily was decently in the ground before they opened it.

57   The violence of breaking down the door seemed to fill this room with pervading dust. A thin, acrid pall as of the tomb seemed to lie everywhere upon this room decked and furnished as for a bridal: upon the valance curtains of faded rose color, upon the rose-shaded lights, upon the dressing table, upon the delicate array of crystal and the man's toilet things backed with tarnished silver, silver so tarnished that the monogram was obscured. Among them lay a collar and tie, as if they had just been removed, which, lifted, left upon the surface a pale crescent in the dust. Upon a chair hung the suit, carefully folded; beneath it the two mute shoes and the discarded socks.

58   The man himself lay in the bed.

59   For a long while we just stood there, looking down at the profound and fleshless grin. The body had apparently once lain in the attitude of an embrace, but now the long sleep that outlasts love, that conquers even the grimace of love, had cuckolded him. What was left of him, rotted beneath what was left of the nightshirt, had become inextricable from the bed in which he lay; and upon him and upon the pillow beside him lay that even coating of the patient and biding dust.

60   Then we noticed that in the second pillow was the indentation of a head. One of us lifted something from it, and leaning foward, that faint and invisible dust dry and acrid in the nostrils, we saw a long strand of iron-gray hair.

_____ CONSIDERATIONS _____

1. The art of narration, some say, is the successful management of a significant sequence of actions through time. But "through time" does not necessarily imply chronological order. Identify the major events of Faulkner's story according to when they actually happened, then arrange them in the order in which they are given by the author. Try the same technique with the story by Eudora Welty (pages 446–454).

2. Faulkner uses the terms "Negro" and "nigger" to refer to nonwhite persons in the story. Does he intend distinction between the two words? If he were writing the story today, instead of in 1930, might he substitute the word "black"? Why? Can you think of parallel terms used to designate other minority peoples, say, Jews, Catholics, Italians, or Japanese? Of what significance is the variety of such terms?

3. In what ways, if any, is Emily Grierson presented as a sympathetic character? Why?

4. In Part III, Faulkner puts considerable emphasis on the phrase *noblesse oblige*. Look up the meaning of that phrase, then comment on the author's use of it.

5. Who is the "we" in the story? Does "we" play any significant part?

6. Obviously death is a significant element in this story. Could Faulkner also have had in mind the death of a particular society or a way of life? Discuss Faulkner's use of symbolism, using examples from the story.

*Robert Frost (1874–1963) was born in California and became
the great poet of New England. He published many books of
poetry and won the Pulitzer Prize three times. A popular figure,
Frost was admired as a gentle, affectionate, avuncular figure
given to country sayings. The private Frost, however, was another man — guilty, jealous, bitter, sophisticated, occasionally
triumphant, and always complicated.*

*"Design" is a brief but complicated poem. As far back as we
find record, humankind has worried about the place of malice
or bad luck in the scheme of things. We have attributed misfortunes to the retribution of a just God, to the Fates, to divine
caprice, to broken taboos, to evil spirtis, witches, demons. It is
possible that Robert Frost here names the greatest fear of all.*

29

Robert Frost

Design

I found a dimpled spider, fat and white,
On a white heal-all, holding up a moth
Like a white piece of rigid satin cloth —
Assorted characters of death and blight
Mixed ready to begin the morning right,
Like the ingredients of a witches' broth —
A snow-drop spider, a flower like a froth,
8   And dead wings carried like a paper kite.

What had that flower to do with being white,
The wayside blue and innocent heal-all?
What brought the kindred spider to that height,
Then steered the white moth thither in the night?
What but design of darkness to appall? —
If design govern in a thing so small.   14

In 1912 Frost sent "In White" to a friend in a letter. At the time he was teaching psychology at the Plymouth Normal School in Plymouth, New Hampshire. In the decade that followed, Frost revised the poem; he first printed "Design" as we know it in 1922.

30

Robert Frost

In White

A dented spider like a snowdrop white
On a white Heal-all, holding up a moth
Like a white piece of lifeless satin cloth —
4   Saw ever curious eye so strange a sight?

Portent in little, assorted death and blight
Like the ingredients of a witches' broth?
The beady spider, the flower like a froth,
8   And the moth carried like a paper kite.

What had that flower to do with being white,
The blue Brunella every child's delight?
What brought the kindred spider to that height?
(Make we no thesis of the miller's plight.)
What but design of darkness and of night?
14   Design, design! Do I use the word aright?

Robert Frost wrote little prose. "The Figure a Poem Makes" appeared in 1939 as the introduction to a volume of his collected poems. This short essay gathers together some of Frost's notions about poetry.

31

ROBERT FROST
The Figure a Poem Makes

Abstraction is an old story with the philosophers, but it has been 1 like a new toy in the hands of the artists of our day. Why can't we have any one quality of poetry we choose by itself? We can have in thought. Then it will go hard if we can't in practice. Our lives for it.

Granted no one but a humanist much cares how sound a poem 2 is if it is only *a* sound. The sound is the gold in the ore. Then we will have the sound out alone and dispense with the inessential. We do till we make the discovery that the object in writing poetry is to make all poems sound as different as possible from each other, and the resources for that of vowels, consonants, punctuation, syntax, words, sentences, meter are not enough. We need the help of context — meaning — subject matter. That is the greatest help towards variety. All that can be done with words is soon told. So also with meters — particularly in our language where there are virtually but two, strict iambic and loose iambic. The ancients with many were still poor if they depended on meters for all tune. It is painful to watch our sprung-rhythmists straining at the point of omitting one short from a foot for relief from monotony.

The possibilities for tune from the dramatic tones of meaning struck across the rigidity of a limited meter are endless. And we are back in poetry as merely one more art of having something to say, sound or unsound. Probably better if sound, because deeper and from wider experience.

3   Then there is this wildness whereof it is spoken. Granted again that it has an equal claim with sound to being a poem's better half. If it is a wild tune, it is a poem. Our problem then is, as modern abstractionists, to have the wildness pure; to be wild with nothing to be wild about. We bring up as aberrationists, giving way to undirected associations and kicking ourselves from one chance suggestion to another in all directions as of a hot afternoon in the life of a grasshopper. Theme alone can steady us down. Just as the first mystery was how a poem could have a tune in such a straightness as meter, so the second mystery is how a poem can have wildness and at the same time a subject that shall be fulfilled.

4   It should be of the pleasure of a poem itself to tell how it can. The figure a poem makes. It begins in delight and ends in wisdom. The figure is the same as for love. No one can really hold that the ecstasy should be static and stand still in one place. It begins in delight, it inclines to the impulse, it assumes direction with the first line laid down, it runs a course of lucky events, and ends in a clarification of life — not necessarily a great clarification, such as sects and cults are founded on, but in a momentary stay against confusion. It has denouement. It has an outcome that though unforeseen was predestined from the first image of the original mood — and indeed from the very mood. It is but a trick poem and no poem at all if the best of it was thought of first and saved for the last. It finds its own name as it goes and discovers the best waiting for it in some final phrase at once wise and sad — the happy-sad blend of the drinking song.

5   No tears in the writer, no tears in the reader. No surprise for the writer, no surprise for the reader. For me the initial delight is in the surprise of remembering something I didn't know I knew. I am in a place, in a situation, as if I had materialized from cloud or risen out of the ground. There is a glad recognition of the long lost and the rest follows. Step by step the wonder of unexpected supply keeps growing. The impressions most useful to my purpose seem always those I was unaware of and so made no note of at the time when taken, and the conclusion is come to that like giants we are always hurling experience ahead of us to pave the future with against the day when we may want to strike a line of purpose across it for somewhere. The line will have the more

charm for not being mechanically straight. We enjoy the straight crookedness of a good walking stick. Modern instruments of precision are being used to make things crooked as if by eye and hand in the old days.

I tell how there may be a better wildness of logic than of inconse- 6 quence. But the logic is backward, in retrospect, after the act. It must be more felt than seen ahead like prophecy. It must be a revelation, or a series of revelations, as much for the poet as for the reader. For it to be that there must have been the greatest freedom of the material to move about in it and to establish relations in it regardless of time and space, previous relation, and everything but affinity. We prate of freedom. We call our schools free because we are not free to stay away from them till we are sixteen years of age. I have given up my democratic prejudices and now willingly set the lower classes free to be completely taken care of by the upper classes. Political freedom is nothing to me. I bestow it right and left. All I would keep for myself is the freedom of my material — the condition of body and mind now and then to summons aptly from the vast chaos of all I have lived through.

Scholars and artists thrown together are often annoyed at the puz- 7 zle of where they differ. Both work from knowledge; but I suspect they differ most importantly in the way their knowledge is come by. Scholars get theirs with conscientious thoroughness along projected lines of logic; poets theirs cavalierly and as it happens in and out of books. They stick to nothing deliberately, but let what will stick to them like burrs where they walk in the fields. No acquirement is on assignment, or even self-assignment. Knowledge of the second kind is much more available in the wild free ways of wit and art. A school boy may be defined as one who can tell you what he knows in the order in which he learned it. The artist must value himself as he snatches a thing from some previous order in time and space into a new order with not so much as a ligature clinging to it of the old place where it was organic.

More than once I should have lost my soul to radicalism if it had 8 been the originality it was mistaken for by its young converts. Originality and initiative are what I ask for my country. For myself the originality need be no more than the freshness of a poem run in the way I have described: from delight to wisdom. The figure is the same as for love. Like a piece of ice on a hot stove the poem must ride on its own melting. A poem may be worked over once it is in being, but may not be worried into being. Its most precious quality will remain its having run itself and carried away the poet with it. Read it a hundred times: it will forever keep its freshness as a metal keeps its fragrance. It can never lose its sense of a meaning that once unfolded by surprise as it went.

——— CONSIDERATIONS ———————————————

1. Frost's title, "The Figure a Poem Makes," suggests something of a pun: "figure" might well refer to the shape the poem takes and/or the importance of figures of speech the poet uses. Name three or four similes and metaphors in the essay. What do they have in common? How do they differ from the serious tone of the overall piece?

2. In Paragraph 4, Frost gives the poem-in-the-making a life of its own, one not controlled by the poet. How does this image contribute to the ideas in Paragraph 5?

3. Perhaps because as a poet, he values compression in writing, Frost's essay is densely packed with an accumulated knowledge of his subject and may be difficult reading for those trained in speed reading. Examine his first paragraph or the first three sentences of Paragraph 6 and try your hand at rewriting them, laying out the ideas more fully.

4. In Paragraph 6, Frost expresses his feelings about "freedom." Are these expressions relevant to the subject of his essay?

5. If you agree with Frost that the figure a poem makes is the same for love, write an essay showing how love, "like a piece of ice on a hot stove . . . must ride on its own melting."

6. Read the two versions of Frost's poem preceding this essay and decide whether either "poem begins in delight and ends in wisdom." Is the later version an improvement? Compare Frost's work with Emily Dickinson's "There's a certain Slant of light," (pages 127–128), Langston Hughes's "Two Poems," (pages 215–219), Etheridge Knight's "The Idea of Ancestry," (pages 226–227), Andrew Marvell's "To His Coy Mistress," (pages 255–256), Leslie Marmon Silko's "Slim Man Canyon," (pages 379–380), and William Stafford's "Traveling in the Dark," (page 393).

Martin Gansberg (b. 1920) edited and reported for The New
York Times *for forty years. This story, written in 1964, has
been widely reprinted. Largely because of Gansberg's account,
the murder of Kitty Genovese has become an infamous example of citizen apathy. When Gansberg returned to the
neighborhood fifteen years afterward, revisiting the place of the
murder with a television crew, the people had not changed:
still, no one wanted to get involved.*

32

MARTIN GANSBERG

38 Who Saw Murder Didn't Call the Police

For more than half an hour 38 respectable, law-abiding citizens in   1
Queens watched a killer stalk and stab a woman in three separate attacks in Kew Gardens.

Twice their chatter and the sudden glow of their bedroom lights   2
interrupted him and frightened him off. Each time he returned, sought
her out, and stabbed her again. Not one person telephoned the police
during the assault; one witness called after the woman was dead.

That was two weeks ago today.   3

Still shocked is Assistant Chief Inspector Frederick M. Lussen, in   4
charge of the borough's detectives and a veteran of 25 years of homicide
investigations. He can give a matter-of-fact recitation on many murders.
But the Kew Gardens slaying baffles him — not because it is a murder,
but because the "good people" failed to call the police.

5   "As we have reconstructed the crime," he said, "the assailant had three chances to kill this woman during a 35-minute period. He returned twice to complete the job. If we had been called when he first attacked, the woman might not be dead now."

6   This is what the police say happened beginning at 3:20 A.M. in the staid, middle-class, tree-lined Austin Street area:

7   Twenty-eight-year-old Catherine Genovese, who was called Kitty by almost everyone in the neighborhood was returning home from her job as manager of a bar in Hollis. She parked her red Fiat in a lot adjacent to the Kew Gardens Long Island Rail Road Station, facing Mowbray Place. Like many residents of the neighborhood, she had parked there day after day since her arrival from Connecticut a year ago, although the railroad frowns on the practice.

8   She turned off the lights of her car, locked the door, and started to walk the 100 feet to the entrance of her apartment at 82–70 Austin Street, which is in a Tudor building, with stores in the first floor and apartments on the second.

9   The entrance to the apartment is in the rear of the building because the front is rented to retail stores. At night the quiet neighborhood is shrouded in the slumbering darkness that marks most residential areas.

10   Miss Genovese noticed a man at the far end of the lot, near a seven-story apartment house at 82–40 Austin Street. She halted. Then, nervously, she headed up Austin Street toward Lefferts Boulevard, where there is a call box to the 102nd Police Precinct in nearby Richmond Hill.

11   She got as far as a street light in front of a bookstore before the man grabbed her. She screamed. Lights went on in the 10-story apartment house at 82–67 Austin Street, which faces the bookstore. Windows slid open and voices punctuated the early-morning stillness.

12   Miss Genovese screamed: "Oh, my God, he stabbed me! Please help me! Please help me!"

13   From one of the upper windows in the apartment house, a man called down: "Let that girl alone!"

14   The assailant looked up at him, shrugged and walked down Austin Street toward a white sedan parked a short distance away. Miss Genovese struggled to her feet.

15   Lights went out. The killer returned to Miss Genovese, now trying to make her way around the side of the building by the parking lot to get to her apartment. The assailant stabbed her again.

16   "I'm dying!" she shrieked. "I'm dying!"

Windows were opened again, and lights went on in many apart-   17
ments. The assailant got into his car and drove away. Miss Genovese
staggered to her feet. A city bus, O–10, the Lefferts Boulevard line to
Kennedy International Airport, passed. It was 3:35 A.M.

The assailant returned. By then, Miss Genovese had crawled to   18
the back of the building, where the freshly painted brown doors to the
apartment house held out hope for safety. The killer tried the first door;
she wasn't there. At the second door, 82–62 Austin Street, he saw her
slumped on the floor at the foot of the stairs. He stabbed her a third
time — fatally.

It was 3:50 by the time the police received their first call, from   19
a man who was a neighbor of Miss Genovese. In two minutes they were
at the scene. The neighbor, a 70-year-old woman, and another woman
were the only persons on the street. Nobody else came forward.

The man explained that he had called the police after much   20
deliberation. He had phoned a friend in Nassau County for advice and
then he had crossed the roof of the building to the apartment of the
elderly woman to get her to make the call.

"I didn't want to get involved," he sheepishly told the police.   21

Six days later, the police arrested Winston Moseley, a 29-year-old   22
business-machine operator, and charged him with homicide. Moseley
had no previous record. He is married, has two children and owns a home
at 133–19 Sutter Avenue, South Ozone Park, Queens. On Wednesday,
a court committed him to Kings County Hospital for psychiatric
observation.

When questioned by the police, Moseley also said that he had slain   23
Mrs. Annie May Johnson, 24, of 146–12 133d Avenue, Jamaica, on Feb.
29 and Barbara Kralik, 15, of 174–17 140th Avenue, Springfield Gardens,
last July. In the Kralik case, the police are holding Alvin L. Mitchell,
who is said to have confessed that slaying.

The police stressed how simple it would have been to have gotten   24
in touch with them. "A phone call," said one of the detectives, "would
have done it." The police may be reached by dialing "O" for operator
or SPring 7–3100.

Today witnesses from the neighborhood, which is made up of one-   25
family homes in the $35,000 to $60,000 range with the exception of the
two apartment houses near the railroad station, find it difficult to explain why they didn't call the police.

A housewife, knowingly if quite casually, said, "We thought it was   26
a lover's quarrel." A husband and wife both said, "Frankly, we were

afraid." They seemed aware of the fact that events might have been different. A distraught woman, wiping her hands in her apron, said, "I didn't want my husband to get involved."

27   One couple, now willing to talk about that night, said they heard the first screams. The husband looked thoughtfully at the bookstore where the killer first grabbed Miss Genovese.

28   "We went to the window to see what was happening," he said, "but the light from our bedroom made it difficult to see the street." The wife, still apprehensive, added: "I put out the light and we were able to see better."

29   Asked why they hadn't called the police, she shrugged and replied: "I don't know."

30   A man peeked out from a light opening in the doorway to his apartment and rattled off an account of the killer's second attack. Why hadn't he called the police at the time? "I was tired," he said without emotion. "I went back to bed."

31   It was 4:25 A.M. when the ambulance arrived to take the body of Miss Genovese. It drove off. "Then," a solemn police detective said, "the people came out."

___ CONSIDERATIONS _____

    1. Obviously — though not overtly — Gansberg's newspaper account condemns the failure of ordinary citizens to feel socially responsible. Explain how the writer makes his purpose obvious without openly stating it. Compare his method with Orwell's use of implication in "A Hanging."

    2. In Paragraph 7, Gansberg tells us that Catherine Genovese was called Kitty and that she drove a red Fiat. Are these essential details? If not, why does this writer use them?

    3. Newspapers use short paragraphs for visual relief. If you were making this story into a narrative essay, how might you change the paragraphing?

    4. Is Gansberg's opening sentence a distortion of the facts? Read his account carefully before you answer; then explain and support your answer with reference to other parts of the story.

    5. Gansberg's newspaper report was published nearly twenty years ago. Are similar incidents more common now? Were they more common in the 1960s than in the 1940s, 1920s, 1900s? In what way does media coverage affect our impressions? What sources could you use to find the facts?

Stephen Jay Gould (b. 1941) is a paleontologist who teaches at Harvard and writes scientific essays for the general reader. He calls himself "an evolutionist," for Darwin and the theory of evolution live at the center of his mind. He has written several books, of which four collect his periodical essays: Ever Since Darwin *(1977),* The Panda's Thumb *(1980),* Hen's Teeth and Horse's Toes *(1983), and* The Flamingo's Smile. *Gould's lively mind, eager to use scientific method for public thinking, seeks out diverse subjects and often discovers a political flavor in matters not usually perceived as political.*

33

STEPHEN JAY GOULD
The Politics of Census

In the constitution of the United States, the same passage that prescribes a census every ten years also includes the infamous statement that slaves shall be counted as three-fifths of a person. Ironically, and however different the setting and motives, black people are still undercounted in the American census because poor people in inner cities are systematically missed.   1

The census has always been controversial because it was established as a political device, not as an expensive frill to satisfy curiosity and feed academic mills. The constitutional passage that ordained the census begins: "Representatives and direct taxes shall be apportioned among the several states which may be included within this union, according to their respective numbers."   2

3   Political use of the census has often extended beyond the alloca-
tion of taxation and representation. The sixth census of 1840 engendered
a heated controversy based upon the correct contention that certain
black people had, for once, been falsely *over*counted. This curious tale
illustrates the principle that copious numbers do not guarantee objectivity and that even the most careful and rigorous surveys are only as
good as their methods and assumptions. (William Stanton tells the story
in *The Leopard's Spots,* his excellent book on the history of scientific
attitudes toward race in America during the first half of the nineteenth
century. I have also read the original papers of the major protagonist,
Edward Jarvis.)

4   The 1840 census was the first to include counts of the mentally
ill and deficient, enumerated by race and by state. Dr. Edward Jarvis,
then a young physician but later to become a national authority on
medical statistics, rejoiced that the frustrations of inadequate data would
soon be overcome. He wrote in 1844:

> The statistics of insanity are becoming more and more an object of
> interest to philanthropists, to political economists, and to men of
> science. But all investigations, conducted by individuals or by
> associations, have been partial, incomplete, and far from satisfac-
> tory. . . . They could not tell the numbers of any class or people,
> among whom they found a definite number of the insane. And
> therefore, as a ground of comparison of the prevalence of insanity
> in one country with that of another, or in one class or race of peo-
> ple with that in another, their reports did not answer their intended
> purpose.

5   Jarvis then praised the marshals of the 1840 census as apostles of
the new, quantitative order:

> As these functionaries were ordered to inquire from house to house,
> and leave no dwelling — neither mansion nor cabin — neither tent
> nor ship unvisited and unexamined, it was reasonably supposed that
> there would be a complete and accurate account of the prevalence
> of insanity among 17 millions of people. A wider field than this had
> never been surveyed for this purpose in any part of the earth, since
> the world began. . . . Never had the philanthropist a better promise
> of truth hitherto undiscovered. . . . Many proceeded at once to
> analyze the tables, in order to show the proportion of lunacy in the
> various states, and among the two races, which constitute our
> population.

6   As scholars and ideologues of varying stripes scrutinized the tables,
one apparent fact rose to obvious prominence in those troubled times.

Among blacks, insanity struck free people in northern states far more often than it afflicted slaves in the South. In fact, one in 162 blacks was insane in free states, but only one in 1,558 in slave states. But freedom and the North posed no mental terror for whites, since their relative sanity did not differ in the North and South.

Moreover, insanity among blacks seemed to decrease in even grada-   7
tion from the harsh North to the congenial South. One in 14 of Maine's black population was either insane or idiotic; in New Hampshire, one in 28; in Massachusetts, one in 43; in New Jersey, one in 279. In Delaware, however, the frequency of insanity among blacks suddenly nose-dived. As Stanton writes: "It appeared that Mason and Dixon had surveyed a line not only between Maryland and Pennsylvania but also — surely all unwitting — between Sanity and Bedlam."

In his first publication on the 1840 census, Jarvis drew the same   8
conclusion that so many other whites would advance: slavery, if not the natural state of black people, must have a remarkably beneficent effect upon them. It must exert "a wonderful influence upon the development of moral faculties and the intellectual powers." A slave gains equanimity by "refusing many of the hopes and responsibilities which the free, self-thinking and self-acting enjoy and sustain," for bondage "saves him from some of the liabilities and dangers of active self-direction."

The basic "fact" of ten times more insanity in freedom than in   9
slavery was widely bruited about in the contemporary press, often in lurid fashion. Stanton quotes a contributor to the *Southern Literary Messenger* (1843) who, concluding that blacks grow "more vicious in a state of freedom," painted a frightful picture of Virginia should it ever become a free state, with "all sympathy on the part of the master to the slave ended." He inquired:

> Where should we find penitentiaries for the thousands of felons? Where, lunatic asylums for the tens of thousands of maniacs? Would it be possible to live in a country where maniacs and felons meet the traveler at every crossroad.

But Jarvis was troubled. The disparity between North and South   10
made sense to him, but its extent was puzzling. Could slavery possibly make such an enormous difference? If the information had not been stamped with a governmental imprimatur, who could have believed it? Jarvis wrote:

> This was so improbable, so contrary to common experience, there was in it such a strong prima facie evidence of error, that nothing but a document, coming forth with all the authority of the national

government, and "corrected in the department of state," could have gained for it the least credence among the inhabitants of the free states, where insanity was stated to abound so plentifully.

11   Jarvis therefore began to examine the tables and was shocked by what he discovered. Somehow, and in a fashion that could scarcely represent a set of random accidents, the number of insane blacks had been absurdly inflated in reported figures for northern states. Jarvis discovered that twenty-five towns in the twelve free states contained not a single black person of sound mind. The figure for "all blacks" had obviously been recopied or misplaced in the column for "insane blacks." But data for 135 additional towns (including thirty-nine in Ohio and twenty in New York) could not be explained so easily, for these towns actually reported a population of insane blacks greater than the total number of blacks, both sane and unhinged!

12   In a few cases, Jarvis was able to track down the source of error. Worcester, Massachusetts, for example, reported 133 insane in a total black population of 151. Jarvis inquired and discovered that these 133 people were white patients living in the state mental hospital located there. With this single correction, the first among many, black insanity in Massachusetts dropped from one in 43 to one in 129. Jarvis, demoralized and angry, began a decade of unsuccessful campaigning to win an official retraction or correction of the 1840 census. He began:

> Such a document as we have described, heavy with its errors and its misstatements, instead of being a messenger of truth to the world to enlighten its knowledge and guide its opinions, it is, in respect to human ailment, a bearer of falsehood to confuse and mislead.

13   This debate was destined for a more significant fate than persistent bickering in literary and scholarly journals. For Jarvis's disclosures caught the ear of a formidable man: John Quincy Adams, then near eighty, and capping a distinguished career as leader of antislavery forces in the House of Representatives. But Adams's opponent was equally formidable. At that time, the census fell under the jurisdiction of the Department of State, and its newly appointed secretary was none other than John C. Calhoun, the cleverest and most vigorous defender of slavery in America.

14   Calhoun, in one of his first acts in office, used the incorrect but official census figures in responding to the expressed hope of the British foreign secretary, Lord Aberdeen, that slavery would not be permitted in the new republic (soon to be state) of Texas. The census proved, Calhoun wrote to Aberdeen, that northern blacks had "invariably sunk

into vice and pauperism, accompanied by the bodily and mental afflictions incident thereto," while states that had retained what Calhoun called, in genteel euphemism, "the ancient relation" between races, contained a black population that had "improved greatly in every respect — in number, comfort, intelligence, and morals."

Calhoun then proceeded to evade the official request from the   15
House, passed on Adams's motion, that the secretary of state report on errors in the census and steps that would be taken to correct them. Adams then accosted Calhoun in his office and recorded the secretary's response in his diary:

> He writhed like a trodden rattlesnake on the exposure of his false report to the House that no material errors had been discovered in the printed Census of 1840, and finally said that there were so many errors they balanced one another, and led to the same conclusion as if they were all correct.

Jarvis, meanwhile, had enlisted the support of the Massachusetts   16
Medical Society and the American Statistical Association. Armed with new data and support, Adams again persuaded the House to ask Calhoun for an official explanation. And again Calhoun wriggled out, finally delivering a report full of obfuscation and rhetoric, and still citing the 1840 figures on insanity as proof that freedom would be "a curse instead of a blessing" for black slaves. Jarvis lived until 1884 and assisted in the censuses of 1850, 1860, and 1870. But he never won official rectification of the errors he had uncovered in the 1840 census; the finagled, if not outrightly fraudulent, data on insanity among blacks continued to be cited as an argument for slavery as the Civil War approached.

There is a world of difference between the overcount of insane   17
blacks in 1840 and the undercount of poor blacks (and other groups) in central cities in 1980. First, although the source of error in the 1840 census has never been determined, we may strongly suspect some systematic, perhaps conscious manipulation by those charged with putting the raw data in tabular form. I think we can be reasonably confident that, with automated procedures and more deliberate care, the systematic errors of the 1980 census are at least honest ones. Second, the politics of 1840 left few channels open to critics, and Calhoun's evasive stubbornness finally prevailed. Today, nearly every census is subjected to legal scrutiny and challenge.

Yet behind these legal struggles stands the fact that we still do not   18
know how to count people accurately. Voluminous numbers and extensive tabulation do not guarantee objectivity. If you can't find peo-

ple, you can't count them — and the American census is, by law, an attempt at exhaustive counting, not a statistical operation based on sampling.

19   If it were possible (however expensive) to count everyone with confidence, then no valid complaint could be raised. But it is not, and the very attempt to do so engenders a systematic error that guarantees failure. For some people are much harder to find than others, either by their direct resistance to being counted (illegal aliens, for example) or by the complex of unfortunate circumstances that renders the poor more anonymous than other Americans.

20   Regions with a concentration of poor people will be systematically undercounted, and such regions are not spread across America at random. They are located in the heart of our major cities. A census that assesses populations by direct counting will be a source of endless contention so long as federal money and representation in Congress reach cities as rewards for greater numbers.

21   Censusing has always been controversial, especially since its historical purpose has usually involved taxation or conscription. When David, inveigled by Satan himself, had the chutzpah to "number" Israel (I Chronicles, chapter 21), the Lord punished him by offering some unpleasant alternatives: three years of famine, three months of devastation by enemy armies, or three days of pestilence (all reducing the population, perhaps to countable levels). The legacy of each American census seems to be ten years of contention.

—— CONSIDERATIONS ————————————————————

1. A writer's thesis sentence unifies his or her essay and at the same time gives it point and direction. Suppose the second sentence of Paragraph 1 and the first sentence of Paragraph 2 were both nominated as Gould's thesis. Which would you choose? Why? Examine your own compositions to see if they might be improved by more careful attention to the thesis statement.

2. "The Politics of Census" could be called a book review, since Gould's principal source was a book-length account published originally in 1960. Gould's essay, however, is not a simple retelling of Stanton's book. What additional research has Gould carried out, and how has he brought the account of census making up-to-date?

3. Although census techniques have greatly improved since the nineteenth century, Gould maintains that a perfect count is still impossible. Why?

4. Is the account of Calhoun's refusal to acknowledge Jarvis's findings a destructive exposé of government corruption or a constructive job of historical

research? Explain, in a short essay, the difference between destructive and constructive criticism.

   5. Gould refers, in Paragraph 18, to the difference between counting and sampling. How are we affected today by research based on sampling? Setting aside the possibility of dishonesty, how can such research produce what scientists call "skewed" results?

   6. Gould was obviously attracted to the story of the 1840 census by the detective story inherent in Jarvis's quest for truth. Is it sensible to think of research as detective work? Discuss, with examples of your own finding. (An interesting source for examples of researcher-detectives is Richard D. Altick's *The Art of Literary Research*. New York: Norton, 1963.)

Lillian Hellman (1905–1984) was a playwright, born in New Orleans, who grew up in New Orleans and New York City. After graduating from New York University, she went to work in publishing. The Children's Hour *(1934), her first great success on Broadway, was followed by her most famous play,* The Little Foxes *(1939), and* Watch on the Rhine *(1941). She also wrote the book for Leonard Bernstein's musical,* Candide.

Hellman's later works were autobiographical, and include Pentimento *(1973),* Scoundrel Time *(1977), and* An Unfinished Woman, *which won the National Book Award in 1970. These narratives were collected into one volume with new commentary by the author:* Three *(1979). In 1980 she published* Maybe: A Story.

The anecdote below, which is from An Unfinished Woman, *tells of a climactic episode in the transition from childhood to adolescence, and shows the rebelliousness, strong feeling, and independence that become themes of the autobiography.*

34

LILLIAN HELLMAN
Runaway

1   It was that night that I disappeared, and that night that Fizzy said I was disgusting mean, and Mr. Stillman said I would forever pain my mother and father, and my father turned on both of them and said he would handle his family affairs himself without comments from strangers. But he said it too late. He had come home very angry with me: the jeweler, after my father's complaints about his unreliability, had found the lock of hair in the back of the watch. What started out

to be a mild reproof on my father's part soon turned angry when I wouldn't explain about the hair. (My father was often angry when I was most like him.) He was so angry that he forgot that he was attacking me in front of the Stillmans, my old rival Fizzy, and the delighted Mrs. Dreyfus, a new, rich boarder who only that afternoon had complained about my bad manners. My mother left the room when my father grew angry with me. Hannah, passing through, put up her hand as if to stop my father and then, frightened of the look he gave her, went out to the porch. I sat on the couch, astonished at the pain in my head. I tried to get up from the couch, but one ankle turned and I sat down again, knowing for the first time the rampage that could be caused in me by anger. The room began to have other forms, the people were no longer men and women, my head was not my own. I told myself that my head had gone somewhere and I have little memory of anything after my Aunt Jenny came into the room and said to my father, "Don't you remember?" I have never known what she meant, but I knew that soon after I was moving up the staircase, that I slipped and fell a few steps, that when I woke up hours later in my bed, I found a piece of angel cake — an old love, an old custom — left by my mother on my pillow. The headache was worse and I vomited out of the window. Then I dressed, took my red purse, and walked a long way down St. Charles Avenue. A St. Charles Avenue mansion had on its back lawn a famous doll's-house, an elaborate copy of the mansion itself, built years before for the small daughter of the house. As I passed this showpiece, I saw a policeman and moved swiftly back to the doll palace and crawled inside. If I had known about the fantasies of the frightened, that ridiculous small house would not have been so terrible for me. I was surrounded by ornate, carved reproductions of the mansion furniture, scaled for children, bisque figurines in miniature, a working toilet seat of gold leaf in suitable size, small draperies of damask with a sign that said "From the damask of Marie Antoinette," a miniature samovar with small bronze cups, and a tiny Madame Récamier couch on which I spent the night, my legs on the floor. I must have slept, because I woke from a nightmare and knocked over a bisque figurine. The noise frightened me, and since it was now almost light, in one of those lovely mist mornings of late spring when every flower in New Orleans seems to melt and mix with the air, I crawled out. Most of that day I spent walking, although I had a long session in the ladies' room of the railroad station. I had four dollars and two bits, but that wasn't much when you meant it to last forever and when you knew it would not be easy for a fourteen-year-old girl to find work in a city where too many people knew her. Three times

I stood in line at the railroad ticket windows to ask where I could go for four dollars, but each time the question seemed too dangerous and I knew no other way of asking.

2   Toward evening, I moved to the French Quarter, feeling sad and envious as people went home to dinner. I bought a few Tootsie Rolls and a half loaf of bread and went to the St. Louis Cathedral in Jackson Square. (It was that night that I composed the prayer that was to become, in the next five years, an obsession, mumbled over and over through the days and nights: "God forgive me, Papa forgive me, Mama forgive me, Sophronia, Jenny, Hannah, and all others, through this time and that time, in life and in death." When I was nineteen, my father, who had made several attempts through the years to find out what my lip movements meant as I repeated the prayer, said, "How much would you take to stop that? Name it and you've got it." I suppose I was sick of the nonsense by that time because I said, "A leather coat and a feather fan," and the next day he bought them for me.) After my loaf of bread, I went looking for a bottle of soda pop and discovered, for the first time, the whorehouse section around Bourbon Street. The women were ranged in the doorways of the cribs, making the first early evening offers to sailors, who were the only men in the streets. I wanted to stick around and see how things like that worked, but the second or third time I circled the block, one of the girls called out to me. I couldn't understand the words, but the voice was angry enough to make me run toward the French Market.

3   The Market was empty except for two old men. One of them called to me as I went past, and I turned to see that he had opened his pants and was shaking what my circle called "his thing." I flew across the street into the coffee stand, forgetting that the owner had known me since I was a small child when my Aunt Jenny would rest from her marketing tour with a cup of fine, strong coffee.

4   He said, in the patois, *"Que faites, ma 'fant? Je suis fermé."*

5   I said, *"Rien. My tante attend"* — Could I have a doughnut?

6   He brought me two doughnuts, saying one was *lagniappe,* but I took my doughnuts outside when he said, *"Mais ou est vo' tante à c'heure?"*

7   I fell asleep with my doughnuts behind a shrub in Jackson Square. The night was damp and hot and through the sleep were many voices and, much later, there was music from somewhere near the river. When all sounds had ended, I woke, turned my head, and knew I was being watched. Two rats were sitting a few feet from me. I urinated on my dress, crawled backwards to stand up, screamed as I ran up the steps

of St. Louis Cathedral and pounded on the doors. I don't know when I stopped screaming or how I got to the railroad station, but I stood against the wall trying to tear off my dress and only knew I was doing it when two women stopped to stare at me. I began to have cramps in my stomach of a kind I had never known before. I went into the ladies' room and sat bent in a chair, whimpering with pain. After a while the cramps stopped, but I had an intimation, when I looked into the mirror, of something happening to me: my face was blotched, and there seemed to be circles and twirls I had never seen before, the straight blonde hair was damp with sweat, and a paste of green from the shrub had made lines on my jaw. I had gotten older.

Sometime during that early morning I half washed my dress, threw away my pants, put cold water on my hair. Later in the morning a cleaning woman appeared, and after a while began to ask questions that frightened me. When she put down her mop and went out of the room, I ran out of the station. I walked, I guess, for many hours, but when I saw a man on Canal Street who worked in Hannah's office, I realized that the sections of New Orleans that were known to me were dangerous for me.

Years before, when I was a small child, Sophronia and I would go to pick up, or try on, pretty embroidered dresses that were made for me by a colored dressmaker called Bibettera. A block up from Bibettera's there had been a large ruin of a house with a sign, ROOMS — CLEAN — CHEAP, and cheerful people seemed always to be moving in and out of the house. The door of the house was painted a bright pink. I liked that and would discuss with Sophronia why we didn't live in a house with a pink door.

Bibettera was long since dead, so I knew I was safe in this Negro neighborhood. I went up and down the block several times, praying that things would work and I could take my cramps to bed. I knocked on the pink door. It was answered immediately by a small young man.

I said, "Hello." He said nothing.

I said, "I would like to rent a room, please."

He closed the door but I waited, thinking he had gone to get the lady of the house. After a long time, a middle-aged woman put her head out of a second-floor window and said, "What you at?"

I said, "I would like to rent a room, please. My mama is a widow and has gone to work across the river. She gave me money and said to come here until she called for me."

Who your mama?"

"Er. My mama."

17   "What you at? Speak out."

18   "I told you. I have money . . ." But as I tried to open my purse, the voice grew angry.

19   "This is a nigger house. Get you off. *Vite.*"

20   I said, in a whisper, "I know. I'm part nigger."

21   The small young man opened the front door. He was laughing. "You part mischief. Get the hell out of here."

22   I said, "Please" — and then, "I'm related to Sophronia Mason. She told me to come. Ask her."

23   Sophronia and her family were respected figures in New Orleans Negro circles, and because I had some vague memory of her stately bow to somebody as she passed this house, I believed they knew her. If they told her about me I would be in trouble, but phones were not usual then in poor neighborhoods, and I had no other place to go.

24   The woman opened the door. Slowly I went into the hall.

25   I said, "I won't stay long. I have four dollars and Sophronia will give more if . . ."

26   The woman pointed up the stairs. She opened the door of a small room. "Washbasin place down the hall. Toilet place behind the kitchen. Two-fifty and no fuss, no bother."

27   I said, "Yes, ma'am, yes ma'am," but as she started to close the door, the young man appeared.

28   "Where your bag?"

29   "Bag?"

30   "Nobody put up here without no bag."

31   "Oh. You mean the bag with my clothes? It's at the station. I'll go and get it later . . ." I stopped because I knew I was about to say I'm sick, I'm in pain, I'm frightened.

32   He said, "I say you lie. I say you trouble. I say you get out."

33   I said, "And I say you shut up."

34   Years later, I was to understand why the command worked, and to be sorry that it did, but that day I was very happy when he turned and closed the door. I was asleep within minutes.

35   Toward evening, I went down the stairs, saw nobody, walked a few blocks and bought myself an oyster loaf. But the first bite made me feel sick, so I took my loaf back to the house. This time, as I climbed the steps, there were three women in the parlor, and they stopped talking when they saw me. I went back to sleep immediately, dizzy and nauseated.

36   I woke to a high, hot sun and my father standing at the foot of the bed staring at the oyster loaf.

He said, "Get up now and get dressed."   37

I was crying as I said, "Thank you, Papa, but I can't."   38

From the hall, Sophronia said, "Get along up now. *Vite.* The mor-   39
ning is late."

My father left the room. I dressed and came into the hall carrying   40
my oyster loaf. Sophronia was standing at the head of the stairs. She
pointed out, meaning my father was on the street.

I said, "He humiliated me. He did. I won't . . ."   41

She said, "Get you going or I will never see you whenever again."   42

I ran past her to the street. I stood with my father until Sophronia 43
joined us, and then we walked slowly, without speaking, to the street-
car line. Sophronia bowed to us, but she refused my father's hand when
he attempted to help her into the car. I ran to the car meaning to ask
her to take me with her, but the car moved and she raised her hand
as if to stop me. My father and I walked again for a long time.

He pointed to a trash can sitting in front of a house. "Please put   44
that oyster loaf in the can."

At Vanalli's restaurant, he took my arm. "Hungry?"   45

I said, "No, thank you, Papa."   46

But we went through the door. It was, in those days, a New Orleans   47
custom to have an early black coffee, go to the office, and after a few
hours have a large breakfast at a restaurant. Vanalli's was crowded, the
headwaiter was so sorry, but after my father took him aside, a very small
table was put up for us — too small for my large father, who was ac-
commodating himself to it in a manner most unlike him.

He said, "Jack, my rumpled daughter would like cold crayfish, a   48
nice piece of pompano, separate bowl of Béarnaise sauce, don't ask me
why, French fried potatoes . . ."

I said, "Thank you, Papa, but I am not hungry. I don't want to be   49
here."

My father waved the waiter away and we sat in silence until the   50
crayfish came. My hand reached out instinctively and then drew back.

My father said, "Your mother and I have had an awful time."   51

I said, "I'm sorry about that. But I don't want to go home, Papa."   52

He said, angrily, "Yes, you do. But you want me to apologize first.   53
I do apologize but you should not have made me say it."

After a while I mumbled, "God forgive me, Papa forgive me, Mama   54
forgive me, Sophronia, Jenny, Hannah . . ."

"Eat your crayfish."   55

I ate everything he had ordered and then a small steak. I suppose   56
I had been mumbling throughout my breakfast.

57   My father said, "You're talking to yourself. I can't hear you. What are you saying.?"

58   "God forgive me, Papa forgive me, Mama forgive me, Sophronia, Jenny . . ."

59   My father said, "Where do we start your training as the first Jewish nun on Prytania Street?"

60   When I finished laughing, I liked him again. I said, "Papa, I'll tell you a secret. I've had very bad cramps and I am beginning to bleed. I'm changing life."

61   He stared at me for a while. Then he said, "Well, it's not the way it's usually described, but it's accurate, I guess. Let's go home now to your mother."

62   We were never, as long as my mother and father lived, to mention that time again. But it was of great importance to them and I've thought about it all my life. From that day on I knew my power over my parents. That was not to be too important: I was ashamed of it and did not abuse it too much. But I found out something more useful and more dangerous: if you are willing to take the punishment, you are halfway through the battle. That the issue may be trivial, the battle ugly, is another point.

___ **CONSIDERATIONS** _____

1. Hellman's recollection of running away at fourteen is complicated by her refusal to tell it in strict chronology. Instead, she interrupts the narratve with flashbacks and episodes of later years. How can one justify such interruptions?

2. On page 202, as she is trying to talk her way into the rooming house in the black district, Hellman tells a young man to shut up and then adds, "Years later, I was to understand why the command worked, and to be sorry that it did." What did she later understand?

3. What was the "power over my parents" that Hellman learned from her runaway experience? Have you ever wielded such power?

4. Accounts of childhood escapades often suffer as the author idealizes or glamorizes them. Does Hellman successfully resist the temptation? What is your evidence?

5. The bases the fourteen-year-old runaway touched in her flight were actually part of a familiar world; a doll's house, a cathedral, a market, a railroad station. How does Hellman give her flight more than a touch of horror?

6. In what specific ways did her first menstrual period heighten and distort some of the things that happened — or seemed to happen — to the fourteen-year-old runaway? Discuss the ways in which physiological and psychological conditions seem to feed upon each other.

Ernest Hemingway (1899–1961) was an ambulance driver and a soldier in World War I, and made use of these experiences in his novel A Farewell to Arms *(1929). One of the Lost Generation of expatriate American writers who lived in Paris in the twenties — a time described in his memoir,* A Moveable Feast *(1964) — he was a great prose stylist and innovator, who received a Nobel Prize for literature in 1954. Other Hemingway novels include* The Sun Also Rises *(1926),* To Have and Have Not *(1937),* For Whom the Bell Tolls *(1940), and* The Garden of Eden, *which was discovered recently and published posthumously in 1986. His* Selected Letters, *edited by Carlos Baker, appeared in 1981.*

Many critics prefer Hemingway's short stories to his novels, and his early stories — "Hills Like White Elephants" among them — to his later ones. This early prose is plain, simple, and clean. This story is dialogue virtually without narrative or description or interpretation; yet when we have finished it we have met two people whom we will not easily forget.

35

ERNEST HEMINGWAY
Hills Like White Elephants

The hills across the valley of the Ebro were long and white. On this side there was no shade and no trees and the station was between two lines of rails in the sun. Close against the side of the station there was the warm shadow of the building and a curtain, made of strings of bamboo beads, hung across the open door into the bar, to keep out 5 flies. The American and the girl with him sat at a table in the shade,

outside the building. It was very hot and the express from Barcelona
would come in forty minutes. It stopped at this junction for two minutes
and went on to Madrid.

10   "What should we drink?" the girl asked. She had taken off her hat
and put it on the table.

"It's pretty hot," the man said.

"Let's drink beer."

"Dos cervezas," the man said into the curtain.

15   "Big ones?" a woman asked from the doorway.

"Yes. Two big ones."

The woman brought two glasses of beer and two felt pads. She put
the felt pads and the beer glasses on the table and looked at the man
and the girl. The girl was looking off at the line of hills. They were white

20 in the sun and the country was brown and dry.

"They look like white elephants," she said.

"I've never seen one." The man drank his beer.

"No, you wouldn't have."

"I might have," the man said. "Just because you say I wouldn't have

25 doesn't prove anything."

The girl looked at the bead curtain. "They've painted something
on it," she said. "What does it say?"

"Anis del Toro. It's a drink."

"Could we try it?"

30   The man called "Listen" through the curtain.

The woman came out from the bar.

"Four reales."

"We want two Anis del Toros."

"With water?"

35   "Do you want it with water?"

"I don't know," the girl said. "Is it good with water?"

"It's all right."

"You want them with water?" asked the woman.

"Yes, with water."

40   "It tastes like licorice," the girl said and put the glass down.

"That's the way with everything."

"Yes," said the girl. "Everything tastes of licorice. Especially all the
things you've waited so long for, like absinthe."

"Oh, cut it out."

45   "You started it," the girl said. "I was being amused. I was having
a fine time."

"Well, let's try and have a fine time."

"All right. I was trying. I said the mountains looked like white elephants. Wasn't that bright?"

"That was bright." 50

"I wanted to try this new drink. That's all we do, isn't it — look at things and try new drinks?"

"I guess so."

The girl looked across at the hills.

"They're lovely hills," she said. "They don't really look like white 55 elephants. I just meant the colouring of their skin through the trees."

"Should we have another drink?"

"All right."

The warm wind blew the bead curtain against the table.

"The beer's nice and cool," the man said. 60

"It's lovely," the girl said.

"It's really an awfully simple operation, Jig," the man said. "It's not really an operation at all."

The girl looked at the ground the table legs rested on.

"I know you wouldn't mind it, Jig. It's really not anything. It's just 65 to let the air in."

The girl did not say anything.

"I'll go with you and I'll stay with you all the time. They just let the air in and then it's all perfectly natural."

"Then what will we do afterwards?" 70

"We'll be fine afterwards. Just like we were before."

"What makes you think so?"

"That's the only thing that bothers us. It's the only thing that's made us unhappy."

The girl looked at the bead curtain, put her hand out and took hold 75 of two of the strings of beads.

"And you think then we'll be all right and be happy."

"I know we will. You don't have to be afraid. I've known lots of people that have done it."

"So have I," said the girl. "And afterward they were all so happy." 80

"Well," the man said, "if you don't want to you don't have to. I wouldn't have you do it if you didn't want to. But I know it's perfectly simple."

"And you really want to?"

"I think it's the best thing to do. But I don't want you to do it if 85 you don't really want to."

"And if I do it you'll be happy and things will be like they were and you'll love me?"

"I love you now. You know I love you."

90   "I know. But if I do it, then it will be nice again if I say things are like white elephants, and you'll like it?"

"I'll love it. I love it now but I just can't think about it. You know how I get when I worry."

"If I do it you won't ever worry?"

95   "I won't worry about that because it's perfectly simple."

"Then I'll do it. Because I don't care about me."

"What do you mean?"

"I don't care about me."

"Well, I care about you."

100   "Oh, yes. But I don't care about me. And I'll do it and then everything will be fine."

"I don't want you to do it if you feel that way."

The girl stood up and walked to the end of the station. Across, on the other side, were fields of grain and trees along the banks of the Ebro.

105   Far away, beyond the river, were mountains. The shadow of a cloud moved across the field of grain and she saw the river through the trees.

"And we could have all this," she said. "And we could have everything and every day we make it more impossible."

"What did you say?"

110   "I said we could have everything."

"We can have everything."

"No, we can't."

"We can have the whole world."

"No, we can't."

115   "We can go everywhere."

"No, we can't. It isn't ours any more."

"It's ours."

"No, it isn't. And once they take it away, you never get it back."

"But they haven't taken it away."

120   "We'll wait and see."

"Come on back in the shade," he said. "You mustn't feel that way."

"I don't feel any way," the girl said. "I just know things."

"I don't want you to do anything that you don't want to do —"

"Nor that isn't good for me," she said. "I know. Could we have an-

125   other beer?"

"All right. But you've got to realize —"

"I realize," the girl said. "Can't we maybe stop talking?"

They sat down at the table and the girl looked across at the hills on the dry side of the valley and the man looked at her and at the table.

"You've got to realize," he said, "that I don't want you to do it if   130
you don't want to. I'm perfectly willing to go through with it if it means
anything to you."

"Doesn't it mean anything to you? We could get along."

"Of course it does. But I don't want anybody but you. I don't want
anyone else. And I know it's perfectly simple."   135

"Yes, you know it's perfectly simple."

"It's all right for you to say that, but I do know it."

"Would you do something for me now?"

"I'd do anything for you."

"Would you please please please please please please please stop   140
talking?"

He did not say anything but looked at the bags against the wall
of the station. There were labels on them from all the hotels where they
had spent nights.

"But I don't want you to," he said, "I don't care anything about it."   145

"I'll scream," the girl said.

The woman came out through the curtains with two glasses of beer
and put them down on the damp felt pads. "The train comes in five
minutes," she said.

"What did she say?" asked the girl.   150

"That the train is coming in five minutes."

The girl smiled brightly at the woman, to thank her.

"I'd better take the bags over to the other side of the station," the
man said. She smiled at him.

"All right. Then come back and we'll finish the beer."   155

He picked up the two heavy bags and carried them around the station to the other tracks. He looked up the tracks but could not see the
train. Coming back, he walked through the bar-room, where people
waiting for the train were drinking. He drank an Anis at the bar and
looked at the people. They were all waiting reasonably for the train.   160
He went out through the bead curtain. She was sitting at the table and
smiled at him.

"Do you feel better?" he asked.

"I feel fine," she said. "There's nothing wrong with me. I feel fine."

_____ **CONSIDERATIONS** _____

1. Nearly all of Hemingway's story is dialogue, often without identifying
phrases such as "he said" or "she said." Does the lack of these phrases make it
difficult to decide which character is speaking? What, if anything, does

Hemingway do to make up for missing dialogue tags? Compare his practice with the way other short story writers in this book handle dialogue.

2. If you have ever questioned the common statement that writers must pay careful attention to *every* word they use, spend a little time examining the way Hemingway uses "it," beginning where the couple start talking about the operation. Try to determine the various possible antecedents for that neutral pronoun in each context where it occurs. Such an effort may help you discover one reason why Hemingway's spare, almost skeletal style is so powerful.

3. Try to put the central conflict of this story in your own words. Imagine yourself the writer suddenly getting the idea for this story and quickly writing a sentence or two to record the idea in your journal. Is that idea anything like the thesis statement of an essay?

4. Why is Hemingway *not* explicit about the kind of operation the two characters are discussing? Is he simply trying to mystify the reader? Does this consideration help you to understand other stories or poems that seem difficult at first?

5. Although Hemingway's description of locale is limited to a few brief passages, he presents a distinct place. How does that place contribute to your understanding the point of the story?

6. Why does Hemingway refuse to describe the two characters? From what the story offers, what do you know about them?

7. Hemingway's story was written in the 1920s. Have the questions he raises about the operation been resolved since then?

Edward Hoagland (b. 1932) was born in New York City and lives there much of the year, alternating between Manhattan and the countryside of northern Vermont. He has written novels but is best known for the essays collected in The Edward Hoagland Reader *(1979) and many other books, including* The Tugman's Passage *(1982) from which we take these notions about the art he practices.*

36

EDWARD HOAGLAND
What I Think, What I Am

Our loneliness makes us avid column readers these days. The personalities in the San Francisco *Chronicle,* Chicago *Daily News,* New York *Post* constitute our neighbors now, some of them local characters but also the opinionated national stars. And movie reviewers thrive on our yearning for somebody emotional who is willing to pay attention to us and return week after week, year after year, through all the to-and-fro of other friends, to flatter us by pouring out his/her heart. They are essayists of a type, as Elizabeth Hardwick is, James Baldwin was.

We sometimes hear that essays are an old-fashioned form, that so-and-so is the "last essayist," but the facts of the marketplace argue quite otherwise. Essays of nearly any kind are so much easier than short stories for a writer to sell, so many more see print, it's strange that though two fine anthologies remain that publish the year's best stories, no comparable collection exists for essays. Such changes in the reading public's taste aren't always to the good, needless to say. The art of telling stories predated even cave painting, surely; and if we ever find ourselves living in caves again, it (with painting and drumming) will be the only art left, after movies, novels, photography, essays, biography, and all the rest have gone down the drain — the art to build from.

3   One has the sense with the short story as a form that while everything may have been done, nothing has been overdone; it has a permanence. Essays, if a comparison is to be made, although they go back four hundred years to Montaigne, seem a mercurial, newfangled, sometimes hokey affair that has lent itself to many of the excesses of the age, from spurious autobiography to spurious hallucination, as well as to the shabby careerism of traditional journalism. It's a greased pig. Essays are associated with the way young writers fashion a name — on plain, crowded newsprint in hybrid vehicles like the *Village Voice, Rolling Stone*, the *New York Review of Books*, instead of the thick paper stock and thin readership of *Partisan Review*.

4   Essays, however, hang somewhere on a line between two sturdy poles: this is what I think, and this is what I am. Autobiographies which aren't novels are generally extended essays, indeed. A personal essay is like the human voice talking, its order the mind's natural flow, instead of a systematized outline of ideas. Though more wayward or informal than an article or treatise, somewhere it contains a point which is its real center, even if the point couldn't be uttered in fewer words than the essayist has used. Essays don't usually boil down to a summary, as articles do, and the style of the writer has a "nap" to it, a combination of personality and originality and energetic loose ends that stand up like the nap on a piece of wool and can't be brushed flat. Essays belong to the animal kingdom, with a surface that generates sparks, like a coat of fur, compared with the flat, conventional cotton of the magazine article writer, who works in the vegetable kingdom, instead. But essays, on the other hand, may have fewer "levels" than fiction, because we are not supposed to argue much about their meaning. In the old distinction between teaching and storytelling, the essayist, however cleverly he camouflages his intentions, is a bit of a teacher or reformer, and an essay is intended to convey the same point to each of us.

5   This emphasis upon mind speaking to mind is what makes essays less universal in their appeal than stories. They are addressed to an educated, perhaps a middle-class, reader, with certain presuppositions, a frame of reference, even a commitment to civility that is shared — not the grand and golden empathy inherent in every man or woman that a storyteller has a chance to tap.

6   Nevertheless, the artful "I" of an essay can be as chameleon as any narrator in fiction; and essays do tell a story quite as often as a short

story stakes a claim to a particular viewpoint. Mark Twain's piece called "Corn-pone Opinions," for example, which is about public opinion, begins with a vignette as vivid as any in *Huckleberry Finn*. Twain says that when he was a boy of fifteen, he used to hang out a back window and listen to the sermons preached by a neighbor's slave standing on top of a woodpile: "He imitated the pulpit style of the several clergymen of the village, and did it well and with fine passion and energy. To me he was a wonder. I believed he was the greatest orator in the United States and would some day be heard from. But it did not happen; in the distribution of rewards he was overlooked. . . . He interrupted his preaching now and then to saw a stick of wood, but the sawing was a pretense — he did it with his mouth, exactly imitating the sound the bucksaw makes in shrieking its way through the wood. But it served its purpose, it kept his master from coming out to see how the work was getting along."

A novel would go on and tell us what happened next in the life   7 of the slave — and we miss that. But the extraordinary flexibility of essays is what has enabled them to ride out rough weather and hybridize into forms that suit the times. And just as one of the first things a fiction writer learns is that he needn't actually be writing fiction to write a short story — that he can tell his own history or anybody else's as exactly as he remembers it and it will be "fiction" if it remains primarily a story — an essayist soon discovers that he doesn't have to tell the whole truth and nothing but the truth; he can shape or shave his memories, as long as the purpose is served of elucidating a truthful point. A personal essay frequently is not autobiographical at all, but what it does keep in common with autobiography is that, through its tone and tumbling progression, it conveys the quality of the author's mind. Nothing gets in the way. Because essays are directly concerned with the mind and the mind's idiosyncrasy, the very freedom the mind possesses is bestowed on this branch of literature that does honor to it, and the fascination of the mind is the fascination of the essay.

_____ CONSIDERATIONS _____

1. Study Hoagland's central idea in the first sentence of Paragraph 4. How closely does his own essay adhere to this statement? Find other pieces in the book to illustrate this thesis.

2. Hoagland's opening sentence could be misread. Do you agree with his generalization about "our loneliness"? What well-known columnists, either local or national, fit the picture he draws in that first paragraph?

3. How else could you describe what Hoagland calls a "nap," in Paragraph 4. Voice? Tone? Personal style?

4. What purpose does Hoagland's excerpt from Mark Twain serve in this essay? Is this an effective technique for getting the point across?

5. Choose three or four selections in this book to illustrate Hoagland's belief that "the flexibility of essays is what has enabled them to . . . hybridize into forms that suit the times."

6. Explain, with examples from this and other essays, what Hoagland means when he states, "A personal essay frequently is not autobiographical at all." Is this true of Berger's "Her Secrets," (pages 57–62), or Berry's "A Native Hill," (pages 63–74), or Shellenbarger's "Selling Off the Family Farm" (pages 373–378)?

Langston Hughes (1902–1967) was a poet, novelist, play-
wright, and essayist who wrote with wit and energy; he was a
leader in the emergence of black American literature in the
twentieth century. More than twenty of his books remain in
print, including Selected Poems; *his autobiography,* I Wonder as
I Wander; *and* The Langston Hughes Reader. *He argues as well*
as he sings the blues — and he knows how to tell a story.

37

LANGSTON HUGHES
Salvation

I was saved from sin when I was going on thirteen. But not really   1
saved. It happened like this. There was a big revival at my Auntie Reed's
church. Every night for weeks there had been much preaching, singing,
praying, and shouting, and some very hardened sinners had been brought
to Christ, and the membership of the church had grown by leaps and
bounds. Then just before the revival ended, they held a special meeting
for children, "to bring the young lambs to the fold." My aunt spoke of
it for days ahead. That night I was escorted to the front row and placed
on the mourners' bench with all the other young sinners, who had not
yet been brought to Jesus.

My aunt told me that when you were saved you saw a light, and   2
something happened to you inside! And Jesus came into your life! And
God was with you from then on! She said you could see and hear and
feel Jesus in your soul. I believed her. I had heard a great many old people say the same thing and it seemed to me they ought to know. So I

sat there calmly in the hot, crowded church, waiting for Jesus to come
to me.

3   The preacher preached a wonderful rhythmical sermon, all moans
and shouts and lonely cries and dire pictures of hell, and then he sang
a song about the ninety and nine safe in the fold, but one little lamb
was left out in the cold. Then he said: "Won't you come? Won't you come
to Jesus? Young lambs, won't you come?" And he held out his arms to
all us young sinners there on the mourners' bench. And the little girls
cried. And some of them jumped up and went to Jesus right away. But
most of us just sat there.

4   A great many old people came and knelt around us and prayed,
old women with jet-black faces and braided hair, old men with work-
gnarled hands. And the church sang a song about the lower lights are
burning, some poor sinners to be saved. And the whole building rocked
with prayer and song.

5   Still I kept waiting to *see* Jesus.

6   Finally all the young people had gone to the altar and were saved,
but one boy and me. He was a rounder's son named Westley. Westley
and I were surrounded by sisters and deacons praying. It was very hot
in the church, and getting late now. Finally Westley said to me in a whisper: "God damn! I'm tired o' sitting here. Let's get up and be saved." So
he got up and was saved.

7   Then I was left all alone on the mourners' bench. My aunt came
and knelt at my knees and cried, while prayers and songs swirled all
around me in the little church. The whole congregation prayed for me
alone, in a mighty wail of moans and voices. And I kept waiting serenely
for Jesus, waiting, waiting — but he didn't come. I wanted to see him,
but nothing happened to me. Nothing! I wanted something to happen
to me, but nothing happened.

8   I heard the songs and the minister saying: "Why don't you come?
My dear child, why don't you come to Jesus? Jesus is waiting for you.
He wants you. Why don't you come? Sister Reed, what is this child's
name?"

9   "Langston," my aunt sobbed.

10   "Langston, why don't you come? Why don't you come and be saved?
Oh, Lamb of God! Why don't you come?"

11   Now it was really getting late. I began to be ashamed of myself,
holding everything up so long. I began to wonder what God thought
about Westley, who certainly hadn't seen Jesus either, but who was now
sitting proudly on the platform, swinging his knickerbockered legs and
grinning down at me, surrounded by deacons and old women on their

knees praying. God had not struck Westley dead for taking his name in vain or for lying in the temple. So I decided that maybe to save further trouble, I'd better lie, too, and say that Jesus had come, and get up and be saved.

So I got up. 12

Suddenly the whole room broke into a sea of shouting, as they saw 13 me rise. Waves of rejoicing swept the place. Women leaped in the air. My aunt threw her arms around me. The minister took me by the hand and led me to the platform.

When things quieted down, in a hushed silence, punctuated by a 14 few ecstatic "Amens," all the new young lambs were blessed in the name of God. Then joyous singing filled the room.

That night, for the last time in my life but one — for I was a big 15 boy twelve years old — I cried. I cried, in my bed alone, and couldn't stop. I buried my head under the quilts, but my aunt heard me. She woke up and told my uncle I was crying because the Holy Ghost had come into my life, and because I had seen Jesus. But I was really crying because I couldn't bear to tell her that I had lied, that I had deceived everybody in the church, and I hadn't seen Jesus, and that now I didn't believe there was a Jesus any more, since he didn't come to help me.

_____ CONSIDERATIONS _____

1. Hughes tells this critical episode of his childhood in a simple, straightforward, unelaborated fashion, almost as though he were still a child telling the story as it happened. Why is it necessary to say *"almost* as though he were still a child"? How would you go about recounting a critical moment in your childhood? Where does simple childhood memory stop and adult judgment take over?

2. Hughes's disillusionment is an example of what people call "an initiation story." Compare it with the Ernest Hemingway short story (pages 205–210), or John Updike's story (pages 427–436), or the autobiographical essay by Lillian Hellman (pages 198–204). Discuss the *degrees* of awareness noticeable among these varied characters.

3. Why is it so important to the congregation of Auntie Reed's church that everyone, children included, acknowledge their salvation?

4. Why does Westley finally proclaim that he is saved?

5. In his final paragraph, Hughes writes, "That night, for the last time in my life but one . . . I cried." He does not tell us, in this account, what that other time was. Read a little more about his life, or simply use your imagination, and write a brief account of the other time.

Langston Hughes's poetry took many forms, and much of it resembled song. If you repeat the first two lines of each stanza of these poems, you will discover the classic form of the blues.

38

LANGSTON HUGHES
Two Poems

BAD LUCK CARD

Cause you don't love me
Is awful, awful hard.
Gypsy done showed me
4 My bad luck card.

There ain't no good left
In this world for me
Gypsy done told me —
8 Unlucky as can be.

I don't know what
Po' weary me can do.
Gypsy says I'd kill my self
12 If I was you.

HOMECOMING

I went back in the alley
And I opened up my door.
All her clothes was gone:
She wasn't home no more.   4

I pulled back the covers.
I made down the bed.
A *whole* lot of room
Was the only thing I had.   8

*Thomas Jefferson (1743–1826) was the third president of the
United States, and perhaps more truly the Father of his Country than George Washington was; or maybe we would only like
to think so, for such paternity flatters the offspring. Jefferson
was a politician, philosopher, architect, inventor, and writer.
With an energy equal to his curiosity, he acted to improve the
world: he wrote the Declaration of Independence; he wrote a
life of Jesus; and he founded the University of Virginia, whose
original buildings he designed. An arch-republican, fearful of
Alexander Hamilton's monarchical reverence for authority,
Jefferson withheld support from the Constitution until he saw
the Bill of Rights added to it.*

We take this text from Garry Wills's Inventing America
*(1978); by juxtaposition, Wills demonstrates the revision of a
classic.*

39

THOMAS JEFFERSON

The Declarations of Jefferson and of the Congress

I will state the form of the declaration as originally reported. The
parts struck out by Congress shall be distinguished by a black line drawn
under them; & those inserted by them shall be placed in the margin
or in a concurrent column:

1   A Declaration by the representatives of the United states of
    America, in [General] Congress assembled.
2   When in the course of human events it becomes necessary for one
    people to dissolve the political bands which have connected them

Taken from Jefferson's Notes and Proceedings — *Papers*, 1:315–319.

with another, and to assume among the powers of the earth the separate & equal station to which the laws of nature and of nature's
god entitle them, a decent respect to the opinions of mankind requires that they should declare the causes which impel them to the
separation.

3   We hold these truths to be self evident: that all men are created
equal; that they are endowed by their creator with ∧ [inherent and]   certain
inalienable rights; that among these are life, liberty & the pursuit
of happiness: that to secure these rights, governments are instituted
among men, deriving their just powers from the consent of the
governed; that whenever any form of government becomes destructive of these ends, it is the right of the people to alter or to abolish
it, & to institute new government, laying it's foundation on such
principles, & organising it's powers in such form, as to them shall
seem most likely to effect their safety & happiness. Prudence indeed will dictate that governments long established should not be
changed for light & transient causes; and accordingly all experience
hath shewn that mankind are more disposed to suffer while evils
are sufferable than to right themselves by abolishing the forms to
which they are accustomed. But when a long train of abuses & usurpations [begun at a distinguished period and] pursuing invariably the
same object, evinces a design to reduce them under absolute
despotism it is their right, it is their duty to throw off such government, & to provide new guards for their future security. Such has
been the patient sufferance of these colonies; & such is now the
necessity which constrains them to ∧ [expunge] their former systems   alter
of government. The history of the present king of Great Britain is
a history of ∧ [unremitting] injuries & usurpations, [among which   repeated
appears no solitary fact to contradict the uniform tenor of the rest
but all have] ∧ in direct object the establishment of an absolute   all having
tyranny over these states. To prove this let facts be submitted to
a candid world [for the truth of which we pledge a faith yet unsullied
by falsehood.]

4   He has refused his assent to laws the most wholesome & necessary
for the public good.

5   He has forbidden his governors to pass laws of immediate & pressing importance, unless suspended in their operation till his assent
should be obtained; & when so suspended, he has utterly neglected
to attend to them.

6   He has refused to pass other laws for the accommodation of large
districts of people, unless those people would relinquish the right
of representation in the legislature, a right inestimable to them, &
formidable to tyrants only.

7   He has called together legislative bodies at places unusual, uncomfortable, and distant from the depository of their public records,

for the sole purpose of fatiguing them into compliance with his measures.

8   He has dissolved representative houses repeatedly [& continually] for opposing with manly firmness his invasions on the rights of the people.

9   He has refused for a long time after such dissolutions to cause others to be elected, whereby the legislative powers, incapable of annihilation, have returned to the people at large for their exercise, the state remaining in the mean time exposed to all the dangers of invasion from without & convulsions within.

10   He has endeavored to prevent the population of these states; for that purpose obstructing the laws for naturalization of foreigners, refusing to pass others to encourage their migrations hither, & raising the conditions of new appropriations of lands.

11   He has ∧ [suffered] the administration of justice [totally to cease in some of these states] ∧ refusing his assent to laws for establishing judiciary powers.   obstructed / by

12   He has made [our] judges dependant on his will alone, for the tenure of their offices, & the amount & paiment of their salaries.

13   He has erected a multitude of new offices [by a self assumed power] and sent hither swarms of new officers to harrass our people and eat out their substance.

14   He has kept among us in times of peace standing armies [and ships of war] without the consent of our legislatures.

15   He has affected to render the military independant of, & superior to the civil power.

16   He has combined with others to subject us to jurisdiction foreign to our constitutions & unacknowleged by our laws, giving his assent to their acts of pretended legislation for quartering large bodies of armed troops among us; for protecting them by a mock-trial from punishment for any murders which they should commit on the inhabitants of these states; for cutting off our trade with all parts of the world; for imposing taxes on us without our consent; for depriving us ∧ of the benefits of trial by jury; for transporting us beyond   in many cases
seas to be tried for pretended offences; for abolishing the free system of English laws in a neighboring province, establishing therein an arbitrary government, and enlarging it's boundaries, so as to render it at once an example and fit instrument for introducing the same absolute rule into these ∧ [states]; for taking away our charters,   colonies
abolishing our most valuable laws, and altering fundamentally the forms of our governments; for suspending our own legislatures, & declaring themselves invested with power to legislate for us in all cases whatsoever.

17   He has abdicated government here ∧ [withdrawing his governors, and declaring us out of his allegiance & protection.]   by declaring u / out of his / protection & / waging war / against us

18   He has plundered our seas, ravaged our coasts, burnt our towns, & destroyed the lives of our people.

19   He is at this time transporting large armies of foreign mercenaries to compleat the works of death, desolation & tyranny already begun with circumstances of cruelty and perfidy ∧ unworthy the head of a civilized nation.

scarcely par   alleled in the most barbarous ages, & totally

20   He has constrained our fellow citizens taken captive on the high seas to bear arms against their country, to become the executioners of their friends & brethren, or to fall themselves by their hands.

21   He has ∧ endeavored to bring on the inhabitants of our frontiers the merciless Indian savages, whose known rule of warfare is an undistinguished destruction of all ages, sexes, & conditions [of existence.]

excited domestic insurrections amongst us, & has

22   [He has incited treasonable insurrections of our fellow-citizens, with the allurements of forfeiture & confiscation of our property.

23   He has waged cruel war against human nature itself, violating it's most sacred rights of life and liberty in the persons of a distant people who never offended him, captivating & carrying them into slavery in another hemisphere or to incur miserable death in their transportation thither. This piratical warfare, the opprobrium of *infidel* powers, is the warfare of the *Christian* king of Great Britain. Determined to keep open a market where *Men* should be bought & sold, he has prostituted his negative for suppressing every legislative attempt to prohibit or to restrain this execrable commerce. And that this assemblage of horrors might want no fact of distinguished die, he is now exciting those very people to rise in arms among us, and to purchase that liberty of which he has deprived them, by murdering the people on whom he also obtruded them: thus paying off former crimes committed against the *Liberties* of one people, with crimes which he urges them to commit against the *lives* of another.]

24   In every stage of these oppressions we have petitioned for redress in the most humble terms: our repeated petitions have been answered only by repeated injuries. A prince whose character is thus marked by every act which may define a tyrant is unfit to be the ruler of a ∧ people [who mean to be free. Future ages will scarcely believe that the hardiness of one man adventured, within the short compass of twelve years only, to lay a foundation so broad & so undisguised for tyranny over a people fostered & fixed in principles of freedom.]

free

25   Nor have we been wanting in attentions to our British brethren. We have warned them from time to time of attempts by their legislature to extend ∧ [a] jurisdiction over ∧ [these our states.] We have reminded them of the circumstances of our emigration & settlement here, [no one of which could warrant so strange a preten-

an unwarrantable   us

sion: that these were effected at the expence of our own blood &
treasure, unassisted by the wealth or the strength of Great Britain:
that in constituting indeed our several forms of government, we had
adopted one common king, thereby laying a foundation for perpetual
league & amity with them: but that submission to their parliament
was no part of our constitution, nor ever in idea, if history may be
credited: and,] we ∧ appealed to their native justice and magnanimity
∧ [as well as to] the ties of our common kindred to disavow these
usurpations which ∧ [were likely to] interrupt our connection and
correspondence. They too have been deaf to the voice of justice &
of consanguinity, [and when occasions have been given them, by
the regular course of their laws, of removing from their councils
the disturbers of our harmony, they have, by their free election, re-
established them in power. At this very time too they are permit-
ting their chief magistrate to send over not only souldiers of our
common blood, but Scotch & foreign mercenaries to invade & destroy us. These facts have given the last stab to agonizing affection,
and manly spirit bids us to renounce for ever these unfeeling brethren. We must endeavor to forget our former love for them, and to
hold them as we hold the rest of mankind enemies in war, in peace
friends. We might have been a free and a great people together; but
a communication of grandeur & of freedom it seems is below their
dignity. Be it so, since they will have it. The road to happiness &
to glory is open to us too. We will tread it apart from them, and] ∧
acquiesce in the necessity which denounces our [eternal] separation ∧ !

have
and we have
conjured ther
by
would
inevitably

we must
therefore
and hold ther
as we hold th
rest of mankii
enemies in w
in peace
friends.

26   We therefore the representatives of the United states of
America in General Congress
assembled do in the name, & by
the authority of the good people
of these [states reject & renounce
all allegiance & subjection to the
kings of Great Britain & all
others who may hereafter claim
by, through or under them: we
utterly dissolve all political connection which may heretofore
have subsisted between us & the
people or parliament of Great
Britain: & finally we do assert &
declare these colonies to be free
& independant states,] & that as
free & independent states, they
have full power to levy war, con-

   We therefore the representatives of the United states of
America in General Congress
assembled, appealing to the supreme judge of the world for the
rectitude of our intentions, do in
the name, & by the authority of
the good people of these colonies, solemnly publish &
declare that these United colonies are & of right ought to be
free & independant states; that
they are absolved from all allegiance to the British crown, and
that all political connection between them & the state of Great
Britain is, & ought to be, totally
dissolved; & that as free & independant states they have full

clude peace, contract alliances, establish commerce, & to do all other acts & things which independant states may of right do. And for the support of this declaration we mutually pledge to each other our lives, our fortunes & our sacred honour.

power to levy war, conclude peace, contract alliances, establish commerce & to do all other acts & things which independant states may of right do.

And for the support of this declaration, with a firm reliance on the protection of divine providence we mutually pledge to each other our lives, our fortunes & our sacred honour.

_____ CONSIDERATIONS _____

1. What part of the original declaration deleted by Congress most surprises you? Why?

2. Make a careful study of the first eight or ten changes imposed by Congress on Jefferson's original declaration. Why do you think each was made? Would any of them have made good examples for George Orwell to use in his "Politics and the English Language"?

3. Garry Wills says in his book, *Inventing America,* that the declaration is easy to misunderstand because it "is written in the lost language of the Enlightenment." What was the Enlightenment? How does the language of that period differ from that of today? Perhaps the declaration should be rewritten in modern English?

4. If you conclude that the declaration should be rewritten, try your hand at it. Try, for instance, rewriting the famous third paragraph: "We hold these truths . . ." Can you be sure you're not writing a parody?

5. How is the declaration organized? Does it break down into distinct parts? If so, what is the function of those parts?

6. For a more thorough exploration of the before-and-after versions of the declaration and of the political and literary motives for the changes, see Carl Becker's *The Declaration of Independence.*

Etheridge Knight (b. 1931) began writing poetry in 1963 while he was an inmate of the Indiana State Prison. Born in Mississippi, he has lived in Memphis, Pittsburgh, Hartford, and most recently in New Hampshire. In each of these locations he has started a Free People's Poetry Workshop. Knight has received fellowships from the Guggenheim Foundation and the National Endowment for the Arts, and has taught at several universities. His many volumes of poetry include The Essential Etheridge Knight, *published by the University of Pittsburgh Press.*

40

ETHERIDGE KNIGHT
The Idea of Ancestry

1

Taped to the wall of my cell are 47 pictures: 47 black
faces: my father, mother, grandmothers (1 dead), grand
fathers (both dead), brothers, sisters, uncles, aunts,
cousins (1st & 2nd), nieces, and nephews. They stare
across the space at me sprawling on my bunk. I know
their dark eyes, they know mine. I know their style,
they know mine. I am all of them, they are all of me;
8   they are farmers, I am a thief, I am me, they are thee.

I have at one time or another been in love with my mother,
1 grandmother, 2 sisters, 2 aunts (1 went to the asylum),

Reprinted from *The Essential Etheridge Knight* by Etheridge Knight by permission of the University of Pittsburgh Press. © 1986 by Etheridge Knight.

and 5 cousins. I am now in love with a 7 yr old niece
(she sends me letters written in large block print, and
her picture is the only one that smiles at me).   13

I have the same name as 1 grandfather, 3 cousins, 3 nephews,
and 1 uncle. The uncle disappeared when he was 15, just took
off and caught a freight (they say). He's discussed each year
when the family has a reunion, he causes uneasiness in
the clan, he is an empty space. My father's mother, who is 93
and who keeps the Family Bible with everybody's birth dates
(and death dates) in it, always mentions him. There is no
place in her Bible for "whereabouts unknown."   21

2

Each Fall the graves of my grandfathers call me, the brown
hills and red gullies of mississippi send out their electric
messages, galvanizing my genes. Last yr/like a salmon quitting
the cold ocean — leaping and bucking up his birthstream/I
hitchhiked my way from L.A. with 16 caps in my pocket and a
monkey on my back. and I almost kicked it with the kinfolks.
I walked barefooted in my grandmother's backyard/I smelled the old
land and the woods/I sipped cornwhiskey from fruit jars with the men/
I flirted with the women/I had a ball till the caps ran out
and my habit came down. That night I looked at my grandmother
and split/my guts were screaming for junk/but I was almost
contented/I had almost caught up with me.
(The next day in Memphis I cracked a croaker's crib for a fix.)

This yr there is a gray stone wall damming my stream, and when
the falling leaves stir my genes, I pace my cell or flop on my bunk
and stare at 47 black faces across the space. I am all of them,
they are all of me, I am me, they are thee, and I have no sons
to float in the space between.

Robin Lakoff (b. 1942) was born in Brooklyn, New York, and received her B.A. and her Ph.D. from Harvard. She is now a professor of linguistics at the University of California at Berkeley. Her first book, Abstract Syntax and Latin Complementation *(MIT Press), was published in 1968 followed, in 1975, by* Language and Woman's Place. *In 1984, in collaboration with Raquel Scherr, she published* Face Value: The Politics of Beauty.

41

ROBIN LAKOFF
You Are What You Say

1   "Women's language" is that pleasant (dainty?), euphemistic, never-aggressive way of talking we learned as little girls. Cultural bias was built into the language we were allowed to speak, the subjects we were allowed to speak about, and the ways we were spoken of. Having learned our linguistic lesson well, we go out in the world, only to discover that we are communicative cripples — damned if we do, and damned if we don't.

2   If we refuse to talk "like a lady," we are ridiculed and criticized for being unfeminine. ("She thinks like a man" is, at best, a left-handed compliment.) If we do learn all the fuzzy-headed, unassertive language of our sex, we are ridiculed for being unable to think clearly, unable to take part in a serious discussion, and therefore unfit to hold a position of power.

3   It doesn't take much of this for a woman to begin feeling she deserves such treatment because of inadequacies in her own intelligence and education.

From *Ms.* magazine, July 1974. Reprinted by permission of the author.

"Women's language" shows up in all levels of English. For example, women are encouraged and allowed to make far more precise discriminations in naming colors than men do. Words like *mauve, beige, ecru, aquamarine, lavender,* and so on, are unremarkable in a woman's active vocabulary, but largely absent from that of most men. I know of no evidence suggesting that women actually *see* a wider range of colors than men do. It is simply that fine discriminations of this sort are relevant to women's vocabularies, but not to men's; to men, who control most of the interesting affairs of the world, such distinctions are trivial — irrelevant.

In the area of syntax, we find similar gender-related peculiarities of speech. There is one construction, in particular, that women use conversationally far more than men: the tag-question. A tag is midway between an outright statement and a yes-no question; it is less assertive than the former, but more confident than the latter.

A *flat statement* indicates confidence in the speaker's knowledge and is fairly certain to be believed; a *question* indicates a lack of knowledge on some point and implies that the gap in the speaker's knowledge can and will be remedied by an answer. For example, if, at a Little League game, I have had my glasses off, I can legitimately ask someone else: "Was the player out at third?" A *tag-question*, being intermediate between statement and question, is used when the speaker is stating a claim, but lacks full confidence in the truth of that claim. So if I say, "Is Joan here?" I will probably not be surprised if my respondent answers "no"; but if I say, "Joan is here, isn't she?" instead, chances are I am already biased in favor of a positive answer, wanting only confirmation. I still want a response, but I have enough knowledge (or think I have) to predict that response. A tag question, then, might be thought of as a statement that doesn't demand to be believed by anyone but the speaker, a way of giving leeway, of not forcing the addressee to go along with the views of the speaker.

Another common use of the tag-question is in small talk when the speaker is trying to elicit conversation: "Sure is hot here, isn't it?"

But in discussing personal feelings or opinions, only the speaker normally has any way of knowing the correct answer. Sentences such as "I have a headache, don't I?" are clearly ridiculous. But there are other examples where it is the speaker's opinions, rather than perceptions, for which corroboration is sought, as in "The situation in Southeast Asia is terrible, isn't it?"

While there are, of course, other possible interpretations of a sentence like this, one possibility is that the speaker has a particular answer in mind — "yes" or "no" — but is reluctant to state it baldly. This sort of tag-question is much more apt to be used by women than by men in conversation. Why is this the case?

10   The tag-question allows a speaker to avoid commitment, and thereby avoid conflict with the addressee. The problem is that, by so doing, speakers may also give the impression of not really being sure of themselves, or looking to the addressee for confirmation of their views. This uncertainty is reinforced in more subliminal ways, too. There is a peculiar sentence intonation-pattern, used almost exclusively by women, as far as I know, which changes a declarative answer into a question. The effect of using the rising inflection typical of a yes-no question is to imply that the speaker is seeking confirmation, even though the speaker is clearly the only one who has the requisite information, which is why the question was put to her in the first place:

(Q) When will dinner be ready?

(A) Oh . . . around six o'clock . . . ?

11   It is as though the second speaker were saying, "Six o'clock — if that's okay with you, if you agree." The person being addressed is put in the position of having to provide confirmation. One likely consequence of this sort of speech-pattern in a woman is that, often unbeknownst to herself, the speaker builds a reputation of tentativeness, and others will refrain from taking her seriously or trusting her with any real responsibilities, since she "can't make up her mind," and "isn't sure of herself."

12   Such idiosyncrasies may explain why women's language sounds much more "polite" than men's. It is polite to leave a decision open, not impose your mind, or views, or claims, on anyone else. So a tag-question is a kind of polite statement, in that it does not force agreement or belicf on the addressee. In the same way a request is a polite command, in that it does not force obedience on the addressee, but rather suggests something be done as a favor to the speaker. A clearly stated order implies a threat of certain consequences if it is not followed, and — even more impolite — implies that the speaker is in a superior position and able to enforce the order. By couching wishes in the form of a request, on the other hand, a speaker implies that if the request is not carried out, only the speaker will suffer; noncompliance cannot harm the addressee. So the decision is really left up to addressee. The distinction becomes clear in these examples:

Close the door.
Please close the door.
Will you close the door?

Will you please the close the door?
Won't you close the door?

In the same ways as words and speech patterns used *by* women   13
undermine their image, those used *to describe* women make matters
even worse. Often a word may be used of both men and women (and
perhaps of things as well); but when it is applied to women, it assumes
a special meaning that, by implications rather than outright assertion,
is derogatory to women as a group.

The use of euphemisms has this effect. A euphemism is a   14
substitute for a word that has acquired a bad connotation by association with something unpleasant or embarrassing. But almost as soon
as the new word comes into common usage, it takes on the same old
bad connotations, since feelings about the things or people referred to
are not altered by a change of name; thus new euphemisms must be
constantly found.

There is one euphemism for *woman* still very much alive. The   15
word, of course, is *lady. Lady* has a masculine counterpart, namely
gentleman, occasionally shortened to *gent*. But for some reason *lady*
is very much commoner than *gent (leman)*.

The decision to use *lady* rather than *woman*, or vice versa, may   16
considerably alter the sense of a sentence, as the following examples
show:

(a) A woman (lady) I know is a dean at Berkeley.
(b) A woman (lady) I know makes amazing things out of shoelaces
     and old boxes.

The use of *lady* in (a) imparts a frivolous, or nonserious, tone to   17
the sentence: the matter under discussion is not one of great moment.
Similarly, in (b), using *lady* here would suggest that the speaker considered the "amazing things" not to be serious art, but merely a hobby or
an aberration. If *woman* is used, she might be a serious sculptor. To
say *lady doctor* is very condescending, since no one ever says *gentleman
doctor* or even *man doctor*. For example, mention in the San Francisco
Chronicle of January 31, 1972, of Madalyn Murray O'Hair as the *lady
atheist* reduces her position to that of scatterbrained eccentric. Even
woman atheist is scarcely defensible: sex is irrelevant to her
philosophical position.

Many women argue that, on the other hand, *lady* carries with it   18
overtones recalling the age of chivalry: conferring exalted stature on the
person so referred to. This makes the term seem polite at first, but we
must also remember that these implications are perilous: they suggest
that a "lady" is helpless, and cannot do things by herself.

19   *Lady* can also be used to infer frivolousness, as in titles of organizations. Those that have a serious purpose (not merely that of enabling "the ladies" to spend time with one another) cannot use the word *lady* in their titles, but less serious ones may. Compare the *Ladies' Auxiliary* of a men's group, or the *Thursday Evening Ladies' Browning and Garden Society* with *Ladies' Liberation* or *Ladies' Strike for Peace*.

20   What is curious about this split is that *lady* is in origin a euphemism — a substitute that puts a better face on something people find uncomfortable — for *woman*. What kind of euphemism is it that subtly denigrates the people to whom it refers? Perhaps *lady* functions as a euphemism for *woman* because it does not contain the sexual implications present in *woman:* it is not "embarrassing" in that way. If this is so, we may expect that, in the future, *lady* will replace woman as the primary word for the human female, since *woman* will have become too blatantly sexual. That this distinction is already made in some contexts at least is shown in the following examples, where you can try replacing *woman* with *lady:*

(a) She's only twelve, but she's already a woman.
(b) After ten years in jail, Harry wanted to find a woman.
(c) She's my woman, see, so don't mess around with her.

21   Another common substitute for *woman* is *girl*. One seldom hears a man past the age of adolescence referred to as a boy, save in expressions like "going out with the boys," which are meant to suggest an air of adolescent frivolity and irresponsibility. But women of all ages are "girls": one can have a man — not a boy — Friday, but only a girl — never a woman or even a lady — Friday; women have girlfriends, but men do not — in a nonsexual sense — have boyfriends. It may be that this use of *girl* is euphemistic in the same way the use of *lady* is: in stressing the idea of immaturity, it removes the sexual connotations lurking in *woman*. *Girl* brings to mind irresponsibility: you don't send a girl to do a woman's errand (or even, for that matter, a boy's errand). She is a person who is both too immature and too far from real life to be entrusted with responsibilities or with decisions of any serious or important nature.

22   Now let's take a pair of words which, in terms of the possible relationships in an earlier society, were simple male-female equivalents, analogous to *bull: cow*. Suppose we find that, for independent reasons, society has changed in such a way that the original meanings now are irrelevant. Yet the words have not been discarded, but have acquired new meanings, metaphorically related to their original senses. But suppose these new metaphorical uses are no longer parallel to each other.

By seeing where the parallelism breaks down, we discover something about the different roles played by men and women in this culture. One good example of such a divergence through time is found in the pair, *master: mistress*. Once used with reference to one's power over servants, these words have become unusable today in their original master-servant sense as the relationship has become less prevalent in our society. But the words are still common.

Unless used with reference to animals, *master* now generally refers to a man who has acquired consummate ability in some field, normally nonsexual. But its feminine counterpart cannot be used this way. It is practically restricted to its sexual sense of "paramour." We start out with two terms, both roughly paraphrasable as "one who has power over another." But the masculine form, once one person is no longer able to have absolute power over another, becomes usable metaphorically in the sense of "having power over *something*." *Master* requires as its object only the name of some activity, something inanimate and abstract. But *mistress* requires a masculine noun in the possessive to precede it. One cannot say: "Rhonda is a mistress." One must be *someone's* mistress. A man is defined by what he does, a woman by her sexuality, that is, in terms of one particular aspect of her relationship to men. It is one thing to be an *old master* like Hans Holbein, and another to be an *old mistress*.   23

The same is true of the words *spinster* and *bachelor* — gender words for "one who is not married." The resemblance ends with the definition. While *bachelor* is a neuter term, often used as a compliment, *spinster* normally is used pejoratively, with connotations of prissiness, fussiness, and so on. To be a bachelor implies that one has the choice of marrying or not, and this is what makes the idea of a bachelor existence attractive, in the popular literature. He has been pursued and has successfully eluded his pursuers. But a spinster is one who has not been pursued, or at least not seriously. She is old, unwanted goods. The metaphorical connotations of *bachelor* generally suggest sexual freedom; of *spinster*, puritanism or celibacy.   24

These examples could be multiplied. It is generally considered a *faux pas*, in society, to congratulate a woman on her engagement, while it is correct to congratulate her fiancé. Why is this? The reason seems to be that it is impolite to remind people of things that may be uncomfortable to them. To congratulate a woman on her engagement is really to say, "Thank goodness! You had a close call." For the man, on the other hand, there was no such danger. His choosing to marry is viewed as a good thing, but not something essential.   25

26   The linguistic double standard holds throughout the life of the relationship. After marriage, bachelor and spinster become man and wife, not man and woman. The woman whose husband dies remains "John's widow"; John, however, is never "Mary's widower."

27   Finally, why is it that salesclerks and others are so quick to call women customers "dear," "honey," and other terms of endearment they really have no business using? A male customer would never put up with it. But women, like children, are supposed to enjoy these endearments, rather than being offended by them.

28   In more ways than one, it's time to speak up.

___ CONSIDERATIONS _____

1. In this informal essay, Lakoff does not provide the documentation and references that she would in a formal paper. The reader is thus asked to take the writer's word for what she says. Given the importance Lakoff places, for example, on the tag-question (Paragraphs 5 through 10) it might be interesting to make your own objective, systematic observation of the use of that locution. Carefully note tag-question usages — including place, time, sex of speaker, and context — and report your findings to your class. Linguistic field research is fascinating, but it makes severe demands upon your accuracy and honesty.

2. In discussing the word "lady" (Paragraphs 15 through 20) Lakoff points out the connotations of the word that work against women. To study the importance of connotative meanings as opposed to denotative meanings, list associative and implied meanings for the terms "lady," "woman," "female," and "girl." Follow through in the same way for "gentleman," "man," "male," and "boy." What are your conclusions?

3. Lakoff states in Paragraph 23 that "It is one thing to be an 'old master' like Hans Holbein, and another to be an 'old mistress.'" Study the paragraph to see how carefully Lakoff leads the reader to an acceptance of this point.

4. Other students of sexism in language usage suggest that it is due chiefly to habit and lack of awareness. Does George Orwell, in his "Politics and the English Language," (pages 292–305) offer any solutions to these problems?

5. While Lakoff writes informally in this essay, you may find a number of unfamiliar words such as "euphemism," "syntax," "gender-related," "subliminal," and "denigrates." List all unfamiliar words, then take the trouble to develop a working acquaintance with each one — an ideal way to build your vocabulary.

6. Would you say that the anxiety suffered by the woman in Nora Ephron's "A Few Words About Breasts" (pages 161–169) is heightened by sexism in language as described by Lakoff? Explain.

Abraham Lincoln (1809–1865) was our sixteenth president, and a consensus of historians ranks him our greatest president — an opinion generally supported by the American people. He grew up self-educated, nurturing his mind on five special books: the King James Version of the Bible, Shakespeare, Parson Weems's Life of Washington, *John Bunyan's* Pilgrim's Progress, *and Daniel Defoe's* Robinson Crusoe. *His speeches and letters are models of a formal, rhythmic, studied English prose. None of Lincoln's utterances is so known — so parodied, so quoted, so misquoted — as the speech he gave at Gettysburg.*

42

ABRAHAM LINCOLN

The Gettysburg Address

Four score and seven years ago our fathers brought forth on this 1
continent, a new nation, conceived in Liberty, and dedicated to the pro
position that all men are created equal.

Now we are engaged in a great civil war, testing whether that na- 2
tion, or any nation so conceived and so dedicated, can long endure. We
are met on a great battle-field of that war. We have come to dedicate
a portion of that field, as a final resting place for those who here gave
their lives that that nation might live. It is altogether fitting and proper
that we should do this.

But, in a larger sense, we can not dedicate — we can not conse- 3
crate — we can not hallow — this ground. The brave men, living and
dead, who struggled here, have consecrated it, far above our poor power
to add or detract. The world will little note, nor long remember what
we say here, but it can never forget what they did here. It is for us the
living, rather, to be dedicated here to the unfinished work which they
who fought here have thus far so nobly advanced. It is rather for us to

be here dedicated to the great task remaining before us — that from these honored dead we take increased devotion to that cause for which they gave the last full measure of devotion — that we here highly resolve that these dead shall not have died in vain — that this nation, under God, shall have a new birth of freedom — and that government of the people, by the people, for the people, shall not perish from the earth.

_____ CONSIDERATIONS _____

1. Lincoln's Gettysburg Address was not subjected to the intense study, criticism, and revision that Congress gave Thomas Jefferson's Declaration of Independence (pages 220–225), but neither did Lincoln give his short speech off the top of his head. He reworked the composition before he delivered it. One of the changes occurred in the last sentence of Paragraph 2, which in an earlier version read, "This we may, in all propriety do." What do you think of his decision to change that sentence?

2. Commentators have noted that Lincoln made telling use of repeated sentence structure. Locate a good example in the address, then compose two sentences of your own, on any subject, but built in the same way.

3. Shortly after Lincoln delivered the address, the *Chicago Times* criticized his phrase, "a new birth of freedom" and called it a misrepresentation of the motives of the men slain at Gettysburg. The *Times* argued that the soldiers had died to maintain the government, the Constitution, and the union — not to advance Lincoln's "odious abolition doctrines." Can an objective reading of the address help you determine whether the *Times* attack had any substance?

4. Note how Lincoln's first reference to place is the word "continent"; his second is to "nation"; his third to "battle-field"; and his fourth to "a portion of that field." What do you make of this progressive narrowing of the field of vision? Can you see a use for such a device in your own writing?

5. Lincoln begins Paragraph 3 with a sentence in which he moves from "dedicate" to "consecrate" to "hallow." Are these words synonyms? If so, why does he say the same thing three times? If they have different meanings, is there any significance in the order in which Lincoln arranges them? Consult a good dictionary or collection of synonyms.

Barry Lopez (b. 1945) was born in New York State and at-
tended Notre Dame. He has made his living as a writer since
the age of twenty-five; Desert Notes *appeared in 1976, and* Of
Wolves and Men *in 1978. The latter book earned Lopez the*
John Burroughs Medal for distinguished writing about natural
history, and nomination for an American Book Award. His
essays and short stories appear in the best American
magazines, where he is a leading defender of the natural world.
Arctic Dreams *came out to critical acclaim in 1985.*

43

BARRY LOPEZ
The Stone Horse

A BLM archaeologist told me, with understandable reluctance,   1
where to find the intaglio. I spread my Automobile Club of Southern
California map of Imperial County out on his desk, and he traced the
route with a pink, felt-tip pen. The line crossed Interstate 8 and then
turned west along the Mexican border.

"You can't drive any farther than about here," he said, marking a   2
small X. "There's boulders in the wash. You walk up past them."

On a separate piece of paper he drew a route in a smaller scale that   3
would take me up the arroyo to a certain point where I was to cross
back east, to another arroyo. At its head, on higher ground just to the
north, I would find the horse.

"It's tough to spot unless you know it's there. Once you pick it   4
up . . ." He shook his head slowly, in a gesture of wonder at its existence.

I waited until I held his eye. I assured him I would not tell anyone   5 else how to get there. He looked at me with stoical despair, like a man who had been robbed twice, whose belief in human beings was offered without conviction.

6   I did not go until the following day because I wanted to see it at dawn. I ate breakfast at 4 A.M. in El Centro and then drove south. The route was easy to follow, though the last section of road proved difficult, broken and drifted over with sand in some spots. I came to the barricade of boulders and parked. It was light enough by then to find my way over the ground with little trouble. The contours of the landscape were stark, without any masking vegetation. I worried only about rattlesnakes.

7   I traversed the stone plain as directed, but, in spite of the frankness of the land, I came on the horse unawares. In the first moment of recognition I was without feeling. I recalled later being startled, and that I held my breath. It was laid out on the ground with its head to the east, three times life size. As I took in its outline I felt a growing concentration of all my senses, as though my attentiveness to the pale rose color of the morning sky and other peripheral images had now ceased to be important. I was aware that I was straining for sound in the windless air and I felt the uneven pressure of the earth hard against my feet. The horse, outlined in a standing profile on the dark ground, was as vivid before me as a bed of tulips.

8   I've come upon animals suddenly before, and felt a similar tension, a precipitate heightening of the senses. And I have felt the inexplicable but sharply boosted intensity of a wild moment in the bush, where it is not until some minutes later that you discover the source of electricity — the warm remains of a grizzly bear kill, or the still moist tracks of a wolverine.

9   But this was slightly different. I felt I had stepped into an unoccupied corridor. I had no familiar sense of history, the temporal structure in which to think: This horse was made by Quechan people three hundred years ago. I felt instead a headlong rush of images: people hunting wild horses with spears on the Pleistocene veld of southern California; Cortés riding across the causeway into Montezuma's Tenochtitlán; a short-legged Comanche, astride his horse like some sort of ferret, slashing through cavalry lines of young men who rode like farmers. A hoof exploding past my face one morning in a corral in Wyoming. These images had the weight and silence of stone.

10   When I released my breath, the images softened. My initial feeling, of facing a wild animal in a remote region, was replaced with a calm sense of antiquity. It was then that I became conscious, like an ordinary tourist, of what was before me, and thought: This horse was probably

laid out by Quechan people. But when, I wondered? The first horses they saw, I knew, might have been those that came north from Mexico in 1692 with Father Eusebio Kino. But Cocopa people, I recalled, also came this far north on occasion, to fight with their neighbors, the Quechan. And *they* could have seen horses with Melchior Díaz, at the mouth of the Colorado River in the fall of 1540. So, it could be four hundred years old. (No one in fact knows.)

I still had not moved. I took my eyes off the horse for a moment 11 to look south over the desert plain into Mexico, to look east past its head at the brightening sunrise, to situate myself. Then, finally, I brought my trailing foot slowly forward and stood erect. Sunlight was running like a thin sheet of water over the stony ground and it threw the horse into relief. It looked as though no hand had ever disturbed the stones that gave it its form.

The horse had been brought to life on ground called desert pave- 12 ment, a tight, flat matrix of small cobbles blasted smooth by sand-laden winds. The uniform, monochromatic blackness of the stones, a patina of iron and magnesium oxides called desert varnish, is caused by long-term exposure to the sun. To make this type of low-relief ground glyph, or intaglio, the artist either selectively turns individual stones over to their lighter side or removes areas of stone to expose the lighter soil underneath, creating a negative image. This horse, about eighteen feet from brow to rump and eight feet from withers to hoof, had been made in the latter way, and its outline was bermed at certain points with low ridges of stone a few inches high to enhance its three-dimensional qualities. (The left side of the horse was in full profile; each leg was extended at 90 degrees to the body and fully visible, as though seen in three-quarter profile.)

I was not eager to move. The moment I did I would be back in 13 the flow of time, the horse no longer quivering in the same way before me. I did not want to feel again the sequence of quotidian events — to be drawn off into deliberation and analysis. A human being, a four-footed animal, the open land. That was all that was present — and a "thoughtless" understanding of the very old desires bearing on this particular animal: to hunt it, to render it, to fathom it, to subjugate it, to honor it, to take it as a companion.

What finally made me move was the light. The sun now filled the 14 shallow basin of the horse's body. The weighted line of the stone berm created the illusion of a mane and the distinctive roundness of an equine belly. The change in definition impelled me. I moved to the left , circling past its rump, to see how the light might flesh the horse out from various points of view. I circled it completely before squatting on my haunches. Ten or fifteen minutes later I chose another view. The third time I moved, to a point near the rear hooves, I spotted a stone tool at my feet. I stared at it a long while, more in awe than disbelief, before reaching out to pick it up. I turned it over in my left palm and took it between my fingers to feel its cutting edge. It is always difficult, especially with something so portable, to rechannel the desire to steal.

15   I spent several hours with the horse. As I changed positions and as the angle of the light continued to change I noticed a number of things. The angle at which the pastern carried the hoof away from the ankle was perfect. Also, stones had been placed within the image to suggest at precisely the right spot the left shoulder above the foreleg. The line that joined thigh and hock was similarly accurate. The muzzle alone seemed distorted — but perhaps these stones had been moved by a later hand. It was an admirably accurate representation, but not what a breeder would call perfect conformation. There was the suggestion of a bowed neck and an undershot jaw, and the tail, as full as a winter coyote's, did not appear to be precisely to scale.

16   The more I thought about it, the more I felt I was looking at an individual horse, a unique combination of generic and specific detail. It was easy to imagine one of Kino's horses as a model, or a horse that ran off from one of Coronado's columns. What kind of horses would these have been, I wondered? In the sixteenth century the most sought-after horses in Europe were Spanish, the offspring of Arabian stock and Barbary horses that the Moors brought to Iberia and bred to the older, eastern European strains brought in by the Romans. The model for this horse, I speculated, could easily have been a palomino, or a descendant of horses trained for lion-hunting in North Africa.

17   A few generations ago, cowboys, cavalry quartermasters, and draymen would have taken this horse before me under consideration and not let up their scrutiny until they had its heritage fixed to their satisfaction. Today, the distinction between draft and harness horses is arcane knowledge, and no image may come to mind for a blue roan or a claybank horse. The loss of such refinement in everyday conversation leaves me unsettled. People praise the Eskimo's ability to distinguish among forty types of snow but forget the skill of others who routinely differentiate between overo and tobiano pintos. Such distinctions are made for the same reason. You have to do it to be able to talk clearly about the world.

18   For parts of two years I worked as a horse wrangler and packer in Wyoming. It is dim knowledge now; I would have to think to remember

if a buckskin was a kind of dun horse. And I couldn't throw a double-diamond hitch over a set of panniers — the packer's basic tie-down — without guidance. As I squatted there in the desert, however, these more personal memories seemed tenuous in comparison with the sweep of this animal in human time. My memories had no depth. I thought of the Hittite cavalry riding against the Syrians 3,500 years ago. And the first of the Chinese emperors, Ch'in Shih Huang, buried in Shensi Province in 210 B.C. with thousands of life-size horses and soldiers, a terra-cotta guardian army. What could I know of what was in the mind of whoever made this horse? Was there some racial memory of it as an animal that had once fed the artist's ancestors and then disappeared from North America? And then returned in this strange alliance with another race of men?

Certainly, whoever it was, the artist had observed the animal very closely. Certainly the animal's speed had impressed him. Among the first things the Quechan would have learned from an encounter with Kino's horses was that their own long-distance runners — men who could run down mule deer — were no match for this animal. 19

From where I squatted I could look far out over the Mexican plain. Juan Bautista de Anza passed this way in 1774, extending El Camino Real into Alta California from Sinaloa. He was followed by others, all of them astride the magical horse; *gente de razón*, the people of reason, coming into the country of *los primitivos*. The horse, like the stone animals of Egypt, urged these memories upon me. And as I drew them up from some forgotten corner of my mind — huge horses carved in the white chalk downs of southern England by an Iron Age people; Spanish horses rearing and wheeling in fear before alligators in Florida — the images seemed tethered before me. With this sense of proportion, a memory of my own — the morning I almost lost my face to a horse's hoof — now had somewhere to fit. 20

I rose up and began to walk slowly around the horse again. I had taken the first long measure of it and was looking now for a way to depart, a new angle of light, a fading of the image itself before the rising sun, that would break its hold on me. As I circled, feeling both heady and serene at the encounter, I realized again how strangely vivid it was. It had been created on a barren bajada between two arroyos, as nondescript a place as one could imagine. The only plant life here was a few wands of ocotillo cactus. The ground beneath my shoes was so hard it wouldn't take the print of a heavy animal even after a rain. The only sounds I had heard were the voices of quail. 21

The archaeologist had been correct. For all its forcefulness, the 22 horse is inconspicuous. If you don't care to see it you can walk right past it. That pleases him, I think. Unmarked on this bleak shoulder of the plain, the site signals to no one; so he wants no protective fences here, no informative plaque, to act as beacons. He would rather take a chance that no motorcyclist, no aimless wanderer with a flair for violence and a depth of ignorance, will ever find his way here.

23   The archaeologist had given me something before I left his office that now seemed peculiar — an aerial photograph of the horse. It is widely believed that an aerial view of an intaglio provides a fair and accurate depiction. It does not. In the photograph the horse looks somewhat crudely constructed; from the ground it appears far more deftly rendered. The photograph is of a single moment, and in that split second the horse seems vaguely impotent. I watched light pool in the intaglio at dawn; I imagine you could watch it withdraw at dusk and sense the same animation I did. In those prolonged moments its shape and so, too, its general character changed — noticeably. The living quality of the image, its immediacy to the eye, was brought out by the light-in-time, not, at least here, in the camera's frozen instant.

24   Intaglios, I thought, were never meant to be seen by gods in the sky above. They were meant to be seen by people on the ground, over a long period of shifting light. This could even be true of the huge figures on the Plain of Nazca in Peru, where people could walk for the length of a day beside them. It is our own impatience that leads us to think otherwise.

25   This process of abstraction, almost unintentional, drew me gradually away from the horse. I came to a position of attention at the edge of the sphere of its influence. With a slight bow I paid my respects to the horse, its maker, and the history of us all, and departed.

_____ CONSIDERATIONS _____

1. In Paragraph 7, on the verge of discovering the stone horse, Lopez speaks of "the frankness of the land . . ." Look up the surprising word in the phrase and decide whether it was an appropriate choice.

2. After discovering the horse, Lopez devotes the bulk of Paragraphs 7 through 11, not to a description of the thing, but to his feelings and reflections. Does this make sense, given the thrust of the essay? Does it make you impatient to *see* what Lopez has stumbled upon? If you can answer "yes" to both questions, explain how *that* makes sense?

3. How successful is Lopez at showing us the horse (Paragraphs 12 and 14)? What qualities of an object should a writer consider if he or she wishes to *show* us that object?

4. Judging by Paragraphs 14, 15, and 21, we might call Lopez a serious, patient, and resourceful observer. Experiment with his methods of observation by spending some time with a sculpture in your campus art gallery or elsewhere. What does such painstaking *seeing* produce besides physical details of the thing observed?

5. There's an important principle for writers in the first sentence of Paragraph 25. Refresh your understanding of "abstraction"; restate the principle in your own words.

6. Lopez worries about the great treasure of the horse lying vulnerable in the desert. How does he change this fear into something positive? See Paragraph 13 and consider why he makes a slight bow to the horse in Paragraph 25.

*Niccolo Machiavelli (1469–1525) was born in Florence, Italy,
where he held office and acted as a diplomat until the Medici
family took power in 1512. After a spell in prison he retired to
an estate where he wrote his books, most especially* The Prince
and the Discourses. *His theories of government and statecraft
have made him proverbial; people use him as an adjective who
have never read him as an author.*

44

NICCOLO MACHIAVELLI
How a Prince Should Keep His Word

1   How praiseworthy it is for a prince to keep his word and to live
by integrity and not by deceit everyone knows; nevertheless, one sees
from the experience of our times that the princes who have accomplished great deeds are those who have cared little for keeping their
promises and who have known how to manipulate the minds of men
by shrewdness; and in the end they have surpassed those who laid their
foundations upon honesty.

2   You must, therefore, know that there are two means of fighting:
one according to the laws, the other with force; the first way is proper
to man, the second to beasts; but because the first, in many cases, is
not sufficient, it becomes necessary to have recourse to the second.
Therefore, a prince must know how to use wisely the natures of the
beast and the man. This policy was taught to princes allegorically by
the ancient writers, who described how Achilles and many other an-

cient princes were given to Chiron[1] the Centaur to be raised and taught under his discipline. This can only mean that, having a half-beast and half-man as a teacher, a prince must know how to employ the nature of the one and the other; and the one without the other cannot endure.

Since, then, a prince must know how to make good use of the nature of the beast, he should choose from among the beasts the fox and the lion; for the lion cannot defend itself from traps and the fox cannot protect itself from wolves. It is therefore necessary to be a fox in order to recognize the traps and a lion in order to frighten the wolves. Those who play only the part of the lion do not understand matters. A wise ruler, therefore, cannot and should not keep his word when such an observance of faith would be to his disadvantage and when the reasons which made him promise are removed. And if men were all good, this rule would not be good; but since men are a sorry lot and will not keep their promises to you, you likewise need not keep yours to them. A prince never lacks legitimate reasons to break his promises. Of this one could cite an endless number of modern examples to show how many pacts, how many promises have been made null and void because of the infidelity of princes; and he who has known best how to use the fox has come to a better end. But it is necessary to know how to disguise this nature well and to be a great hypocrite and a liar: and men are so simpleminded and so controlled by their present necessities that one who deceives will always find another who will allow himself to be deceived. 3

I do not wish to remain silent about one of these recent instances. Alexander VI[2] did nothing else, he thought about nothing else, except to deceive men, and he always found the occasion to do this. And there never was a man who had more forcefulness in his oaths, who affirmed a thing with more promises, and who honored his word less; nevertheless, his tricks always succeeded perfectly since he was well acquainted with this aspect of the world. 4

Therefore, it is not necessary for a prince to have all of the above-mentioned qualities, but it is very necessary for him to appear to have them. Furthermore, I shall be so bold as to assert this: that having them and practicing them at all times is harmful; and appearing to have them is useful; for instance, to seem merciful, faithful, humane, forthright, 5

---

[1]**Chiron** A mythical figure, a centaur (half man, half horse). Unlike most centaurs, he was wise and benevolent; he was also a legendary physician.

[2]**Alexander VI (1431–1503)** Roderigo Borgia, pope from 1492 to 1503. He was Cesare Borgia's father and a corrupt but immensely powerful pope.

religious, and to be so; but his mind should be disposed in such a way that should it become necessary not to be so, he will be able and know how to change to the contrary. And it is essential to understand this: that a prince, and especially a new prince, cannot observe all those things by which men are considered good, for in order to maintain the state he is often obliged to act against his promise, against charity, against humanity, and against religion. And therefore, it is necessary that he have a mind ready to turn itself according to the way the winds of Fortune and the changeability of affairs require him; and, as I said above, as long as it is possible, he should not stray from the good, but he should know how to enter into evil when necessity commands.

6   A prince, therefore, must be very careful never to let anything slip from his lips which is not full of the five qualities mentioned above: he should appear, upon seeing and hearing him, to be all mercy, all faithfulness, all integrity, all kindness, all religion. And there is nothing more necessary than to seem to possess this last quality. And men in general judge more by their eyes than their hands; for everyone can see but few can feel. Everyone sees what you seem to be, few perceive what you are, and those few do not dare to contradict the opinion of the many who have the majesty of the state to defend them; and in the actions of all men, and especially of princes, where there is no impartial arbiter, one must consider the final result.[3] Let a prince therefore act to seize and to maintain the state; his methods will always be judged honorable and will be praised by all; for ordinary people are always deceived by appearances and by the outcome of a thing; and in the world there is nothing but ordinary people; and there is no room for the few, while the many have a place to lean on. A certain prince[4] of the present day, whom I shall refrain from naming, preaches nothing but peace and faith, and to both one and the other he is entirely opposed; and both, if he had put them into practice, would have cost him many times over either his reputation or his state.

_____ **CONSIDERATIONS** _____

1. The translators of this edition of Machiavelli's *Prince* point out, in a footnote to the fourth sentence of Paragraph 6, that the Italian "has often been

---

[3]The Italian original, *si guarda al fine*, has often been mistranslated as "the ends justify the means," something Machiavelli never wrote. [Translators' note]

[4]**A certain prince** Probably King Ferdinand V of Spain (1452–1516).

mistranslated as the ends justify the means, something Machiavelli never wrote."
Rewrite the debatable sentence in your own words.

2. Are there any limits to the extent to which a prince — a leader or
ruler — should keep his word and live by integrity? How and where in his essay
does Machiavelli answer that question?

3. In Paragraph 4, Machiavelli cites an example from his own time of a
man notable for promises made, "who honored his word less." Can you name
an important figure in your time who might be so described? In what instances
would such a judgment merit punitive action?

4. Of the five qualities that a prince should appear to possess, which, according to Machiavelli, is the most important?

5. How does Machiavelli use mythology and analogy to support his ideas?

Beryl Markham (1902–1986) moved from England to East
Africa when she was four years old with her father, who was a
farmer and breeder of horses. She grew up playing with her
neighbors and learning to hunt. Later she became a pilot, and
from 1931 to 1936 flew mail, passengers, supplies, and
medicine into the Sudan, Tanganyika, and Kenya. In 1936
Markham made the first solo flight across the Atlantic east to
west, crash landing in Nova Scotia twenty-one hours and
twenty-five minutes after takeoff in England.

Her account of her adventures, West with the Night, *was*
published in 1942, and praised by Ernest Hemingway as a
"bloody, wonderful book."

45

BERYL MARKHAM
He Was a Good Lion

1   One day, when we were riding to Elkington's, my father spoke
about lions.

2   'Lions are more intelligent than some men,' he said, 'and more
courageous than most. A lion will fight for what he has and for what
he needs; he is contemptuous of cowards and wary of his equals. But
he is not afraid. You can always trust a lion to be exactly what he is —
and never anything else.'

3   'Except,' he added, looking more paternally concerned than usual,
'that damned lion of Elkington's!'

4   The Elkington lion was famous within a radius of twelve miles

in all directions from the farm, because, if you happened to be anywhere inside that circle, you could hear him roar when he was hungry, when he was sad, or when he just felt like roaring. If, in the night, you lay sleepless on your bed and listened to an intermittent sound that began like the bellow of a banshee trapped in the bowels of Kilimanjaro and ended like the sound of that same banshee suddenly at large and arrived at the foot of your bed, you knew (because you had been told) that this was the song of Paddy.

Two or three of the settlers in East Africa at that time had caught 5 lion cubs and raised them in cages. But Paddy, the Elkington lion, had never seen a cage.

He had grown to full size, tawny, black-maned and muscular, with- 6 out a worry or a care. He lived on fresh meat, not of his own killing. He spent his waking hours (which coincided with everybody else's sleeping hours) wandering through Elkington's fields and pastures like an affable, if apostrophic, emperor, a-stroll in the gardens of his court.

He thrived in solitude. He had no mate, but pretended indifference 7 and walked alone, not toying too much with imaginings of the unattainable. There were no physical barriers to his freedom, but the lions of the plains do not accept into their respected fraternity an individual bearing in his coat the smell of men. So Paddy ate, slept, and roared, and perhaps he sometimes dreamed, but he never left Elkington's. He was a tame lion, Paddy was. He was deaf to the call of the wild.

'I'm always careful of that lion,' I told my father, 'but he's really 8 harmless. I have seen Mrs. Elkington stroke him.'

'Which proves nothing,' said my father. 'A domesticated lion is only 9 an unnatural lion — and whatever is unnatural is untrustworthy.'

Whenever my father made an observation as deeply philosophical 10 as that one, and as inclusive, I knew there was nothing more to be said.

I nudged my horse and we broke into a canter covering the remain- 11 ing distance to Elkington's.

It wasn't a big farm as farms went in Africa before the First World 12 War, but it had a very nice house with a large veranda on which my father, Jim Elkington, Mrs. Elkington, and one or two other settlers sat and talked with what to my mind was always unreasonable solemnity.

There were drinks, but beyond that there was a tea-table lavishly 13 spread, as only the English can spread them. I have sometimes thought since of the Elkingtons' tea-table — round, capacious, and white, standing with sturdy legs against the green vines of the garden, a thousand miles of Africa receding from its edge.

It was a mark of sanity, I suppose, less than of luxury. It was 14 evidence of the double debt England still owes to ancient China for her two gifts that made expansion possible — tea and gunpowder.

15   But cakes and muffins were no fit bribery for me. I had pleasures of my own then, or constant expectations. I made what niggardly salutations I could bring forth from a disinterested memory and left the house at a gait rather faster than a trot.

16   As I scampered past the square hay shed a hundred yards or so behind the Elkington house, I caught sight of Bishon Singh whom my father had sent ahead to tend our horses.

17   I think the Sikh must have been less than forty years old then, but his face was never any indication of his age. On some days he looked thirty and on others he looked fifty, depending on the weather, the time of day, his mood, or the tilt of his turban. If he had ever disengaged his beard from his hair and shaved the one and clipped the other, he might have astonished us all by looking like one of Kipling's elephant boys, but he never did either, and so, to me at least, he remained a man of mystery, without age or youth, but burdened with experience, like the wandering Jew.

18   He raised his arm and greeted me in Swahili as I ran through the Elkington farmyard and out toward the open country.

19   Why I ran at all or with what purpose in mind is beyond my answering, but when I had no specific destination I always ran as fast as I could in the hope of finding one — and I always found it.

20   I was within twenty yards of the Elkington lion before I saw him. He lay sprawled in the morning sun, huge, black-maned, and gleaming with life. His tail moved slowly, stroking the rough grass like a knotted rope end. His body was sleek and easy, making a mould where he lay, a cool mould, that would be there when he had gone. He was not asleep; he was only idle. He was rusty-red, and soft, like a strokable cat.

21   I stopped and he lifted his head with magnificent ease and stared at me out of yellow eyes.

22   I stood there staring back, scuffling my bare toes in the dust, pursing my lips to make a noiseless whistle — a very small girl who knew about lions.

23   Paddy raised himself then, emitting a little sigh, and began to contemplate me with a kind of quiet premeditation, like that of a slow-witted man fondling an unaccustomed thought.

24   I cannot say that there was any menace in his eyes, because there wasn't, or that his 'frightful jowls' were drooling, because they were handsome jowls and very tidy. He did sniff the air, though, with what im-

pressed me as being close to audible satisfaction. And he did not lie down again.

I remembered the rules that one remembers. I did not run. I walked   25
very slowly, and I began to sing a defiant song.

'Kali coma Simba sisi,' I sang, 'Asikari yoti ni udari! — Fierce like   26
the lion are we, Askari all are brave!'

I went in a straight line past Paddy when I sang it, seeing his eyes   27
shine in the thick grass, watching his tail beat time to the metre of my
ditty.

'Twendi, twendi — ku pigana — piga aduoi — piga sana! — Let   28
us go, let us go — to fight — beat down the enemy! Beat hard, beat hard!'

What lion would be unimpressed with the marching song of the   29
King's African Rifles?

Singing it still, I took up my trot toward the rim of the low hill   30
which might, if I were lucky, have Cape gooseberry bushes on its slopes.

The country was grey-green and dry, and the sun lay on it closely,   31
making the ground hot under my bare feet. There was no sound and
no wind.

Even Paddy made no sound, coming swiftly behind me.   32

What I remember most clearly of the moment that followed are   33
three things — a scream that was barely a whisper, a blow that struck
me to the ground, and, as I buried my face in my arms and felt Paddy's
teeth close on the flesh of my leg, a fantastically bobbing turban, that
was Bishon Singh's turban, appear over the edge of the hill.

I remained conscious, but I closed my eyes and tried not to be. It   34
was not so much the pain as it was the sound.

The sound of Paddy's roar in my ears will only be duplicated, I   35
think, when the doors of hell slip their wobbly hinges, one day, and give
voice and authenticity to the whole panorama of Dante's poetic
nightmares. It was an immense roar that encompassed the world and
dissolved me in it.

I shut my eyes very tight and lay still under the weight of Paddy's   36
paws.

Bishon Singh said afterward that he did nothing. He said he had   37
remained by the hay shed for a few minutes after I ran past him, and
then, for no explainable reason, had begun to follow me. He admitted,
though, that, a little while before, he had seen Paddy go in the direction I had taken.

The Sikh called for help, of course, when he saw the lion meant   38
to attack, and a half-dozen of Elkington's syces had come running from

the house. Along with them had come Jim Elkington with a rawhide whip.

39   Jim Elkington, even without a rawhide whip, was very impressive. He was one of those enormous men whose girths alone seem to preclude any possibility of normal movement, much less of speed. But Jim had speed — not to be loosely compared with lightning, but rather like the speed of something spherical and smooth and relatively irresistible, like the cannon balls of the Napoleonic Wars. Jim was, without question, a man of considerable courage, but in the case of my Rescue From the Lion, it was, I am told, his momentum rather than his bravery for which I must forever be grateful.

40   It happened like this — as Bishon Singh told it;

41   'I am resting against the walls of the place where hay is kept and first the large lion and then you, Beru, pass me going toward the open field, and a thought comes to me that a lion and a young girl are strange company, so I follow. I follow to the place where the hill that goes up becomes the hill that goes down, and where it goes down deepest I see that you are running without much thought in your head and the lion is running behind you with many thoughts in his head, and I scream for everybody to come very fast.

42   'Everybody comes very fast, but the large lion is faster than anybody, and he jumps on your back and I see you scream but I hear no scream. I only hear the lion, and I begin to run with everybody, and this includes Bwana Elkington, who is saying a great many words I do not know and is carrying a long kiboko which he holds in his hand and is meant for beating the large lion.

43   'Bwana Elkington goes past me the way a man with lighter legs and fewer inches around his stomach might go past me, and he is waving the long kiboko so that it whistles over all of our heads like a very sharp wind, but when we get close the lion it comes to my mind that that lion is not of the mood to accept a kiboko.

44   'He is standing with the front of himself on your back, Beru, and you are bleeding in three or five places, and he is roaring. I do not believe Bwana Elkington could have thought that that lion at that moment would consent to being beaten, because the lion was not looking the way he had ever looked before when it was necessary for him to be beaten. He was looking as if he did not wish to be disturbed by a kiboko, or the Bwana, or the syces, or Bishon Singh, and he was saying so in a very large voice.

45   'I believe that Bwana Elkington understood this voice when he was still more than several feet from the lion, and I believe the Bwana con-

sidered in his mind that it would be the best thing not to beat the lion just then, but the Bwana when he runs very fast is like the trunk of a great baobob tree rolling down a slope, and it seems that because of this it was not possible for him to explain the thought of his mind to the soles of his feet in a sufficient quickness of time to prevent him from rushing much closer to the lion than in his heart he wished to be.

'And it was this circumstance, as I am telling it,' said Bishon Singh,   46
'which in my considered opinion made it possible for you to be alive, Beru.'

'Bwana Elkington rushed at the lion then, Bishon Singh?'   47

'The lion, as of the contrary, rushed at Bwana Elkington,' said   48
Bishon Singh. 'The lion deserted you for the Bwana, Beru. The lion was of the opinion that his master was not in any honest way deserving of a portion of what he, the lion, had accomplished in the matter of fresh meat through no effort by anybody except himself.'

Bishon Singh offered this extremely reasonable interpretation with   49
impressive gravity, as if he were expounding the Case For the Lion to a chosen jury of Paddy's peers.

'Fresh meat'. . . I repeated dreamily, and crossed my fingers.   50

'So then what happened . . . ?'   51

The Sikh lifted his shoulders and let them drop again 'What could   52
happen, Beru? The lion rushed for Bwana Elkington, who in his turn rushed from the lion, and in so rushing did not keep in his hand the long kiboko, but allowed it to fall upon the ground, and in accomplishing this the Bwana was free to ascend a very fortunate tree, which he did.'

'And you picked me up, Bishon Singh?'   53

He made a little dip with his massive turban. 'I was happy with   54
the duty of carrying you back to this very bed, Beru, and of advising your father, who had gone to observe some of Bwana Elkington's horses, that you had been moderately eaten by the large lion. Your father returned very fast, and Bwana Elkington some time later returned very fast, but the large lion has not returned at all.'

The large lion had not returned at all. That night he killed a horse,   55
and the next night he killed a yearling bullock, and after that a cow fresh for milking.

In the end he was caught and finally caged, but brought to no   56
rendezvous with the firing squad at sunrise. He remained for years in his cage, which, had he managed to live in freedom with his inhibitions, he might never have seen at all.

It seems characteristic of the mind of man that the repression of   57
what is natural to humans must be abhorred, but that what is natural

to an infinitely more natural animal must be confined within the bounds of a reason peculiar only to men — more peculiar sometimes than seems reasonable at all.

58 Paddy lived, people stared at him and he stared back, and this went on until he was an old, old lion. Jim Elkington died, and Mrs. Elkington, who really loved Paddy, was forced, because of circumstances beyond her control or Paddy's, to have him shot by Boy Long, the manager of Lord Delamere's estates.

59 This choice of executioners was, in itself, a tribute to Paddy, for no one loved animals more or understood them better, or could shoot more cleanly than Boy Long.

60 But the result was the same to Paddy. He had lived and died in ways not of his choosing. He was a good lion. He had done what he could about being a tame lion. Who thinks it just to be judged by a single error?

61 I still have the scars of his teeth and claws, but they are very small now and almost forgotten, and I cannot begrudge him his moment.

_____ CONSIDERATIONS _____

1. If Markham's descriptive simile about Paddy the lion (see last sentence of Paragraph 6) is not clear, take special note of her word choices, particularly "apostrophic." Then rewrite the sentence in your own words. How does an unfamiliar word strike you as you read? Do you resent the bother it causes you? Do you see it as an opportunity?

2. To what extent, in her descriptions of the lion, is the writer guilty of anthropomorphism? (Here's another word to add to your vocabulary.) Point out words or phrases to support your answer.

3. What object, according to Markham, symbolized sanity in the enormous chaos and mystery called Africa? Are there comparable objects in your own environment?

4. In Paragraph 40, Markham turns the telling of the story over to the Sikh employee, Bishon Singh. Isolate some of his characteristic turns of speech.

5. Describing the moment when the lion leaped on her, Markham uses none of the expected phrases, "I was terrified," "It was the most frightening moment in my life," or "You cannot imagine my horror." What would her account gain — or lose — by such expressions?

6. "I cannot begrudge him his moment," Markham writes in her closing sentence. What does this tell us of her attitude toward animals? (See Paragraph 57.)

Andrew Marvell (1621–1678) lived in a time of turmoil in England — during Cromwell's revolution, the beheading of a king, and the restoration of the monarchy. He was a political man, a member of Parliament, and at different times espoused different sides, without ever turning hypocrite. Some of his poems are political; the best are not, unless "To His Coy Mistress" is a manifesto of sexual politics. Many readers find it less concerned with sexuality than with mortality.

46

ANDREW MARVELL
To His Coy Mistress

Had we but world enough, and time,
This coyness, lady, were no crime.
We would sit down, and think which way
To walk, and pass our long love's day.
Thou by the Indian Ganges' side   5
Shouldst rubies find; I by the tide
Of Humber would complain. I would
Love you ten years before the flood,
And you should, if you please, refuse
Till the conversion of the Jews.   10
My vegetable love should grow
Vaster than empires and more slow;
An hundred years should go to praise
Thine eyes, and on thy forehead gaze;
Two hundred to adore each breast,   15
But thirty thousand to the rest;
An age at least to every part,
And the last age should show your heart.

For, lady, you deserve this state,
20 Nor would I love at lower rate
    But at my back I always hear
    Time's wingéd chariot hurrying near;
    And yonder all before us lie
    Deserts of vast eternity.
25 Thy beauty shall no more be found;
    Nor, in thy marble vault, shall sound
    My echoing song; then worms shall try
    That long-preserved virginity,
    And your quaint honor to dust,
30 And into ashes all my lust:
    The grave's a fine and private place,
    But none, I think, do there embrace.
        Now therefore, while the youthful hue
    Sits on thy skin like morning dew,
35 And while thy willing soul transpires
    At every pore with instant fires,
    Now let us sport us while we may,
    And now, like amorous birds of prey,
    Rather at once our time devour
40 Than languish in his slow-chapped° power.
    Let us roll all our strength and all
    Our sweetness up into one ball,
    And tear our pleasures with rough strife
    Thorough the iron gates of life:
45 Thus, though we cannot make our sun
    Stand still, yet we will make him run.

°slow-jawed.

47

JOYCE CAROL OATES

On Boxing

No sport is more physical, more direct, than boxing. No sport appears more powerfully homoerotic: the confrontation in the ring — the disrobing — the sweaty, heated combat that is part dance, courtship, coupling — the frequent urgent pursuit by one boxer of the other in the fight's natural and violent movement toward the "knockout." Surely boxing derives much of its appeal from this mimicry of a species of erotic love in which one man overcomes the other in an exhibition of superior strength.

Most fights, however fought, lead to an embrace between the boxers after the final bell — a gesture of mutual respect and apparent affection that appears to the onlooker to be more than perfunctory. Rocky Graziano, often derided for being a slugger rather than a "classic" boxer, sometimes kissed his opponents out of gratitude for the fight. Does the boxing match, one almost wonders, lead irresistibly to this moment: the public embrace of two men who otherwise, in public or in private, could not approach each other with such passion. Are men privileged to embrace with love only after having fought? A woman is struck by the tenderness men will express for boxers who have been hurt, even if it is only by way of commentary on photographs: the startling picture of Ray (Boom Boom) Mancini after his second losing fight with Livingstone Bramble, for instance, when Mancini's face was hideously battered (photographs in *Sports Illustrated* and elsewhere were gory, near-pornographic); the much-reprinted photograph of the defeatd Thomas Hearns being carried to his corner in the arms of an enormous black man in formal attire — the "Hit Man" from Detroit now helpless, only semiconscious, looking precisely like a black Christ taken from the cross. These are powerful, haunting, unsettling images, cruelly beautiful, very much bound up with the primitive appeal of the sport.

3   Yet to suggest that men might love one another directly without the violent ritual of combat is to misread man's greatest passion — for war, not peace. Love, if there is to be love, comes second.

4   Boxing is, after all, about lying. It is about cultivating a double personality. As José Torres, the ex-light-heavyweight champion who is now the New York State Boxing Commissioner, says: "We fighters understand lies. What's a feint? What's a left hook off the jab? What's an opening? What's thinking one thing and doing another . . . ?"

5   There is nothing fudamentally playful about boxing, nothing that seems to belong to daylight, to pleasure. At its moments of greatest intensity it seems to contain so complete and so powerful an image of life — life's beauty, vulnerability, despair, incalculable and often reckless courage — that boxing *is* life, and hardly a mere game. During a superior boxing match we are deeply moved by the body's communion with itself by way of another's flesh. The body's dialogue with its shadow-self — or Death. Baseball, football, basketball — these quintessentially American pastimes are recognizably sports because they involve play: They are games. One *plays* football; one doesn't *play* boxing.

6   Observing team sports, teams of adult men, one sees how men are children in the most felicitous sense of the word. But boxing in its elemental ferocity cannot be assimilated into childhood — though very young men box, even professionally, and numerous world champions began boxing when they were hardly more than children. Spectators at public games derive much of their pleasure from reliving the communal emotions of childhood, but spectators at boxing matches relive the murderous infancy of the race. Hence the notorious cruelty of boxing crowds and the excitement when a man begins to bleed. ("When I see blood," says Marvin Hagler, "I become a bull." He means his own.)

The boxing ring comes to seem an altar of sorts, one of those   7
legendary magical spaces where the laws of a nation are suspended: Inside the ropes, during an officially regulated three-minute round, a man
may be killed at his opponent's hands but he cannot be legally murdered.
Boxing inhabits a sacred space predating civilization; or, to use D. H.
Lawrence's phrase, before God was love. If it suggests a savage ceremony
or a rite of atonement, it also suggests the futility of such rites. For what
atonement is the fight waged, if it must shortly be waged again . . . ?

All this is to speak of the paradox of boxing — its obsessive appeal   8
for many who find in it not only a spectacle involving sensational feats
of physical skill but an emotional experience impossible to convey in
words; an art form, as I have suggested, with no natural analogue in the
arts. And of course this accounts, too, for the extreme revulsion it
arouses in many people. ("Brutal," "disgusting," "barbaric," "inhuman,"
"a terrible, terrible sport" — typical comments on the subject.)

In December 1984, the American Medical Association passed a   9
resolution calling for the abolition of boxing on the principle that it is
the only sport in which the *objective* is to cause injury. This is not surprising. Humanitarians have always wanted to reform boxing — or
abolish it altogether. The 1896 heavyweight title match between Ruby
Robert Fitzsimmons and Peter Maher was outlawed in many parts of
the United States, so canny promoters staged it across the Mexican border four hundred miles from El Paso. (Some three hundred people made
the arduous journey to see what must have been one of the most disap-
pointing bouts in boxing history — Fitzsimmons knocked out his opponent in a mere ninety-five seconds.)

During the prime of Jack Dempsey's career in the 1920s, boxing   10
was illegal in many states, like alcohol, and like alcohol, seems to have
aroused a hysterical public enthusiasm. Photographs of jammed outdoor
arenas taken in the 1920s with boxing rings like postage-sized altars at
their centers, the boxers themselves scarcely visible, testify to the extraordinary emotional appeal boxing had at that time, even as reform
movements were lobbying against it. When Jack Johnson won the heavyweight title in 1908 (he had to pursue the white champion Tommy Burns
all the way to Australia to confront him), the special "danger" of boxing
was also that it might expose and humiliate white men in the ring. After
Johnson's victory over the "White Hope" contender Jim Jeffries, there
were race riots and lynchings throughout the United States; even films
of some of Johnson's fights were outlawed in many states. And because
boxing has become a sport in which black and Hispanic men have lately
excelled, it is particularly vulnerable to attack by white middle-class
reformers, who seem uninterested in lobbying against equally dangerous

but "establishment" sports like football, auto racing, and thoroughbred horse racing.

11   There is something peculiarly American in the fact that, while boxing is our most controversial sport, it is also the sport that pays its top athletes the most money. In spite of the controversy, boxing has never been healthier financially. The three highest paid athletes in the world in both 1983 and 1984 were boxers; a boxer with a long career like heavyweight champion Larry Holmes — forty-eight fights in thirteen years as a professional — can expect to earn somewhere beyond $50 million. (Holmes said that after retirement what he would miss about boxing is his million-dollar checks.) Dempsey, who said that a man fights for one thing only — money — made somewhere beyond $3,500,000 in the ring in his long and varied career. Now $1.5 million is a fairly common figure for a single fight. Thomas Hearns made at least $7 million in his fight with Hagler while Hagler made at least $7.5 million. For the first of his highly publicized matches with Roberto Duran in 1980 — which he lost on a decision — the popular black welterweight champion Sugar Ray Leonard received a staggering $10 million to Duran's $1.3 million. And none of these figures takes into account various subsidiary earnings (from television commercials, for instance) which in Leonard's case are probably as high as his income was from boxing.

12   Money has drawn any number of retired boxers back into the ring, very often with tragic results. The most notorious example is perhaps Joe Louis, who, owing huge sums in back taxes, continued boxing well beyond the point at which he could perform capably. After a career of seventeen years he was stopped by Rocky Marciano — who was said to have felt as upset by his victory as Louis by the defeat. (Louis then went on to a degrading second career as a professional wrestler. This, too, ended abruptly when 300-pound Rocky Lee stepped on the forty-two-year-old Louis's chest and damaged his heart.) Ezzard Charles, Jersey Joe Walcott, Joe Frazier, Muhammad Ali — each continued fighting when he was no longer in condition to defend himself against young heavyweight boxers on the way up. Of all heavyweight champions, only Rocky Marciano, to whom fame and money were not of paramount significance, was prudent enough to retire before he was defeated. In any case, the prodigious sums of money a few boxers earn do not account for the sums the public is willing to pay them.

13   Though boxing has long been popular in many countries and under many forms of government, its popularity in the United States since the days of John L. Sullivan has a good deal to do with what is felt as the spirit of the individual — his "physical" spirit — in conflict with

the constrictions of the state. The rise of boxing in the 1920s in particular might well be seen as a consequence of the diminution of the individual vis-à-vis society; the gradual attrition of personal freedom, will, and strength — whether "masculine" or otherwise. In the Eastern bloc of nations, totalitarianism is a function of the state; in the Western bloc it has come to seem a function of technology, or history — "fate." The individual exists in his physical supremacy, but does the individual matter?

In the magical space of the boxing ring so disquieting a question   14
has no claim. There, as in no other public arena, the individual as a unique physical being asserts himself; there, for a dramatic if fleeting period of time, the great world with its moral and political complexities, its terrifying impersonality, simply ceases to exist. Men fighting one another with only their fists and their cunning are all contemporaries, all brothers, belonging to no historical time. "He can run, but he can't hide" — so said Joe Louis before his famous fight with young Billy Conn in 1941. In the brightly lighted ring, man is *in extremis*, performing an atavistic rite or agon for the mysterious solace of those who can participate only vicariously in such drama: the drama of life in the flesh. Boxing has become America's tragic theater.

——— CONSIDERATIONS ———

1. In her opening paragraph, Oates uses the term "homoerotic." How does this differ from "homosexual"? Or does it?

2. What, according to Oates, is "man's greatest passion"? How does she try to support this assertion?

3. In Paragraphs 11 and 12, Oates cites remarks by great fighters like Larry Holmes and Jack Dempsey, who claim that the most important thing about boxing is the money. How do their statements affect the writer's assertion (in Paragraph 5) that boxing is hardly a game, it is life itself?

4. A research question: What happened to the resolution passed in 1984 by the American Medical Association calling for the abolition of boxing? Does Oates's essay provide any answers? How would you go about finding an answer in your college library?

5. In what way does it make sense for Oates to describe gory photographs of battered boxers as "near-pornographic"?

6. Oates compares boxing to love (Paragraph 2), sacrifice (Paragraph 6), religious rites (Paragraph 7), and the theater (Paragraph 14). Are such notions merely fanciful or do they point up significant aspects of the sport?

Flannery O'Connor (1925–1964) was born in Savannah, and moved with her family to her mother's birthplace, Milledgeville, Georgia, at the age of twelve. When she was fifteen her father died of the inherited degenerative disease, lupus. She took her B.A. at Milledgeville's Georgia State College for Women (now Georgia College) and then studied fiction writing at the University of Iowa. From 1947 until 1951 she spent time in New York, Connecticut, and Georgia. When she discovered that she was ill, she returned to live with her mother on the Milledgeville farm called Andalusia, surrounded by pet peacocks and peahens, writing her remarkable fiction and staying in touch with friends by letter. She died of lupus when she was thirty-eight.

Flannery O'Connor also wrote essays, collected after her death in a volume called Mystery and Manners *(1969). This essay appeared in the* Georgia Bulletin *in 1963, addressed to local and immediate problems; in the American eighties its insights remain urgent, as our culture, in O'Connor's word, becomes increasingly "fractured."*

48

FLANNERY O'CONNOR

The Total Effect
and the Eighth Grade

In two recent instances in Georgia, parents have objected to their   1
eighth- and ninth-grade children's reading assignments in modern fiction.
This seems to happen with some regularity in cases throughout the
country. The unwitting parent picks up his child's book, glances through
it, comes upon passages of erotic detail or profanity, and takes off at
once to complain to the school board. Sometimes, as in one of the Georgia cases, the teacher is dismissed and hackles rise in liberal circles
everywhere.

The two cases in Georgia, which involved Steinbeck's *East of Eden*   2
and John Hersey's *A Bell for Adano*, provoked considerable newspaper
comment. One columnist, in commending the enterprise of the teachers,
announced that students do not like to read the fusty works of the nineteenth century, that their attention can best be held by novels dealing
with the realities of our own time, and that the Bible, too, is full of racy
stories.

Mr. Hersey himself addressed a letter to the State School   3
Superintendent in behalf of the teacher who had been dismissed. He
pointed out that his book is not scandalous, that it attempts to convey
an earnest message about the nature of democracy, and that it falls well
within the limits of the principle of "total effect," that principle followed
in legal cases by which a book is judged not for isolated parts but by
the final effect of the whole book upon the general reader.

4   I do not want to comment on the merits of these particular cases. What concerns me is what novels ought to be assigned in the eighth and ninth grades as a matter of course, for if these cases indicate anything, they indicate the haphazard way in which fiction is approached in our high schools. Presumably there is a state reading list which contains "safe" books for teachers to assign; after that it is up to the teacher.

5   English teachers come in Good, Bad, and Indifferent, but too frequently in high schools anyone who can speak English is allowed to teach it. Since several novels can't easily be gathered into one textbook, the fiction that students are assigned depends upon their teacher's knowledge, ability, and taste: variable factors at best. More often than not, the teacher assigns what he thinks will hold the attention and interest of the students. Modern fiction will certainly hold it.

6   Ours is the first age in history which has asked the child what he would tolerate learning, but that is a part of the problem with which I am not equipped to deal. The devil of Educationism that possesses us is the kind that can be "cast out only by prayer and fasting." No one has yet come along strong enough to do it. In other ages the attention of children was held by Homer and Virgil, among others, but, by the reverse evolutionary process, that is no longer possible; our children are too stupid now to enter the past imaginatively. No one asks the student if algebra pleases him or if he finds it satisfactory that some French verbs are irregular, but if he prefers Hersey to Hawthorne, his taste must prevail.

7   I would like to put forward the proposition, repugnant to most English teachers, that fiction, if it is going to be taught in the high schools, should be taught as a subject and as a subject with a history. The total effect of a novel depends not only on its innate impact, but upon the experience, literary and otherwise, with which it is approached. No child needs to be assigned Hersey or Steinbeck until he is familiar with a certain amount of the best work of Cooper, Hawthorne, Melville, the early James, and Crane, and he does not need to be assigned these until he has been introduced to some of the better English novelists of the eighteenth and nineteenth centuries.

8   The fact that these works do not present him with the realities of his own time is all to the good. He is surrounded by the realities of his own time, and he has no perspective whatever from which to view them. Like the college student who wrote in her paper on Lincoln that he went to the movies and got shot, many students go to college unaware that the world was not made yesterday; their studies began with the

present and dipped backward occasionally when it seemed necessary or unavoidable.

There is much to be enjoyed in the great British novels of the nine- 9 teenth century, much that a good teacher can open up in them for the young student. There is no reason why these novels should be either too simple or too difficult for the eighth grade. For the simple, they offer simple pleasures; for the more precocious, they can be made to yield subtler ones if the teacher is up to it. Let the student discover, after reading the nineteenth-century British novel, that the nineteenth-century American novel is quite different as to its literary characteristics, and he will thereby learn something not only about these individual works but about the sea-change which a new historical situation can effect in a literary form. Let him come to modern fiction with this experience behind him, and he will be better able to see and to deal with the more complicated demands of the best twentieth-century fiction.

Modern fiction often looks simpler than the fiction that preceded 10 it, but in reality is more complex. A natural evolution has taken place. The author has for the most part absented himself from direct participation in the work and has left the reader to make his own way amid experiences dramatically rendered and symbolically ordered. The modern novelist merges the reader in experience; he tends to raise the passions he touches upon. If he is a good novelist, he raises them to effect by their order and clarity a new experience — the total effect — which is not in itself sensuous or simply of the moment. Unless the child has had some literary experience before, he is not going to be able to resolve the immediate passions the book arouses into any true, total picture.

It is here the moral problem will arise. It is one thing for a child 11 to read about adultery in the Bible or in *Anna Karenina,* and quite another for him to read about it in most modern fiction. This is not only because in both the former instances adultery is considered a sin, and in the latter, at most, an inconvenience, but because modern writing involves the reader in the action with a new degree of intensity, and literary mores now permit him to be involved in any action a human being can perform.

In our fractured culture, we cannot agree on morals; we cannot 12 even agree that moral matters should come before literary ones when there is a conflict between them. All this is another reason why the high schools would do well to return to their proper business of preparing foundations. Whether in the senior year students should be assigned modern novelists should depend both on their parents' consent and on what they have already read and understood.

13   The high-school English teacher will be fulfilling his responsibility if he furnishes the student a guided opportunity, through the best writing of the past, to come, in time, to an understanding of the best writing of the present. He will teach literature, not social studies or little lessons in democracy or the customs of many lands.

14   And if the student finds that this is not to his taste? Well, that is regrettable. Most regrettable. His taste should not be consulted; it is being formed.

_____ **CONSIDERATIONS** _____

1. How far must you read in O'Connor's essay before you know her chief concern? Does it occupy her attention in her first three paragraphs? If not, how can you defend the organization of this essay?

2. O'Connor argues in Paragraph 8 that "it is all to the good" that the so-called classics do not present the child with realities of his own time. How does her reference to the college student writing about Lincoln apply to her argument? How would she offset a reader's insistence that the child's reading be relevant to his or her own time?

3. To what extent does O'Connor's Paragraph 10 help explain the principle of "total effect" mentioned in Paragraph 3? Do you consider that principle a reasonable means of sorting out acceptable from unacceptable reading matter?

4. How would Margaret Atwood ("Pornography," pages 40–46) respond to O'Connor's solution to the moral problem mentioned in Paragraph 12?

5. Write a response to O'Connor's answer to her question at the beginning of Paragraph 14. Take into account the rest of her essay as well as your own feelings.

6. What nineteenth-century British and American novels do you remember well enough to compare with modern novels? If your answer is "none," are you in any position to argue with O'Connor?

Flannery O'Connor's first novel, Wise Blood, *appeared in 1952, her second and last,* The Violent Bear It Away, *in 1960. Most readers believe her short stories to be her best fiction; they are available in* The Collected Stories of Flannery O'Connor *(1972). During her lifetime she published one volume of stories, bearing the title of the story that follows. This was the story she usually read aloud when asked to read.*

49

FLANNERY O'CONNOR
A Good Man Is Hard to Find

The grandmother didn't want to go to Florida. She wanted to visit some of her connections in east Tennessee and she was seizing every chance to change Bailey's mind. Bailey was the son she lived with, her only boy. He was sitting on the edge of his chair at the table, bent over the orange sports section of the *Journal.* "Now look here, Bailey," she said, "see here, read this," and she stood with one hand on her thin hip and the other rattling the newspaper at his bald head. "Here this fellow that calls himself The Misfit is aloose from the Federal Pen and headed toward Florida and you read here what it says he did to these people. Just you read it. I wouldn't take my children in any direction with a criminal like that aloose in it. I couldn't answer to my conscience if I did." 1

Bailey didn't look up from his reading so she wheeled around then and faced the children's mother; a young woman in slacks, whose face was as broad and innocent as a cabbage and was tied around with a green 2 headkerchief that had two points on the top like rabbit's ears. She was sitting on the sofa, feeding the baby his apricots out of a jar. "The children have been to Florida before," the old lady said. "You all ought to take them somewhere else for a change so they would see different parts of the world and be broad. They never have been to east Tennessee."

3   The children's mother didn't seem to hear her, but the eight-year-old boy, John Wesley, a stocky child with glasses, said, "If you don't want to go to Florida, why dontcha stay at home?" He and the little girl, June Star, were reading the funny papers on the floor.

4   "She wouldn't stay at home to be queen for a day," June Star said without raising her yellow head.

5   "Yes, and what would you do if this fellow, The Misfit, caught you?" the grandmother asked.

6   "I'd smack his face," John Wesley said.

7   "She wouldn't stay at home for a million bucks," June Star said. "Afraid she'd miss something. She has to go everywhere we go."

8   "All right, Miss," the grandmother said. "Just remember that the next time you want me to curl your hair."

9   June Star said her hair was naturally curly.

10   The next morning the grandmother was the first one in the car, ready to go. She had her big black valise that looked like the head of a hippopotamus in one corner, and underneath it she was hiding a basket with Pitty Sing, the cat, in it. She didn't intend for the cat to be left alone in the house for three days because he would miss her too much and she was afraid he might brush against one of the gas burners and accidentally asphyxiate himself. Her son, Bailey, didn't like to arrive at a motel with a cat.

11   She sat in the middle of the back seat with John Wesley and June Star on either side of her. Bailey and the children's mother and the baby sat in the front and they left Atlanta at eight forty-five with the mileage on the car at 55890. The grandmother wrote this down because she thought it would be interesting to say how many miles they had been when they got back. It took them twenty minutes to reach the outskirts of the city.

12   The old lady settled herself comfortably, removing her white cotton gloves and putting them up with her purse on the shelf in front of the back window. The children's mother still had on slacks and still had her head tied up in a green kerchief, but the grandmother had on a navy blue straw sailor hat with a bunch of white violets on the brim and a navy blue dress with a small white dot in the print. Her collar

and cuffs were white organdy trimmed with lace and at her neckline she had pinned a purple spray of cloth violets containing a sachet. In case of an accident, anyone seeing her dead on the highway would know at once that she was a lady.

She said she thought it was going to be a good day for driving, nei- 13 ther too hot nor too cold, and she cautioned Bailey that the speed limit was fifty-five miles an hour and that the patrolmen hid themselves behind bill-boards and small clumps of trees and sped out after you before you had a chance to slow down. She pointed out interesting details of the scenery: Stone Mountain; the blue granite that in some places came up to both sides of the highway; the brilliant red clay banks slightly streaked with purple; and the various crops that made rows of green lace-work on the ground. The trees were full of silver-white sunlights and the meanest of them sparkled. The children were reading comic magazines and their mother had gone back to sleep.

"Let's go through Georgia fast so we don't have to look at it much," 14 John Wesley said.

"If I were a little boy," said the grandmother, "I wouldn't talk about 15 my native state that way. Tennessee has the mountains and Georgia has the hills."

"Tennessee is just a hillbilly dumping ground," John Wesley said, 16 "and Georgia is a lousy state too."

"You said it," June Star said. 17

"In my time," said the grandmother, folding her thin veined fingers, 18 "children were more respectful of their native states and their parents and everything else. People did right then. Oh look at the cute little pickaninny!" she said and pointed to a Negro child standing in the door of a shack. "Wouldn't that make a picture, now?" she asked and they all turned and looked at the little Negro out of the back window. He waved.

"He didn't have any britches on," June Star said. 19

"He probably didn't have any," the grandmother explained. "Little 20 niggers in the country don't have things like we do. If I could paint, I'd paint that picture," she said.

The children exchanged comic books. 21

The grandmother offered to hold the baby and the children's 22 mother passed him over the front seat to her. She set him on her knee and bounced him and told him about the things they were passing. She rolled her eyes and screwed up her mouth and stuck her leathery thin face into his smooth bland one. Occasionally he gave her a faraway smile. They passed a large cotton field with five or six graves fenced in the middle of it, like a small island. "Look at the graveyard!" the grandmother said, pointing it out. "That was the old family burying ground. That belonged to the plantation."

23   "Where's the plantation?" John Wesley asked.

24   "Gone With the Wind," said the grandmother. "Ha. Ha."

25   When the children finished all the comic books they had brought, they opened the lunch and ate it. The grandmother ate a peanut butter sandwich and an olive and would not let the children throw the box and the paper napkins out the window. When there was nothing else to do they played a game by choosing a cloud and making the other two guess what shape it suggested. John Wesley took one the shape of a cow and June Star guessed a cow and John Wesley said, no, an automobile, and June Star said he didn't play fair, and they began to slap each other over the grandmother.

26   The grandmother said she would tell them a story if they would keep quiet. When she told a story, she rolled her eyes and waved her head and was very dramatic. She said once when she was a maiden lady she had been courted by a Mr. Edgar Atkins Teagarden from Jasper, Georgia. She said he was a very good-looking man and a gentleman and that he brought her a watermelon every Saturday afternoon with his initials cut in it, E.A.T. Well, one Saturday, she said, Mr. Teagarden brought the watermelon and there was nobody at home and he left it on the front porch and returned in his buggy to Jasper, but she never got the watermelon, she said, because a nigger boy ate it when he saw the initials, E.A.T.! This story tickled John Wesley's funny bone and he giggled and giggled but June Star didn't think it was any good. She said she wouldn't marry a man that just brought her a watermelon on Saturday. The grandmother said she would have done well to marry Mr. Teagarden because he was a gentleman and had bought Coca-Cola stock when it first came out and that he had died only a few years ago, a very wealthy man.

27   They stopped at The Tower for barbecued sandwiches. The Tower was a part-stucco and part-wood filling station and dance hall set in a clearing outside of Timothy. A fat man named Red Sammy Butts ran it and there were signs stuck here and there on the building and for miles up and down the highway saying, TRY RED SAMMY'S FAMOUS BARBECUE. NONE LIKE FAMOUS RED SAMMY'S! RED SAM! THE FAT BOY WITH THE HAPPY LAUGH. A VETERAN! RED SAMMY'S YOUR MAN!

28   Red Sammy was lying on the bare ground outside The Tower with his head under a truck while a gray monkey about a foot high, chained to a small chinaberry tree, chattered nearby. The monkey sprang back

into the tree and got on the highest limb as soon as he saw the children jump out of the car and run toward him.

Inside, The Tower was a long dark room with a counter at one end 29 and tables at the other and dancing space in the middle. They all sat down at a broad table next to the nickelodeon and Red Sam's wife, a tall burnt-brown woman with hair and eyes lighter than her skin, came and took their order. The children's mother put a dime in the machine and played "The Tennessee Waltz," and the grandmother said that tune always made her want to dance. She asked Bailey if he would like to dance but he only glared at her. He didn't have a naturally sunny disposition like she did and trips made him nervous. The grandmother's brown eyes were very bright. She swayed her head from side to side and pretended she was dancing in her chair. June Star said play something she could tap to so the children's mother put in another dime and played a fast number and June Star stepped out onto the dance floor and did her tap routine.

"Ain't she cute?" Red Sam's wife said, leaning over the counter. 30 "Would you like to come be my little girl?"

"No, I certainly wouldn't," June Star said. "I wouldn't live in a 31 broken-down place like this for a million bucks!" and she ran back to the table.

"Ain't she cute?" the woman repeated, stretching her mouth 32 politely.

"Aren't you ashamed?" hissed the grandmother. 33

Red Sam came in and told his wife to quit lounging on the counter 34 and hurry up with these people's order. His khaki trousers reached just to his hip bones and his stomach hung over them like a sack of meal swaying under his shirt. He came over and sat down at a table nearby and let out a combination sigh and yodel. "You can't win," he said. "You can't win," and he wiped his sweating red face off with a gray handkerchief. "These days you don't know who to trust," he said. "Ain't that the truth?"

"People are certainly not nice like they used to be," said the 35 grandmother.

"Two fellers come in here last week," Red Sammy said, "driving 36 a Chrysler. It was an old beat-up car but it was a good one and these boys looked all right to me. Said they worked at the mill and you know I let them fellers charge the gas they bought? Now why did I do that?"

"Because you're a good man!" the grandmother said at once. 37

"Yes'm, I suppose so," Red Sam said as if he were struck with this 38 answer.

39   His wife brought the orders, carrying the five plates all at once without a tray, two in each hand and one balanced on her arm. "It isn't a soul in this green world of God's that you can trust," she said. "And I don't count nobody out of that, not nobody," she repeated, looking at Red Sammy.

40   "Did you read about that criminal, The Misfit, that's escaped?" asked the grandmother.

41   "I wouldn't be a bit surprised if he didn't attack this place right here," said the woman. "If he hears about it being here, I wouldn't be none surprised to see him. If he hears it's two cent in the cash register, I wouldn't be a tall surprised if he . . ."

42   "That'll do," Red Sam said. "Go bring these people their Co'-Colas," and the woman went off to get the rest of the order.

43   "A good man is hard to find," Red Sammy said. "Everything is getting terrible. I remember the day you could go off and leave your screen door unlatched. Not no more."

44   He and the grandmother discussed better times. The old lady said that in her opinion Europe was entirely to blame for the way things were now. She said the way Europe acted you would think we were made of money and Red Sam said it was no use talking about it, she was exactly right. The children ran outside into the white sunlight and looked at the monkey in the lacy chinaberry tree. He was busy catching fleas on himself and biting each one carefully between his teeth as if it were a delicacy.

45   They drove off again into the hot afternoon. The grandmother took cat naps and woke up every few minutes with her own snoring. Outside of Toombsboro she woke up and recalled an old plantation that she had visited in this neighborhood once when she was a young lady. She said the house had six white columns across the front and that there was an avenue of oaks leading up to it and two little wooden trellis arbors on either side in front where you sat down with your suitor after a stroll in the garden. She recalled exactly which road to turn off to get to it. She knew that Bailey would not be willing to lose any time looking at an old house, but the more she talked about it, the more she wanted to see it once again and find out if the little twin arbors were still standing. "There was a secret panel in this house," she said craftily, not telling the truth but wishing that she were, "and the story went that all the family silver was hidden in it when Sherman came through but it was never found. . . ."

46   "Hey!" John Wesley said. "Let's go see it! We'll find it! We'll poke

all the wood work and find it! Who lives there? Where do you turn off at? Hey Pop, can't we turn off there?"

"We never have seen a house with a secret panel!" June Star   47
shrieked. "Let's go to the house with the secret panel! Hey, Pop, can't we go see the house with the secret panel!"

"It's not far from here, I know," the grandmother said. "It wouldn't   48
take over twenty minutes."

Bailey was looking straight ahead. His jaw was as rigid as a   49
horseshoe. "No," he said.

The children began to yell and scream that they wanted to see the   50
house with the secret panel. John Wesley kicked the back of the front seat and June Star hung over her mother's shoulder and whined desperately into her ear that they never had any fun even on their vacation, that they could never do what THEY wanted to do. The baby began to scream and John Wesley kicked the back of the seat so hard that his father could feel the blows in his kidney.

"All right!" he shouted and drew the car to a stop at the side of   51
the road. "Will you all shut up? Will you all just shut up for one second? If you don't shut up, we won't go anywhere."

"It would be very educational for them," the grandmother   52
murmured.

"All right," Bailey said, "but get this. This is the only time we're   53
going to stop for anything like this. This is the one and only time."

"The dirt road that you have to turn down is about a mile back,"   54
the grandmother directed. "I marked it when we passed."

"A dirt road," Bailey groaned.   55

After they had turned around and were headed toward the dirt road,   56
the grandmother recalled other points about the house, the beautiful glass over the front doorway and the candle lamp in the hall. John Wesley said that the secret panel was probably in the fireplace.

"You can't go inside the house," Bailey said. "You don't know who   57
lives there."

"While you all talk to the people in front, I'll run around behind   58
and get in a window," John Wesley suggested.

"We'll all stay in the car," his mother said.   59

They turned onto the dirt road and the car raced roughly along in   60
a swirl of pink dust. The grandmother recalled the times when there were no paved roads and thirty miles was a day's journey. The dirt road was hilly and there were sudden washes in it and sharp curves on dangerous embankments. All at once they would be on a hill, looking

down over the blue tops of trees for miles around, then the next minute, they would be in a red depression with the dust-coated trees looking down on them.

61   "This place had better turn up in a minute," Bailey said, "or I'm
going to turn around."

62   The road looked as if no one had traveled on it in months.

63   "It's not much farther," the grandmother said and just as she said
it, a horrible thought came to her. The thought was so embarrassing
that she turned red in the face and her eyes dilated and her feet jumped
up, upsetting her valise in the corner. The instant the valise moved,
the newspaper top she had over the basket under it rose with a snarl
and Pitty Sing, the cat, sprang onto Bailey's shoulder.

64   The children were thrown to the floor and their mother, clutching
the baby, was thrown out the door onto the ground; the old lady was
thrown into the front seat. The car turned over once and landed right-
side-up in a gulch on the side of the road. Bailey remained in the driver's
seat with the cat — gray-striped with a broad white face and an orange
nose — clinging to his neck like a caterpillar.

65   As soon as the children saw they could move their arms and legs,
they scrambled out of the car shouting, "We've had an ACCIDENT!" The
grandmother was curled up under the dashboard, hoping she was injured so that Bailey's wrath would not come down on her all at once.
The horrible thought she had had before the accident was that the house
she had remembered so vividly was not in Georgia but in Tennessee.

66   Bailey removed the cat from his neck with both hands and flung
it out the window against the side of a pine tree. Then he got out of
the car and started looking for the children's mother. She was sitting
against the side of the red gutted ditch, holding the screaming baby, but
she only had a cut down her face and a broken shoulder. "We've had
an ACCIDENT!" the children screamed in a frenzy of delight.

67   "But nobody's killed," June Star said with disappointment as the
grandmother limped out of the car, her hat still pinned to her head but
the broken front brim standing up at a jaunty angle and the violet spray
hanging off the side. They all sat down in the ditch, except the children,
to recover from the shock. They were all shaking.

68   "Maybe a car will come along," said the children's mother hoarsely.

69   "I believe I have injured an organ," said the grandmother, pressing
her side, but no one answered her. Bailey's teeth were clattering. He
had on a yellow sport shirt with bright blue parrots designed in it and
his face was as yellow as the shirt. The grandmother decided that she
would not mention that the house was in Tennessee.

The road was about ten feet above and they could see only the tops
of the trees on the other side of it. Behind the ditch they were sitting
in there were more woods, tall and dark and deep. In a few minutes they
saw a car some distance away on top of a hill, coming slowly as if the
occupants were watching them. The grandmother stood up and waved
both arms dramatically to attract their attention. The car continued to
come on slowly, disappeared around a bend and appeared again, moving even slower, on top of the hill they had gone over. It was a big black
battered hearselike automobile. There were three men in it. 70

It came to a stop just over them and for some minutes, the driver
looked down with a steady expressionless gaze to where they were sitting, and didn't speak. Then he turned his head and muttered something
to the other two and they got out. One was a fat boy in black trousers
and a red sweat shirt with a silver stallion embossed on the front of
it. He moved around on the right side of them and stood staring, his
mouth partly open in a kind of loose grin. The other had on khaki pants
and a blue striped coat and a gray hat pulled down very low, hiding most
of his face. He came around slowly on the left side. Neither spoke. 71

The driver got out of the car and stood by the side of it, looking
down at them. He was an older man than the other two. His hair was
just beginning to gray and he wore silver-rimmed spectacles that gave
him a scholarly look. He had a long creased face and didn't have on any
shirt or undershirt. He had on blue jeans that were too tight for him
and he was holding a black hat and a gun. The two boys also had guns. 72

"We've had an ACCIDENT!" the children screamed. 73

The grandmother had the peculiar feeling that the bespectacled
man was someone she knew. His face was as familiar to her as if she
had known him all her life but she could not recall who he was. He
moved away from the car and began to come down the embankment,
placing his feet carefully so that he wouldn't slip. He had on tan and
white shoes and no socks, and his ankles were red and thin. "Good afternoon," he said, "I see you all had you a little spill." 74

"We turned over twice!" said the grandmother. 75

"Oncet," he corrected. "We see it happen. Try their car and see will
it run, Hiram," he said quietly to the boy with the gray hat. 76

"What you got that gun for?" John Wesley asked. "Whatcha gonna
do with that gun?" 77

"Lady," the man said to the children's mother, "would you mind
calling them children to sit down by you? Children make me nervous.
I want all you all to sit down right together there were you're at." 78

"What are you telling us what to do for?" June Star asked. 79

80   Behind them the line of woods gaped like a dark open mouth. "Come here," said their mother.

81   "Look here now," Bailey began suddenly, "we're in a predicament! We're in . . ."

82   The grandmother shrieked. She scrambled to her feet and stood staring.

83   "You're The Misfit!" she said. "I recognized you at once!"

84   "Yes'm," the man said, smiling slightly as if he were pleased in spite of himself to be known. "But it would have been better for all of you, lady, if you hadn't of reckernized me."

85   Bailey turned his head sharply and said something to his mother that shocked even the children. The old lady began to cry and The Misfit reddened.

86   "Lady," he said, "don't you get upset. Sometimes a man says things he don't mean. I don't reckon he meant to talk to you thataway."

87   "You wouldn't shoot a lady, would you?" the grandmother said and removed a clean handkerchief from her cuff and began to slap at her eyes with it.

88   The Misfit pointed the toe of his shoe into the ground and made a little hole and then covered it up again. "I would hate to have to," he said.

89   "Listen," the grandmother almost screamed, "I know you're a good man. You don't look a bit like you have common blood. I know you must come from nice people!"

90   "Yes mam," he said, "finest people in the world." When he smiled he showed a row of strong white teeth. "God never made a finer woman than my mother and my daddy's heart was pure gold," he said. The boy with the red sweat shirt had come around behind them and was standing with his gun at his hip. The Misfit squatted down on the ground. "Watch them children, Bobby Lee," he said. "You know they make me nervous." He looked at the six of them huddled together in front of him and he seemed to be embarrassed as if he couldn't think of anything to say. "Ain't a cloud in the sky," he remarked, looking up at it. "Don't see no sun but don't see no cloud neither."

91   "Yes, it's a beautiful day," said the grandmother. "Listen," she said, "you shouldn't call yourself The Misfit because I know you're a good man at heart. I can just look at you and tell."

92   "Hush!" Bailey yelled. "Hush! Everybody shut up and let me handle this!" He was squatting in the position of a runner about to spring forward but he didn't move.

"I pre-chate that, lady," The Misfit said and drew a little circle in   93
the ground with the butt of his gun.

"It'll take a half a hour to fix this here car," Hiram called, looking   94
over the raised hood of it.

"Well, first you and Bobby Lee get him and that little boy to step   95
over yonder with you," The Misfit said, pointing to Bailey and John
Wesley. "The boys want to ask you something," he said to Bailey. "Would
you mind stepping back in them woods there with them?"

"Listen," Bailey began, "we're in a terrible predicament! Nobody   96
realizes what this is," and his voice cracked. His eyes were as blue and
intense as the parrots in his shirt and he remained perfectly still.

The grandmother reached up to adjust her hat brim as if she were   97
going to the woods with him but it came off in her hand. She stood staring at it and after a second she let it fall on the ground. Hiram pulled
Bailey up by the arm as if he were assisting an old man. John Wesley
caught hold of his father's hand and Bobby Lee followed. They went off
toward the woods and just as they reached the dark edge, Bailey turned
and supporting himself against a gray naked pine trunk, he shouted, "I'll
be back in a minute, Mamma, wait on me!"

"Come back this instant!" his mother shrilled but they all disap-   98
peared into the woods.

"Bailey Boy!" the grandmother called in tragic voice but she found   99
she was looking at The Misfit squatting on the ground in front of her.
"I just know you're a good man," she said desperately. "You're not a bit
common!"

"Nome, I ain't a good man," The Misfit said after a second as if he   100
had considered her statement carefully, "but I ain't the worst in the world
neither. My daddy said I was a different breed of dog from my brothers
and sisters. 'You know,' Daddy said, 'it's some that can live their whole
life out without asking about it and it's others has to know why it is,
and this boy is one of the latters. He's going to be into everything!'" He
put on his black hat and looked up suddenly and then away deep into
the woods as if he were embarrassed again. "I'm sorry, I don't have on
a shirt before you ladies," he said, hunching his shoulders slightly. "We
buried our clothes that we had on when we escaped and we're just making do until we can get better. We borrowed these from some folks we
met," he explained.

"That's perfectly all right," the grandmother said. "Maybe Bailey   101
has an extra shirt in his suitcase."

"I'll look and see terrectly," The Misfit said.   102

103   "Where are they taking him?" the children's mother screamed.

104   "Daddy was a card himself," The Misfit said. "You couldn't put anything over on him. He never got in trouble with the Authorities though. Just had the knack of handling them."

105   "You could be honest too if you'd only try," said the grandmother. "Think how wonderful it would be to settle down and live a comfortable life and not have to think about somebody chasing you all the time."

106   The Misfit kept scratching in the ground with the butt of his gun as if he were thinking about it. "Yes'm, somebody is always after you," he murmured.

107   The grandmother noticed how thin his shoulder blades were just behind his hat because she was standing up looking down on him. "Do you ever pray?" she asked.

108   He shook his head. All she saw was the black hat wiggle between his shoulder blades. "Nome," he said.

109   There was a pistol shot from the woods, followed closely by another. Then silence. The old lady's head jerked around. She could hear the wind move through the tree tops like a long satisfied insuck of breath. "Bailey Boy!" she called.

110   "I was a gospel singer for a while," The Misfit said. "I been most everything. Been in the arm service, both land and sea, at home and abroad, been twict married, been an undertaker, been with the railroads, plowed Mother Earth, been in a tornado, seen a man burnt alive oncet," and he looked up at the children's mother and the little girl who were sitting close together, their faces white and their eyes glassy; "I even seen a woman flogged," he said.

111   "Pray, pray," the grandmother began, "pray, pray . . ."

112   "I never was a bad boy that I remember of," The Misfit said in an almost dreamy voice, "but somewheres along the line I done something wrong and got sent to the penitentiary. I was buried alive," and he looked up and held her attention to him by a steady stare.

113   "That's when you should have started to pray," she said. "What did you do to get sent to the penitentiary that first time?"

114   "Turn to the right, it was a wall," The Misfit said, looking up again at the cloudless sky. "Turn to the left, it was a wall. Look up it was a ceiling, look down it was a floor. I forgot what I done, lady. I set there and set there, trying to remember what it was I done and I ain't recalled it to this day. Oncet in a while, I would think it was coming to me, but it never come."

"Maybe they put you in by mistake," the old lady said vaguely.   115

"Nome," he said. "It wasn't no mistake. They had the papers on me."   116

"You must have stolen something," she said.   117

The Misfit sneered slightly. "Nobody had nothing I wanted," he   118
said. "It was a head-doctor at the penitentiary said what I had done was
kill my daddy but I known that for a lie. My daddy died in nineteen
ought nineteen of the epidemic flu and I never had a thing to do with
it. He was buried in the Mount Hopewell Baptist churchyard and you
can go there and see for yourself."

"If you would pray," the old lady said, "Jesus would help you."   119

"That's right," The Misfit said.   120

"Well then, why don't you pray?" she asked trembling with delight   121
suddenly.

"I don't want no hep," he said, "I'm doing all right by myself."   122

Bobby Lee and Hiram came ambling back from the woods. Bobby   123
Lee was dragging a yellow shirt with bright blue parrots in it.

"Throw me that shirt, Bobby Lee," The Misfit said. The shirt came   124
flying at him and landed on his shoulder and he put it on. The grandmother couldn't name what the shirt reminded her of. "No, lady," The
Misfit said while he was buttoning it up, "I found out the crime don't
matter. You can do one thing or you can do another, kill a man or take
a tire off his car, because sooner or later you're going to forget what it
was you done and just be punished for it."

The children's mother had begun to make heaving noises as if she   125
couldn't get her breath. "Lady," he asked, "would you and that little girl
like to step off yonder with Bobby Lee and Hiram and join your husband?"

"Yes, thank you," the mother said faintly. Her left arm dangled   126
helplessly and she was holding the baby, who had gone to sleep, in the
other. "Hep that lady up, Hiram," The Misfit said as she struggled to
climb out of the ditch, "and Bobby Lee, you hold onto that little girl's
hand."

"I don't want to hold hands with him," June Star said. "He reminds   127
me of a pig."

The fat boy blushed and laughed and caught her by the arm and   128
pulled her off into the woods after Hiram and her mother.

Alone with The Misfit, the grandmother found that she had lost   129
her voice. There was not a cloud in the sky nor any sun. There was
nothing around her but woods. She wanted to tell him that he must
pray. She opened and closed her mouth several times before anything

came out. Finally she found herself saying, "Jesus. Jesus," meaning, Jesus will help you, but the way she was saying it, it sounded as if she might be cursing.

130   "Yes'm," The Misfit said as if he agreed. "Jesus thrown everything off balance. It was the same case with Him as with me except He hadn't committed any crime and they could prove I had committed one because they had the papers on me. Of course," he said, "they never shown me any papers. That's why I sign myself now, I said long ago, you get you a signature and sign everything you do and keep a copy of it. Then you'll know what you done and you can hold up the crime to the punishment and see do they match and in the end you'll have something to prove you ain't been treated right. I call myself The Misfit," he said, "because I can't make what all I done wrong fit what all I gone through in punishment."

131   There was a piercing scream from the woods, followed closely by a pistol report. "Does it seem right to you, lady, that one is punished a heap and another ain't punished at all?"

132   "Jesus!" the old lady cried. "You've got blood! I know you wouldn't shoot a lady! I know you come from nice people! Pray! Jesus, you ought not to shoot a lady. I'll give you all the money I've got!"

133   "Lady," The Misfit said, looking beyond her far into the woods, "there was never a body that give the undertaker a tip."

134   There were two more pistol reports and the grandmother raised her head like a parched old turkey hen crying for water and called, "Bailey Boy, Bailey Boy!" as if her heart would break.

135   "Jesus was the only One that ever raised the dead," The Misfit continued, "and He shouldn't have done it. He thrown everything off balance. If He did what He said, then it's nothing for you to do but throw away everything and follow Him, and if He didn't then it's nothing for you to do but enjoy the few minutes you got left the best way you can — by killing somebody or burning down his house or doing some other meanness to him. No pleasure but meanness," he said and his voice had become almost a snarl.

136   "Maybe He didn't raise the dead," the old lady mumbled, not knowing what she was saying and feeling so dizzy that she sank down in the ditch with her legs twisted under her.

137   "I wasn't there so I can't say He didn't," The Misfit said. "I wisht I had of been there," he said, hitting the ground with his fist. "It ain't right I wasn't there because if I had of been there I would of known. Listen lady," he said in a high voice, "if I had of been there I would of

known and I wouldn't be like I am now." His voice seemed about to crack and the grandmother's head cleared for an instant. She saw the man's face twisted close to her own as if he were going to cry and she murmured, "Why, you're one of my babies. You're one of my own children!" She reached out and touched him on the shoulder. The Misfit sprang back as if a snake had bitten him and shot her three times through the chest. Then he put his gun down on the ground and took off his glasses and began to clean them.

Hiram and Bobby Lee returned from the woods and stood over the ditch, looking down at the grandmother who half sat and half lay in a puddle of blood with her legs crossed under her like a child's and her face smiling up at the cloudless sky.   138

Without his glasses, The Misfit's eyes were red-rimmed and pale and defenseless-looking. "Take her off and throw her where you thrown the others," he said, picking up the cat that was rubbing itself against his leg.   139

"She was a talker, wasn't she?" Bobby Lee said, sliding down the ditch with a yodel.   140

"She would of been a good woman," The Misfit said, "if it had been somebody there to shoot her every minute of her life."   141

"Some fun!" Bobby Lee said.   142

"Shut up, Bobby Lee," The Misfit said. "It's no real pleasure in life."   143

_____ CONSIDERATIONS _____

1. In order to keep the children quiet, the grandmother tells the ridiculous story of Mr. Edgar Atkins Teagarden, who cut his initials, E.A.T., in a watermelon. How do you account for O'Connor's including such an anecdote in a story about a psychopathic murderer?

2. One respected scholar and critic describes O'Connor's story as a "satire on the half-and-half Christian faced with nihilism and death." In what sense would the grandmother qualify as a "half-and-half Christian"? Is there anything in O'Connor's letters to John Hawkes and Alfred Corn (see pages 283–289) that might help you understand what O'Connor thought a real Christian was?

3. Does this story contain characteristics of satire as seen in Jonathan Swift's "A Modest Proposal," Don Sharp's "Under the Hood," or Woody Allen's "Death Knocks"?

4. O'Connor borrows a line from her own story to serve as a title. Find the line, study the context and comment on it as a title.

5. When the Misfit tells the grandmother, "it would have been better for all of you, lady, if you hadn't of reckernized me," what purpose does his warning serve, in furthering the story?

6. Study three elderly women: the grandmother in this story, Faulkner's Emily, and Welty's Phoenix Jackson. Do you think it fair to say that all three are used to convey the point of their respective authors' stories? Explain.

In 1979 a selection of Flannery O'Connor's letters, edited by Sally Fitzgerald, appeared as The Habit of Being. *The letters are affectionate, ofen funny, rich with literary and religious thought.*

The following excerpts begin with passages from two letters about "A Good Man Is Hard to Find." The letter To a Professor of English is prefaced by Sally Fitzgerald's explanatory note. The other passage comes from a letter addressed to the novelist John Hawkes, a leading writer of O'Connor's generation, author of The Lime Twig, Blood Oranges, *and* The Passion Artist *among other novels. Here O'Connor speaks of the theology of her story. In the letter that follows, also to John Hawkes, O'Connor's Catholicism is clear and certain; Hawkes is of another mind. The last letter is addressed to Alfred Corn, who is now a well-known poet. In 1962 he was an undergraduate at Emory University in Atlanta, Georgia; when he heard Flannery O'Connor speak to an English class, he wrote her about a subject that troubled him.*

50

FLANNERY O'CONNOR
From Flannery O'Connor's Letters

To John Hawkes

14 April 60

Thanks for your letter of some time back. I have been busy keep- 1
ing my blood pressure down while reading various reviews of my book. Some of the favorable ones are as bad as the unfavorable; most reviewers seem to have read the book in fifteen minutes and written the review in ten. . . . I hope that when your comes out you'll fare better.

2   It's interesting to me that your students naturally work their way to the idea that the Grandmother in "A Good Man" is not pure evil and may be a medium for Grace. If they were Southern students I would say this was because they all had grandmothers like her at home. These old ladies exactly reflect the banalities of the society and the effect of the comical rather than the seriously evil. But Andrew [Lytle] insists that she is a witch, even down to the cat. These children, yr. students, know their grandmothers aren't witches.

3   Perhaps it is a difference in theology, or rather the difference that ingrained theology makes in the sensibility. Grace, to the Catholic way of thinking, can and does use as its medium the imperfect, purely human, and even hypocritical. Cutting yourself off from Grace is a very decided matter, requiring a real choice, act of will, and affecting the very ground of the soul. The Misfit is touched by the Grace that comes through the old lady when she recognizes him as her child, as she has been touched by the Grace that comes through him in his particular suffering. His shooting her is a recoil, a horror at her humanness, but after he has done it and cleaned his glasses, the Grace has worked in him and he pronounces his judgment: she would have been a good woman if *he* had been there every moment of her life. True enough. In the Protestant view, I think Grace and nature don't have much to do with each other. The old lady, because of her hypocrisy and humanness and banality couldn't be a medium for Grace. In the sense that I see things the other way, I'm a Catholic writer.

TO A PROFESSOR OF ENGLISH

A professor of English had sent Flannery the following letter: "I am writing as spokesman for three members of our department and some ninety university students in three classes who for a week now have been discussing your story 'A Good Man Is Hard to Find.' We have debated at length several possible interpretations, none of which fully satisfies us. In general we believe that the appearance of the Misfit is not "real" in the same sense that the incidents of the first half of the story are real. Bailey, we believe, imagines the appearance of the Misfit, whose activities have been called to his attention on the night before the trip and again during the stopover at the roadside restaurant. Bailey, we further believe, identifies himself with the Misfit and so plays two roles in the imaginary last half of the story. But we cannot, after great effort, determine the point at which reality fades into illusion or reverie. Does the accident literally occur, or is it a part of Bailey's dream? Please believe me when I say we are not seeking an easy way out of our difficulty. We admire your story and have examined it with great care, but we are convinced that we are missing something important which you intended for us to grasp. We will all be very grateful if you comment on the interpretation which I have outlined above and if you will give us further comments about your intention in writing 'A Good Man Is Hard to Find.'"

She replied:

28 March 61

1 The interpretation of your ninety students and three teachers is fantastic and about as far from my intentions as it could get to be. If it were a legitimate interpretation, the story would be little more than a trick and its interest would be simply for abnormal psychology. I am not interested in abnormal psychology.

2 There is a change of tension from the first part of the story to the second where the Misfit enters, but this is no lessening of reality. This story is, of course, not meant to be realistic in the sense that it portrays the everyday doings of people in Georgia. It is stylized and its conventions are comic even though its meaning is serious.

3 Bailey's only importance is as the Grandmother's boy and the driver of the car. It is the Grandmother who first recognizes the Misfit and who is most concerned with him throughout. The story is a duel of sorts between the Grandmother and her superficial beliefs and the Misfit's more profoundly felt involvement with Christ's action which set the world off balance for him.

4 The meaning of a story should go on expanding for the reader the more he thinks about it, but meaning cannot be captured in an interpretation. If teachers are in the habit of approaching a story as if it were a research problem for which any answer is believable so long as it is not obvious, then I think students will never learn to enjoy fiction. Too much interpretation is certainly worse than too little, and where feeling for a story is absent, theory will not supply it.

5 My tone is not mean to be obnoxious. I am in a state of shock.

TO JOHN HAWKES

28 November 61

1 I have been fixing to write you ever since last summer when we saw the goat man.[1] We went up to north Georgia to buy a bull and when

[1]The founder of the Free Thinking Christian Mission, a wandering witness who traveled with a cart and a clutch of goats.

we were somewhere above Conyers we saw up ahead a pile of rubble some eight feet high on the side of the road. When we got about fifty feet from it, we could begin to make out that some of the rubble was distributed around something like a cart and that some of it was alive. Then we began to make out the goats. We stopped in front of it and looked back. About half the goats were asleep, venerable and exhausted, in a kind of heap. I didn't see Chess. Then my mother located an arm around the neck of one of the goats. We also saw a knee. The old man was lying on the road, asleep amongst them, but we never located his face.

2   That is wonderful about the new baby. I can't equal that but I do have some new additions to my ménage. For the last few years I have been hunting a pair of swans that I could afford. Swans cost $250 a pair and that was beyond me. My friend in Florida, the one I wrote you about once, took upon herself to comb Florida for cheap swans. What she sets out to do, she does. . . . So now I am the owner of a one-eyed swan and her consort. They are Polish, or immutable swans and very tractable and I radiate satisfaction every time I look at them.

3   I had brief notes from Andrew [Lytle][2] a couple of times lately. In fact he has a story of mine but I haven't heard from him whether he's going to use it or not. He said he had asked you to write an article about my fiction and that if he used my story I might want to send it to you. If he does take it and you write an article and want to see the story ["The Lame Shall Enter First"], I'll send it. It's about one of Tarwater's terrible cousins, a lad named Rufus Johnson, and it will add fuel to your theory though not legitimately I think.

4   You haven't convinced me that I write with the Devil's will or belong in the romantic tradition and I'm prepared to argue some more with you on this if I can remember where we left off at. I think the reason we can't agree on this is because there is a difference in our two devils. My Devil has a name, a history and a definite plan. His name is Lucifer, he's a fallen angel, his sin is pride, and his aim is the destruction of the Divine plan. Now I judge that your Devil is co-equal to God, not his creature; that pride is his virtue, not his sin; and that his aim is not to destroy the Divine plan because there isn't any Divine plan to destroy. My Devil is objective and yours is subjective. You say one becomes "evil" when one leaves the herd. I say that depends entirely on what the herd is doing.

5   The herd has been known to be right, in which case the one who

[2]Novelist, editor at this time of the *Sewanee Review.*

leaves it is doing evil. When the herd is wrong, the one who leaves it is not doing evil but the right thing. If I remember rightly, you put that word, evil, in quotation marks which means the standards you judge it by there are relative; in fact you would be looking at it there with the eyes of the herd.

I think I would admit to writing what Hawthorne called 6 "romances," but I don't think that has anything to do with the romantic mentality. Hawthorne interests me considerably. I feel more of a kinship with him than with any other American, though some of what he wrote I can't make myself read through to the end.

I didn't write the note to *Wise Blood.* I just let it go as is. I thought 7 here I am wasting my time saying what I've written when I've already written it and I could be writing something else. I couldn't hope to convince anybody anyway. A friend of mine wrote me that he had read a review in one of the university magazines of *The Violent Bear etc.* that said that since the seeds that had opened one at a time in Tarwater's blood were put there in the first place by the great uncle that the book was about homosexual incest. When you have a generation of students who are being taught to think like that, there's nothing to do but wait for another generation to come along and hope it won't be worse. . . .

I've introduced *The Lime Twig* to several people and they're all en- 8 thusiastic. Somebody has gone off with my copy now. I hope you are at another one.

TO ALFRED CORN

30 May 62

I think that this experience you are having of losing your faith, 1 or as you think, of having lost it, is an experience that in the long run belongs to faith; or at least it can belong to faith if faith is still valuable to you, and it must be or you would not have written me about this.

I don't know how the kind of faith required of a Christian living 2 in the 20th century can be at all if it is not grounded on this experience that you are having right now of unbelief. This may be the case always and not just in the 20th century. Peter said, "Lord, I believe. Help my unbelief." It is the most natural and most human and most agonizing prayer in the gospels, and I think it is the foundation prayer of faith.

As a freshman in college you are bombarded with new ideas, or 3 rather pieces of ideas, new frames of reference, an activation of the intellectual life which is only beginning, but which is already running

ahead of your lived experience. After a year of this, you think you cannot believe. You are just beginning to realize how difficult it is to have
faith and the measure of a commitment to it, but you are too young
to decide you don't have faith just because you feel you can't believe.
About the only way we know whether we believe or not is by what we
do, and I think from your letter that you will not take the path of least
resistance in this matter and simply decide that you have lost your faith
and that there is nothing you can do about it.

4   One result of the stimulation of your intellectual life that takes
place in college is usually a shrinking of the imaginative life. This sounds
like a paradox, but I have often found it to be true. Students get so bound
up with difficulties such as reconciling the clashing of so many different
faiths such as Buddhism, Mohammedanism, etc., that they cease to look
for God in other ways. Bridges once wrote Gerard Manley Hopkins and
asked him to tell him how he, Bridges, could believe. He must have expected from Hopkins a long philosophical answer. Hopkins wrote back,
"Give alms." He was trying to say to Bridges that God is to be experienced
in Charity (in the sense of love for the divine image in human beings).
Don't get so entangled with intellectual difficulties that you fail to look
for God in this way.

5   The intellectual difficulties have to be met, however, and you will
be meeting them for the rest of your life. When you get a reasonable
hold on one, another will come to take its place. At one time, the clash
of the different world religions was a difficulty for me. Where you have
absolute solutions, however, you have no need of faith. Faith is what
you have in the absence of knowledge. The reason this clash doesn't
bother me any longer is because I have got, over the years, a sense of
the immense sweep of creation, of the evolutionary process in
everything, of how incomprehensible God must necessarily be to be the
God of heaven and earth. You can't fit the Almighty into your intellectual categories. I might suggest that you look into some of the works
of Pierre Teilhard de Chardin (*The Phenomenon of Man* et al.). He was
a paleontologist—helped to discover Peking man—and also a man of
God. I don't suggest you go to him for answers but for different questions, for that stretching of the imagination that you need to make you
a sceptic in the face of much that you are learning, much of which is
new and shocking but which when boiled down becomes less so and
takes its place in the general scheme of things. What kept me a sceptic
in college was precisely my Christian faith. It always said: wait, don't
bite on this, get a wider picture, continue to read.

6   If you want your faith, you have to work for it. It is a gift, but for
very few is it a gift given without any demand for equal time devoted

to its cultivation. For every book you read that is anti-Christian, make it your business to read one that presents the other side of the picture; if one isn't satisfactory read others. Don't think that you have to abandon reason to be a Christian. A book that might help you is *The Unity of Philosophical Experience* by Etienne Gilson. Another is Newman's *The Grammar of Assent.* To find out about faith, you have to go to the people who have it and you have to go to the most intelligent ones if you are going to stand up intellectually to agnostics and the general run of pagans that you are going to find in the majority of people around you. Much of the criticism of belief that you find today comes from people who are judging it from the standpoint of another and narrower discipline. The Biblical criticism of the 19th century, for instance, was the product of historical disciplines. It has been entirely revamped in the 20th century by applying broader criteria to it, and those people who lost their faith in the 19th century because of it, could better have hung on in blind trust.

Even in the life of a Christian, faith rises and falls like the tides   7
of an invisible sea. It's there, even where he can't see it or feel it, if he wants it to be there. You realize, I think, that it is more valuable, more mysterious, altogether more immense than anything you can learn or decide upon in college. Learn what you can, but cultivate Christian scepticism. It will keep you free — not free to do anything you please, but free to be formed by something larger than your own intellect or the intellects of those around you.

I don't know if this is the kind of answer that can help you, but   8
any time you care to write me, I can try to do better.

_____ **CONSIDERATIONS** _____

Letter to John Hawkes: April 14, 1960

1. What does O'Connor mean when she says that some of the favorable reviews of her book "are as bad as the unfavorable"? How do you go about judging the quality of a book review? As a writer, how do you judge your instructors' comments on your own papers?

2. In Paragraph 2 O'Connor suggests that the grandmother in her story is like a lot of grandmothers in the South, but in her letter to the Professor of English (page 285) she says her story is not realistic in the "everyday" sense. Can you reconcile this apparent contradiction?

3. O'Connor's comments on the term "grace" in Paragraph 3 might be more understandable if you pursued the word itself in a good dictionary where you will find at least a dozen different definitions of the word. Keep in mind that she is using the word according to her own view of Catholic theology.

4. O'Connor says at the end of Paragraph 3 that she is a Catholic writer. Does she mean that Protestant readers are not welcome or that Protestants could not understand her work? Is it possible to disagree with—or even disapprove of—a writer's ideas and still appreciate that writer's work? Explain.

5. While she does not always agree with John Hawkes's interpretations of her stories, O'Connor's letters to him (see also that of 11/28/61) express a good deal more respect for his ideas than can be found in her letter to a professor of English. Read a little of the work of John Hawkes to see if you can discover qualities he shares with O'Connor.

Letter to a Professor of English, March 28, 1961

1. O'Connor says her story is realistic, not in an "everyday" but "stylized" sense. Compare a paragraph or two of her story with a passage in Eudora Welty's "A Worn Path" to see if you can determine what O'Connor means by "stylized." You might also get some help on that word by consulting a history of art.

2. Find passages in "A Good Man Is Hard to Find" that will illustrate what O'Connor means by the grandmother's "superficial beliefs" and the Misfit's "more profoundly felt involvement." Does such a close examination of the story push you closer to or further away from O'Connor's belief that the heart of the story is a "duel of sorts" between the grandmother and the Misfit?

3. In Paragraph 4 O'Connor makes an interesting distinction between "meaning" and "interpretation" as she deplores the "habit of approaching a story as if it were a research problem for which any answer is believable so long as it is not obvious." Discuss some experience of your own in which insistence upon a particular interpretation (yours or anyone else's) interfered with the expanded meaning O'Connor mentions.

4. O'Connor says in her last paragraph that her tone in the letter "is not meant to be obnoxious." If you were the professor to whom she had written, what particular lines or words in the letter might you think gave it an obnoxious tone? Can you find any other writers in this book whose tone is obnoxious? Explain.

5. In what sense, if any, do you think a short story (or poem or novel or play or essay for that matter) can be taught? What assistance do you expect or want from your own instructor and/or text in reading a story like O'Connor's?

Letter to John Hawkes, November 28, 1961

1. O'Connor's remarkable versatility in the use of the English language is demonstrated in her letters as well as in her stories. This letter to John Hawkes, for example, shows her ability to shift from one voice to another at will. Find examples.

2. At the end of Paragraph 4, O'Connor tells Hawkes, "You say one becomes 'evil' when one leaves the herd. I say that depends entirely on what the herd is doing." Write an essay on relative versus absolute morality.

3. O'Connor, speaking of her interest in Hawthorne, makes a distinction between writing "romances" and having a "romantic mentality." What did Hawthorne mean by "romances," and why does O'Connor "feel more of a kinship with him than with any other American"?

4. O'Connor's letters are filled with brief reports on local events and people, like the one on the goat man in the letter to John Hawkes. Eudora Welty, in discussing one of her own short stories—see her essay "The Point of the Story"—says that her story began when she observed an old woman in Mississippi. How might O'Connor's observations of her surroundings have contributed to "A Good Man Is Hard to Find"?

Letter to Alfred Corn, May 30, 1962

1. "You can't fit the Almighty into your intellectual categories," says O'Connor. Does she advise her correspondent to ignore the intellectual challenges of college? Study her discussion of the clash between intellectual inquiry and faith, especially in Paragraphs 5 and 6, and write an essay on her conclusions.

2. How, according to O'Connor, can we know whether we believe or not?

3. Look over Consideration 1 regarding O'Connor's 1961 letter to John Hawkes and think about voice. How would you describe the voice in this letter to Alfred Corn? Does O'Connor play with changes of voice in this letter? Why?

4. Read Langston Hughes's essay "Salvation"; how might O'Connor have consoled the disillusioned boy?

George Orwell (1903–1950) was the pen name of Eric Blair, who was born in India of English parents, attended Eton on a scholarship, and returned to the East as a member of the Imperial Police. He quit his position after five years because he wanted to write, and because he came to feel that imperialism was "very largely a racket." For eight years he wrote with small success and lived in considerable poverty. His first book, Down and Out in Paris and London (1933), described those years. Further memoirs and novels followed, including Burmese Days (1935) and Keep the Aspidistra Flying (1938). His last books were the political fable Animal Farm (1945) and his great anti-utopia 1984, which appeared in 1949, shortly before his death. He died of tuberculosis, his health first afflicted when he was a policeman in Burma, undermined by years of poverty, and further worsened by a wound he received during the civil war in Spain.

Best known for his fiction, Orwell was essentially an essayist; even his novels are essays. He made his living most of his adult life by writing reviews and articles for English weeklies. His collected essays, reviews, and letters form an impressive four volumes. Politics is at the center of his work—a personal politics. After his disaffection from imperialism, he became a leftist, and fought on the Loyalist side against Franco in Spain. (Homage to Catalonia comes out of this time.) But his experience of Communist duplicity there, and his early understanding of the paranoid totalitarianism of Stalin, turned him anti-Communist. He could swear allegiance to no party. His anti-Communism made him in no way conservative; he considered himself a socialist until his death, but other socialists would have nothing to do with him. He found politics shabby and politicians dishonest. With an empirical, English turn of mind, he looked skeptically at all saviors and panaceas. In this famous essay, he attacks the rhetoric of politics. He largely attacks the left—because his audience was an English intellectual class that was largely leftist.

51

GEORGE ORWELL
Politics and the English Language

Most people who bother with the matter at all would admit that   1
the English language is in a bad way, but it is generally assumed that
we cannot by conscious action do anything about it. Our civilization
is decadent and our language — so the argument runs — must inevitably
share in the general collapse. It follows that any struggle against the
abuse of language is a sentimental archaism, like preferring candles to
electric light or hansom cabs to aeroplanes. Underneath this lies the
half-conscious belief that language is a natural growth and not an instrument which we shape for our own purposes.

Now, it is clear that the decline of a language must ultimately have   2
political and economic causes: it is not due simply to the bad influence
of this or that individual writer. But an effect can become a cause, reinforcing the original cause and producing the same effect in an inten-
sified form, and so indefinitely. A man may take to drink because he
feels himself to be a failure, and then fail all the more completely because
he drinks. It is rather the same thing that is happening to the English
language. It becomes ugly and inaccurate because our thoughts are
foolish, but the slovenliness of our language makes it easier for us to
have foolish thoughts. The point is that the process is reversible. Modern English, especially written English, is full of bad habits which spread
by imitation and which can be avoided if one is willing to take the
necessary trouble. If one gets rid of these habits one can think more
clearly, and to think clearly is a necessary first step towards political
regeneration: so that the fight against bad English is not frivolous and

is not the exclusive concern of professional writers. I will come back to this presently, and I hope that by that time the meaning of what I have said here will have become clearer. Meanwhile, here are five specimens of the English language as it is now habitually written.

3   These five passages have not been picked out because they are especially bad—I could have quoted far worse if I had chosen—but because they illustrate various of the mental vices from which we now suffer. They are a little below the average, but are fairly representative samples. I number them so that I can refer back to them when necessary:

(1) I am not, indeed, sure whether it is not true to say that the Milton who once seemed not unlike a seventeenth-century Shelley had not become, out of an experience ever more bitter in each year, more alien [*sic*] to the founder of that Jesuit sect which nothing could induce him to tolerate.

> Professor Harold Laski
> [Essay in *Freedom of Expression*].

(2) Above all, we cannot play ducks and drakes with a native battery of idioms which prescribes such egregious collocations of vocables as the Basic *put up with* for *tolerate* or *put at a loss* for *bewilder.*

> Professor Lancelot Hogben [*Interglossa*].

(3) On the one side we have the free personality: by definition it is not neurotic, for it has neither conflict nor dream. Its desires, such as they are, are transparent, for they are just what institutional approval keeps in the forefront of consciouness; another institutional pattern would alter their number and intensity, there is little in them that is natural, irreducible, or culturally dangerous. But *on the other side,* the social bond itself is nothing but the mutual reflection of these self-secure integrities. Recall the definition of love. Is not this the very picture of a small academic? Where is there a place in this hall of mirrors for either personality or fraternity?

> Essay on psychology in *Politics* [New York].

(4) All the "best people" from the gentlemen's clubs, and all the frantic fascist captains, united in common hatred of Socialism and bestial horror of the rising tide of the mass revolutionary movement, have turned to acts of provocation, to foul incendiarism, to medieval legends of poisoned wells, to legalize their own destruction of proletarian organizations, and rouse the agitated petty-bourgeoisie to chauvinistic fervor on behalf of the fight against the revolutionary way out of the crisis.

> Communist pamphlet

(5) If a new spirit is to be infused into this old country, there is one thorny and contentious reform which must be tackled, and that is the humanization and galvanization of the B.C.C. Timidity here will bespeak canker and atrophy of the soul. The heart of Britain may be sound and of strong beat, for instance, but the British lion's roar at present is like that of Bottom in Shakespeare's *Midsummer Night's Dream*—as gentle as any sucking dove. A virile new Britain cannot continue indefinitely to be traduced in the eyes, or rather ears, of the world by the effete languors of Langham Place brazenly masquerading as "standard English." When the Voice of Britain is heard at nine o'clock, better far and infinitely less ludicrous to hear aitches honestly dropped than the present priggish, inflated, inhibited, school-ma'amish arch braying of blameless bashful mewing maidens!

Letter in Tribune

Each of these passages has faults of its own, but, quite apart from avoidable ugliness, two qualities are common to all of them. The first is staleness of imagery; the other is lack of precision. The writer either has a meaning and cannot express it, or he inadvertently says something else, or he is almost indifferent as to whether his words mean anything or not. This mixture of vagueness and sheer incompetence is the most marked characteristic of modern English prose, and especially of any kind of political writing. As soon as certain topics are raised, the concrete melts into the abstract and no one seems able to think of turns of speech that are not hackneyed: prose consists less and less of *words* chosen for the sake of their meaning, and more and more of *phrases* tacked together like the sections of a prefabricated hen-house. I list below, with notes and examples, various of the tricks by means of which the work of prose-construction is habitually dodged: 4

DYING METAPHORS

A newly invented metaphor assists thought by evoking a visual image, while on the other hand a metaphor which is technically "dead" (e.g. *iron resolution*) has in effect reverted to being an ordinary word and can generally be used without loss of vividness. But in between these two classes there is a huge dump of worn-out metaphors which have lost all evocative power and are merely used because they save people the trouble of inventing phrases for themselves. Examples are: *Ring the changes on, take up the cudgels for, toe the line, ride roughshod over, stand shoulder to shoulder with, play into the hands of, no axe to grind,*   5 *grist to the mill, fishing in troubled waters, on the order of the day, Achilles' heel, swan song, hotbed.* Many of these are used without knowledge of their meaning (what is a "rift," for instance?), and incompatible metaphors are frequently mixed, a sure sign that the writer is not interested in what he is saying. Some metaphors now current have been twisted out of their original meaning without those who use them even being aware of the fact. For example, *toe the line* is sometimes written *tow the line.* Another example is *the hammer and the anvil,* now always used with the implication that the anvil gets the worst of it. In real life it is always the anvil that breaks the hammer, never the other way about: a writer who stopped to think what he was saying would be aware of this, and would avoid perverting the original phrase.

OPERATORS OR VERBAL FALSE LIMBS

6   These save the trouble of picking out appropriate verbs and nouns, and at the same time pad each sentence with extra syllables which give it an appearance of symmetry. Characteristic phrases are *render inoperative, militate against, make contact with, be subjected to, give rise to, give grounds for, have the effect of, play a leading part (role) in, make itself felt, take effect, exhibit a tendency to, serve the purpose of,* etc., etc. The keynote is the elimination of simple verbs. Instead of being a single word, such as *break, stop, spoil, men, kill* a verb becomes a *phrase,* made up of a noun or adjective tacked on to some general-purpose verb such as *prove, serve, form, play, render.* In addition, the passive voice is wherever possible used in preference to the active, and noun constructions are used instead of gerunds *(by examination of* instead of *by examining).* The range of verbs is further cut down by means of the *-ize* and *de-* formations, and the banal statements are given an appearance of profundity by means of the *not un-* formation. Simple conjunctions and prepositions are replaced by such phrases as *with respect to, having regard to, the fact that, by dint of, in view of, in the interests of, on the hypothesis that;* and the ends of sentences are saved from anticlimax by such resounding commonplaces as *greatly to be desired, cannot be left out of account, a development to be expected in the near future, deserving of serious consideration, brought to a satisfactory conclusion* and so on and so forth.

PRETENTIOUS DICTION

7   Words like *phenomenon, element, individual* (as noun), *objective, categorical, effective, virtual, basic, primary, promote, constitute, exhibit, exploit, utilize, eliminate, liquidate,* are used to dress up simple

statements and give an air of scientific impartiality to biased judgments. Adjectives like *epoch-making, epic, historic, unforgettable, triumphant, age-old, inevitable, inexorable, veritable,* are used to dignify the sordid processes of international politics, while writing that aims at glorifying war usually takes on an archaic color, its characteristic words being: *realm, throne, chariot, mailed fist, trident, sword, shield, buckler, banner, jackboot, clarion.* Foreign words and expressions such as *cul de sac, ancien régime, deux ex machina, mutatis mutandis, status quo, gleichschaltung, weltanschauung,* are used to give an air of culture and elegance. Except for the useful abbrecations *i.e., e.g.,* and *etc.,* there is no real need for any of the hundreds of foreign phrases now current in English. Bad writers, and especially scientific, political and sociological writers, are nearly always haunted by the notion that Latin or Greek words are grander than Saxon ones, and unnecessary words like *expedite, ameliorate, predict, extraneous, deracinated, clandestine, subaqueous* and hundreds of others constantly gain ground from their Anglo-Saxon opposite numbers.[1] The jargon peculiar to Marxist writing *(hyena, hangman, cannibal, petty bourgeois, these gentry, lacquey, flunkey, mad dog, White Guard,* etc.) consists largely of words and phrases translated from Russian, German or French; but the normal way of coining a new word is to use a Latin or Greek root with the appropriate affix and, where necessary, the *-ize* formation. It is often easier to make up words of this kind *(deregionalize, impermissible, extramarital, nonfragmentary* and so forth) than to think up the English words that will cover one's meaning. The result, in general, is an increase in slovenliness and vagueness.

MEANINGLESS WORDS

In certain kinds of writing, particularly in art criticism and literary 8 criticism, it is normal to come across long passages which are almost completely lacking in meaning.[2] Words like *romantic, plastic, values,*

---

[1]An interesting illustration of this is the way in which the English flower names which were in use till very recently are being ousted by Greek ones, *snapdragon* becoming *antirrhinum, forget-me-not* becoming *myosotis,* etc. It is hard to see any practical reason for this change of fashion: it is probably due to an instinctive turning-away from the more homely word and a vague feeling that the Greek is scientific.

[2]Example: "Comfort's catholicity of perception and image, strangely Whitmanesque in range, almost the exact opposite in aesthetic compulsion, continues to evoke that trembling atmospheric accumulative hinting at a cruel, an inexorably serene timelessness. . . . Wrey Gardiner scores by aiming at simple bull's-eyes with precision. Only they are not so simple, and through his contented sadness runs more than the surface bitter-sweet of resignation." (Poetry Quarterly.)

human, dead, sentimental, natural, vitality, as used in art criticism, are strictly meaningless, in the sense that they not only do not point to any discoverable object, but are hardly ever expected to do so by the reader. When one critic writes, "The outstanding feature of Mr. X's work is its living quality," while another writes, "The immediately striking thing about Mr. X's work is its peculiar deadness," the reader accepts this as a simple difference of opinion. If words like *black* and *white* were involved, instead of the jargon words *dead* and *living,* he would see at once that language was being used in an improper way. Many political words are similarly abused. The word *Fascism* has now no meaning in so far as it signifies "something not desirable." The words *democracy, socialism, freedom, patriotic, realistic, justice,* have each of them several different meanings which cannot be reconciled with one another. In the case of a word like *democracy,* not only is there no agreed definition, but the attempt to make one is resisted from all sides. It is almost universally felt that when we call a country democratic we are praising it: consequently the defenders of every kind of régime claim that it is a democracy, and fear that they might have to stop using the word if it were tied down to any one meaning. Words of this kind are often used in a consciously dishonest way. That is, the person who uses them has his own private definition, but allows his hearer to think he means something quite different. Statements like *Marshal Pétain was a true patriot, The Soviet Press is the freest in the world, The Catholic Church is opposed to persecution,* are almost always made with intent to deceive. Other words used in variable meanings, in most cases more or less dishonestly, are: *class, totalitarian, science, progressive, reactionary, bourgeois, equality.*

9   Now that I have made this catalogue of swindles and perversions, let me give another example of the kind of writing that they lead to. This time it must of its nature be an imaginary one. I am going to translate a passage of good English into modern English of the worst sort. Here is a well-known verse from *Ecclesiastes:*

> *I returned and saw under the sun, that the race is not to the swift, nor the battle to the strong, neither yet bread to the wise, nor yet riches to men of understanding, nor yet favour to men of skill, but time and chance happeneth to them all.*

10   Here it is in modern English:

> Objective consideration of contemporary phenomena compels the conclusion that success or failure in competitive activities exhibits no tendency to be commensurate with innate capacity, but that a

considerable element of the unpredictable must invariably be taken into account.

This is a parody, but not a very gross one. Exhibit (3), above, for 11 instance, contains several patches of the same kind of English. It will be seen that I have not made a full translation. The beginning and ending of the sentence follow the original meaning fairly closely, but in the middle the concrete illustrations—race, battle, bread—dissolve into the vague phrase "success or failure in competitive activities." This had to be so, because no modern writer of the kind I am discussing—no one capable of using phrases like "objective consideration of contemporary phenomena"—would ever tabulate his thoughts in that precise and detailed way. The whole tendency of modern prose is away from concreteness. Now analyse these two sentences a little more closely. The first contains forty-nine words but only sixty syllables, and all its words are those of everyday life. The second contains thirty-eight words of ninety syllables: eighteen of its words are from Latin roots, and one from Greek. The first sentence contains six vivid images, and only one phrase ("time and chance") that could be called vague. The second contains not a single fresh, arresting phrase, and in spite of its ninety syllables it gives only a shortened version of the meaning contained in the first. Yet without a doubt it is the second kind of sentence that is gaining ground in modern English. I do not want to exaggerate. This kind of writing is not yet universal, and outcrops of simplicity will occur here and there in the worst-written page. Still, if you or I were told to write a few lines on the uncertainty of human fortunes, we should probably come much nearer to my imaginary sentence than to the one from *Ecclesiastes*.

As I have tried to show, modern writing at its worst does not consist in picking out words for the sake of their meaning and inventing images in order to make the meaning clearer. It consists in gumming together long strips of words which have already been set in order by someone else, and making the results presentable by sheer humbug. The attraction of this way of writing is that it is easy. It is easier—even quicker, once you have the habit—to say *In my opinion it is not an unjustifiable assumption that* than to say *I think*. If you use ready-made phrases, you not only don't have to hunt about for words; you also don't have to bother with the rhythms of your sentences, since these phrases are generally so arranged as to be more or less euphonious. When you are composing in a hurry—when you are dictating to a stenographer, for instance, or making a public speech—it is natural to fall into a pretentious, Latinized style. Tags like *a consideration which we should do well to bear in mind* or *a conclusion to which all of us would readily assent* will save many a sentence from coming down with a bump. By using stale metaphors, similes and idioms, you save much mental effort, at the cost of leaving your meaning vague, not only for your reader but for yourself. This is the significance of mixed metaphors. The sole aim of a metaphor is to call up visual image. When these images clash—as in *The Fascist octopus has sung its swan song, the jackboot is thrown into the melting pot*—it can be taken as certain that the writer is not seeing a mental image of the objects he is naming; in other words he is not really thinking. Look again at the examples I gave at the beginning of this essay. Professor Laski (1) uses five negatives in fifty-three words. One of these is superfluous, making nonsense of the whole passage, and in addition there is the slip *alien* for *akin*, making further nonsense, and several avoidable pieces of clumsiness which increase the general vagueness. Professor Hogben (2) plays ducks and drakes with a battery which is able to write prescriptions, and, while disapproving of the everyday phrase *put up with*, is unwilling to look *egregious* up in the dictionary and see what it means; (3), if one takes an uncharitable attitude towards it, is simply meaningless: probably one could work out its intended meaning by reading the whole of the article in which it occurs. In (4), the writer knows more or less what he wants to say, but an accumulation of stale phrases chokes him, like tea leaves blocking a sink. In (5), words and meaning have almost parted company. People who write in this manner usually have a general emotional meaning—they dislike one thing and want to express solidarity with another—but they are not interested in the detail of what they are saying. A scrupulous writer, in every sentence that he writes, will ask himself at least four questions, thus: What am I trying to say? What words will express it? What image or idiom will make it clearer? Is this image fresh enough to have an effect? And he will probably ask himself two more: Could I put it more shortly? Have I said anything that is avoidably ugly? But you are not obliged to go to all this trouble. You can shirk it by simply throwing your mind open and letting the ready-made phrases come crowding in. They will construct your sentences for you—even think your thoughts for you, to a certain extent—and at need they will perform the important service of partially concealing your meaning even from yourself. It is at this point that the special connection between politics and the debasement of language becomes clear.

13   In our time it is broadly true that political writing is bad writing. Where it is not true, it will generally be found that the writer is some kind of rebel, expressing his private opinions and not a "party line." Orthodoxy, of whatever color, seems to demand a lifeless, imitative style.

The political dialects to be found in pamphlets, leading articles, manifestos, White Papers and the speeches of undersecretaries do, of course, vary from party to party, but they are all alike in that one almost never finds in them a fresh, vivid, home-made turn of speech. When one watches some tired hack on the platform mechanically repeating the familiar phrases—*bestial atrocities, iron heel, blood-stained tyranny, free people of the world, stand shoulder to shoulder*—one often has a curious feeling that one is not watching a live human being but some kind of dummy: a feeling which suddenly becomes stronger at moments when the light catches the speaker's spectacles and turns them into blank discs which seem to have no eyes behind them. And this is not altogether fanciful. A speaker who uses that kind of phraseology has gone some distance towards turning himself into a machine. The appropriate noises are coming out of his larynx, but his brain is not involved as it would be if he were choosing his words for himself. If the speech he is making is one that he is accustomed to make over and over again, he may be almost unconscious of what he is saying, as one is when one utters the responses in church. And this reduced state of consciousness, if not indispensable, is at any rate favorable to political conformity.

In our time, political speech and writing are largely the defence 14 of the indefensible. Things like the continuance of British rule in India, the Russian purges and deportations, the dropping of the atom bombs on Japan, can indeed be defended, but only by arguments which are too brutal for most people to face, and which do not square with the professed aims of political parties. Thus political language has to consist largely of euphemism, question-begging and sheer cloudy vagueness. Defenceless villages are bombarded from the air, the inhabitants driven out into the countryside, the cattle machine-gunned, the huts set on fire with incendiary bullets: this is called *pacification*. Millions of peasants are robbed of their farms and sent trudging along the roads with no more than they can carry: this is called *transfer of population* or *rectification of frontiers*. People are imprisoned for years without trial, or shot in the back of the neck or sent to die of scurvy in Arctic lumber camps: this is called *elimination of unreliable elements*. Such phraseology is needed if one wants to name things without calling up mental pictures of them. Consider for instance some comfortable English professor defending Russian totalitarianism. He cannot say outright: "I believe in killing off your opponents when you can get good results by doing so." Probably, therefore, he will say something like this:

"While freely conceding that the Soviet régime exhibits certain 15 features which the humanitarian may be inclined to deplore, we must,

I think, agree that a certain curtailment of the right to political opposi-
tion is an unavoidable concomitant of transitional periods, and that the
rigors which the Russian people have been called upon to undergo have
been amply justified in the sphere of concrete achievement."

16   The inflated style is itself a kind of euphemism. A mass of Latin
words falls upon the facts like soft snow, blurring the outlines and covering up all the details. The great enemy of clear language is insincerity.
When there is a gap between one's real and one's declared aims, one turns
as it were instinctively to long words and exhausted idioms, like a cut-
tlefish squirting out ink. In our age there is no such thing as "keeping
out of politics." All issues are political issues, and politics itself is a mass
of lies, evasions, folly, hatred and schizophrenia. When the general atmosphere is bad, language must suffer. I should expect to find—this is
a guess which I have not sufficient knowledge to verify—that the German, Russian and Italian languages have all deteriorated in the last ten
or fifteen years, as a result of dictatorship.

17   But if thought corrupts language, language can also corrupt
thought. A bad usage can spread by tradition and imitation, even among
people who should and do know better. The debased language that I have
been discussing is in some ways very convenient. Phrases like *a not
unjustifiable assumption, leaves much to be desired, would serve no
good purpose, a consideration which we should do well to bear in mind,*
are a continuous temptation, a packet of aspirins always at one's elbow.
Look back through this essay, and for certain you will find that I have
again and again committed the very faults I am protesting against. By
this morning's post I have received a pamphlet dealing with conditions
in Germany. The author tells me that he "felt impelled" to write it. I
open it at random, and here is almost the first sentence that I see: "[The
Allies] have an opportunity not only of achieving a radical transformation of Germany's social and political structure in such a way as to avoid
a nationalistic reaction in Germany itself, but at the same time of laying the foundations of a co-operative and unified Europe." You see, he
"feels impelled" to write—feels, presumably, that he has something new
to say—and yet his words, like cavalry horses answering the bugle, group
themselves automatically into the familiar dreary pattern. This invasion of one's mind by ready-made phrases *(lay the foundations, achieve
a radical transformation)* can only be prevented if one is constantly on
guard against them, and every such phrase anaesthetizes a portion of
one's brain.

18   I said earlier that the decadence of our language is probably curable.
Those who deny this would argue, if they produced an argument at all,

that language merely reflects existing social conditions, and that we cannot influence its development by any direct tinkering with words and constructions. So far as the general tone or spirit of a language goes, this may be true, but it is not true in detail. Silly words and expressions have often disappeared, not through any evolutionary process but owing to the conscious action of a minority. Two recent examples were *explore every avenue* and *leave no stone unturned*, which were killed by the jeers of a few journalists. There is a long list of flyblown metaphors which could similarly be got rid of if enough people would interest themselves in the job; and it should also be possible to laugh the *not un-* formation out of existence,[3] to reduce the amount of Latin and Greek in the average sentence, to drive out foreign phrases and strayed scientific words, and, in general, to make pretentiousness unfashionable. But all these are minor points. The defence of the English language implies more than this, and perhaps it is best to start by saying what it does *not* imply.

To begin with it has nothing to do with archaism, with the salvaging of obsolete words and turns of speech, or with the setting up of a "standard English" which must never be departed from. On the contrary, it is especially concerned with the scrapping of every word or idiom which has outworn its usefulness. It has nothing to do with correct grammar and syntax, which are of no importance so long as one makes one's meaning clear, or with the avoidance of Americanisms, or with having what is called a "good prose style." On the other hand it is not concerned with fake simplicity and the attempt to make written English colloquial. Nor does it even imply in every case preferring the Saxon word to the Latin one, though it does imply using the fewest and shortest words that will cover one's meaning. What is above all needed is to let the meaning choose the word, and not the other way about. In prose, the worst thing one can do with words is to surrender to them. When you think of a concrete object, you think wordlessly, and then, if you want to describe the thing you have been visualizing you probably hunt about till you find the exact words that seem to fit it. When you think of something abstract you are more inclined to use words from the start, and unless you make a conscious effort to prevent it, the existing dialect will come rushing in and do the job for you, at the expense of blurring or even changing your meaning. Probably it is better to put off using words as long as possible and get one's meaning as clear as one can

19

---

[3]One can cure oneself of the *not un-* formation by memorizing this sentence: *A not unblack dog was chasing a not unsmall rabbit across a not ungreen field.*

through pictures or sensations. Afterwards one can choose — not simply *accept* — the phrases that will best cover the meaning, and then switch round and decide what impression one's words are likely to make on another person. This last effort of the mind cuts out all stale or mixed images, all prefabricated phrases, needless repetitions, and humbug and vagueness generally. But one can often be in doubt about the effect of a word or a phrase, and one needs rules that one can rely on when instinct fails. I think the following rules will cover most cases:

(i) Never use a metaphor, simile or other figure of speech which you are used to seeing in print.

(ii) Never use a long word where a short one will do.

(iii) If it is possible to cut a word out, always cut it out.

(iv) Never use the passive where you can use the active.

(v) Never use a foreign phrase, a scientific word or a jargon word if you can think of an everyday English equivalent.

(vi) Break any of these rules sooner than say anything outright barbarous.

These rules sound elementary, and so they are, but they demand a deep change of attitude in anyone who has grown used to writing in the style now fashionable. One could keep all of them and still write bad English, but one could not write the kind of stuff that I quoted in those five specimens at the beginning of this article.

20   I have not here been considering the literary use of language, but merely language as an instrument for expressing and not for concealing or preventing thought. Stuart Chase and others have come near to claiming that all abstract words are meaningless, and have used this as a pretext for advocating a kind of political quietism. Since you don't know what Fascism is, how can you struggle aganst Fascism? One need not swallow such absurdities as this, but one ought to recognize that the present political chaos is connected with the decay of language, and that one can probably bring about some improvement by starting at the verbal end. If you simplify your English, you are freed from the worst follies of orthodoxy. You cannot speak any of the necessary dialects, and when you make a stupid remark its stupidity will be obvious, even to yourself. Political language — and with variations this is true of all political parties, from Conservatives to Anarchists — is designed to make lies sound truthful and murder respectable, and to give an appearance of solidity to pure wind. One cannot change this all in a moment, but one can at least change one's own habits, and from time to

time one can even, if one jeers loudly enough, send some worn-out and useless phrase — some *jackboot, Achilles' heel, hotbed, melting pot, acid test, veritable inferno* or other lump of verbal refuse — into the dustbin where it belongs.

_____ **CONSIDERATIONS** _____

1. "Style is the man himself." How well, and in what ways, does Orwell's essay illustrate Buffon's aphorism? Select another author in the text, someone with a distinct style, and test it against Buffon's statement.

2. Assuming that Orwell's statement in Paragraph 2, "the fight against bad English is not frivolous and is not the exclusive concern of professional writers," is the conclusion of a syllogism, reconstruct the major and minor premises of that syllogism by studying the steps Orwell takes to reach his conclusion.

3. Orwell documents his argument by quoting five passages by writers who wrote in the forties. From comparable sources, assemble a gallery of current specimens to help confirm or refute his contention that "the English language is in a bad way."

4. Orwell concludes with six rules. From the rest of his essay, how do you think he would define "anything outright barbarous" (in rule vi)?

5. Has Orwell broken some of his own rules? Point out and explain any examples you find. Look over his "Shooting an Elephant" and "A Hanging" as well as "Politics and the English Language."

6. In Paragraph 16, Orwell asserts that "The inflated style is itself a kind of euphemism." Look up the meaning of "euphemism" and compile examples from your local newspaper. Do you agree with Orwell that they are "swindles and perversions"? Note how Ambrose Bierce counts on our understanding of euphemisms in his Devil's Dictionary (pages 75–78).

*Two of George Orwell's best essays derive from his ex-
perience as a colonial policeman, upholder of law and order for
the British empire. Many political thinkers develop an ideology
from thought and theory; Orwell's politics grew empirically
from the life he lived. He provides us models for learning by
living — and for learning by writing out of one's life.*

52

GEORGE ORWELL
Shooting an Elephant

1   In Moulmein, in Lower Burma, I was hated by large numbers of
people — the only time in my life that I have been important enough
for this to happen to me. I was sub-divisional police officer of the town,
and in an aimless, petty kind of way anti-European feeling was very bitter. No one had the guts to raise a riot, but if a European woman went
through the bazaars alone somebody would probably spit betel juice over
her dress. As a police officer I was an obvious target and was baited whenever it seemed safe to do so. When a nimble Burman tripped me up on
the football field and the referee (another Burman) looked the other way,
the crowd yelled with hideous laughter. This happened more than once.
In the end the sneering yellow faces of young men that met me
everywhere, the insults hooted after me when I was at a safe distance,
got badly on my nerves. The young Buddhist priests were the worst of
all. There were several thousands of them in the town and none of them
seemed to have anything to do except stand on street corners and jeer
at Europeans.

All this was perplexing and upsetting. For at that time I had already 2
made up my mind that imperialism was an evil thing and the sooner
I chucked up my job and got out of it the better. Theoretically — and
secretly, of course — I was all for the Burmese and all against their op-
pressors, the British. As for the job I was doing, I hated it more bitterly
than I can perhaps make clear. In a job like that you see the dirty work
of Empire at close quarters. The wretched prisoners huddling in the
stinking cages of the lock-ups, the grey, cowed faces of the long-term
convicts, the scarred buttocks of the men who had been flogged with
bamboos — all these oppressed me with an intolerable sense of guilt.
But I could get nothing into perspective. I was young and ill-educated
and I had had to think out my problems in the utter silence that is imposed on every Englishman in the East. I did not even know that the
British Empire is dying, still less did I know that it is a great deal better
than the younger empires that are going to supplant it. All I knew was
that I was stuck between my hatred of the empire I served and my rage
against the evil-spirited little beasts who tried to make my job impossible. With one part of my mind I thought of the British Raj as an un-
breakable tyranny, as something clamped down, in *saecula saeculorum*,
upon the will of prostrate peoples; with another part I thought that the
greatest joy in the world would be to drive a bayonet into a Buddhist
priest's guts. Feelings like these are the normal by-products of imperialism; ask any Anglo-Indian official, if you can catch him off duty.

One day something happened which in a roundabout way was 3
enlightening. It was a tiny incident in itself, but it gave me a better
glimpse than I had had before of the real nature of imperialism — the
real motives for which despotic governments act. Early one morning
the sub-inspector at a police station the other end of town rang me up
on the phone and said that an elephant was ravaging the bazaar. Would
I please come and do something about it? I did not know what I could
do, but I wanted to see what was happening and I got on to a pony and
started out. I took my rifle, an old .44 Winchester and much too small
to kill an elephant, but I thought the noise might be useful *in terrorem*.
Various Burmans stopped me on the way and told me about the elephant's doings. It was not, of course, a wild elephant, but a tame one
which had gone "must." It had been chained up, as tame elephants always
are when their attack of "must" is due, but on the previous night it had
broken its chain and escaped. Its mahout, the only person who could
manage it when it was in that state, had set out in pursuit, but had taken
the wrong direction and was now twelve hours' journey away, and in
the morning the elephant had suddenly reappeared in the town. The

Burmese population had no weapons and were quite helpless against it. It had already destroyed somebody's bamboo hut, killed a cow and raided some fruit-stalls and devoured the stock; also it had met the municipal rubbish van and, when the driver jumped out and took to his heels, had turned the van over and inflicted violences upon it.

4   The Burmese sub-inspector and some Indian constables were waiting for me in the quarter where the elephant had been seen. It was a very poor quarter, a labyrinth of squalid bamboo huts, thatched with palmleaf, winding all over a steep hillside. I remember that it was a cloudy, stuffy morning at the beginning of the rains. We began questioning the people as to where the elephant had gone and, as usual, failed to get any definite information. That is invariably the case in the East; a story always sounds clear enough at a distance, but the nearer you get to the scene of events the vaguer it becomes. Some of the people said that the elephant had gone in one direction, some said that he had gone in another, some professed not even to have heard of any elephant. I had almost made up my mind that the whole story was a pack of lies, when we heard yells a little distance away. There was a loud, scandalized cry of "Go away, child! Go away this instant!" and an old woman with a switch in her hand came round the corner of hut, violently shooing away a crowd of naked children. Some more women followed, clicking their tongues and exclaiming; evidently there was something that the children ought not to have seen. I rounded the hut and saw a man's dead body sprawling in the mud. He was an Indian, a black Dravidian coolie, almost naked, and he could not have been dead many minutes. The people said that the elephant had come suddenly upon him round the corner of the hut, caught him with its trunk, put its foot on his back and ground him into the earth. This was the rainy season and the ground was soft, and his face had scored a trench a foot deep and a couple of yards long. He was lying on his belly with arms crucified and head sharply twisted to one side. His face was coated with mud, the eyes wide open, the teeth bared and grinning with an expression of unendurable agony. (Never tell me, by the way, that the dead look peaceful. Most of the corpses I have seen looked devilish.) The friction of the great beast's foot had stripped the skin from his back as neatly as one skins a rabbit. As soon as I saw the dead man I sent an orderly to a friend's house nearby to borrow an elephant rifle. I had already sent back the pony, not wanting it to go mad with fright and throw me if it smelt the elephant.

5   The orderly came back in a few minutes with a rifle and five cartridges, and meanwhile some Burmans had arrived and told us that the

elephant was in the paddy fields below, only a few hundred yards away. As I started forward practically the whole population of the quarter flocked out of the houses and followed me. They had seen the rifle and were all shouting excitedly that I was going to shoot the elephant. They had not shown much interest in the elephant when he was merely ravaging their homes, but it was different now that he was going to be shot. It was a bit of fun to them, as it would be to an English crowd; besides they wanted the meat. It made me vaguely uneasy. I had no intention of shooting the elephant — I had merely sent for the rifle to defend myself if necessary — and it is always unnerving to have a crowd following you. I marched down the hill, looking and feeling a fool, with the rifle over my shoulder and an ever-growing army of people jostling at my heels. At the bottom, when you got away from the huts, there was a metalled road and beyond that a miry waste of paddy fields a thousand yards across, not yet ploughed but soggy from the first rains and dotted with coarse grass. The elephant was standing eight yards from the road, his left side towards us. He took not the slightest notice of the crowd's approach. He was tearing up bunches of grass, beating them against his knees to clean them and stuffing them into his mouth.

I had halted on the road. As soon as I saw the elephant I knew with   6 perfect certainty that I ought not to shoot him. It is a serious matter to shoot a working elephant — it is comparable to destroying a huge and costly piece of machinery — and obviously one ought not to do it if it can possibly be avoided. And at that distance, peacefully eating, the elephant looked no more dangerous than a cow. I thought then and I think now that his attack of "must" was already passing off; in which case he would merely wander harmlessly about until the mahout came back and caught him. Moreover, I did not in the least want to shoot him. I decided that I would watch him for a little while to make sure that he did not turn savage again, and then go home.

But at that moment, I glanced round at the crowd that had followed   7 me. It was an immense crowd, two thousand at the least and growing every minute. It blocked the road for a long distanc on either side. I looked at the sea of yellow faces above the garish clothes — faces all happy and excited over this bit of fun, all certain that the elephant was going to be shot. They were watching me as they would watch a conjuror about to perform a trick. They did not like me, but with the magical rifle in my hands I was momentarily worth watching. And suddenly I realized that I should have to shoot the elephant after all. The people expected it of me and I had got to do it; I could feel their two thousand wills pressing me forward, irresistibly. And it was at this moment, as

I stood there with the rifle in my hands, that I first grasped the hollowness, the futility of the white man's dominion in the East. Here was I, the white man with his gun, standing in front of the unarmed native crowd — seemingly the leading actor of the piece; but in reality I was only an absurd puppet pushed to and fro by the will of those yellow faces behind. I perceived in this moment that when the white man turns tyrant it is his own freedom that he destroys. He becomes a sort of hollow, posing dummy, the conventionalized figure of a sahib. For it is the condition of his rule that he shall spend his life in trying to impress the "natives," and so in every crisis he has got to do what the "natives" expect of him. He wears a mask, and his face grows to fit it. I had got to shoot the elephant. I had committed myself to doing it when I sent for the rifle. A sahib has got to act like a sahib; he has got to appear resolute, to know his own mind and do definite things. To come all that way, rifle in hand, with two thousand people marching at my heels, and then to trail feebly away, having done nothing — no, that was impossible. The crowd would laugh at me. And my whole life, every white man's life in the East, was one long struggle not to be laughed at.

8   But I did not want to shoot the elephant. I watched him beating his bunch of grass against his knees, with that preoccupied grandmotherly air that elephants have. It seemed to me that it would be murder to shoot him. At that age I was not squeamish about killing animals, but I had never shot an elephant and never wanted to. (Somehow it always seems worse to kill a *large* animal.) Besides, there was the beast's owner to be considered. Alive, the elephant was worth at least a hundred pounds; dead, he would only be worth the value of his tusks, five pounds, possibly. But I had got to act quickly. I turned to some experienced-looking Burmans who had been there when we arrived, and asked them how the elephant had been behaving. They all said the same things: he took no notice of you if you left him alone, but he might charge if you went too close to him.

9   It was perfectly clear to me what I ought to do. I ought to walk up to within, say, twenty-five yards of the elephant and test his behavior. If he charged, I could shoot; if he took no notice of me, it would be safe to leave him until the mahout came back. But also I knew that I was going to do no such thing. I was a poor shot with a rifle and the ground was soft mud into which one would sink at every step. If the elephant charged and I missed him, I should have about as much chance as a toad under a steam-roller. But even then I was not thinking particularly of my own skin, only of the watchful yellow faces behind. For at that moment, with the crowd watching me, I was not afraid in the ordinary

sense, as I would have been if I had been alone. A white man mustn't
be frightened in front of "natives"; and so, in general, he isn't frightened.
The sole thought in my mind was that if anything went wrong those
two thousand Burmans would see me pursued, caught, trampled on and
reduced to a grinning corpse like that Indian up the hill. And if that
happened it was quite probable that some of them would laugh. That
would never do. There was only one alternative. I shoved the cartridges
into the magazine and lay down on the road to get a better aim.

The crowd grew very still, and a deep, low, happy sigh, as of peo- 10
ple who see the theatre curtain go up at last, breathed from innumerable
throats. They were going to have their bit of fun after all. The rifle was
a beautiful German thing with cross-hair sights. I did not then know
that in shooting an elephant one would shoot to cut an imaginary bar
running from ear-hole to ear-hole. I ought, therefore, as the elephant
was sideways on, to have aimed striaght at his ear-hole; actually I aimed
several inches in front of this, thinking the brain would be further
forward.

When I pulled the trigger I did not hear the bang or feel the kick — 11
one never does when a shot goes home — but I heard the devilish roar
of glee that went up from the crowd. In that instant, in too short a time,
one would have thought, even for the bullet to get there, a mysterious,
terrible change had come over the elephant. He neither stirred nor fell,
but every line of his body had altered. He looked suddenly stricken,
shrunken, immensely old, as though the frightful impact of the bullet
had paralysed him without knocking him down. At last, after what
seemed a long time — it might have been five seconds, I dare say —
he sagged flabbily to his knees. His mouth slobbered. An enormous
senility seemed to have settled upon him. One could have imagined him
thousands of years old. I fired again into the same spot. At the second
shot he did not collapse but climbed with desperate slowness to his feet
and stood weakly upright, with legs sagging and head drooping. I fired
a third time. That was the shot that did for him. You could see the agony
of it jolt his whole body and knock the last remnant of strength from
his legs. But in falling he seemed for a moment to rise, for as his hind
legs collapsed beneath him he seemed to tower upward like a huge rock
toppling, his trunk reaching skywards like a tree. He trumpeted, for the
first and only time. And then down he came, his belly towards me, with
a crash that seemed to shake the ground even where I lay.

I got up. The Burmans were already racing past me across the mud. 12
It was obvious that the elephant would never rise again, but he was not
dead. He was breathing very rhythmically with long rattling gasps, his

great mound of a side painfully rising and falling. His mouth was wide open. I could see far down into caverns of pale pink throat. I waited a long time for him to die, but his breathing did not weaken. Finally I fired my two remaining shots into the spot where I thought his heart must be. The thick blood welled out of him like red velvet, but still he did not die. His body did not even jerk when the shots hit him, the tortured breathing continued without pause. He was dying, very slowly and in great agony, but in some world remote from me where not even a bullet could damage him further. I felt I had got to put an end to that dreadful noise. It seemed dreadful to see the great beast lying there, powerless to move and yet powerless to die, and not even to be able to finish him. I sent back for my small rifle and poured shot after shot into his head and down his throat. They seemed to make no impression. The tortured gasps continued as steadily as the ticking of a clock.

13   In the end I could not stand it any longer and went away. I heard later that it took him half an hour to die. Burmans were bringing dahs and baskets even before I left, and I was told they had stripped his body almost to the bones by the afternoon.

14   Afterwards, of course, there were endless discussions about the shooting of the elephant. The owner was furious, but he was only an Indian and could do nothing. Besides, legally I had done the right thing, for a mad elephant has to be killed, like a mad dog, if its owner fails to control it. Among the Europeans opinion was divided. The older men said I was right, the younger men said it was a damn shame to shoot an elephant for killing a coolie, because the elephant was worth more than any damn Coringhee coolie. And afterwards I was very glad that the coolie had been killed; it put me legally in the right and it gave me sufficient pretext for shooting the elephant. I often wondered whether any of the others grasped that I had done it solely to avoid looking a fool.

——— CONSIDERATIONS ————————————————————

1. Some of Orwell's remarks about the Burmese make him sound like a racist; collect a half dozen of them on a separate sheet of paper, then look for lines or phrases that counter the first samples. Discuss your findings, bearing in mind the purpose of Orwell's essay.

2. "In a job like that you see the dirty work of Empire at close quarters." If you ponder Orwell's capitalizing "Empire" (Paragraph 2) and then substitute other abstract terms for "Empire" — say, Government, Poverty, War, Hatred — you may discover one of the most important principles of effective writing, a principle beautifully demonstrated by Orwell's whole account.

3. In Paragraph 4, Orwell says, "the nearer you get to the scene of events the vaguer it becomes." Have you had an experience that would help you understand his remark? Would it hold true for the soldier caught in battle, a couple suffering a divorce, a football player caught in a pile-up on the scrimmage line?

4. Some years after his experience in Burma, Orwell became a well-known opponent of fascism. How might shooting the elephant have taught him to detest totalitarianism?

5. "Somehow it always seems worse to kill a *large* animal," Orwell writes in Paragraph 8. Why? Are some lives more equal than others?

6. In Paragraph 10, Orwell describes his rifle as a "beautiful German thing." Does he use the word "beautiful" in the same way Don Sharp uses it in the last paragraph of his essay "Under the Hood"? Neither of the writers means "pulchritude" when he uses "beautiful." What synonyms might fit their sense of the word?

7. After two substantial paragraphs of agonizing detail, Orwell's elephant is still dying. Why does the writer inflict this punishment on the reader?

53

GEORGE ORWELL
A Hanging

1   It was in Burma, a sodden morning of the rains. A sickly light, like yellow tinfoil, was slanting over the high walls into the jail yard. We were waiting outside the condemned cells, a row of sheds fronted with double bars, like small animal cages. Each cell measured about ten feet by ten and was quite bare within except for a plank bed and a pot for drinking water. In some of them brown, silent men were squatting at the inner bars, with their blankets draped round them. These were the condemned men, due to be hanged within the next week or two.

2   One prisoner had been brought out of his cell. He was a Hindu, a puny wisp of a man, with a shaven head and vague liquid eyes. He had a thick, sprouting moustache, absurdly too big for his body, rather like the moustache of a comic man on the films. Six tall Indian warders were guarding him and getting him ready for the gallows. Two of them stood by with rifles and fixed bayonets, while the others handcuffed him, passed a chain through his handcuffs and fixed it to their belts, and lashed his arms tight to his sides. They crowded very close about him, with their hands always on him in a careful, caressing grip, as though all the while feeling him to make sure he was there. It was like men handling a fish which is still alive and may jump back into the water. But he stood quite unresisting, yielding his arms limply to the ropes, as though he hardly noticed what was happening.

3   Eight o'clock struck and a bugle call, desolately thin in the wet air, floated from the distant barracks. The superintendent of the jail,

who was standing apart from the rest of us, moodily prodding the gravel with his stick, raised his head at the sound. He was an army doctor, with a grey toothbrush moustache and a gruff voice. "For God's sake hurry up, Francis," he said irritably. "The man ought to have been dead by this time. Aren't you ready yet?"

Francis, the head jailer, a fat Dravidian in a white drill suit and   4
gold spectacles, waved his black hand. "Yes sir, yes sir," he bubbled. "All iss satisfactorily prepared. The hangman iss waiting. We shall proceed."

"Well, quick march, then. The prisoners can't get their breakfast   5
till this job's over."

We set out for the gallows. Two warders marched on either side   6
of the prisoner, with their rifles at the slope; two others marched close against him, gripping him by arm and shoulder, as though at once pushing and supporting him. The rest of us, magistrates and the like, followed behind. Suddenly, when we had gone ten yards, the procession stopped short without any order or warning. A dreadful thing had happened — a dog, come goodness knows whence, had appeared in the yard. It came bounding among us with a loud volley of barks and leapt round us wagging its whole body, wild with glee at finding so many human beings together. It was a large woolly dog, half Airedale, half pariah. For a moment it pranced round us, and then, before anyone could stop it, it had made a dash for the prisoner, and jumping up tried to lick his face. Everybody stood aghast, too taken aback even to grab the dog.

"Who let that bloody brute in here?" said the superintendent   7
angrily. "Catch it, someone!"

A warder detached from the escort, charged clumsily after the dog,   8
but it danced and gambolled just out of his reach, taking everything as part of the game. A young Eurasian jailer picked up a handful of gravel and tried to stone the dog away, but it dodged the stones and came after us again. Its yaps echoed from the jail walls. The prisoner, in the grasp of the two warders, looked on incuriously, as though this was another formality of the hanging. It was several minutes before someone managed to catch the dog. Then we put my handkerchief through its collar and moved off once more, with the dog still straining and whimpering.

It was about forty yards to the gallows. I watched the bare brown   9
back of the prisoner marching in front of me. He walked clumsily with his bound arms, but quite steadily, with that bobbing gait of the Indian who never straightens his knees. At each step his muscles slid neatly into place, the lock of hair on his scalp danced up and down, his feet

printed themselves on the wet gravel. And once, in spite of the men who gripped him by each shoulder, he stepped lightly aside to avoid a puddle on the path.

10   It is curious; but till that moment I had never realized what it means to destroy a healthy, conscious man. When I saw the prisoner step aside to avoid the puddle I saw the mystery, the unspeakable wrongness, of cutting a life short when it is in full tide. This man was not dying, he was alive just as we are alive. All the organs of his body were working — bowels digesting food, skin renewing itself, nails growing, tissues forming — all toiling away in solemn foolery. His nails would still be growing when he stood on the drop, when he was falling through the air with a tenth-of-a-second to live. His eyes saw the yellow gravel and the grey walls, and his brain still remembered, foresaw, reasoned — even about puddles. He and we were a party of men walking together, seeing, hearing, feeling, understanding the same world; and in two minutes, with a sudden snap, one of us would be gone — one mind less, one world less.

11   The gallows stood in a small yard, separate from the main grounds of the prison, and overgrown with tall prickly weeds. It was a brick erection like three sides of a shed, with planking on top, and above that two beams and a crossbar with the rope dangling. The hangman, a greyhaired convict in the white uniform of the prison, was waiting beside his machine. He greeted us with a servile crouch as we entered. At a word from Francis the two wards, gripping the prisoner more closely than ever, half led, half pushed him to the gallows and helped him clumsily up the ladder. Then the hangman climbed up and fixed the rope round the prisoner's neck.

12   We stood waiting, five yards away. The warders had formed in a rough circle round the gallows. And then, when the noose was fixed, the prisoner began crying out to his god. It was a high, reiterated cry of "Ram! Ram! Ram! Ram!" not urgent and fearful like a prayer or cry for help, but steady, rhythmical, almost like the tolling of a bell. The dog answered the sound with a whine. The hangman, still standing on the gallows, produced a small cotton bag like a flour bag and drew it down over the prisoner's face. But the sound, muffled by the cloth, still persisted, over and over again: "Ram! Ram! Ram! Ram! Ram!"

13   The hangman climbed down and stood ready, holding the lever. Minutes seemed to pass. The steady, muffled crying from the prisoner went on and on, "Ram! Ram! Ram!" never faltering for an instant. The superintendent, his head on his chest, was slowly poking the ground with his stick; perhaps he was counting the cries, allowing the prisoner a fixed number — fifty, perhaps, or a hundred. Everyone had changed

colour. The Indians had gone grey like bad coffee, and one or two of the bayonets were wavering. We looked at the lashed, hooded man on the drop, and listened to his cries — each cry another second of life; the same thought was in all our minds; oh, kill him quickly, get it over, stop that abominable noise!

Suddenly the superintendent made up his mind. Throwing up his 14 head he made a swift motion with his stick. "Chalo!" he shouted almost fiercely.

There was a clanking noise, and then dead silence. The prisoner 15 had vanished, and the rope was twisting on itself. I let go of the dog, and it galloped immediately to the back of the gallows; but when it got there it stopped short, barked, and then retreated into a corner of the yard, where it stood among the weeds, looking timorously out at us. We went round the gallows to inspect the prisoner's body. He was dangling with his toes pointed straight downwards, very slowly revolving, as dead as a stone.

The superintendent reached out with his stick and poked the bare 16 brown body; it oscillated slightly. "*He's* all right," said the superintendent. He backed out from under the gallows, and blew out a deep breath. the moody look had gone out of his face quite suddenly. He glanced at his wrist-watch. "Eight minutes past eight. Well, that's all for this morning, thank God."

The warders unfixed bayonets and marched away. The dog, sobered 17 and conscious of having misbehaved itself, slipped after them. We walked out of the gallows yard, past the condemned cells with their waiting prisoners, into the big central yard of the prison. The convicts, under the command of warders armed with lathis, were already receiving their breakfast. They squatted in long rows, each man holding a tin pannikin, while two warders with buckets marched round ladling out rice; it seemed quite a homely, jolly scene, after the hanging. An enormous relief had come upon us now that the job was done. One felt an impulse to sing, to break into a run, to snigger. All at once everyone began chatting gaily.

The Eurasian boy walking beside me nodded towards the way we 18 had come, with a knowing smile: "Do you know, sir, our friend (he meant the dead man) when he heard his appeal had been dismissed, he pissed on the floor of his cell. From fright. Kindly take one of my cigarettes, sir. Do you not admire my new silver case, sir? From the boxwallah, two rupees eight annas. Classy European style."

Several people laughed — at what, nobody seemed certain. 19

Francis was walking by the superintendent, talking garrulously: 20 "Well, sir, all has passed off with the utmost satisfactoriness. It was all finished — flick! Like that. It iss not always so — oah, no! I have known cases where the doctor wass obliged to go beneath the gallows and pull the prissoner's legs to ensure decease. Most disagreeable!"

21   "Wriggling about, eh? That's bad," said the superintendent.

22   "Ach, sir, it iss worse when they become refractory! One man, I recall, clung to the bars of hiss cage when we went to take him out. You will scarcely credit, sir, that it took six wards to dislodge him, three pulling at each leg. We reasoned with him, 'My dear fellow,' we said, 'think of all the pain and trouble you are causing to us!' But no, he would not listen! Ach, he wass very troublesome!"

23   I found that I was laughing quite loudly. Everyone was laughing. Even the superintendent grinned in a tolerant way. "You'd better all come out and have a drink," he said quite genially. "I've got a bottle of whiskey in the car. We could do with it."

24   We went through the big double gates of the prison into the road. "Pulling at his legs!" exclaimed a Burmese magistrate suddenly, and burst into a loud chuckling. We all began laughing again. At that moment Francis' anecdote seemed extraordinarily funny. We all had a drink together, native and European alike, quite amicably. The dead man was a hundred yards away.

____ CONSIDERATIONS _____

1. Many readers have described Orwell's "A Hanging" as a powerful condemnation of capital punishment. Study Orwell's technique in drawing from his readers the desired inference. It might be helpful to read another master of implication — Ernest Hemingway in his short story "Hills Like White Elephants."

2. Point out examples of Orwell's skillful use of detail to establish the place and mood of "A Hanging." Adapt his technique to your purpose in your next essay.

3. What minor incident caused Orwell suddenly to see "the unspeakable wrongness . . . of cutting a life short"? Why?

4. What effect, in Paragraph 6, does the boisterous dog have on the players of this scene? On you, the reader? Explain in terms of the whole essay.

5. "One mind, one world less" is the way Orwell sums up the demise of the Hindu prisoner. Obviously, Orwell's statement is highly compressed, jamming into its short length many ideas, hopes, and fears. Write a short essay, opening up his aphorism so that your readers get some idea of what can be packed into five short words. For additional examples of compressed expression, see Ambrose Bierce's "Devil's Dictionary," and any of the poems in this book.

6. The warden and others present were increasingly disconcerted by the prisoner's continued cry, "Ram! Ram! Ram! Ram!" But note Orwell's description of that cry in Paragraphs 12 and 13. Does that description give you a clue as to the nature of the man's cry? Why doesn't Orwell explain it?

Eleanor Perényi (b. 1918) was born in Washington, D.C.; her mother was a novelist, and her father a naval officer. She lived in Europe, China, the West Indies, and all over the United States. After marrying the Baron Zsigmond Perényi she lived in Hungary for some years, and later wrote about her Hungarian experience in a book called More Was Lost. *She has worked on magazines in New York; written a book about* Liszt; *and published essays in* The Atlantic, Harper's, Esquire, *and* Harper's Bazaar. *Perényi currently lives in Stonington, Connecticut, where she spends much of her time gardening.*

"Partly Cloudy" comes from Green Thoughts, *whose accurate subtitle is "A Writer in the Garden."*

54

ELEANOR PERÉNYI
Partly Cloudy

1   The drought is serious, the corn crop threatened, lawns are burning up and water restrictions forbid us to water them. Turn to the evening weather forecast and there is a grinning young man surrounded with weather maps and radarscopes to assure us we haven't a worry in the world; 'The threat of shower activity has passed and it looks like a gorgeous weekend.' Or it is winter and a snowfall in prospect. Panic: 'It could be as much as four inches and travelers' warnings are out for the metropolitan area and eastern Long Island.' Nightly, some variation on these themes is enacted in the grotesque ritual called a weather forecast but more accurately described as pandering to infantilism. It is a frightening revelation of how insulated we have become from the natural world.

I assume that in those parts of the country where sufficient rain   2
is still a life-and-death matter the forecasters show a little more sensitivity, though I wouldn't bet on it; and surely the states whose economy
depends on snow to activate the ski resorts don't allow an imminent
storm to be forecast as though it were a plague of locusts. Elsewhere,
the weather is treated as something between a threat and a joke. The
'meteorologist,' having read out the figures we can see for ourselves on
the screen and relayed predictions that come to him from computers
at the National Weather Service as though they were his own, then
engages in heavy banter with the fellow who broadcasts the news: 'Don't
give us any more the white stuff, Bill.' 'I'll do my best, Jim.' Thus is the
power once attributed to Jove and his thunderbolts transferred to a man
in a sports jacket — a quaint conceit indeed in a scientific age, and one
with disturbing implications that the viewer is a child on perpetual holi-
day, his only interest in going out to play.

Unfortunately, that assumption seems to be correct. Americans   3
resent the vagaries of weather to a degree unknown to other peoples.
England's generally abominable climate is forecast in positively poetic
terms — 'Intervals of sun and cloud over East Anglia' — and in Italy
a light chop on the Mediterranean sounds Vergilian. The majority of
Americans crave a sunlit perfection, as if hell itself weren't a warm, well-
lighted place, and have accordingly migrated by the millions to the Sun
Belt, where the real prediction, not often uttered, is that they and their
crops, planted in areas never intended by nature to support such exploitation, will die of thirst within twenty years unless a miracle occurs. Not
only that: Bulldozed and overbuilt southern California is regularly burnt
over by man-kindled fires and bids fair to be destroyed by mudslides
well before the long-predicted earthquake comes along. Californians are
only continuing the well-worn practice of building where floods and
washouts are regular events — all our alluvial plains are examples of
the same recklessness. We aren't, of course, the only people who have
chosen to live on the brink. Ancient history testifies to that. From the
flood plains of Mesopotamia to volcanic regions around the world,
always heavily populated, the record is of one catastrophe after another,
beginning with the Flood. But we are surely, in modern times, the least
realistic and least equipped to deal with quite ordinary and predictable
happenings. Our cars are so constructed (they didn't used to be) that an
inch or two of snow is enough to swamp the roads with accidents. I
don't know how they do it, but in northern and Alpine Europe (and Japan's northernmost island, Hokkaido), trains race through blizzards and
arrive on the minute. In the United States, a commuter railroad like

the Long Island, with no mountain passes to cross, no elaborate connections to be made with other international trains, can and has collapsed for more than a week after a snowstorm. No wonder the prospect
of a little bad weather makes us nervous. We aren't equipped to handle
it physically or — what is more important in the long run —
psychologically either.

4   Weather is a force we have lost touch with. We feel entitled to
dominate it, like everything else in the environment, and when we can't
are more panic-stricken than primitives who know that when nature
is out of control they can only pray to the gods. We pray, too — to the
electric company on whose vulnerable wires our lives depend. When
we first moved here, the local company was called the Mystic Light &
Power, a name that made me laugh whenever I made out a check. Now
it is Northeast Utilities, which doesn't inspire the same confidence. Nor
has Northeast moved to change the scary system of wires, strung
overhead where they can be smitten by lightning and tree limbs, that
was installed about the turn of the century. In Europe, these tangles
are underground and not allowed to disfigure the streets and endanger
the citizenry. Why are they here? Nobody can tell me. There they hang,
one more reason to fear the winds that can't be stopped from blowing.
Only last week, lightning struck the maple across the street, bringing
down the wires interlaced in its branches and leaving us powerless for
a night and half a day. Powerless is the word. It was almost comic that
I couldn't even brew a cup of coffee.

5   It probably goes without saying that that particular storm didn't
figure in the evening forecast — neither its violence nor where it would
strike. 'Possible late afternoon or late evening thundershowers' is a
prediction we hear day after day all summer and have learned to ignore
until wc see the thunderheads. It is the forecasters' way of not getting
caught, just as ever since the unannounced 1938 hurricane of terrible
memory they have been careful to inform us of the least tropical depression developing in the Caribbean. But having lived through many later
hurricanes, I have noticed that the nearer the storm, the less accurate
the plotting of its probable strike. We are told the 'eye' will pass over
Montauk (which on the usual north by east course means, in short order, us), or no — it will pass over Bridgeport (which doesn't), or it has
already gone out to sea. The same with snow, which will accumulate
to two inches, four inches or, suddenly, amount to little or nothing. Not
the least of the sins of the forecasters is their unreliability. Many years
ago, my father believed there would be a revolution in forecasting as
soon as Arctic weather stations and an efficient system of radio com-

munication were established at various points across the globe. A Navy man, he had a particular interest in the subject, especially as it applied to military operations like the Normandy landings, which it will be recalled nearly foundered on account of an unforeseen storm. He died before the invention of weather satellites and other advanced technology like computers, which would have given him even higher hopes. What would have been his feelings to learn, thirty years later, that our military weathermen in the Arabian Sea were unaware of a vast sandstorm hovering over the Iranian plateau at a critical moment — a locality where such storms are common at that time of year? Is it reasonable to expect the little chap on the TV screen, who gets his information from a less vitally concerned source, to do better? I would rather trust the farmer who holds his finger to the wind, anyone, indeed, who lives outside the technological cocoon. I remember that when my father was in charge of a naval station on a West Indian island in the 1920's, he had received no official word of an approaching hurricane. It was the inhabitants who gave him warning of the need to take precautions. Reading the motion of the sea, the clouds, feeling in the barometer of their bones a sudden drop a thousand miles away, they muttered for days, 'Hurricane coming, hurricane coming.' They were right. A couple of hours after the official warning arrived, the storm struck the island like a sand-blasting machine and nearly blew us off the map.

Such skills have largely been lost. Hence, in part, the inordinate fear of weather and the dependence on the idiot box to feed the dream of eternal sunshine, or the nightmare of a couple of inches of snow. In our civilization, if that is what it is, only farmers and gardeners are free of these fantasies. We don't care if your weekend *is* ruined by the rain we need. We curse the wind the Sunday sailor wants for his outing (it dries up our peas, just coming to perfection), and bless the snow that blocks your roads but keeps our plants and the winter wheat safe. We must collaborate with nature whether we like it or not and perhaps need a special weather service of our own.   6

Something of the sort exists, and I don't mean the old black magic, not but what I don't rely on it on occasion, and in the short run. Rain really is imminent when the leaves turn their backs to the wind, smoke goes to ground and the earthworms rise to the surface. It may not be true that if St. Martin's Day is fair and cold the winter will be short, but I would give it a try. A Mexican-Indian gardener once told me at the beginning of the dry season in October that it would rain heavily for three days in February — I forgot which saint's fiesta was involved and anyway the saint was undoubtedly a thinly disguised Aztec god —   7 and not thereafter for three months. The prediction was correct and amazed me at the time. It doesn't amaze me now. It never pays to underestimate folk wisdom. Neither does it pay to overestimate it. The 'natives' don't know everything or they wouldn't be 'natives.' But neither do we, or we wouldn't be in the awful pickle we are. What I seek is a scientific approach that takes into account information gathered down the ages by observant human beings — and goes on from there.

8   Such a minor discipline is at hand in a development called phenology: the study of the growth stages of plants, which can be used to predict the approach of spring and all that implies about planting dates, the emergence of insects and other data vital to farmers and gardeners. The name is modern, the practice as old as the hills. The Chinese and the ancient Romans were using phenological calendars a couple of thousand years ago, and real farmers, as opposed to those engaged in mass agriculture, have always been aware of the principle — which simply consists in noting the dates when one or more plants known as 'indicators' burst into leaf or bloom. Given this information, it is then possible to predict other events like the warming of the soil, the likelihood of one area remaining persistently colder than another, and so on. It has long been understood that plants are sensitive weather instruments, registering temperature and humidity. Indicator plants are simply more reliable than others. The common lilac, for instance, won't open its buds until it is safe to do so (which is why the flowering can vary by as much as three weeks from one season to another), and the farmer or gardener who takes phenology for his guide will watch for this flowering rather than go by the books and perform certain tasks at a fixed date. In Montana, the blooming of the lilacs tells farmers they have ten days to cut the alfalfa and eliminate the first brood of alfalfa weevils. Truck farmers in Long Island count on the flowering forsythia to signal the arrival of the cabbage-root maggot. In New England we used to plant our corn when the elm leaves were the size of a squirrel's ear, knowing the ground would then be warm enough for the seed to germinate. The elms are nearly gone but oak or maple will do as well. Using the lilac, or the dogwood — another indicator plant — it should also be possible to locate the best place on a property to plant a tender fruit tree like an apricot. Where either of these flowered consistently earlier than others of their kind would be a warm spot that could save the fruit buds from late freezes.

9   A number of countries in Europe maintain networks to gather phenological information as part of their national weather services. We don't. Such a network was established here in 1904 by the Weather Bu-

reau but abandoned for lack of funds. Now, however, there seems to be a revival of interest. A few states are developing programs and the Department of Agriculture is collaborating with some of them. Phenological maps have been compiled. But it will be a long time before the nightly forecast includes the latest word on lilac time. Meanwhile, there is nothing to stop the amateur from making his own observations. I scored a minor success, though not with phenology, in long-range forecasting in the fall of 1979, when we had an exceptionally early snowfall, one that took place while the roses were still in bloom and the leaves green on the trees. That, I announced grandly, meant we would have no more snow until February and an exceptionally dry winter. This was based on nothing more than notes in my garden log which recorded two similarly premature snowfalls in the early 1970's, both followed by dry winters. It may well have been coincidence, but I turned out to be right. On the number of times I have been wrong, misled by the behavior of squirrels with nuts and the amount of moss on the north sides of trees, time-honored omens, I naturally don't enlarge. But then I notice that those who predict weather never do mention, or apologize for, their failures.

––––– **CONSIDERATIONS** –––––––––––––––––––––––––––

1. Perényi's paragraphs run longer than most contemporary writers'. Can you see any advantage to larger sections? If her essay were yours, would you break any of these paragraphs? No. 3? No. 5? Why?

2. "Weather is a force we have lost touch with," writes Perényi. Beginning with your car, make a list of the devices and features of your daily life that screen you from the elements. Would such "protections" explain our occasional impulse to go walking in a rainstorm? Why is it unfortunate to lose touch with the weather?

3. Perényi says that the name of her local electric company, "Mystic Light & Power," made her laugh, but that she lost confidence in it when the name changed to "Northeast Utilities." Connect this notion with her later remark that she "would rather trust the farmer who holds his finger to the wind, anyone, indeed, who lives outside the technological cocoon."

4. How does she develop her distrust of TV weathermen in the "technological cocoon" in Paragraphs 5 and 6?

5. If Perényi distrusts modern meteorology and admits the fallibility of folk methods, what does she consider a reliable weather indicator? Find an example of how it works.

6. What do Pernýi's style and tone reveal about her as a person?

Sylvia Plath (1932–1963) grew up in Massachusetts and graduated from Smith College. She was a precocious writer, publishing professionally even as an undergraduate. While her first devotion was to poetry, she also worked in fiction and the essay. On a Fulbright Fellowship to England she met and married the English poet Ted Hughes, with whom she had two children. Her first book of poetry, The Colossus, *was published in 1960, her novel* The Bell Jar *in 1963. The poems of* Ariel *(1965) are her best work — poems of intense suffering and power, including "The Bee Meeting." In February of 1963 she killed herself.*

The journal entry that follows is from Johnny Panic and the Bible of Dreams *(1978), a posthumous collection of short stories and miscellaneous prose. Other posthumous works include* The Collected Poems *(1981) and* The Journals of Sylvia Plath *(1982). Here we watch a young writer at work — first on her journal — observant, careful, distinctive; then we watch her refine her prose into the lines of the finished poem.*

55

SYLVIA PLATH

Journal Entries:
Charlie Pollard and
the Beekeepers

JUNE 7 [1962]

The midwife stopped to see Ted at noon to remind him that the   1
Devon beekeepers were having a meeting at six at Charlie Pollard's. We
were interested in starting a hive, so dumped the babies in bed and
jumped in the car and dashed down the hill past the old factory to Mill
Lane, a row of pale orange stucco cottages on the Taw, which gets
flooded whenever the river rises. We drove into the dusty, ugly paved
parking lot under the gray peaks of the factory buildings, unused since
1928 and now only used for wool storage. We felt very new & shy, I
hugging my bare arms in the cool of the evening, for I had not thought
to bring a sweater. We crossed a little bridge to the yard where a group
of miscellaneous Devonians were standing — an assortment of shapeless
men in brown-speckled, bulgy tweeds, Mr. Pollard in white shirtsleeves,
with his dark, nice brown eyes and oddly Jewy head, tan, balding, dark-
haired. I saw two women, one very large, tall, stout, in a glistening aqua-
blue raincoat, the other cadaverous as a librarian in a dun raincoat. Mr.
Pollard glided toward us & stood for a moment on the bridge end, talking. He indicated a pile of hives, like white and green blocks of wood
with little gables, & said we could have one, if we would like to fix it

up. A small pale blue car pulled into the yard: the midwife. Her moony beam came at us through the windshield. Then the rector came pontificating across the bridge, & there was a silence that grew round him. He carried a curious contraption — a dark felt hat with a screen box built on under it, and cloth for a neckpiece under that. I thought the hat a clerical beekeeping hat, and that he must have made it for himself. Then I saw, on the grass, and in hands, everybody was holding a bee hat, some with netting of nylon, most with box screening, some with khaki round hats. I felt barer and barer. People became concerned. Have you no hat? Have you no coat? Then a dry little woman came up, Mrs. P, the secretary of the society, with tired, short blond hair. "I have a boiler suit." She went to her car and came back with a small white silk button-down smock, the sort pharmacist's assistants use. I put it on and buttoned it & felt more protected. Last year, said the midwife, Charlie Pollard's bees were bad-tempered and made everybody run. Everyone seemed to be waiting for someone. But then we all slowly filed after Charlie Pollard to his beehives. We threaded our way through neatly weeded allotment gardens, one with bits of tinfoil and a fan of black and white feathers on a string, very decorative, to scare the birds, and twiggy lean-tos over the plants. Black-eyed sweetpea-like blooms: broad beans, somebody said. The gray ugly backs of the factory. Then we came to a clearing, roughly scythed, with one hive, a double-brood hive, two layers. From this hive Charlie Pollard wanted to make three hives. I understood very little. The men gathered round the hive. Charlie Pollard started squirting smoke from a little funnel with a hand bellows attached to it round the entry at the bottom of the hive. "Too much smoke," hissed the large, blue-raincoated woman next to me. "What do you do if they sting?" I whispered, as the bees, now Charlie had lifted the top off the hive, were zinging out and dancing round as at the end of long elastics. (Charlie had produced a fashionable white straw Italian hat for me with a black nylon veil that collapsed perilously into my face in the least wind. The rector had tucked it into my collar, much to my surprise. "Bees always crawl up, never down," he said. I had drawn it down loose over my shoulders.) The woman said, "Stand behind me, I'll protect you." I did. (I had spoken to her husband earlier, a handsome, rather sarcastic man standing apart, silver hair, a military blue eye. Plaid tie, checked shirt, plaid vest, all different. Tweedy suit, navy blue beret. His wife, he had said, kept twelve hives & was the expert. The bees always stung him. His nose & lips, his wife later said.)

2   The men were lifting out rectangular yellow slides, crusted with bees, crawling, swarming. I felt prickles all over me, & itches. I had one pocket & was advised to keep my hands in this and not move. "See all

the bees round the rector's dark trousers!" whispered the woman. "They don't seem to like white." I was grateful for my white smock. The rector was somehow an odd man out, referred to now and then by Charlie jestingly: "Eh, rector?" "Maybe they want to join his church," one man, emboldened by the anonymity of the hats, suggested.

The donning of the hats had been an odd ceremony. Their ugliness 3 & anonymity very compelling, as if we were all party to a rite. They were brown or gray or faded green felt, mostly, but there was one white straw boater with a ribbon. All faces, shaded, became alike. Commerce became possible with complete strangers.

The men were lifting slides, Charlie Pollard squirting smoke, into 4 another box. They were looking for queen cells — long, pendulous, honey-colored cells from which the new queens would come. The blue-coated woman pointed them out. She was from British Guiana, had lived alone in the jungle for eighteen years, lost £25 on her first bees there — there had been no honey for them to eat. I was aware of bees buzzing and stalling before my face. The veil seemed hallucinatory. I could not see it for moments at a time. Then I became aware I was in a bone-stiff trance, intolerably tense, and shifted round to where I could see better. "Spirit of my death father, protect me!" I arrogantly prayed. A dark, rather nice, "unruly"-looking man came up through the cut grasses. Everyone turned, murmured, "O Mr. Jenner, we didn't think you were coming."

This, then, the awaited expert, the "government man" from Exeter. 5 An hour late. He donned a white boiler suit and a very expert bee hat — a vivid green dome, square black screen box for head, joined with yellow cloth at the corners, and a white neckpiece. The men muttered, told what had been done. They began looking for the old queen. Slide after slide was lifted, examined on both sides. To no avail. Myriads of crawling, creeping bees. As I understood it from my blue bee-lady, the first new queen out would kill the old ones, so the new queen cells were moved to different hives. The old queen would be left in hers. But they couldn't find her. Usually the old queen swarmed before the new queen hatched. This was to prevent swarming. I heard words like "supersede," "queen excluder" (a slatted screen of metal only workers could crawl through). The rector slipped away unnoticed, then the midwife. "He used too much smoke" was the general criticism of Charlie Pollard. The queen hates smoke. She might have swarmed earlier. She might be hiding. She was not marked. It grew later. Eight. Eight-thirty. The hives were parceled up, queen excluders put on. An old beamy brown man wisely jutted a forefinger as we left. "She's in that one." The beekeepers clustered around Mr. Jenner with questions. The secretary sold chances for a bee festival.

FRIDAY, JUNE 8

6   Ted & I drove down to Charlie Pollard's about nine tonight to collect our hive. He was standing at the door of his cottage in Mill Lane, the corner one, in white shirtsleeves, collar open, showing dark chest hairs & white mail-knit undershirt. His pretty blond wife smiled & waved. We went over the bridge to the shed, with its rotovator, orange, resting at the end. Talked of floods, fish, Ash Ridge: the Taw flooded his place over & over. He was wanting to move up, had an eye on the lodge at Ash Ridge, had hives up there. His father-in-law had been head gardener when they had six gardeners. Told of great heaters to dry hay artificially & turn it to meal: two thousand, four thousand, the machines cost, were lying up there now, hardly used. He hadn't been able to get any more flood insurance once he had claimed. Had his rugs cleaned, but they were flat: you can live with them, I can't, he told the inspector. Had to have the upholstered sofa & chairs all redone at the bottom. Walked down the first step from the second floor one night & put his foot in water. A big salmon inhabited his reach of the Taw. "To be honest with you," he said, over & over. "To be honest with you." Showed us his big barny black offices. A honey ripener with a beautiful sweet-smelling, slow gold slosh of honey at the bottom. Loaned us a bee book. We loaded with our creaky old wood hive. He said if we cleaned it and painted it over Whitsun, he'd order a swarm of docile bees. Had showed us his beautiful red-told Italian queen the day before, with her glossy green mark on the thorax, I think. He had made it. To see her the better. The bees were bad-tempered, though. She would lay a lot of docile bees. We said: Docile, be sure now, & drove home.

These few lines were typed at the top margin of the original MS:

Noticed: a surround of tall white cow parsley, pursy yellow gorse bloom, an old Christmas tree, white hawthorn, strong-smelling.

56

SYLVIA PLATH
The Bee Meeting

Who are these people at the bridge to meet me? They are the villagers —
The rector, the midwife, the sexton, the agent for bees.
In my sleeveless summery dress I have no protection,
And they are all gloved and covered, why did nobody tell me?
They are smiling and taking out veils tacked to ancient hats.   5

I am nude as a chicken neck, does nobody love me?
Yes, here is the secretary of bees with her white shop smock,
Buttoning the cuffs at my wrists and the slit from my neck to my knees.
Now I am milkweed silk, the bees will not notice.
They will not smell my fear, my fear, my fear.   10

Which is the rector now, is it that man in black?
Which is the midwife, is that her blue coat?
Everybody is nodding a square black head, they are knights in visors,
Breastplates of cheesecloth knotted under the armpits.
Their smiles and their voices are changing. I am led through a   15
    beanfield.

Strips of tinfoil winking like people,
Feather dusters fanning their hands in a sea of bean flowers,
Creamy bean flowers with black eyes and leaves like bored hearts.
Is it blood clots the tendrils are dragging up that string?
No, no, it is scarlet flowers that will one day be edible.   20

331

Now they are giving me a fashionable white straw Italian hat
And a black veil that moulds to my face, they are making me one of
    them.

They are leading me to the shorn grove, the circle of hives.
Is it the hawthorn that smells so sick?
25   The barren body of hawthorn, etherizing its children.

Is it some operation that is taking place?
It is the surgeon my neighbors are waiting for,
This apparition in a green helmet,
Shining gloves and white suit.
30   Is it the butcher, the grocer, the postman, someone I know?

I cannot run, I am rooted, and the gorse hurts me
With its yellow purses, its spiky armoury.
I could not run without having to run forever.
The white hive is snug as a virgin,
35   Sealing off her brood cells, her honey, and quietly humming.

Smoke rolls and scarves in the grove.
The mind of the hive thinks this is the end of everything.
Here they come, the outriders, on their hysterical elastics.
If I stand very still, they will think I am cow parsley,
40   A gullible head untouched by their animosity.

Not even nodding, a personage in a hedgerow.
The villagers open the chambers, they are hunting the queen.
Is she hiding, is she eating honey? She is very clever.
She is old, old, old, she must live another year, and she knows it.
While in their fingerjoint cells the new virgins

Dream of a duel they will win inevitably,
A curtain of wax dividing them from the bride flight,
The upflight of the murderess into a heaven that loves her.
The villagers are moving the virgins, there will be no killing.
45   The old queen does not show herself, is she so ungrateful?

I am exhausted, I am exhausted —
Pillar of white in a blackout of knives.
I am the magician's girl who does not flinch.

The villagers are untying their disguises, they are shaking hands.
Whose is that long white box in the grove, what have they accomplished,   50
   why am I cold?

_____ CONSIDERATIONS _____

1. To what extent did Sylvia Plath draw upon her notebook for material in writing her poem, "The Bee Meeting"? Read both pieces carefully and list any phrases, characters, events, and ideas that notebook and poem share. Note changes in the material as it moved from notebook to poem.

2. Compare Plath's notebook entries with passages from other notebooks appearing in this book — those of Joan Didion and Henry David Thoreau. Discuss differences and similarities. Compare your own daily writing or journal.

3. Study the brief but graphic description of each of the people Plath meets at the gathering of beekeepers. How do they differ? What do her observations reveal, other than the physical appearance of the subjects?

4. Study the details Plath notes of the places themselves — the parking lot, the gardens. Do these details reveal Plath's feelings, or are they incidental?

5. "Commerce became possible with complete strangers," writes Plath at the end of Paragraph 3. Consider this curious phenomenon: that strangers often will speak more freely than will acquaintances. Can you explain this behavior?

6. Reread Plath's notebook account, looking especially for points that would allow you to explain either that Plath felt very much a part of the beekeeping crowd or that she remained aloof, an interested but uninvolved observer. It might be helpful to look at Henry David Thoreau's position, described in his journal entry of June 16, 1854 (pages 413–416).

David Quammen (b. 1948) writes a column for Outside *called "Natural Acts," and collected his witty and eccentric essays on science in a volume under that title. He has written two novels, and his essays have appeared in the* New York Times Book Review, Audubon, Esquire, *and* Rolling Stone. *He graduated from Yale University in 1970 and attended Oxford University on a Rhodes Scholarship, where he earned a B. Litt. in 1973.*

After studying literature at both Oxford and Yale, Quammen pursued graduate studies in zoology at the University of Montana. His interests have always varied, ranging from the novels of William Faulkner to the history of nuclear weapons. He once worked as a trout fishing guide, but quit when he discovered that he "sympathized too much with the fish."

57

DAVID QUAMMEN
The Big Goodbye

1   There are extinctions, and then again there are Extinctions.

2   Inevitably every once in a while a single species passes quietly into oblivion. At other and much rarer times large groups of species — entire genera and families of animals and plants, entire civilizations of interrelated organisms — disappear suddenly in a great catastrophic wipeout. During the Permian Extinction, for instance, roughly 225 million years ago, half of all the families of marine creatures (which were then the predominant form of life) died away in a brief few million years. No one knows why, and the question is still debated, but most

likely the cause was habitat loss, when the rich oceanic shelfs were left high and dry by falling sea levels. The Cretaceous Extinction, 65 million years ago, was equally drastic and even more puzzling: After more than 100 million years of unrivaled success, the dinosaurs rather abruptly disappeared, as did the various flying and fishlike reptiles, and many more groups of marine invertebrates. Again there is no proven explanation but the suggested causes include global temperature change, reversal of the polar magnetic field, and the impact of a hypothetical asteroid six miles across which raised such an atmospheric dust cloud that no sunlight could penetrate and no green plants could grow for ten years. Finally and most dramatically, the Late Quaternary Extinction, during which more than a million species of living things perished within just a century. This quickest of all mass extinctions occurred (according to the local time system) in the span 1914–2014 A.D. The main cause was once again habitat loss, and the agent of that loss was the killer-primate *Homo sapiens*, now itself extinct. *Sapiens* unaccountably violated the first rule of a successful parasite: moderation. *Sapiens* was suicidally rapacious.

That's the way it will look to some being on the planet   3
Tralfamadore with an idle interest in the paleontology of Earth. Life has existed on this mudball for about 3½ billion years, and we are just now in the midst of what looks to shape up as the third great mass extinction of species. This episode threatens to be larger in consequence than the Permian and the Cretaceous and the other major die-offs put together: One-fifth of all forms of earthly organism could be gone within thirty years.

After that, things would get ugly for the survivors. Global climatic   4
conditions would change, with accelerated buildup of carbon dioxide in the atmosphere, disruption of wind currents, cycles of vastly increasing erosion despite decreasing rainfall, breakdown of natural processes for the purification of fresh water, warmer average temperatures, the eventual failure of domestic food crops — and that would only be the beginning. We have all heard about snail darters and whooping cranes until our eyes glaze over, but what in fact is at issue here is the overall biological stability of a world. The Late Quaternary Extinction wants *you*.

In a broad sense the LQE began about 400 years ago, with the Euro-   5
pean age of empires, when humankind reached a stage smart enough to sail all over the planet and still stupid enough to kill much of what

we found when we got there. Dutch settlers arrived on the island of
Mauritius in 1598 and the dodo was extinct by 1681. On Bering Island
off Alaska, the last Steller's sea cow was killed by a party of Russian
sealers in 1768. Icelandic hunters killed a lonely pair of great auk in
June of 1844, and no great auk has been seen alive since. But these were
just the preliminaries. In a stricter sense the start of the Late Quaternary Extinction can be set, with precision that is artificial but
emblematic, as September 1, 1914. That day the last passenger pigeon,
name of Martha, died in the Cincinnati Zoo.

6   Martha is significant because her species — despite incredibly intense hunting pressure against them — succumbed chiefly to loss of
habitat. The passenger pigeon, which had once been perhaps the most
numerous bird on earth, needed huge, continuous areas of oak and
beechnut forest for its gregarious patterns of feeding and nesting. With
the great hardwood forests east of the Mississippi cut back to small
pockets, the passenger pigeon had no more chance of surviving than,
literally, a fish out of water. And at this end of the century the same
thing is happening, say eminent biologists like Thomas Lovejoy and Norman Myers, to hundreds of species — *poof:* gone forever — each year.

7   Eventual extinction is as natural for every species as eventual death
is for every individual creature. What matters for biological stability
are (1) patterns of extinction, and (2) rate of extinction. As long as extinctions occur no more rapidly than new species arise, and are not so
clustered in particular areas as to destroy the conditions from which
new species *can* arise, then ecosystems remain stable and healthy. While
the Cretaceous Extinction was in full swing, paleontologists estimate,
the rate of disappearance was one species every thousand years. Between
1600 and 1900 A.D., with our improved capabilities for travel and hunting, mankind eliminated roughly seventy-five species of known mammals and birds. Since 1900 we have killed off another seventy-five
species of conspicuous animal — just less than one per year. For a single
new species of bird to diverge from another species probably takes at
least 10,000 years.

8   A bad balance, but growing still worse: Norman Myers, having
studied the problem for years from his base in Nairobi, figures we might
say goodbye to *one million* further species by the year 2000. That
amounts to about 100 species driven extinct every day.

9   Numbers, yes. Boggling, dulling numbers. Finally it doesn't sound
real. *What are all these vanishing species? Where are they? And what's
killing them?*

10   But it is real. They are, for the most part, inconspicuous but
ecologically crucial organisms: plants, insects, fungi, crustaceans, mites,

nematode worms. They inhabit those ecological zones that are richest in living diversity but have been least investigated by man: estuaries, shallow oceanic shelfs, coral reefs, and in particular, tropical rainforests. They are being extinguished, like the passenger pigeon, by human activities that alter their habitats.

We are poisoning the estuaries with our industrial and municipal   11
wastes, we are drilling for oil and spilling it on the ocean shelfs; but most egregious and most critical is the destruction of tropical rainforests. Rainforests comprise only 6 percent of the Earth's land surface, yet may hold as many as half the Earth's total number of species, and two-thirds of all species of plant. The rainforests of Central America and the Amazon are today being mown down for pulpwood, and to graze cattle on the cleared land so that American hamburger chains can buy cheap beef. Rainforests of the Philippines, Indonesia and other parts of tropical Asia are being lumbered, to fill the demand for plywood and exotic hardwoods in more affluent countries. In West Africa the forests are falling chiefly to slash-and-burn agricultural methods by starving peasants who can't feed their growing families off small permanent fields, partly because world oil demand has priced them out of any chance for petroleum-based fertilizer. Altogether the planet may be losing 3,000 acres of rainforest — and four irreplaceable living species — every hour. We are gaining rosewood and mahogany trinkets, profligate use of personal autos, and the Big Mac.

There is complicity involved here, more than a share for us all.   12
Norman Myers says that "the main problem for declining wildlife is not the person with conscious intent to exploit or kill: it is the citizen who, by virtue of his consumerist lifestyle, stimulates economic processes that lead to disruption of natural environments."

All of this is tenaciously intertangled — the guilt, the patterns of   13
demand, the good selfish considerations that should dictate species preservation — as intertangled as the life cycles of the species themselves.

Plants, for instance. The educated guess is that each species of plant   14
supports ten to thirty species of dependent animal. Eliminate just one species of insect and you may have destroyed the sole specific pollinator for a flowering plant; when that plant consequently vanishes, so may another twenty-nine species of insects that rely on it for food; each of those twenty-nine species might be an important parasite upon still another species of insect, a pest, which when left uncontrolled by parasitism will destroy further whole populations of trees, which themselves had been important because. . . .

And so on, into the endless reticulation, the endless fragile chain   15 of interdependence that is a tropical ecosystem. Of course it is possible that the most dire projections will not become reality, that the trend will change, that mankind at the last minute will show unexpected forebearance — as economist Julian Simon and other bullish anthropocentrists are fond of predicting. Possible, yes. It is *possible*, for that matter, that with a hundred years of trying genetic engineers at the General Electric laboratories might find a way to re-invent the passenger pigeon. (If so, they would probably patent it.) Possible but not likely. Neither of those cheerful miracles can sensibly be counted on.

16   What seems all *too* likely is that the present trend will continue; that mankind will have cut down and bulldozed away most of the world's rainforests before the year 2000. If so, by direct action alone we will have thereby exterminated perhaps 150,000 species of plants — with indirect consequences, among other creatures and for the biosphere as a whole, that would be geometrically larger. Maybe 900,000 species of insect lost; and the 291 species of tropical bird already known to be threatened; and the fewer than fifty remaining Sumatran rhino; and the nine surviving representatives of the Mauritius kestrel. Enough numbers.

17   No, one final number: 300. Just that many years have passed since 1681. In this tricentennial year of the extinction of *Raphus cucullatus*, the giant flightless Mauritian pigeon, it is worth remembering that *Homo sapiens* too could become part of the Late Quaternary Extinction, engineering ourselves a place among the next group of species bidding this planet the Dodo's Farewell.

―――― CONSIDERATIONS ――――――――――――――――――

1. As David Quammen demonstrates, there is more than one way to begin an essay. Compare his opening with half a dozen other selections in your text. How would you characterize his strategy? As science fiction?

2. Who was "Martha," and what is "emblematic" about her demise? If you find her disappearance interesting or significant, you might like to read John James Audubon's dramatic recording of the mass slaughter of her species in his *Ornithological Biography* (1831–1839).

3. Occasionally, Quammen makes use of that forbidden device, the sentence fragment. Why do professional writers use the fragment, so frowned upon by composition teachers? Can you justify Quammen's opening to Paragraph 14?

4. Quammen has an easy-going style that mixes different levels of vocabulary: from "Cretaceous Extinction" in Paragraph 2 to "poof: gone forever"

in Paragraph 6, "endless reticulation," and "bullish anthropocentrists" in Paragraph 15. Use your dictionary and your good judgment: is Quammen's usage effective; is he guilty of inappropriate diction?

5. Who, according to this author, is chiefly responsible for the destruction of rain forests in Central America and the Amazon? What are his and her motives?

6. There's a little more than meets the eye in the last two words of Quammen's essay. Look up the slang meaning of "dodo," then read his final line again for an interesting and clever surprise.

7. Are any species expendable (e.g., the mosquito)? Might Quammen's last four or five Paragraphs convince you to respect such a species?

8. Compare the *tone* of Quammen's essay with Edward Abbey's (pages 1–7), another man deeply concerned about the environment.

Chet Raymo (b. 1936) teaches physics and astronomy at Stonehill College in Massachusetts. He writes a weekly column about science for the Boston Globe, *from which we take this essay. His six books on science include* The Soul of the Night, *which became a Book of the Month Club selection. In 1987 he published* Honey from Stone.

58

CHET RAYMO
Dinosaurs and Creationists

1   Down on the Paluxy River in Texas there are fossil footprints of human beings in the stratum of sedimentary rock that bears the tracks of dinosaurs. Or so claim the adherents of some fundamentalist religious groups. The Paluxy tracks, and similar markings at other sites in the American West, have become one of the centerpieces of the fundamentalist anti-evolution crusade. For a decade, the purported "man tracks" in Texas have been touted by creationists as proof, once and for all, of the falsity of evolution.

2   The Paluxy River sedimentary strata date from the Cretaceous Period of geologic history, 120 million years ago. Creationists claim the rocks are only thousands of years old, and, they say, the Paluxy River tracks show that humans and dinosaurs coexisted, most likely in the time preceding the flood of Noah.

3   Of course, there are no human footprints in the Cretaceous rocks of Texas, or in any other rocks that date from the time of the dinosaurs. The purported man tracks have been examined by geologists. Some are

From *The Boston Globe*, November 17, 1986. Reprinted by permission of the author.

not tracks at all, but only erosion features that are typical of river beds. Other, poorly defined "human" footprints are similar to dinosaur tracks in size, pace and step angles. So devastatng has been the scientific critique that in recent months some creationists have begun to hedge their bets regarding a human origin for the Paluxy River tracks.

None of this would be worth talking about if it were not for the 4 fact that science is under a growing attack by people who take things like the Paluxy River "man tracks" seriously. In Louisiana the state legislature has mandated that "creation science" be taught in schools along with evolution. The law has been judged unconstitutional by lower federal courts and is now before the US Supreme Court.

In spite of setbacks in the courts, fundamentalists maintain 5 pressure on school boards, state legislatures and textbook publishers to include creation science in school curricula or, failing that, to end the teaching of evolution.

At issue is not freedom of religion. People have the right to believe 6 what they want about how and when the world was made. At issue is whether there is such a thing as creation science that should be taught in our public schools.

Science is not a collection of truths about the world. If I say that 7 "the Earth is 4.5 billion years old," or that "humans evolved from lower orders of life," I have made a scientific statement, but such a statement is not itself science. Science is not what we know; science is a way of knowing.

Observation is an important criteron for the validity of scientific 8 truth, but it is not the only criterion. Different people can interpret the same observations differently. The Paluxy River tracks are a case in point. An equally important criterion for truth in science is consistency. What we hold to be true in one area of science must not contradict what is held to be true in another area.

Science is not a smorgasbord of truths from which we can pick 9 and choose. A better image for science is a spider's web. Confidence in any one strand of the web is maintained by the tension and resiliency of the entire web. If one strand of the web is broken, a certain relaxation of tension is felt throughout the web.

Our belief in the evolution of life through geologic time is based 10 on what we have learned in many other areas of science. Our confidence is assured by the success of the entire ensemble of scientific truths. Scientific truths are tentative and partial, and subject to continual revision and refinement, but as we tinker with truth in science we always keep our ear attuned to the timbre of the web.

11   Fundamentalists use film, video, electronics, computer and communication satellites to spread the anti-evolution message. Ironically, these technologies are based on the same ensemble of physical principles that lead us to believe that life evolved over eons of geologic time. You can't tear down one part of the web of science unless you are willing and able to rebuild a structure of understanding that works as well or better than the one you have disassembled. This is what the creationists are unable to do. And this is why there is no such thing as creation science.

12   There is more at risk in the anti-evolution crusade than a particular view of the origin of the world. At risk is the ability of the next generation of Americans to distinguish science from nonscience. Science is confidence in the human mind to discover some measure of truth about the world. Science is humility in the face of nature's complexity. And above all, science is a respect for consistency as a hallmark of truth.

13   In at least one thing the creationists are right. If humans walked with dinosaurs, then evolution is false. And by the same test, much of what we know about geology, astronomy, physics, chemistry, biology, and medicine can be thrown out too.

_____ CONSIDERATIONS _____

1. How does Raymo distinguish a "scientific statement" from "science" itself? Why does he pause in his argument against "creation science" to make that distinction?

2. Raymo uses the metaphor of "the web" in his argument. Is he being fanciful or is the metaphor integral to his explanation? Explain.

3. What is Raymo's strategy in delaying his thesis statement until Paragraph 4?

4. Is Raymo chiefly concerned about freedom of religion, the integrity of science, or the nature of tracks found along the Paluxy River in Texas? Does the organization of his essay help you decide?

James C. Rettie (1904–1969) was born and reared on a ranch in eastern Oregon; he attended Willamette University in Oregon, Yale University, and the University of London. Conservation was the passion of his life and he became an economist of natural resources. He acted as economic adviser to Stewart Udall, who was Secretary of the Interior under Presidents Kennedy and Johnson.

Rettie wrote this essay in 1938 while working as an ecologist for the United States Forest Service. Although in his government work he produced hundreds of documents and reports, he wrote nothing else that resembles this essay. It first appeared in a Department of Agriculture Bulletin, and was reprinted in Cornet Magazine *in March 1951.*

59

JAMES C. RETTIE

"But a Watch in the Night": A Scientific Fable[1]

1   Out beyond our solar system there is a planet called Copernicus. It came into existence some four or five billion years before the birth of our Earth. In due course of time it became inhabited by a race of intelligent men.

2   About 750 million years ago the Copernicans had developed the motion picture machine to a point well in advance of the stage that we have reached. Most of the cameras that we now use in motion picture work are geared to take twenty-four pictures per second on a continuous strip of film. When such film is run through a projector, it throws a series of images on the screen and these change with a rapidity that gives

the visual impression of normal movement. If a motion is too swift for the human eye to see it in detail, it can be captured and artificially slowed down by means of the slow-motion camera. This one is geared to take many more shots per second — ninety-six or even more than that. When the slow-motion film is projected at the normal speed of twenty-four pictures per second, we can see just how the jumping horse goes over a hurdle.

What about motion that is too slow to be seen by the human eye?   3
That problem has been solved by the use of the time-lapse camera. In this one, the shutter is geared to take only one shot per second, or one per minute or even one per hour — depending upon the kind of movement that is being photographed. When the time-lapse film is projected at the normal speed of twenty-four pictures per second, it is possible to see a bean sprout growing up out of the ground. Time-lapse films are useful in the study of many types of motion too slow to be observed by the unaided human eye.

The Copernicans, it seems, had time-lapse cameras some 757   4
million years ago and they also had superpowered telescopes that gave them a clear view of what was happening upon this Earth. They decided to make a film record of the life history of Earth and to make it on the scale of one picture per year. The photography has been in progress during the last 757 million years.

In the near future, a Copernican interstellar expedition will arrive   5
upon our Earth and bring with it a copy of the time-lapse film. Arrangements will be made for showing the entire film in one continuous run. This will begin at midnight of New Year's eve and continue day and night without a single stop until midnight of December 31. The rate of projection will be twenty-four pictures per second. Time on the screen will thus seem to move at the rate of twenty-four years per second; 1,440 years per minute; 86,400 years per hour; approximately two million years per day; and 62 million years per month. The normal lifespan of individual man will occupy about three seconds. The full period of Earth history that will be unfolded on the screen (some 757 million years) will extend from what the geologists call Pre-Cambrian times up to the present. This will, by no means, cover the full time-span of the Earth's geological history but it will embrace the period since the advent of living organisms.

During the months of January, February and March the picture will   6
be desolate and dreary. The shape of the land masses and the oceans will bear little or no resemblance to those that we know. The violence of geological erosion will be much in evidence. Rains will pour down

on the land and promptly go booming down to the seas. There will be no clear streams anywhere except where the rains fall upon hard rock. Everywhere on the steeper ground the stream channels will be filled with boulders hurled down by rushing waters. Raging torrents and dry stream beds will keep alternating in quick succession. High mountains will seem to melt like so much butter in the sun. The shifting of land into the seas, later to be thrust up as new mountains, will be going on a grand scale.

7   Early in April there will be some indication of the presence of single-celled living organisms in some of the warmer and sheltered coastal waters. By the end of the month it will be noticed that some of these organisms have become multicellular. A few of them, including the Trilobites, will be encased in hard shells.

8   Toward the end of May, the first vertebrates will appear, but they will still be aquatic creatures. In June about 60 percent of the land area that we know as North America will be under water. One broad channel will occupy the space where the Rocky Mountains now stand. Great deposits of limestone will be forming under some of the shallower seas. Oil and gas deposits will be in process of formation — also under shallow seas. On land there will be no sign of vegetation. Erosion will be rampant, tearing loose particles and chunks of rock and grinding them into sand and silt to be spewed out by the streams into bays and estuaries.

9   About the middle of July the first land plants will appear and take up the tremendous job of soil building. Slowly, very slowly, the mat of vegetation will spread, always battling for its life against the power of erosion. Almost foot by foot, the plant life will advance, lacing down with its root structures whatever pulverized rock material it can find. Leaves and stems will be giving added protection against the loss of the soil foothold. The increasing vegetation will pave the way for the land animals that will live upon it.

10   Early in August the seas will be teeming with fish. This will be what geologists call the Devonian period. Some of the races of these fish will be breathing by means of lung tissue instead of through gill tissues. Before the month is over, some of the lung fish will go ashore and take on a crude lizard-like appearance. Here are the first amphibians.

11   In early September the insects will put in their appearance. Some will look like huge dragon flies and will have a wingspread of 24 inches. Large portions of the land masses will now be covered with heavy vegetation that will include the primitive spore-propagating trees. Layer upon layer of this plant growth will build up, later to appear as the coal deposits. About the middle of this month, there will be evidence of the first seed-bearing plants and the first reptiles. Heretofore, the land

animals will have been amphibians that could reproduce their kind only by depositing a soft egg mass in quiet waters. The reptiles will be shown to be freed from the aquatic bond because they can reproduce by means of a shelled egg in which the embryo and its nurturing liquids are sealed in and thus protected from destructive evaporation. Before September is over, the first dinosaurs will be seen — creatures destined to dominate the animal realm for about 140 million years and then to disappear.

In October there will be a series of mountain uplifts along what is now the eastern coast of the United States. A creature with feathered limbs — half bird and half reptile in appearance — will take itself into the air. Some small and rather unpretentious animals will be seen to bring forth their young in a form that is a miniature replica of the parents and to feed these young on milk secreted by mammary glands in the female parent. The emergence of this mammalian form of animal life will be recognized as one of the great events in geologic time. October will also witness the high water mark of the dinosaurs — creatures ranging in size from that of the modern goat to monsters like Brontosaurus that weighed some 40 tons. Most of them will be placid vegetarians, but a few will be hideous-looking carnivores, like Allosaurus and Tyrannosaurus. Some of the herbivorous dinosaurs will be clad in body armor for protection against their flesh-eating comrades. 12

November will bring pictures of a sea extending from the Gulf of Mexico to the Arctic in space now occupied by the Rocky Mountains. A few of the reptiles will take to the air on bat-like wings. One of these, called Pteranodon, will have a wingspread of 15 feet. There will be a rapid development of the modern flowering plants, modern trees, and modern insects. The dinosaurs will disappear. Toward the end of the month there will be a tremendous land disturbance in which the Rocky Mountains will rise out of the sea to assume a dominating place in the North American landscape. 13

As the picture runs on into December it will show the mammals in command of the animal life. Seed-bearing trees and grasses will have covered most of the land with a heavy mantle of vegetation. Only the areas newly thrust up from the sea will be barren. Most of the streams will be crystal clear. The turmoil of geologic erosion will be confined to localized areas. About December 25 will begin the cutting of the Grand Canyon of the Colorado River. Grinding down through layer after layer of sedimentary strata, this stream will finally expose deposits laid down in Pre-Cambrian times. Thus in the walls of that canyon will appear geological formations dating from recent times to the period when the earth had no living organisms upon it. 14

The picture will run on through the latter days of December and 15 even up to its final day with still no sign of mankind. The spectators will become alarmed in the fear that man has somehow been left out. But not so; sometime about noon on December 31 (one million years ago) will appear a stooped, massive creature of man-like proportions. This will be Pithecanthropus, the Java ape man. For tools and weapons he will have nothing but crude stone and wooden clubs. His children will live a precarious existence threatened on the one side by hostile animals and on the other by tremendous climatic changes. Ice sheets — in places 4000 feet deep — will form in the northern parts of North America and Eurasia. Four times this glacial ice will push southward to cover half the continents. With each advance the plant and animal life will be swept under or pushed southward. With each recession of the ice, life will struggle to reestablish itself in the wake of the retreating glaciers. The wooly mammoth, the musk ox, and the caribou all will fight to maintain themselves near the ice line. Sometimes they will be caught and put into cold storage — skin, flesh, blood, bones and all.

16   The picture will run on through supper time with still very little evidence of man's presence on the Earth. It will be about 11 o'clock when Neanderthal man appears. Another half hour will go by before the appearance of Cro-Magnon man living in caves and painting crude animal pictures on the walls of his dwelling. Fifteen minutes more will bring Neolithic man, knowing how to chip stone and thus produce sharp cutting edges for spears and tools. In a few minutes more it will appear that man has domesticated the dog, the sheep and, possibly, other animals. He will then begin the use of milk. He will also learn the arts of basket weaving and the making of pottery and dugout canoes.

17   The dawn of civilization will not come until about five or six minutes before the end of the picture. The story of the Egyptians, the Babylonians, the Greeks, and the Romans will unroll during the fourth, the third and the second minute before the end. At 58 minutes and 43 seconds past 11:00 P.M. (just 1 minute and 17 seconds before the end) will come the beginning of the Christian era. Columbus will discover the new world 20 seconds before the end. The Declaration of Independence will be signed just 17 seconds before the final curtain comes down.

18   In those few moments of geologic time will be the story of all that has happened since we became a nation. And what a story it will be! A human swarm will sweep across the face of the continent and take it away from the . . . red men. They will change it far more radically than it has ever been changed before in a comparable time. The great virgin forests will be seen going down before ax and fire. The soil, covered for aeons by its protective mantle of trees and grasses, will be laid bare to the ravages of water and wind erosion. Streams that had

been flowing clear will, once again, take up a load of silt and push it toward the seas. Humus and mineral salts, both vital elements of productive soil, will be seen to vanish at a terrifying rate. The railroads and highways and cities that will spring up may divert attention, but they cannot cover up the blight of man's recent activities. In great sections of Asia, it will be seen that man must utilize cow dung and every scrap of available straw or grass for fuel to cook his food. The forests that once provided wood for this purpose will be gone without a trace. The use of these agricultural wastes for fuel, in place of returning them to the land, will be leading to increasing soil impoverishment. Here and there will be seen a dust storm darkening the landscape over an area a thousand miles across. Man-creatures will be shown counting their wealth in terms of bits of printed paper representing other bits of a scarce but comparatively useless yellow metal that is kept buried in strong vaults. Meanwhile, the soil, the only real wealth that can keep mankind alive on the face of this Earth is savagely being cut loose from its ancient moorings and washed into the seven seas.

We have just arrived upon this Earth. How long will we stay?   19

_____ CONSIDERATIONS _____

1. Rettie's essay, opening somewhat like a science-fiction story, is an ingenious example of the extended analogy. What are the advantages and disadvantages of this device?

2. Rettie's Copernican film spins out a large segment of evolutionary history. Compare it with any other account of evolution readily available, such as that in a biology text or encyclopedia. How do different styles and purposes affect the presentation of similar material? Where do we find Rettie's purpose?

3. An unusual feature of Rettie's style is that he writes almost entirely in the future tense. Why? What tense do most writers use? Why?

4. In Paragraph 12, Rettie mentions the emergence of mammals as an event that "will be recognized as one of the great events in geologic time." Recognized by whom? Might the answer to that question explain why Rettie describes the event as "great"? Would the Copernican audiences of Rettie's imaginary film likely use the same adjective?

5. Do our feelings and ideas have "ancestral forms" and evolutionary histories, as do our bodies? What device might an inventive writer employ to discuss such a topic?

6. "How long will we stay?" asks Rettie at the close of his hypothetical movie depicting 757 million years of earth history. The question is a rhetorical one because it is asked not so much to elicit an answer as to force a moment of reflection against the backdrop of his 750-million-year movie. What kinds of reflection would be appropriate?

Rainer Maria Rilke (1875–1926) wrote his Letters to a Young Poet *while he was himself still a young poet. The student poet, Franz Kappus (1883–1966), addressed him in 1903 at the age of twenty, when Rilke was only twenty-eight years old. Rilke, famously solitary, relieved his solitude with much correspondence. We excerpt this passage from Rilke's seventh letter to Kappus, dated May 14, 1904, and written while he visited Rome.*

Rilke is acknowledged to be the greatest modern German poet and one of the greatest in any language. There are many translations of his poetry into English, notably the Selected Poems *translated by Stephen Mitchell, who also translated the* Letters to a Young Poet. *(Note that what follows is* not *from the poems.) Mitchell lives in Berkeley, California, and has won prizes for his translations of Rilke's poems and his novel* The Notebooks of Malte Laurids Brigge.

60

RAINER MARIA RILKE
On Love

1   It is also good to love: because love is difficult. For one human being to love another human being: that is perhaps the most difficult task that has been entrusted to us, the ultimate task, the final test and proof, the work for which all other work is merely preparation. That is why young people, who are beginners in everything, are not yet *capable* of love: it is something they must learn. With their whole being, with all their forces, gathered around their solitary, anxious, upward-beating

hcart, they must learn to love. But learning-time is always a long, secluded time, and therefore loving, for a long time ahead and far on into life, is —: solitude, a heightened and deepened kind of aloneness for the person who loves. Loving does not at first mean merging, surrendering, and uniting with another person (for what would a union be of two people who are unclarified, unfinished, and still incoherent —?), it is a high inducement for the individual to ripen, to become something in himself, to become world, to become world in himself for the sake of another person; it is a great, demanding claim on him, something that chooses him and calls him to vast distances. Only in this sense, as the task of working on themselves ("to hearken and to hammer day and night"), may young people use the love that is given to them. Merging and surrendering and every kind of communion is not for them (who must still, for a long, long time, save and gather themselves); it is the ultimate, is perhaps that for which human lives are as yet barely large enough.

But this is what young people are so often and so disastrously 2 wrong in doing: they (who by their very nature are impatient) fling themselves at each other when love takes hold of them, they scatter themselves, just as they are, in all their messiness, disorder, bewilderment . . . : And what can happen then? What can life do with this heap of half-broken things that they call their communion and that they would like to call their happiness, if that were possible, and their future? And so each of them loses himself for the sake of the other person, and loses the other, and many others who still wanted to come. And loses the vast distances and possibilities, gives up the approaching and fleeing of gentle, prescient Things in exchange for an unfruitful confusion, out of which nothing more can come; nothing but a bit of disgust, disappointment, and poverty, and the escape into one of the many conventions that have been put up in great numbers like public shelters on this most dangerous road. No area of human experience is so extensively provided with conventions as this one is: there are life-preservers of the most varied invention, boats and water wings; society has been able to create refuges of every sort, for since it preferred to take love-life as an amusement, it also had to give it an easy form, cheap, safe, and sure, as public amusements are.

It is true that many young people who love falsely, i.e., simply sur- 3 rendering themselves and giving up their solitude (the average person will of course always go on doing that —), feel oppressed by their failure and want to make the situation they have landed in livable and fruitful in their own, personal way —. For their nature tells them that the questions of love, even more than everything else that is important, cannot be resolved publicly and according to this or that agreement; that they are questions, intimate questions from one human being to another, which in any case require a new, special, *wholly* personal answer —. But how can they, who have already flung themselves together and can no longer tell whose outlines are whose, who thus no longer possess anything of their own, how can they find a way out of themselves, out of the depths of their already buried solitude?

4   They act out of mutual helplessness, and then if, with the best of intentions, they try to escape the convention that is approaching them (marriage, for example), they fall into the clutches of some less obvious but just as deadly conventional solution. For then everything around them is — convention. Wherever people act out of a prematurely fused, muddy communion, *every* action is conventional: every relation that such confusion leads to has its own convention, however unusual (i.e., in the ordinary sense immoral) it may be; even separating would be a conventional step, an impersonal, accidental decision without strength and without fruit.

5   Whoever looks seriously will find that neither for death, which is difficult, nor for difficult love has any clarification, any solution, any hint of a path been perceived; and for both these tasks, which we carry wrapped up and hand on without opening, there is no general, agreed-upon rule that can be discovered. But in the same measure in which we begin to test life as individuals, these great Things will come to meet us, the individuals, with greater intimacy. The claims that the difficult work of love makes upon our development are greater than life, and we, as beginners, are not equal to them. But if we nevertheless endure and take this love upon us as burden and apprenticeship, instead of losing ourselves in the whole easy and frivolous game behind which people have hidden from the most solemn solemnity of their being, — then a small advance and a lightening will perhaps be perceptible to those who come long after us. That would be much.

6   We are only just now beginning to consider the relation of one individual to a second individual objectively and without prejudice, and our attempts to live such relationships have no model before them. And yet in the changes that time has brought about there are already many things that can help our timid novitiate.

7   The girl and the woman, in their new, individual unfolding, will only in passing be imitators of male behavior and misbehavior and repeaters of male professions. After the uncertainty of such transitions, it will become obvious that women were going through the abundance

and variation of those (often ridiculous) disguises just so that they could purify their own essential nature and wash out the deforming influences of the other sex. Women, in whom life lingers and dwells more immediately, more fruitfully, and more confidently, must surely have become riper and more human in their depths than light, easygoing man, who is not pulled down beneath the surface of life by the weight of any bodily fruit and who, arrogant and hasty, undervalues what he thinks he loves. This humanity of woman, carried in her womb through all her suffering and humiliation, will come to light when she has stripped off the conventions of mere femaleness in the transformations of her outward status, and those men who do not yet feel it approaching will be astonished by it. Someday (and even now, especially in the countries of northern Europe, trustworthy signs are already speaking and shining), someday there will be girls and women whose name will no longer mean the mere opposite of the male, but something in itself, something that makes one think not of any complement and limit, but only of life and reality: the female human being.

This advance (at first very much against the will of the out- 8 distanced men) will transform the love experience, which is now filled with error, will change it from the ground up, and reshape it into a relationship that is meant to be between one human being and another, no longer one that flows from man to woman. And this more human love (which will fulfill itself with infinite consideration and gentleness, and kindness and clarity in binding and releasing) will resemble what we are now preparing painfully and with great struggle: the love that consists in this: that two solitudes protect and border and greet each other.

_____ CONSIDERATIONS _____

1. Rilke's disquisition — one is tempted to call it a sermon, for he certainly urges and proclaims as a preacher might — differs from almost every other essay in this text, and thus may prove difficult to read. What contributes to this difficulty?

2. What is his principal reason for saying that the young are incapable of love? How does this belief relate to his comments later in the essay on the evolution of women?

3. Rilke mentions marriage as one of the conventional escapes that so many take instead of persisting along the "dangerous" road to love. He does not specify others. Can you derive some of them from his discussion?

4. In Paragraph 5, Rilke speaks of both death and love — or, rather, our understanding of them — as "tasks which we carry wrapped up and hand on

without opening." Read John Berger's "Her Secrets" (pages 57–62), paying particular attention to Paragraphs 9 and 10. Would Rilke have found Berger's statements about "wrapped secrets" akin to his own?

5. Rilke's letter was written in May 1904. Does Paragraph 7 prophesy stages of women's liberation? What examples or illustrations can you cite to support your answer?

6. Put into your own words Rilke's definition of love, which closes his final sentence in this selection. What difficulties do you find in accomplishing this task? Why?

Carl Sagan (b. 1934) is an astronomer and writer, whose thirteen-part Cosmos *series appeared on public television in 1980. His books include* Intelligent Life in the Universe *(1966),* Other Worlds *(1975),* The Dragons of Eden *(1977), for which he received a Pulitzer Prize,* Broca's Brain *(1979), and* Cosmos *(1980). He is director of the Laboratory for Planetary Studies and David Duncan Professor of Astronomy and Space Sciences at Cornell University.*

Sagan's first paper on the subject of nuclear winter, written in collaboration with four other scientists, appeared in Science *in 1983; later he wrote "Nuclear War and Climatic Consequences: Some Policy Implications" for a different audience in* Foreign Affairs *(1984). The following account, for the more general audience of* Parade, *appeared in 1983 after the paper in* Science.

61

CARL SAGAN
Nuclear Winter

"Into the eternal darkness, into fire, into ice."
                                        –Dante, *The Inferno*

Except for fools and madmen, everyone knows that nuclear war   1
would be an unprecedented human catastrophe. A more or less typical
strategic warhead has a yield of 2 megatons, the explosive equivalent
of 2 million tons of TNT. But 2 million tons of TNT is about the same
as all the bombs exploded in World War II — a single bomb with the
explosive power of the entire Second World War but compressed into
a few seconds of time and an area 30 or 40 miles across. . . .

2   In a 2-megaton explosion over a fairly large city, buildings would be vaporized, people reduced to atoms and shadows, outlying structures blown down like matchsticks, and raging fires ignited. And if the bomb were exploded on the ground, an enormous crater, like those that can be seen through a telescope on the surface of the Moon, would be all that remained where midtown once had been. There are now more than 50,000 nuclear weapons, more than 13,000 megatons of yield, deployed in the arsenals of the United States and the Soviet Union — enough to obliterate a million Hiroshimas.

3   But there are fewer than 3000 cities on the Earth with populations of 100,000 or more. You cannot find anything like a million Hiroshimas to obliterate. Prime military and industrial targets that are far from cities are comparatively rare. Thus, there are vastly more nuclear weapons than are needed for any plausible deterrence of a potential adversary.

4   Nobody knows, of course, how many megatons would be exploded in a real nuclear war. There are some who think that a nuclear war can be "contained," bottled up before it runs away to involve much of the world's arsenals. But a number of detailed analyses, war games run by the U.S. Department of Defense, and official Soviet pronouncements all indicate that this containment may be too much to hope for: Once the bombs begin exploding, communications failures, disorganization, fear, the necessity of making in minutes decisions affecting the fates of millions, and the immense psychological burden of knowing that your own loved ones may already have been destroyed are likely to result in a nuclear paroxysm. Many investigations, including a number of studies for the U.S. government, envision the explosion of 5000 to 10,000 megatons — the detonation of tens of thousands of nuclear weapons that now sit quietly, inconspicuously, in missile silos, submarines, and long-range bombers, faithful servants awaiting orders.

5   The World Health Organization, in a recent detailed study chaired by Sune K. Bergstrom (the 1982 Nobel laureate in physiology and medicine), concludes that 1.1 billion people would be killed outright in such a nuclear war, mainly in the United States, the Soviet Union, Europe, China, and Japan. An additional 1.1 billion people would suffer serious injuries and radiation sickness, for which medical help would be unavailable. It thus seems possible that more than 2 billion people — almost half of all humans on Earth — would be destroyed in the immediate aftermath of a global thermonuclear war. This would represent by far the greatest disaster in the history of the human species and, with no other adverse effects, would probably be enough to reduce at least

the Northern Hemisphere to a state of prolonged agony and barbarism. Unfortunately, the real situation would be much worse.

In technical studies of the consequences of nuclear weapons ex-   6
plosions, there has been a dangerous tendency to underestimate the results. This is partly due to a tradition of conservatism which generally works well in science but which is of more dubious applicability when the lives of billions of people are at stake. In the Bravo test of March 1, 1954, a 15-megaton thermonuclear bomb was exploded in Bikini Atoll. It had about double the yield expected, and there was an unanticipated last-minute shift in the wind direction. As a result, deadly radioactive fallout came down on Rongelap in the Marshall Islands, more than 200 kilometers away. Almost all children on Rongelap subsequently developed thyroid nodules and lesions, and other long-term medical problems, due to the radioactive fallout.

Likewise, in 1973, it was discovered that high-yield airbursts will   7
chemically burn the nitrogen in the upper air, converting it into oxides of nitrogen; these, in turn, combine with and destroy the protective ozone in the Earth's stratosphere. The surface of the Earth is shielded from deadly solar ultraviolet radiation by a layer of ozone so tenuous that, were it brought down to sea level, it would be only 3 millimeters thick. Partial destruction of this ozone layer can have serious consequences for the biology of the entire planet.

These discoveries, and others like them, were made by chance.   8
They were largely unexpected. And now another consequence — by far the most dire — has been uncovered, again more or less by accident.

The U.S. Mariner 9 spacecraft, the first vehicle to orbit another   9
planet, arrived at Mars in late 1971. The planet was enveloped in a global dust storm. As the fine particles slowly fell out, we were able to measure temperature changes in the atmosphere and on the surface. Soon it became clear what had happened.

The dust, lofted by high winds off the desert into the upper Mar-   10
tian atmosphere, had absorbed the incoming sunlight and prevented much of it from reaching the ground. Heated by the sunlight, the dust warmed the adjacent air. But the surface, enveloped in partial darkness, became much chillier than usual. Months later, after the dust fell out of the atmosphere, the upper air cooled and the surface warmed, both returning to their normal conditions. We were able to calculate accurately, from how much dust there was in the atmosphere, how cool the Martian surface ought to have been.

11   Afterwards, I and my colleagues, James B. Pollack and Brian Toon of NASA's Ames Research Center, were eager to apply these insights to the Earth. In a volcanic explosion, dust aerosols are lofted into the high atmosphere. We calculated by how much the Earth's global temperature should decline after a major volcanic explosion and found that our results (generally a fraction of a degree) were in good accord with actual measurements. Joining forces with Richard Turco, who has studied the effects of nuclear weapons for many years, we then began to turn our attention to the climatic effects of nuclear war. [The scientific paper, "Global Atmospheric Consequences of Nuclear War," is written by R. P. Turco, O. B. Toon, T. P. Ackerman, J. B. Pollack and Carl Sagan. From the last names of the authors, this work is generally referred to as "TTAPS."]

12   We knew that nuclear explosions, particularly groundbursts, would lift an enormous quantity of fine soil particles into the atmosphere (more than 100,000 tons of fine dust for every megaton exploded in a surface burst). Our work was further spurred by Paul Crutzen of the Max Planck Institute for Chemistry in Mainz, West Germany, and by John Birks of the University of Colorado, who pointed out that huge quantities of smoke would be generated in the burning of cities and forests following a nuclear war.

13   Groundbursts — at hardened missile silos, for example — generate fine dust. Airbursts — over cities and unhardened military installations — make fires and therefore smoke. The amount of dust and soot generated depends on the conduct of the war, the yields of the weapons employed, and the ratio of groundbursts to airbursts. So we ran computer models for several dozen different nuclear war scenarios. Our baseline case, as in many other studies, was a 5000-megaton war with only a modest fraction of the yield (20 percent) expended on urban or industrial targets. Our job, for each case, was to follow the dust and smoke generated, see how much sunlight was absorbed and by how much the temperatures changed, figure out how the particles spread in longitude and latitude, and calculate how long before it all fell out of the air back onto the surface. Since the radioactivity would be attached to these same fine particles, our calculations also revealed the extent and timing of the subsequent radioactive fallout.

14   Some of what I am about to describe is horrifying. I know, because it horrifies me. There is a tendency — psychiatrists call it "denial" — to put it out of our minds, not think about it. But if we are to deal intelligently, wisely, with the nuclear arms race, then we must steel ourselves to contemplate the horrors of nuclear war.

The results of our calculations astonished us. In the baseline case,   15
the amount of sunlight at the ground was reduced to a few percent of
normal — much darker, in daylight, than in a heavy overcast and too
dark for plants to make a living from photosynthesis. At least in the
Northern Hemisphere, where the great preponderance of strategic targets
lies, an unbroken and deadly gloom would persist for weeks.

Even more unexpected were the temperatures calculated. In the   16
baseline case, land temperatures, except for narrow strips of coastline,
dropped to minus 25° Celsius (minus 13° Fahrenheit) and stayed below
freezing for months — even for a summer war. (Because the atmospheric
structure becomes much more stable as the upper atmosphere is heated
and the lower air is cooled, we may have severely *under*estimated how
long the cold and the dark would last.) The oceans, a significant heat
reservoir, would not freeze, however, and a major ice age would probably not be triggered. But because the temperatures would drop so
catastrophically, virtually all crops and farm animals, at least in the
Northern Hemisphere, would be destroyed, as would most varieties of
uncultivated or undomesticated food supplies. Most of the human survivors would starve.

In addition, the amount of radioactive fallout is much more than   17
expected. Many previous calculations simply ignored the intermediate
time-scale fallout. That is, calculations were made for the prompt fallout — the plumes of radioactive debris blown downwind from each
target — and for the long-term fallout, the fine radioactive particles lofted
into the stratosphere that would descend about a year later, after most
of the radioactivity had decayed. However, the radioactivity carried into
the upper atmosphere (but not as high as the stratosphere) seems to have
been largely forgotten. We found for the baseline case that roughly 30
percent of the land at northern midlatitudes could receive a radioactive dose greater than 250 rads, and that about 50 percent of northern
midlatitudes could receive a dose greater than 100 rads. A 100-rad dose
is the equivalent of about 1000 medical X-rays. A 400-rad dose will, more
likely than not, kill you.

The cold, the dark, and the intense radioactivity, together lasting   18
for months, represent a severe assault on our civilization and our species.
Civil and sanitary services would be wiped out. Medical facilities, drugs,
the most rudimentary means for relieving the vast human suffering,
would be unavailable. Any but the most elaborate shelters would be
useless, quite apart from the question of what good it might be to emerge
a few months later. Synthetics burned in the destruction of the cities
would produce a wide variety of toxic gases, including carbon monox-

ide, cyanides, dioxins, and furans. After the dust and soot settled out, the solar ultraviolet flux would be much larger than its present value. Immunity to disease would decline. Epidemics and pandemics would be rampant, especially after the billion or so unburied bodies began to thaw. Moreover, the combined influence of these severe and simultaneous stresses on life are likely to produce even more adverse consequences — biologists call them synergisms — that we are not yet wise enough to foresee.

19   So far, we have talked only of the Northern Hemisphere. But it now seems — unlike the case of a single nuclear weapons test — that in a real nuclear war, the heating of the vast quantities of atmospheric dust and soot in northern midlatitudes will transport these fine particles toward and across the Equator. We see just this happening in Martian dust storms. The Southern Hemisphere would experience effects that, while less severe than in the Northern Hemisphere, are nevertheless extremely ominous. The illusion with which some people in the Northern Hemisphere reassure themselves — catching an Air New Zealand flight in a time of serious international crisis, or the like — is now much less tenable, even on the narrow issue of personal survival for those with the price of a ticket.

20   But what if nuclear wars *can* be contained, and much less than 5000 megatons is detonated? Perhaps the greatest surprise in our work was that even small nuclear wars can have devastating climatic effects. We considered a war in which a mere 100 megatons were exploded, less than one percent of the world arsenals, and only in low-yield airbursts over cities. This scenario, we found, would ignite thousands of fires, and the smoke from these fires alone would be enough to generate an epoch of cold and dark almost as severe as in the 5000-megaton case. The threshold for what Richard Turco has called The Nuclear Winter is very low.

21   Could we have overlooked some important effect? The carrying of dust and soot from the Northern to the Southern Hemisphere (as well as more local atmospheric circulation) will certainly thin the clouds out over the Northern Hemisphere. But, in many cases, this thinning would be insufficient to render the climatic consequences tolerable — and every time it got better in the Northern Hemisphere, it would get worse in the Southern.

22   Our results have been carefully scrutinized by more than 100 scientists in the United States, Europe, and the Soviet Union. There are still arguments on points of detail. But the overall conclusion seems to be agreed upon: There are severe and previously unanticipated global consequences of nuclear war — subfreezing temperatures in a twilit radioac-

tive gloom lasting for months or longer.

Scientists initially underestimated the effects of fallout, were   23
amazed that nuclear explosions in space disabled distant satellites, had
no idea that the fireballs from high-yield thermonuclear explosions could
deplete the ozone layer, and missed altogether the possible climatic
effects of nuclear dust and smoke. What else have we overlooked?

Nuclear war is a problem that can be treated only theoretically.   24
It is not amenable to experimentation. Conceivably, we have left
something important out of our analysis, and the effects are more modest than we calculate. On the other hand, it is also possible — and, from
previous experience, even likely — that there are further adverse effects
that no one has yet been wise enough to recognize. With billions of lives
at stake, where does conservatism lie — in assuming that the results
will be better than we calculate, or worse?

Many biologists, considering the nuclear winter that these calcula-   25
tions describe, believe they carry somber implications for life on Earth.
Many species of plants and animals would become extinct. Vast numbers
of surviving humans would starve to death. The delicate ecological relations that bind together organisms on Earth in a fabric of mutual
dependency would be torn, perhaps irreparably. There is little question
that our global civilization would be destroyed. The human population
would be reduced to prehistoric levels, or less. Life for any survivors
would be extremely hard. And there seems to be a real possibility of
the extinction of the human species.

It is now almost 40 years since the invention of nuclear weapons.   26
We have not yet experienced a global thermonuclear war — although
on more than one occasion we have come tremulously close. I do not
think our luck can hold forever. Men and machines are fallible, as recent events remind us. Fools and madmen do exist, and sometimes rise
to power. Concentrating always on the near future, we have ignored
the long-term consequences of our actions. We have placed our civilization and our species in jeopardy.

Fortunately, it is not yet too late. We can safeguard the planetary   27
civilization and the human family if we so choose. There is no more
important or more urgent issue.

———— **CONSIDERATIONS** ————————————————————

1. From what predictable results of a thermonuclear war does Sagan draw
the title of his essay?

2. Sagan points out in Paragraph 24 that we cannot experiment with nuclear wars to determine their effects. What is the primary basis for his and his colleagues' calculations about probable atmospheric disturbances?

3. Like the essays of several other writers in the text — David Quammen (pages 334–339), Stephen Jay Gould (pages 191–197), and Caroline Bird (pages 79–89) — "Nuclear Winter" relies upon statistics. How does Sagan handle this data so that the reader will not shrug them off as mere numbers?

4. Sagan's nuclear war scenarios presuppose that the major strikes would occur in the Northern Hemisphere. Why, then, would one be disappointed by flying for safety to the Southern Hemisphere?

5. What characteristic of science, usually highly valued, does Sagan mention as dangerous? Is this tendency evident in his own report?

6. In Paragraph 18, Sagan uses, without defining it, a word probably unknown to many of his readers: synergisms. Must you turn to a dictionary, or does he provide clues to its meaning?

William Shakespeare (1564–1616) wrote three long poems and a sequence of sonnets, as well as the plays for which we know him best. He was born in Stratford-on-Avon to a middle-class family, moved to London in his twenties, and began his theatrical career as an actor. His writing for the theater started with plays based on English history: the three parts of Henry VI *and* Richard III. The Tempest *was his last play, and by 1611 he had retired to Stratford with the money he had made upon the stage.*

This sonnet develops a common poetic theme with metaphors at once profuse and precise.

62

WILLIAM SHAKESPEARE

That time of year thou mayst in me behold

That time of year thou mayst in me behold
When yellow leaves, or none, or few, do hang
Upon those boughs which shake against the cold,
Bare ruined choirs, where late the sweet birds sang.
In me thou see'st the twilight of such day   5
As after sunset fadeth in the west;
Which by and by black night doth take away,
Death's second self, that seals up all in rest.
In me thou see'st the glowing of such fire,
That on the ashes of his youth doth lie,   10
As the deathbed whereon it must expire,
Consumed with that which it was nourished by.
This thou perceiv'st, which makes thy love more strong,
To love that well which thou must leave ere long.

Don Sharp (b. 1938) has taught in Alaska, Hawaii, and Australia, and once owned and operated a garage in Pennsylvania called Discriminating Services. He now lives in Massachusetts, where he writes for magazines and works on old cars. This essay won the Ken Purdy Award for Excellence in Automobile Journalism in 1981.

63

DON SHARP
Under the Hood

1   The owner of this 1966 Plymouth Valiant has made the rounds of car dealers. They will gladly sell him a new car — the latest model of government regulation and industrial enterprise — for $8,000, but they don't want his clattering, emphysemic old vehicle in trade. It isn't worth enough to justify the paperwork, a classified ad, and space on the used-car lot. "Sell it for junk," they tell him. "Scrap iron is high now, and they'll give you $25 for it."

2   The owner is hurt. He likes this car. It has served him well for 90,000-odd miles. It has a functional shape and he can get in and out of it easily. He can roll down his window in a light rain and not get his shoulder wet. The rear windows roll down, and he doesn't need an air conditioner. He can see out of it fore, aft, and abeam. He can hazard it on urban parking lots without fear of drastic, insurance-deductible casualty loss. His teenage children reject it as passé, so it is always available to him. It has no buzzers, and the only flashing lights are those he controls himself when signaling a turn. The owner, clearly one of

a vanishing tribe, brings the car to a kindred spirit and asks me to rebuild it.

    We do not discuss the cost. I do not advertise my services and my   3
sign is discreet. My shop is known by word of mouth, and those who
spread the word emphasize my house rule: "A blank check and a free
hand." That is, I do to your car what I think it needs and you pay for
it; you trust me not to take advantage, I guarantee you good brakes,
sound steering, and prompt starting, and you pay without quarrel. This
kind of arrangement saves a lot of time spent in making estimates and
a lot of time haggling over the bill. It also imposes a tremendous burden
of responsibility on me and on those who spread the word, and it puts
a burden of trust on those who deliver their cars into my custody.

    A relationship of that sort is about as profound as any that two   4
people can enjoy, even if it lasts no longer than the time required to
reline a set of brakes. I think of hometown farmers who made sharecrop-
ping deals for the season on a handshake; then I go into a large garage
and see the white-coated service writer noting the customer's every
specification, calling attention to the fine print at the bottom of the work
order, and requiring a contractual signature before even a brake-light
bulb is replaced. I perceive in their transaction that ignorance of cause
and effect breeds suspicion, and I wonder who is the smaller, the
customer or the service writer, and how they came to be so small of
spirit.

    Under the hood of this ailing Valiant, I note a glistening line of   5
seeping oil where the oil pan meets the engine block. For thousands
of miles, a piece of cork — a strip of bark from a Spanish tree — has
stood firm between the pan and block against churning oil heated to
nearly 200 degrees, oil that sought vainly to escape its duty and was
forced back to work by a stalwart gasket. But now, after years of
perseverance, the gasket has lost its resilience and the craven oil escapes.
Ecclesiastes allows a time for all things, and the time for this gasket
has passed.

    Higher up, between the block casting that forms the foundation   6
of the engine and the cylinder-head casting that admits fresh air and
exhausts oxidized air and fuel, is the head gasket, a piece of sheet metal
as thin as a matchbook cover that has confined the multiple fires built
within the engine to their proper domains. Now, a whitish-gray deposit
betrays an eroded area from which blue flame spits every time the cyl-
inder fires. The gasket is "blown."

    Let us stop and think of large numbers. In the four-cycle engines   7 that power all modern cars, a spark jumps a spark-plug gap and sets off a fire in a cylinder every time the crankshaft goes around twice. The crankshaft turns the transmission shaft, which turns the driveshaft, which turns the differential gears, which turn the rear axles, which turn the wheels (what could Aquinas have done with something like that, had he addressed himself to the source of the spark or to the final destination of the wheels?). In 100,000 miles — a common life for modern engines — the engine will make some 260 million turns, and in half of those turns, 130 million of them, a gasoline-fueled fire with a maximum temperature of 2,000 degrees (quickly falling to about 1,200 degrees) is built in each cylinder. The heat generated by the fire raises the pressure in the cylinder to about 700 pounds per square inch, if only for a brief instant before the piston moves and the pressure falls. A head gasket has to contend with heat and pressure like this all the time the engine is running, and, barring mishap, it will put up with it indefinitely.

8 This Plymouth has suffered mishap. I know it as soon as I raise the hood and see the telltale line of rust running across the underside of the hood: the mark of overheating. A water pump bearing or seal gave way, water leaked out, and was flung off the fan blades with enough force to embed particles of rust in the undercoating. Without cooling water, the engine grew too hot, and that's why the head gasket blew. In an engine, no cause exists without an effect. Unlike a court of law, wherein criminals are frequently absolved of wrongdoing, no engine component is without duty and responsibility, and failure cannot be mitigated by dubious explanations such as parental neglect or a crummy neighborhood.

9 Just as Sherlock Holmes would not be satisfied with one clue if he could find others, I study the oil filter. The block and oil pan are caked with seepings and drippings, but below the filter the caking is visibly less thick and somewhat soft. So: once upon a time, a careless service-station attendant must have ruined the gasket while installing a new oil filter. Oil en route to the bearings escaped and washed away the grime that had accumulated. Odds are that the oil level fell too low and the crankshaft bearings were starved for oil.

10 Bearings are flat strips of metal, formed into half-circles about as thick as a matchbook match and about an inch wide. The bearing surface itself — the surface that *bears* the crankshaft and that *bears* the load imposed by the fire-induced pressure above the piston — is half as thick. Bearing metal is a drab, gray alloy, the principal component of which is *babbitt*, a low-friction metal porous enough to absorb oil

but so soft that it must be allowed to withstand high pressures. (I like to think that Sinclair Lewis had metallurgy in mind when he named his protagonist George Babbitt.) When the fire goes off above the piston and the pressure is transmitted to the crankshaft via the connecting rod, the babbitt-alloyed bearing pushes downward with a force of about 3,500 pounds per square inch. And it must not give way, must not be peened into foil and driven from its place in fragments.

Regard the fleshy end joint of your thumb and invite a 100-pound woman (or a pre-teen child, if no such woman be near to hand) to stand on it. Multiply the sensation by thirty-five and you get an idea of what the bearing is up against. Of course, the bearing enjoys a favorable handicap in the comparison because it works in a metal-to-metal environment heated to 180 degrees or so. The bearing is equal to its task so long as it is protected from direct metal-to-metal contact by a layer of lubricating oil, oil that must be forced into the space between the bearing and the crankshaft against that 3,500 pounds of force. True, the oil gets a lot of help from hydrodynamic action as the spinning crankshaft drags oil along with it, but lubrication depends primarily on a pump that forces oil through the engine at around 40 pounds of pressure. 11

If the oil level falls too low, the oil pump sucks in air. The oil gets as frothy as whipped cream and doesn't flow. In time, oil pressure will fall so low that the "idiot" light on the dashboard will flash, but long before then the bearing may have run "dry" and suffered considerable amounts of its metal to be peened away by those 3,500-pound hammer blows. "Considerable" may mean only .005 inches, or about the thickness of one sheet of 75-percent-cotton, 25-pound-per-ream dissertation bond — not much metal, but enough to allow oil to escape from the bearing even after the defective filter gasket is replaced and the oil supply replenished. From the time of oil starvation onward, the beaten bearing is a little disaster waiting to spoil a vacation or a commute to an important meeting. 12

Curious, that an unseen .005 inches of drab, gray metal worthy only to inspire the name of a poltroonish bourgeois should enjoy more consequence for human life than almost any equal thickness of a randomly chosen doctoral dissertation. Life is full of ironies. 13

The car I confront does not have an "idiot" light. It has an old-fashioned oil-pressure gauge. As the driver made his rounds from condominium to committee room, he could — if he cared or was ever so alert — monitor the health of his engine bearings by noting the oil pressure. Virtually all cars had these gauges in the old days, but they began to disappear in the mid-'50s, and nowadays hardly any cars have 14 them. In eliminating oil-pressure gauges, the car makers pleaded that, in their dismal experience, people didn't pay much attention to gauges. Accordingly, Detroit switched to the warning light, which was cheaper to manufacture anyway (and having saved a few bucks on the mechanicals, the manufacturer could afford to etch a design in the opera windows; this is called "progress"). Curious, in the midst of all this, that Chrysler Corporation, the maker of Plymouths and the victim of so much bad management over the past fifteen years, should have been the one car manufacturer to constantly assert, via a standard-equipment oil-pressure gauge, a faith in the awareness, judgment, and responsibility of drivers. That Chrysler did so may have something to do with its current problems.

15   The other car makers were probably right. Time was when most men knew how to replace their own distributor points, repair a flat tire, and install a battery. Women weren't assumed to know as much, but they were expected to know how to put a gear lever in neutral, set a choke and throttle, and crank a car by hand if the battery was dead. Now, odds are that 75 percent of men and a higher percentage of women don't even know how to work the jacks that come with their cars. To be sure, a bumper jack is an abominable contraption — the triumph of production economies over good sense — but it will do what it is supposed to do, and the fact that most drivers cannot make one work says much about the way motorists have changed over the past forty years.

16   About all that people will watch on the downslide of this century is the fuel gauge, for they don't like to be balked in their purpose. A lack of fuel will stop a car dead in its tracks and categorically prevent the driver from arriving at the meeting to consider tenure for a male associate professor with a black grandfather and a Chinese mother. Lack of fuel will stall a car in mid-intersection and leave dignity and image prey to the honks and curses of riffraff driving taxicabs and beer trucks, so people watch the fuel gauge as closely as they watch a pubescent daughter or a bearish stock.

17   But for the most part, once the key goes into the ignition, people assign responsibility for the car's smooth running to someone else — to anybody but themselves. If the engine doesn't start, that's not because the driver has abused it, but because the manufacturer was remiss or the mechanic incompetent. (Both suspicions are reasonable, but they do not justify the driver's spineless passivity.) The driver considers himself merely a client of the vehicle. He proudly disclaims, at club and luncheon, any understanding of the dysfunctions of the machine. He must so disclaim, for to admit knowledge or to seek it actively would

require an admission of responsibility and fault. To be wrong about inflation or the political aspirations of the Albanians doesn't cost anybody anything, but to claim to know why the car won't start and then to be proved wrong is both embarrassing and costly.

Few people would remove $500 from someone's pocket without a qualm and put it in their own. Yet, the job-lot run of mechanics do it all the time. Mechanics and drivers are alike: they gave up worrying long ago about the intricacies and demands of cause and effect. The mechanics do not attend closely to the behavior of the vehicle. Rather, they consult a book with flow-charts that says, "Try this, and if it doesn't work, try that." Or they hook the engine up to another machine and read gauges or cathode-ray-tube squiggles, but without realizing that gauges and squiggles are not reality but only tools used to aid perception of reality. A microscope is also a wonderful tool, but you still have to comprehend what you're looking for; else, like James Thurber, you get back the reflection of your own eye. 18

Mechanics, like academics and bureaucrats, have retreated too far from the realities of their tasks. An engine runs badly. They consult the book. The book says to replace part A. They replace A. The engine still runs badly, but the mechanic can deny the fact as handily as a socialist can deny that minimum-wage laws eventually lead to unemployment. Just as the driver doesn't care to know why his oil pressure drops from 40 to 30 to 20 pounds and then to zero, so the mechanic cares little for the casuistic distinctions that suggest that part A is in good order but that some subtle conjunction of wholesome part B with defective part C may be causing the trouble. (I don't know about atheists in foxholes, but I doubt that many Jesuits are found among incompetent mechanics.) 19

And why should the mechanic care? He gets paid in any event. From the mechanic's point of view, he should get paid, for he sees a federal judge hire academic consultants to advise about busing, and after the whites have fled before the imperious column of yellow buses and left the schools blacker than ever, the judge hires the consultants again to find out why the whites moved out. The consultant gets paid in public money, whatever effects his action have, even when he causes things he said would never happen. 20

Consider the garden-variety Herr Doktor who has spent a pleasant series of warm fall weekends driving to a retreat in the Catskills; his car has started with alacrity and run well despite a stuck choke. Then, when the first blue norther of the season sends temperatures to- 21 ward zero, the faithful machine must be haggled into action and proceeds haltingly down the road, gasping and backfiring. "Needs a new carburetor," the mechanic says, and, to be sure, once a new carburetor is installed, the car runs well again. Our Herr Doktor is happy. His car did not run well; it got a new carburetor and ran well again; ergo, the carburetor was at fault. Q.E.D.

22   Curious that in personal matters the classic *post hoc* fallacy should be so readily accepted when it would be mocked in academic debate. Our Herr Doktor should know, or at least suspect, that the carburetor that functioned so well for the past several months could hardly have changed its nature overnight, and we might expect of him a more diligent inquiry into its problems. But "I'm no mechanic," he chuckles to his colleagues, and they nod agreeably. Such skinned-knuckle expertise would be unfitting in a man whose self-esteem is equivalent to his uselessness with a wrench. Lilies of the postindustrial field must concern themselves with weighty matters beyond the ken of greasy laborers who drink beer at the end of a workday.

23   Another example will illustrate the point. A battery cable has an end that is designed to connect to a terminal on the battery. Both cable-end and battery-terminal surfaces look smooth, but aren't. Those smooth surfaces are pitted and peaked, and only the peaks touch each other. The pits collect water from the air, and the chemistry of electricity-carrying metals causes lead oxides to form in the pits. The oxides progressively insulate the cable end and battery terminal from each other until the day that turning the key produces only a single, resounding *clunk* and no more. The road service mechanics installs a new $75 battery and collects $25 for his trouble. Removing the cables from the old battery cleans their ends somewhat, so things work for a few days, and then the car again fails to start. The mechanic installs a $110 alternator, applies a $5 charge to the battery, and collects another $25; several days later he gives the battery another $5 charge, installs a $75 starter, and collects $25 more. In these instances, to charge the battery — to send current backwards from cable end to battery terminal — disturbs the oxides and temporarily improves their conductivity. Wriggling the charger clamps on the cable ends probably helps too. On the driver's last $25 visit, the mechanic sells another $5 battery charge and a pair of $25 battery cables. Total bill $400, and all the car needed was to have its cable ends and battery terminals cleaned. The mechanic wasn't necessarily a thief. Perhaps, like academic education consultants, he just wasn't very smart — and his ilk abound; they are as plentiful as

the drivers who will pay generously for the privilege of an aristocratic disdain of elementary cause and effect in a vehicular electrical system.

After a tolerably long practice as a mechanic, I firmly believe that   24 at least two-thirds of the batteries, starters, alternators, ignition coils, carburetors, and water pumps that are sold are not needed. Batteries, alternators, and starters are sold because battery-cable ends are dirty. A maladjusted or stuck automatic choke is cured by a new carburetor. Water pumps and alternators are sold to correct problems from loose fan belts. In the course of the replacement, the fan belt gets properly tightened, so the original problem disappears in the misguided cure, with mechanic and owner never the wiser.

I understand the venality (and laziness and ignorance) of mechanics,   25 and I understand the shop owner's need to pay a salary to someone to keep up with the IRS and OSHA forms. The shop marks up parts by 50 to 100 percent. When the car with the faulty choke comes in the door, the mechanic must make a choice: he can spend fifteen minutes fixing it and charge a half-hour's labor, or he can spend a half-hour replacing the carburetor (and charge for one hour) with one he buys for $80 and sells for $135. If the shop is a profit-making enterprise, the mechanic can hardly be blamed for selling the unneeded new carburetor, especially if the customer will stand still to be fleeced. Whether the mechanic acts from ignorance or larceny (the odds are about equal), the result is still a waste, one that arises from the driver's refusal to study the cause and effect of events that occur under the hood of his car.

The willingness of a people to accept responsibility for the   26 machines they depend on is a fair barometer of their sense of individual worth and of the moral strength of a culture. According to popular reports, the Russian working folk are a sorrowfully vodka-besotted lot; likewise, reports are that Russian drivers abuse their vehicles atrociously. In our unhappy country, as gauges for battery-charging (ammeters), cooling-water temperature, and oil pressure disappeared from the dashboards, they were replaced by a big-brotherly series of cacophonous buzzers and flashing lights, buzzers and lights mandated by regulatory edict for the sole purpose of reminding the driver that the government considers him a hopeless fool. Concurrent with these developments has come social agitation and law known as "consumer protection," which is, in fact, an extension of that philosophy that people are morons for whom the government must provide outpatient care. People pay handsome taxes to be taught that they are not responsible and do not need to be. This is a long way from what the Puritans paid their tithes for, and, Salem witch trials aside, the Puritans got a better product for their money.

27   What is astounding and dismaying is how quickly people came to believe in their own incompetence. In 1951, Eric Hoffer noted in *The True Believer* that a leader so disposed could make free people into slaves easier than he could turn slaves into free people (cf. Moses). Hoffer must be pained by the accuracy of his perception.

28   I do not claim that Everyman can be his own expert mechanic, for I know that precious few can. I do claim that disdain for the beautiful series of cause-and-effect relationships ("beautiful" in the way that provoked Archimedes to proclaim "Eureka!") that move machines, and particularly the automobile, measures not only a man's wit but also a society's morals.

_____ CONSIDERATIONS _____

1. At the end of Paragraph 4, Sharp poses a question. What sentence toward the end of his essay answers this question? Is that sentence the thesis of his essay? What do you think of his choice of a moral barometer?

2. What would James Thurber think of Sharp's use of "which" in Paragraph 7? (See Thurber's short essay "Which.")

3. In Paragraphs 10, 11, and 12, Sharp offers an exposition of a process. Study his success in explaining technical matters without lapsing into terminology too specialized for the general reader.

4. Sharp calls a particular device on the dashboard an "idiot light." Why? Connect this epithet with other ideas in his essay.

5. Sharp refers (in Paragraph 9) to Sherlock Holmes's renowned skill in deduction, and (in Paragraph 22) to a common logical fallacy called *post hoc ergo propter hoc.* Consult a good dictionary for the meaning of this Latin phrase.

6. Note Sharp's distinctive word choice throughout the essay. How do his words affect the tone?

Sue Shellenbarger (b. 1951) grew up in Michigan, attended Michigan State University, and went on to study journalism at Northwestern University. Upon graduating, she began her career as a reporter for the Chicago Tribune, *later worked as a lecturer at Northwestern, and as a reporter and business writer for the Associated Press. In 1980 she went to the* Wall Street Journal — *first as a reporter and editor — where she is currently chief of the Chicago Bureau.*

64

SUE SHELLENBARGER
Selling Off the Family Farm

The harvester, two stories tall and wide as a country road, groans   1
and begins to roar. A cylindrical auger unfolds from its side like a gull's
wing and plunges toward our heads. A cloud of grain dust rises from
its guts, and the smell of past harvests settles on us like manna. "Wow!"
breathes my stepson at my side.

To him, as to me as a child, the combine with its spouts, belts   2
and churning blades is an awesome mechanical monster. Luke recalls
aloud the first time he saw it five years ago. He followed it into a field
and buried himself up to the neck in a wagonload of freshly harvested
corn. "Do we still have that wagon?" he asks, looking around my father's
farmyard.

We don't. Like most of my father's farm equipment, the wagon was   3
sold on this recent day at auction. Almost 100 brightly colored pickups
are lined up on our four corners in southwestern Michigan, and 175 men

in coveralls and duckbilled caps are swarming over our muddy hilltop farmyard. Like nails on a magnet, they follow the auctioneer, a man conspicuous in a short-brimmed Fedora, among the red barns and rows of farm implements, finally gathering in a respectful ring near the combine. The last item on the sale bill, it thunders before us in a demonstration of its soundness.

4   For the first time in 44 years, my father won't need any equipment this spring. With my brother, sister and me long departed for distant cities and occupations, he is selling out and leasing the farm. The auction ends our family's generations in farming so numerous no one ever bothered to count them.

5   We have plenty of company in that exodus. For a variety of reasons, traditional, medium-sized family farms like ours are vanishing; Luther Tweeten, professor of agricultural economics at Oklahoma State University, estimates that 600,000 are left, one-fourth as many as in the 1930s. The number has dropped especially fast since 1980, as falling farmland values and diminished expectations for the farm economy accelerated the shakeout.

6   I'm not sure that's a bad thing. The full-time farmers who persist today are the most determined and efficient managers. Straightforward and unaffected, those here today play their roles in this modern Farm Belt ritual with pride and subtlety. As they bid, the tension of making split-second decisions to spend $5,000, $10,000, is evident only in the pulsing of jaw muscles and the shifting of their rubber-booted feet.

7   Their bodies testify to the harshness of their work, an element of farming that alone was enough to make me reject it. A steel hook extends from the sleeve of one man, his hand lost to a farm-machinery accident. The arm of another's coat is sewn empty across his chest. A longtime friend from a neighboring farm is absent; surgeons are realigning his knee joint, ground by overwork into an instrument of pain.

8   My father's lungs are dotted with lesions from years of breathing dust and pesticides, before we knew those things were harmful. I'd no sooner regret the end of his half-century of hard work on the land than I'd like to relive the Industrial Revolution. I'm glad he's free from it.

9   But still, as Luke trails me around the farmyard to watch the auction, I feel a sense of loss. Memories cloud my thinking as bidding on the combine begins. As Luke studies the big machine with awe, I wish I somehow could pass on to him and his children my headful of memories of a farm childhood, with its small challenges, its solitude and beauty. Perhaps that's the loss in what's happening here — the opportunity for children of future generations to grow up on a farm and take away with them recollections of a peaceful, more pastoral past.

Not a very dramatic tale, my young life; I'm not sure why it means   10
so much. I spent it gathering mostly useless skills and irrelevant knowledge. We learned to rollerskate on layers of spilled soybeans, to make
wads of chewing gum from mouthfuls of wheat.

We were expert, too, at chasing escaped piglets back through holes   11
in their pens. (Defying that presumed expertise, a frenzied porker once
upended me in a mud puddle by making a clean escape straight between
my feet.)

I escaped, by dint of my puny muscles, learning how to "pick   12
stone" — the art of wrenching boulders like impacted teeth from the
earth, where they lie in wait to break a plowshare. But I can still, to
my husband's amusement, box eggs six at a handful with their small
ends down (to prevent the air bubble inside from moving to the wrong
end of the egg — don't ask me why that's important).

Admittedly, our nighttimes were livelier. Every few months, when   13
several hundred of our chickens were ready for market, we'd wait until
dark and stalk them silently in their barn, trying to keep the dozing
birds from panicking. We'd seize the chickens by their scaley legs and
pull them from their nests, thrusting them six at a time into crates
bound for the slaughterhouse. Other evenings, we went "haunted housing" — a teen-age amusement that entailed raiding abandoned farm-
houses in an attempt to scare oneself to death.

Failing that, we found the weather entertaining. Orion the soldier   14
marched conspicuously across the nighttime sky, ending the season
where the Northern lights flickered undimmed by competing city lights.
Sundogs and halos around the moon were the stuff of family fortune;
like red sunrises, they might portend a change in the weather that would
alter or halt our work.

The sky's shapes and colors dictated the rhythm of our days, and   15
destroyed any illusion that we could fully control our fates. Storms were
periodic dramas. My father, cutting his time as short as an urban ex-
ecutive catching a plane, would work in the field until lightning or wind
drove him, drenched, to shelter. Then we'd gather on the front porch,
often humbled by the storm's violence, to watch the rain sweep in silver
sheets across the fields.

If the storm broke a drought or nurtured new plantings, my father   16
would say "Well, that's a $2,000 rain" or "That's a $5,000 rain." If it rotted a $10,000 harvest still standing in the fields, the loss weighed on
us all.

Believing tacitly that we shared somehow in creation, we grew up   17
lacking a sense of scale, of urban proportion. We made our vegetable
gardens with an 8-foot-wide plow and harvested enough green beans an-

nually for the Fifth Army. When one year we decided to plant a pickle patch, it turned out a quarter-mile long; we strained our backs and sweated mud to pick the tons of cucumbers. On occasional trips to the city, we were bewildered by the housing stacked into the sky and backyards the size of calling cards. "How do all these people make a living on this little patch of land?" my father would wonder.

18   Back home, distant from our friends and neighbors, the animals — a cast of characters worthy of Moliere — leavened the solitude. The farm-yard patriarch was a stringy rooster named Mortimer, who attacked anyone who approached. Neck feathers flaring and stubby legs pump-ing like pistons, Mortimer would dash up to trespassers on his turf, heedless of their size, and bury his talons deep in their legs. In self-defense, I walked backward for years on Mortimer's territory. My fa-ther, his most frequent victim, sometimes drop-kicked the bird high overhead, but we never slaughtered Mortimer for Sunday dinner; he'd be too tough, we knew. He died of natural causes at five, a staggering age for a chicken.

19   In those days on the farm before televised kung fu or GI Joe toys, violence always had a purpose. When I chased a beheaded chicken around the slaughtering block, I knew we'd be eating her for dinner. A cat or squirrel maimed in the road must be put out of its misery. A pet dog that acquired a taste for the neighbor's sheep must be killed. But reasonless violence — the Kitty Genovese murder, or snipers from ur-ban windows — puzzled us in the way a moon landing or the theory of relativity surpassed comprehension.

20   Life was so tenacious that it commanded respect. Sometimes, when I rode the tractor across the barren spring fields with my father, a mother killdeer would emerge from the furrows and scrabble across the earth, feigning injury in an attempt to lure the approaching machine away from the chicks in her ground nest. One wing dragging in the dust, the spin-dly bird would charge the giant tractor, then dodge its grinding front wheels in a last-minute feint away from her nest. My father, in a sort of tribute, would lift the plow and circumnavigate her dust-colored home.

21   The seeds sown, we'd tour the fields at dusk to eye the size of seed-lings, the moisture in the soil, the evenness of our rows compared with our neighbors'. Seeing a plum-sized stone newly askew, my father would lean down and turn it aside. Beneath often lay a soybean the size of a pea, unfolding its yellowish sprout like a coiled fist to force aside a rock perhaps 50 times its size. "That's how bad it wants to live," my father would say. "That's how much life it has."

Bidding for the harvester comes to a close. My father shakes the   22
hand of a friend. "Well," he says, "I guess I'm out of business." Dozens
of farmers swoop down on the implements they've bought, from the tractor to a tin dishpan filled with bolts. In 10 minutes, the farmyard is almost empty.

One of the few implements unsold, a vestige of a past time, lies   23
rusting in a pile of old iron — a single-bladed plow. My father first
hitched mules to it in the era of the Model A and Franklin Roosevelt;
to use it, he had to curse, cajole and bully the stubborn creatures slowly
across the fields.

My stepson wanders up, eyes the simple tool, and turns away un-   24
comprehending. My brother and I study the plow and muse about restor-
ing it, replacing its broken handle and polishing its rusted blade. We
each envision it in our suburban houses, a testament to the life we've
left behind.

A neighbor passes. "There aren't many like that any more," he   25
remarks.

Suddenly, the effort of lifting the plow and carrying it away seems   26
too symbolic. We turn away, leaving it to sit, rusting into dust, on the
family farm.

_____ CONSIDERATIONS _____

1. "Selling Off the Family Farm" is told, except for one long section, in
the present tense. Identify the exception and speculate on the author's switching from present to past and back again. What can the present tense contribute
to writing? Why isn't it used more often?

2. Does Shellenbarger avoid falling into sentimentality as she remembers
her childhood on the farm? Elaborate.

3. Violence and death were part of life on the farm. How does the author
justify them as preferable to what she calls "reasonless violence"? See essays
by Jimmy Breslin (pages 96–99) and Martin Gansberg (pages 187–190) for examples of the latter.

4. Find three or four specific details that the author makes more
memorable than the statistics she mentions in Paragraph 5. What makes the
details stick and the statistics fade from our memories? What does this suggest
to you as a writer?

5. "Life was so tenacious," Shellenbarger writes, "that it commanded respect." How does she make that generalization credible? Find examples of the
same technique in other essays in this book.

6. Why, after the auction was over, did the one remaining old-fashioned, single-bladed plow seem so heavy?

7. To what extent does Shellenbarger's essay represent the more general plight of farmers in the Midwest? Read about this ongoing crisis and write an essay, making references to "Selling Off the Family Farm."

Leslie Marmon Silko (b. 1948), born in Albuquerque, New Mexico, is partly Mexican, partly native American, and partly Caucasian. She grew up on the Laguna Pueblo Reservation in a hundred-year-old house of rock and adobe, with walls two feet thick — the same house in which her father was born. Next-door lived her great-grandmother, who took care of her while her mother went to work. A writer of short stories, novels, and poems, she calls her work "the attempt to identify what it is to be a half-breed or mixed blooded person; what it is to grow up neither white nor fully traditional Indian."

Silko studied at the University of New Mexico. Married and the mother of two children, she has written many other books including Laguna Woman *(1974),* Ceremony *(1977), and* Storyteller *(1981). In 1984 she received a MacArthur Foundation Award.*

65

LESLIE MARMON SILKO

Slim Man Canyon

early summer Navajo Nation, 1972 for John

---

700 years ago
         people were living here
         water was running gently
         and the sun was warm
             on pumpkin flowers.   5
It was 700 years ago
         deep in this canyon
         with sandstone rising high above

The rock   the silence   tall sky and flowing water
                    sunshine through cottonwood leaves
                    the willow smell in the wind

12   700 years.
The rhythm
                the horses feet   moving strong through
                                   white deep sand.
Where I come from is like this
            the warmth, the fragrance, the silence.
Blue sky and rainclouds in the distance
                we ride together
                          past cliffs with stories and songs
                        painted on rock.

22   700 years ago.

*Page Smith (b. 1917) has written a long narrative history in
eight volumes called* The People's History of the United States.
*He taught at the University of California at Santa Cruz, where
he was also Provost, but he has also worked outside the
academy. He has written editorials for the* Los Angeles Times
*and collaborated on a famous compendium from the barnyard
called* The Chicken Book. *This essay first appeared in the*
Newsletter *of the Research Center for Nonviolence.*

66

PAGE SMITH
The New Abolitionism

The notion of human slavery, of owning human beings as prop-   1
erty, of beating or mutilating them as punishment, of selling children
away from their mothers and wives from their husbands, is an idea so
repugnant to the modern consciousness that it is hard to comprehend
the fact that such practices were commonplace in the United States a
little more than a hundred years ago. When we think of such matters
they seem infinitely remote, as though they had happened ages past.
Such an institution could never have survived into the present age, we
assure ourselves. If the Civil War had not plucked up slavery, an
enlightened nation would, by the opening decades of the twentieth century, have renounced it as incompatible with everything that America
stands for. "Progress," in its inevitable march, would have made slavery
an anachronism. Industrialization would have made it uneconomic.

The facts are otherwise. From the beginning of the Republic, the   2 institution of slavery put down deeper and deeper roots, becoming increasingly brutal and repressive with each passing decade. Far from deploring the institution, Southerners began to glorify it, comparing the culture it had produced in the South to that of ancient Greece, another slave-holding society. It was the settled determination of the South to extend the protection of the federal government to slaves as property westward to the Pacific Ocean and northward as far as Canada. Indeed, they wished to add Cuba to the slave empire.

3   "Progress," however we define that often ambiguous word, has demonstrated no built-in capacity for regenerating the moral fibre of a people. It has, if anything, displayed a disconcerting capacity to come to terms with exploitation and repression in the name of progress.

4   How then were the slaves freed? Quite simply, by the heroic efforts of individuals who dedicated their lives to the antislavery cause. They took the name abolitionists. Moral gadflies, tireless agitators, proclaimers of a moral order in the universe, champions of Christian brotherhood, they pricked the conscience of their fellow citizens. They allowed them no rest on the issue of slavery. Day in and day out, year in and year out, relentless and indefatigable, they pressed the issue. Mobbed, beaten, denounced, shut out from the company of respectable people, they persisted. They grew from a handful into an army. When Richard Henry Dana undertook to defend runaway slaves in Boston, friends of a lifetime cut him dead on the streets.

5   The great mass of Americans north of Mason's and Dixon's Line were quite ready to concede the iniquity of slavery, but they simply wished to forget about the whole subject. They didn't want trouble; they didn't like agitators. Agitators were bad for business. Northerners had other things on their minds like making a living or "dropping out" West, or quarreling over "hard" money versus "soft" money. Their relative indifference to the moral dimensions of the slavery issue demonstrated the ability of a people to ignore or suppress crucial moral issues. In this respect Americans were no different from the vast majority of species. We are all disposed to accept things-as-they-are as having a kind of inevitability about them. They seem part of the landscape, part of the complex set of ideas that define the society as a whole. Dangerous things to tamper with.

6   We find ourselves today in much the same situation that our forefathers did in the era before the Civil War (which of course was not fought primarily to free the slaves). We have allowed an evil, a horror of almost incomprehensible proportions, to grow up in our midst and come indeed to seem like part of the natural order of things, as inevitable

as the sunrise in the morning or the passage of the seasons. We have knowingly and deliberately armed ourselves with the most terrible weapons of destruction conceivable. As people originally dedicated to "emancipating" the world, we have devised and built weapons capable of destroying it many times over. Most astonishing of all (and, one might add, most obscene), we have done this in the name of peace. We have solemnly declared a moral enormity of staggering proportions to be our regretted but necessary duty.

To inform the world that we may have to destroy the greater part   7
of it in order to save it from communism (or anything else) is an arrogant presumption which, so far as I know, is without precedent in history. (Perhaps the will has been there before but never the capacity.) Indeed, having stated it, one stares at it unbelievingly on the page. Clearly what is involved in part is a dangerously diminished moral sensibility, but perhaps even more important, a badly flawed notion of the meaning of human existence. The world, believe me, was not created (or has not evolved) to be the creature of the United States, to be shaped or destroyed, in accordance with our Will, reinforced by stockpiles of atomic weapons.

Peoples throughout history have lived and suffered under govern-   8
ments far more egregiously tyrannical than any communist regime presently existing in the world. At least they or their children survived to see better times. Now the United States declares that it is prepared, if it deems it necessary to do so, to foreclose a future for the human race by employing nuclear weapons against its communist adversary. Assuming the worst scenario — an impending communist global takeover — I suspect that the peoples of the world might prefer, for a time at least, to live under communist regimes rather than not to live at all, to have no successors that could be called human. Or at the very least to have a say in the matter.

Perhaps the crowning irony is that at the same time that we are   9
preparing to destroy millions upon millions of Russians because they live under a system called communism, we announce that the system itself is collapsing, to quote Karl Marx, from its internal inconsistencies (as every "system" must in time). Moreover, there seems to be some evidence to support the assertion.

I do not covet the mantle of prophecy (I have my hands full with   10
the past) but I see no conceivable reasons to believe that the human race will follow undeviatingly either the path of Russian Communism or American Capitalism (indeed the best thing that can be said of the latter is that it has avoided the worst excesses of the former). Surely

the future, if we allow it to happen, must hold something better than either.

11   Which brings us back to the abolitionists. There is only one overriding issue facing the United States and the world, a single issue beside which *all* other issues fade to relative insignificance, and that is the complete outlawing and destruction of all nuclear weapons and weapons systems, beginning in the United States. We must begin in the United States, because the United States is still a democracy, if a highly imperfect one, and the citizens of this nation can still make their convictions felt through their elected representatives.

12   If the day comes when 75 percent of all Americans (or even, perhaps, 55 percent) announce with clarity and conviction, "We will not tolerate the existence of a nuclear arsenal in a nation that once called itself Christian and professed to be dedicated to improving the condition of all peoples, everywhere," that nuclear arsenal will be dismantled and mankind will breathe more freely. To bring the people of this Republic to such a conviction will not be quickly or easily accomplished. It may take as long as it took the abolitionists to free the slaves and as much heroism and devotion, as much willingness to endure hostility and abuse, charges of being unpatriotic or of being a "commie lover" (as the abolitionists were accused of being "nigger lovers" and proudly confessed to being).

13   I, for one, am willing to confess myself as a "commie lover," because my faith so instructs me. Indeed, I love the commies more than the capitalists — though I deplore the system under which they live — because I suspect they are substantially more in need of love. Certainly, the thought of destroying millions or dozens or *one of them* because they give their allegiance to a different political system than I do fills me with repugnance and dismay (not to mention, of course, the millions upon millions of those who will, it seems clear, be quite coincidentally annihilated).

14   IN THE NAME OF GOD, LET US ABOLISH NUCLEAR WEAPONS.

15   Our leaders tell us that such talk is defeatist, un-American. It is true I have no nerve or will for these murderous games, these scenarios of destruction with their insane calculations of kills and overkills. Nations as well as individuals can go insane. It seems clear to me that the United States is at this moment collectively insane in its policies and attitudes toward the Soviet Union. I know of no other way to explain our continuing accumulation of the deadliest weapons.

Slavery was such a madness; the cure was slow and ultimately terri-   16
ble, but we must never for a moment lose sight of the fact that it was
accomplished finally by the conscious, intelligent, sacrificial efforts of
a host of individuals not strikingly different from ourselves. A group
of pacifist organizations have joined forces recently to distribute "The
New Abolitionist Covenant." It is most appropriately named. Only a
modern abolitionist covenant to do away with nuclear arms, utterly and
completely, can save mankind from something very like destruction
and the United States from bearing the primary guilt for the holocaust
(though most of us presumably will be dead in any event).

—— **CONSIDERATIONS** ————————————————————

1. What is the curious feature of Page Smith's opening paragraph, a
paragraph commonly used to set forth a writer's thesis?

2. How might Smith have used passages from the journals of Henry David
Thoreau (see pages 413–423) to amplify the idea developed in Paragraph 2?

3. Is "Better Red than Dead" an acceptable summary of Smith's Paragraph
8? In what sense is that expression unacceptable — rhetorical, political,
philosophical, religious? Explain.

4. "I have no nerve or will for these murderous games, these scenarios
of destruction," writes Smith in Paragraph 15. He refers to "the worst scenario"
in Paragraph 8. Read Carl Sagan's "Nuclear Winter," (pages 355–372), especially
Paragraphs 4 and 13, comparing his references to war games and scenarios to
Smith's.

5. With the exception of Paragraph 14, Smith's paragraphs are about the
same length. Does its unusual length add to the effect of Paragraph 14? Make
a brief study of the functions and sizes of paragraphs, comparing Smith with
other writers in the text.

6. What precepts of (presumably) religious faith does Smith have in mind
when he says, in Paragraph 13, that his faith instructs him to be a "commie
lover"?

William Stafford (b. 1914) is a poet who grew up in Kansas and taught for many years at Lewis and Clark College in Oregon. Traveling through the Dark *won the National Book Award in 1963, and in 1977, Stafford collected his poems into one volume called* Stories That Could Be True. A Glass Face in the Rain *followed in 1982. His essays appear in* Writing the Australian Crawl *(1978). Stafford's poetry and his personal account of writing poetry look simple at first glance, but their simplicity deepens as we return and reread. His poetry is simple and deep, rather than complex and superficial. Reading about his way of writing, we feel the style of the man as intensely in his prose as in his poems.*

67

WILLIAM STAFFORD
A Way of Writing

1   A writer is not so much someone who has something to say as he is someone who has found a process that will bring about new things he would not have thought of if he had not started to say them. That is, he does not draw on a reservoir; instead, he engages in an activity that brings to him a whole succession of unforeseen stories, poems, essays, plays, laws, philosophies, religions, or — but wait!

2   Back in school, from the first when I began to try to write things, I felt this richness. One thing would lead to another; the world would give and give. Now, after twenty years or so of trying, I live by that certain richness, an idea hard to pin, difficult to say, and perhaps offensive to some. For there are strange implications in it.

From *Field: Contemporary Poetry and Poetics*, #2. Spring 1970. Reprinted by permission of *Field*, Oberlin College, Oberlin, Ohio.

One implication is the importance of just plain receptivity. When 3
I write, I like to have an interval before me when I am not likely to
be interrupted. For me, this means usually the early morning, before
others are awake. I get pen and paper, take a glance out the window
(often it is dark out there), and wait. It is like fishing. But I do not wait
very long, for there is always a nibble — and this is where receptivity
comes in. To get started I will accept anything that occurs to me.
Something always occurs, of course, to any of us. We can't keep from
thinking. Maybe I have to settle for an immediate impression: it's cold,
or hot, or dark, or bright, or in between! Or — well, the possibilities
are endless. If I put down something, that thing will help the next thing
come, and I'm off. If I let the process go on, things will occur to me that
were not at all in my mind when I started. These things, odd or trivial
as they may be, are somehow connected. And if I let them string out,
surprising things will happen.

If I let them string out. . . . Along with initial receptivity, then, 4
there is another readiness: I must be willing to fail. If I am to keep on
writing, I cannot bother to insist on high standards. I must get into action and not let anything stop me, or even slow me much. By "standards" I do not mean "correctness" — spelling, punctuation, and so on.
These details become mechanical for anyone who writes for awhile. I
am thinking about what many people would consider "important" standards, such matters as social significance, positive values, consistency,
etc. I resolutely disregard these. Something better, greater, is happening! I am following a process that leads so wildly and originally into
new territory that no judgment can at the moment be made about values,
significance, and so on. I am making something new, something that
has not been judged before. Later others — and maybe I myself — will
make judgments. Now, I am headlong to discover. Any distraction may
harm the creating.

So, receptive, careless of failure, I spin out things on the page. And 5
a wonderful freedom comes. If something occurs to me, it is all right
to accept it. It has one justification: it occurs to me. No one else can
guide me. I must follow my own weak, wandering, diffident impulses.

A strange bonus happens. At times, without my insisting on it, 6
my writings become coherent; the successive elements that occur to
me are clearly related. They lead by themselves to new connections.
Sometimes the language, even the syllables that happen along, may start
a trend. Sometimes the materials alert me to something waiting in my
mind, ready for sustained attention. At such times, I allow myself to
be eloquent, or intentional, or for great swoops (treacherous! not to be

trusted!) reasonable. But I do not insist on any of that; for I know that back of my activity there will be the coherence of my self, and that indulgence of my impulses will bring recurrent patterns and meanings again.

7   This attitude toward the process of writing creatively suggests a problem for me, in terms of what others say. They talk about "skills" in writing. Without denying that I do have experience, wide reading, automatic orthodoxies and maneuvers of various kinds, I still must insist that I am often baffled about what "skill" has to do with the precious little area of confusion when I do not know what I am going to say and then I find out what I am going to say. That precious interval I am unable to bridge by skill. What can I witness about it? It remains mysterious, just as all of us must feel puzzled about how we are so inventive as to be able to talk along through complexities with our friends, not needing to plan what we are going to say, but never stalled for long in our confident foward progress. Skill? If so, it is the skill we all have, something we must have learned before the age of three or four.

8   A writer is one who has become accustomed to trusting that grace, or luck, or — skill.

9   Yet another attitude I find necessary: most of what I write, like most of what I say in casual conversation, will not amount to much. Even I will realize, and even at the time, that it is not negotiable. It will be like practice. In conversation I allow myself random remarks — in fact, as I recall, that is the way I learned to talk —, so in writing I launch many expendable efforts. A result of this free way of writing is that I am not writing for others, mostly; they will not see the product at all unless the activity eventuates in something that later appears to be worthy. My guide is the self, and its adventuring in the language brings about communication.

10   This process-rather-than-substance view of writing invites a final, dual reflection:

1. Writers may not be special — sensitive or talented in any usual sense. They are simply engaged in sustained use of a language skill we all have. Their "creations" come about through confident reliance on stray impulses that will, with trust, find occasional patterns that are satisfying.

2. But writing itself is one of the great, free human activities. There is scope for individuality, and elation, and discovery, in writing. For the person who follows with trust and forgiveness what occurs to him, the world remains always ready and deep, an inexhaustible environment, with the combined vividness of an actuality and flexibility of a dream.

Working back and forth between experience and thought, writers have more than space and time can offer. They have the whole unexplored realm of human vision.

A sample daily-writing sheet and the poem as revised.

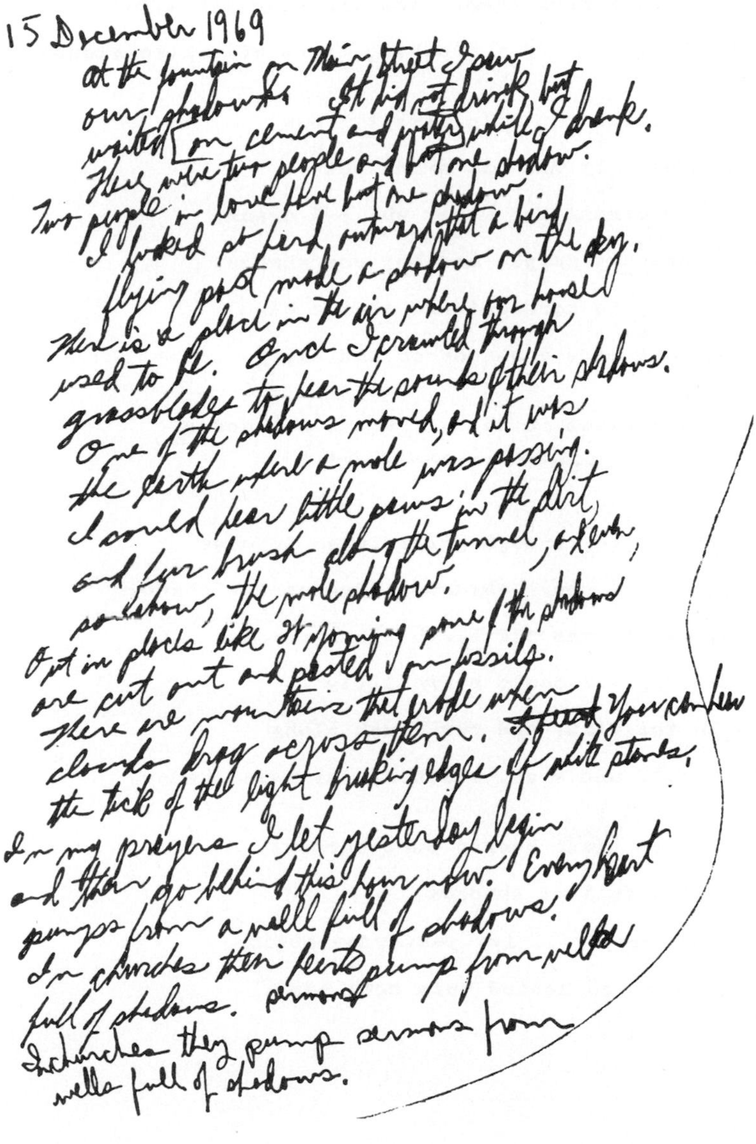
15 December 1969
At the fountain on Main Street I saw
our shadows. It did not drink but
waited on cement and water while I drank.
There were two people and but one shadow.
Two people in love have but one shadow
I looked at first, [illegible] a bird
flying past made a shadow on the sky.
There is a place in the air where our house
used to be. Once I crawled through
grassblades to hear the sounds of their shadows.
One of the shadows moved, and it was
the earth where a mole was passing.
I could hear little paws in the dirt,
and fur brush along the tunnel, and even,
somehow, the mole shadow.
Out in places like Wyoming some of the shadows
are cut out and pasted on fossils.
There are mountains that wade when
clouds drag across them. ~~[illegible]~~ You can hear
the tick of the light breaking edges of white stones.
In my prayers I let yesterday begin
and then go behind this hour now. Every heart
pumps from a well full of shadows.
In churches their hearts pump from wells
full of shadows. sermons
In churches they pump sermons from
wells full of shadows.

Shadows

I

Out in places like Wyoming some of the shadows

are cut out and pasted on fossils.

There are mountains that erode when
clouds drag across them. You can hear the tick

~~the noise~~ of the light breaking edges off white stones.

At a fountain on Main Street I saw

our shadow. It did not drink but

waited on cement and water while I drank.

There were two people and but one shadow.

I looked up so hard outward that a bird

flying past made a shadow on the sky.

There is a place in the air where our house
used to be.

Once I crawled through grassblades to hear

the sounds of their shadows. One of the shadows

moved, and it was the earth where a mole

was passing. I could hear little

paws in the dirt, and fur brush along

the tunnel, and even, somehow, the mole shadow.

In churches where hearts pump sermons

from wells full of shadows.

In my prayers I let yesterday begin
and then go behind this hour now,

SHADOWS

Out in places like Wyoming some of the shadows
are cut out and pasted on fossils.
There are mountains that erode when
clouds drag across them. You hear the tick
of sunlight breaking edges off white stones.

At a fountain on Main Street I saw
our shadow. It did not drink but
waited on cement and water while I drank.
There were two people and but one shadow.
I looked up so hard outward that a bird
flying past made a shadow on the sky.
There is a place in the air where
our old house used to be.

Once I crawled through grassblades to hear
the sounds of their shadows. One shadow
moved, and it was the earth where a mole
was passing. I could hear little
paws in the dirt, and fur brush along
the tunnel, and even, somehow, the mole shadow.

In my prayers I let yesterday begin
and then go behind this hour now,
in churches where hearts pump sermons
from wells full of shadows.

――― **CONSIDERATIONS** ―――――――――――――――――――――――

1. Stafford is clearly and openly talking about himself — how *he* writes, what writing means to *him* — and yet most readers agree that he successfully avoids the egotism or self-consciousness that sours many first-person essays. Compare his style with three or four other first-person pieces in this book to see how he does it.

2. In his first paragraph, Stafford tells of an idea that might be called writing as discovery. Thinking back through your own writing, can you recall this experience — when, after struggling to write an essay or letter that you *had* to write, you discovered something you *wanted* to write? What did you do about it? More important, what might you do next time it happens?

3. What, according to Stafford, is more important to a writer than "social significance, or positive values, or consistency"?

4. Stafford is talking about writing a poem. How do his discoveries and conclusions bear on *your* problems in writing an essay? Be specific.

5. Do the opening and closing paragraphs differ in style? If so, what is the difference, and why does Stafford allow it?

6. Study the three versions of Stafford's poem "Shadows." Do you find anything that belies the easygoing impression his essay gives of Stafford at work? Explain.

7. Compare Stafford's advice with the suggestions of other people in the text who talk about writing: Joan Didion (pages 129–136), Edward Hoagland (pages 211–214), James Baldwin (pages 51–56), or Ralph Ellison (pages 153–160). What advice is most relevant to your current writing tasks?

"Traveling Through the Dark" is William Stafford's most
famous poem.

68

WILLIAM STAFFORD
Traveling Through the Dark

Traveling through the dark I found a deer
dead on the edge of the Wilson River road.
It is usually best to roll them into the canyon:
that road is narrow; to swerve might make more dead.   4

By glow of the tail-light I stumbled back of the car
and stood by the heap, a doe, a recent killing;
she had stiffened already, almost cold.
I dragged her off; she was large in the belly.   8

My fingers touching her side brought me the reason —
her side was warm; her fawn lay there waiting,
alive, still, never to be born.
Beside that mountain road I hesitated.   12

The car aimed ahead its lowered parking lights;
under the hood purred the steady engine.
I stood in the glare of the warm exhaust turning red;
around our group I could hear the wilderness listen.   16

I thought hard for us all — my only swerving —,
then pushed her over the edge into the river.   18

Jonathan Swift (1667–1745), the author of Gulliver's Travels,
*was a priest, a poet, and a master of English prose. Some of his
strongest satire took the form of reasonable defense of the unthinkable, like his argument in favor of abolishing Christianity
in the British Isles. Born in Dublin, he was angry all his life at
England's misuse and mistreatment of the subject Irish people.
In 1729, he made this modest proposal for solving the Irish
problem.*

69

JONATHAN SWIFT
A Modest Proposal

FOR PREVENTING THE CHILDREN OF POOR PEOPLE IN IRELAND
FROM BEING A BURDEN TO THEIR PARENTS OR COUNTRY,
AND FOR MAKING THEM BENEFICIAL TO THE PUBLIC

1   It is a melancholy object to those who walk through this great town
or travel in the country, when they see the streets, the roads, and cabin
doors, crowded with beggars of the female sex, followed by three, four,
or six children, all in rags and importuning every passenger for an alms.
These mothers, instead of being able to work for their honest livelihood,
are forced to employ all their time in strolling to beg sustenance for
their helpless infants, who, as they grow up, either turn thieves for want
of work, or leave their dear native country to fight for the Pretender
in Spain, or sell themselves to the Barbadoes.

2   I think it is agreed by all parties that this prodigious number of
children in the arms, or on the backs, or at the heels of their mothers,
and frequently of their fathers, is in the present deplorable state of the
kingdom a very great additional grievance; and therefore whoever could
find out a fair, cheap, and easy method of making these children sound,

useful members of the commonwealth would deserve so well of the
public as to have his statue set up for a preserver of the nation.

But my intention is very far from being confined to provide only   3
for the children of professed beggars; it is of a much greater extent, and
shall take in the whole number of infants at a certain age who are born
of parents in effect as little able to support them as those who demand
our charity in the streets.

As to my own part, having turned my thoughts for many years   4
upon this important subject, and maturely weighed the several schemes
of other projectors, I have always found them grossly mistaken in their
computation. It is true, a child just dropped from its dam may be supported by her milk for a solar year, with little other nourishment; at
most not above the value of two shillings, which the mother may certainly get, or the value in scraps, by her lawful occupation of begging;
and it is exactly at one year old that I propose to provide for them in
such a manner as instead of being a charge upon their parents or the
parish, or wanting food and raiment for the rest of their lives, they shall
on the contrary contribute to the feeding, and partly to the clothing,
of many thousands.

There is likewise another great advantage in my scheme, that it   5
will prevent those voluntary abortions, and that horrid practice of
women murdering their bastard children, alas, too frequent among us,
sacrificing the poor innocent babes, I doubt, more to avoid the expense
than the shame, which would move tears and pity in the most savage
and inhuman breast.

The number of souls in this kingdom being usually reckoned one   6
million and a half, of these I calculate there may be about two hundred
thousand couples whose wives are breeders; from which number I subtract thirty thousand couples who are able to maintain their own
children, although I apprehend there cannot be so many under the present distress of the kingdom; but this being granted, there will remain
an hundred and seventy thousand breeders. I again subtract fifty thousand for those women who miscarry, or whose children die by accident
or disease within the year. There only remain an hundred and twenty
thousand children of poor parents actually born. The question therefore
is, how this number shall be reared and provided for, which, as I have
already said, under the present situation of affairs, is utterly impossible by all the methods hitherto proposed. For we can neither employ
them in handicraft or agriculture; we neither build houses (I mean in
the country) nor cultivate land. They can very seldom pick up a
livelihood by stealing till they arrive at six years old, except where they

are of towardly parts; although I confess they learn the rudiments much earlier, during which time they can however be looked upon only as probationers, as I have been informed by a principal gentleman in the country of Cavan, who protested to me that he never knew above one or two instances under the age of six, even in a part of the kingdom so renowned for the quickest proficiency in that art.

7   I am assured by our merchants that a boy or a girl before twelve years old is no salable commodity; and even when they come to this age they will not yield above three pounds, or three pounds and half a crown at most on the Exchange; which cannot turn to account either to the parents or the kingdom, the charge of nutriment and rags having been at least four times that value.

8   I shall now therefore humbly propose my own thoughts, which I hope will not be liable to the least objection.

9   I have been assured by a very knowing American of my acquaintance in London, that a young healthy child well nursed is at a year old a most delicious, nourishing, and wholesome food, whether stewed, roasted, baked, or boiled; and I make no doubt that it will equally serve in a fricassee or a ragout.

10   I do therefore humbly offer it to public consideration that of the hundred and twenty thousand children, already computed, twenty thousand may be reserved for breed, whereof only one fourth part to be males, which is more than we allow to sheep, black cattle, or swine; and my reason is that these children are seldom the fruits of marriage, a circumstance not much regarded by our savages, therefore one male will be sufficient to serve four females. That the remaining hundred thousand may at a year old be offered in sale to the persons of quality and fortune through the kingdom, always advising the mother to let them suck plentifully in the last month, so as to render them plump and fat for a good table. A child will make two dishes at an entertainment for friends; and when the family dines alone, the fore or hind quarter will make a reasonable dish, and seasoned with a little pepper or salt will be very good boiled on the fourth day, especially in the winter.

11   I have reckoned upon a medium that a child just born will weigh twelve pounds, and in a solar year if tolerably nursed increaseth to twenty-eight pounds.

12   I grant this food will be somewhat dear, and therefore very proper for landlords, who, as they have already devoured most of the parents, seem to have the best title to the children.

13   Infant's flesh will be in season throughout the year, but more plentiful in March, and a little before and after. For we are told by a grave

author, an eminent French physician, that fish being a prolific diet, there are more children born in Roman Catholic countries about nine months after Lent than at any other season; therefore, reckoning a year after Lent, the markets will be more glutted than usual, because the number of popish infants is at least three to one in this kingdom; and therefore it will have one other collateral advantage, by lessening the number of Papists among us.

    I have already computed the charge of nursing a beggar's child (in 14 which list I reckon all cottagers, laborers, and four fifths of the farmers) to be about two shillings per annum, rags included; and I believe no gentleman would repine to give ten shillings for the carcass of a good fat child, which, as I have said, will make four dishes of excellent nutritive meat, when he hath only some particular friend or his own family to dine with him. Thus the squire will learn to be a good landlord, and grow popular among the tenants; the mother will have eight shillings net profit, and be fit for work till she produces another child.

    Those who are more thrifty (as I must confess the times require) 15 may flay the carcass; the skin of which artificially dressed will make admirable gloves for ladies, and summer boots for fine gentlemen.

    As to our city of Dublin, shambles may be appointed for this pur- 16 pose in the most convenient parts of it, and butchers we may be assured will not be wanting; although I rather recommend buying the children alive, and dressing them hot from the knife as we do roasting pigs.

    A very worthy person, a true lover of his country, and whose vir- 17 tues I highly esteem, was lately pleased in discoursing on this matter to offer a refinement upon my scheme. He said that many gentlemen of his kingdom, having of late destroyed their deer, he conceived that the want of venison might be well supplied by the bodies of young lads and maidens, not exceeding fourteen years of age nor under twelve, so great a number of both sexes in every county being now ready to starve for want of work and service; and these to be disposed of by their parents, if alive, or otherwise by their nearest relations. But with due deference to so excellent a friend and so deserving a patriot, I cannot be altogether in his sentiments; for as to the males, my American acquaintance assured me from frequent experience that their flesh was generally tough and lean, like that of our schoolboys, by continual exercise, and their taste disagreeable; and to fatten them would not answer the charge. Then as to the females, it would, I think with humble submission, be a loss to the public, because they soon would become breeders themselves: and besides, it is not improbable that some scrupulous people might be apt to censure such a practice (although indeed very unjustly) as a little bordering upon cruelty; which, I confess, hath always been with me the strongest objection against any project, how well soever intended.

18   But in order to justify my friend, he confessed that this expedient was put into his head by the famous Psalmanazar, a native of the island Formosa, who came from thence to London above twenty years ago, and in conversation told my friend that in his country when any young person happened to be put to death, the executioner sold the carcass to persons of quality as a prime dainty; and that in his time the body of a plump girl of fifteen, who was crucified for an attempt to poison the emperor, was sold to his Imperial Majesty's prime minister of state, and other great mandarins of the court, in joints from the gibbet, at four hundred crowns. Neither indeed can I deny that if the same use were made of several plump young girls in this town, who without one single groat to their fortunes cannot stir abroad without a chair, and appear at the playhouse and assemblies in foreign fineries which they never will pay for, the kingdom would not be the worse.

19   Some persons of a desponding spirit are in great concern about that vast number of poor people who are aged, diseased, or maimed, and I have been desired to employ my thoughts what course may be taken to ease the nation of so grievous an encumbrance. But I am not in the least pain upon that matter, because it is very well known that they are every day dying and rotting by cold and famine, and filth and vermin, as fast as can be reasonably expected. And as to the younger laborers, they are now in almost as hopeful a condition. They cannot get work, and consequently pine away for want of nourishment to a degree that if at any time they are accidentally hired to common labor, they have not strength to perform it; and thus the country and themselves are happily delivered from the evils to come.

20   I have too long digressed, and therefore shall return to my subject. I think the advantages by the proposal which I have made are obvious and many, as well as of the highest importance.

21   For first, as I have already observed, it would greatly lessen the number of Papists, with whom we are yearly overrun, being the principal breeders of the nation as well as our most dangerous enemies; and who stay at home on purpose to deliver the kingdom to the Pretender, hoping to take their advantage by the absence of so many good Protestants, who have chosen rather to leave their country than to stay at home and pay tithes against their conscience to an Episcopal curate.

22   Secondly, the poorer tenants will have something valuable of their own, which by law may be made liable to distress, and help to pay their

landlord's rent, their corn and cattle being already seized and money a thing unknown.

Thirdly, whereas the maintenance of an hundred thousand 23 children, from two years old and upwards, cannot be computed at less than ten shillings a piece per annum, the nation's stock will be thereby increased fifty thousand pounds per annum, besides the profit of a new dish introduced to the tables of all gentlemen of fortune in the kingdom who have any refinement in taste. And the money will circulate among ourselves, the goods being entirely of our own growth and manufacture.

Fourthly, the constant breeders, besides the gain of eight shillings 24 sterling per annum by the sale of their children, will be rid of the charge of maintaining them after the first year.

Fifthly, this food would likewise bring great custom to taverns, 25 where the vintners will certainly be so prudent as to procure the best receipts for dressing it to perfection, and consequently have their houses frequented by all the fine gentlemen, who justly value themselves upon their knowledge in good eating; and a skillful cook, who understands how to oblige his guests, will contrive to make it as expensive as they please.

Sixthly, this would be a great inducement to marriage, which all 26 wise nations have either encouraged by rewards or enforced by laws and penalties. It would increase the care and tenderness of mothers toward their children, when they were sure of a settlement for life to the poor babes, provided in some sort by the public, to their annual profit instead of expense. We should see an honest emulation among the married women, which of them could bring the fattest child to the market. Men would become as fond of their wives during the time of their pregnancy as they are now of their mares in foal, their cows in calf, or sows when they are ready to farrow; nor offer to beat or kick them (as is too frequent a practice) for fear of a miscarriage.

Many other advantages might be enumerated. For instance, the ad- 27 dition of some thousand carcasses in our exportation of barreled beef, the propagation of swine's flesh, and improvements in the art of making good bacon, so much wanted among us by the great destruction of pigs, too frequent at our tables, which are no way comparable in taste or magnificence to a well-grown, fat, yearling child, which roasted whole will make a considerable figure at a lord mayor's feast or any other public entertainment. But this and many others I omit, being studious of brevity.

Supposing that one thousand families in this city would be con- 28 stant customers for infants' flesh, besides others who might have it at merry meetings, particularly weddings and christenings, I compute that Dublin would take off annually about twenty thousand carcasses, and the rest of the kingdom (where probably they will be sold somewhat cheaper) the remaining eighty thousand.

29   I can think of no one objection that will possibly be raised against this proposal, unless it should be urged that the number of people will be thereby much lessened in the kingdom. This I freely own, and it was indeed one principal design in offering it to the world. I desire the reader will observe, that I calculate my remedy for this one individual kingdom of Ireland and for no other that ever was, is, or I think ever can be upon earth. Therefore let no man talk to me of other expedients: of taxing our absentees at five shillings a pound: of using neither clothes nor household furniture except what is of our own growth and manufacture; of utterly rejecting the materials and instruments that promote foreign luxury: of curing the expensiveness of pride, vanity, idleness, and gaming in our women: of introducing a vein of parsimony, prudence, and temperance: of learning to love our country, in the want of which we differ even from Laplanders and the inhabitants of Topinamboo: of quitting our animosities and factions, nor acting any longer like the Jews, who were murdering one another at the very moment their city was taken: of beng a little cautious not to sell our country and conscience for nothing: of teaching landlords to have at least one degree of mercy toward their tenants: lastly, of putting a spirit of honesty, industry, and skill into our shopkeepers; who, if a resolution could now be taken to buy only our native goods, would immediately unite to cheat and exact upon us in the price, the measure, and the goodness, nor could ever yet be brought to make one fair proposal of just dealing, though often and earnestly invited to it.

30   Therefore, I repeat, let no man talk to me of these and the like expedients, till he hath at least some glimpse of hope that there will ever be some hearty and sincere attempt to put them in practice.

31   But as to myself, having been wearied out for many years with offering vain, idle, visionary thoughts, and at length utterly despairing of success, I fortunately fell upon this proposal, which, as it is wholly new, so it hath something solid and real, of no expense and little trouble, full in our own power, and whereby we can incur no danger in disobliging England. For this kind of commodity will not bear exportation, the flesh being of too tender a consistence to admit a long continuance in salt, although perhaps I could name a country which would be glad to eat up our whole nation without it.

After all, I am not so violently bent upon my own opinion as to   32
reject any offer proposed by wise men, which shall be found equally
innocent, cheap, easy, and effectual. But before something of that kind
shall be advanced in contradiction to my scheme, and offering a better,
I desire the author or authors will be pleased maturely to consider two
points. First, as things now stand, how they will be able to find food
and raiment for an hundred thousand useless mouths and backs. And
secondly, there being a round million of creatures in human figure
throughout this kingdom, whose sole subsistence put into a common
stock would leave them in debt two millions of pounds sterling, adding
those who are beggars by profession to the bulk of farmers, cottagers,
and laborers, with their wives and children who are beggars in effect;
I desire those politicians who dislike my overture, and may perhaps be
so bold to attempt an answer, that they will first ask the parents of these
mortals whether they would not at this day think it a great happiness
to have been sold for food at a year old in this manner I prescribe, and
thereby have avoided such a perpetual scene of misfortunes as they have
since gone through by the oppression of landlords, the impossibility of
paying rent without money or trade, the want of common sustenance,
with neither house nor clothes to cover them from the inclemencies
of the weather, and the most inevitable prospect of entailing the like
or greater miseries upon their breed forever.

I profess, in the sincerity of my heart, that I have not the least per-   33
sonal interest in endeavoring to promote this necessary work, having
no other motive than the public good of my country, by advancing our
trade, providing for infants, relieving the poor, and giving some pleasure
to the rich. I have no children by which I can propose to get a single
penny; the youngest being nine years old, and my wife past childbearing.

_____ CONSIDERATIONS _____

1. The biggest risk a satirist runs is that his reader will be too literal-
minded to understand that he or she is reading satire. Can you imagine a reader
missing the satiric nature of Swift's "A Modest Proposal"? It has happened many
times. What might such a reader think of the author? Consider the same problem with regard to Ambrose Bierce (pages 75–78), Nora Ephron (pages 161–169),
Woody Allen (pages 20–28), Eleanor Perényi (pages 320–325), or E.B. White (pages
469–471).

2. One clue to the satire is Swift's diction in certain passages. In Paragraph
4, for example, note the phrase, "just dropped from its dam," in reference to a

newborn child. How do these words make a sign to the reader? Look for other such words.

3. What words and phrases does Swift use to give the impression of straightforward seriousness?

4. How does Swift turn his satirical talent against religious intolerance?

5. What is the chief target of his satire toward the end of the essay?

6. If you have read Swift's *Gulliver's Travels* only in the version usually offered to children, you are in for a surprise when you read the complete unexpurgated *Gulliver's Travels*, a devastating satire of British political, moral, and religious values.

Studs Terkel (b. 1912) has been an actor on stage and television, and has conducted a successful radio interview show in Chicago. His best known books, collections of interviews, are Division Street America *(1966),* Hard Times *(1970),* Working *(1974) — from which we take this example of American speech — and* The Good War *(1984). In 1977, he published* Talking to Myself, *his autobiography, and in 1980* American Dreams Lost and Found.

70

STUDS TERKEL
Phil Stallings, Spot Welder

He is a spot-welder at the Ford assembly plant on the far South 1
Side of Chicago. He is twenty-seven years old; recently married. He works the third shift: 3:30 P.M. to midnight.

"I start the automobile, the first welds. From there it goes to an- 2
other line, where the floor's put on, the roof, the trunk hood, the doors. Then it's put on a frame. There is hundreds of lines.

"The welding gun's got a square handle, with a button on the top 3
for high voltage and a button on the bottom for low. The first is to clamp the metal together. The second is to fuse it.

"The gun hangs from a ceiling, over tables that ride on a track. 4
It travels in a circle, oblong, like an egg. You stand on a cement platform, maybe six inches from the ground."

I stand in one spot, about two- or three-feet area, all night. The 5
only time a person stops is when the line stops. We do about thirty-two

jobs per car, per unit. Forty-eight units an hour, eight hours a day. Thirty-two times forty-eight times eight. Figure it out. That's how many times I push that button.

6   The noise, oh it's tremendous. You open your mouth and you're liable to get a mouthful of sparks. (Shows his arms.) That's a burn, these are burns. You don't compete against the noise. You go to yell and at the same time you're straining to maneuver the gun to where you have to weld.

7   You got some guys that are uptight, and they're not sociable. It's too rough. You pretty much stay to yourself. You get involved with yourself. You dream, you think of things you've done. I drift back continuously to when I was a kid and what me and my brothers did. The things you love most are the things you drift back into.

8   Lots of times I worked from the time I started to the time of the break and I never realized I had even worked. When you dream, you reduce the chances of friction with the foreman or with the next guy.

9   It don't stop. It just goes and goes and goes. I bet there's men who have lived and died out there, never seen the end of that line. And they never will — because it's endless. It's like a serpent. It's just all body, no tail. It can do things to you . . . (Laughs.)

10   Repetition is such that if you were to think about the job itself, you'd slowly go out of your mind. You'd let your problems build up, you'd get to a point where you'd be at the fellow next to you — his throat. Every time the foreman came by and looked at you, you'd have something to say. You just strike out at anything you can. So if you involve yourself by yourself, you overcome this.

11   I don't like the pressure, the intimidation. How would you like to go up to someone and say, "I would like to go to the bathroom?" If the foreman doesn't like you, he'll make you hold it, just ignore you. Should I leave this job to go to the bathroom I risk being fired. The line moves all the time.

12   I work next to Jim Grayson and he's preoccupied. The guy on my left, he's a Mexican, speaking Spanish, so it's pretty hard to understand him. You just avoid him. Brophy, he's a young fella, he's going to college. He works catty-corner from me. Him and I talk from time to time. If he ain't in the mood, I don't talk. If I ain't in the mood, he knows it.

13   Oh sure, there's tension here. It's not always obvious, but the whites stay with the whites and the coloreds stay with the coloreds. When you go into Ford, Ford says, "Can you work with other men?" This stops a lot of trouble, 'cause when you're working side by side with a guy, they can't afford to have guys fighting. When two men don't

socialize, that means two guys are gonna do more work, know what I mean?

I don't understand how come more guys don't flip. Because you're 14 nothing more than a machine when you hit this type of thing. They give better care to that machine than they will to you. They'll have more respect, give more attention to that machine. And you *know* this. Somehow you get the feeling that the machine is better than you are. (Laughs.)

You really begin to wonder. What price do they put on me? Look 15 at the price they put on the machine. If that machine breaks down, there's somebody out there to fix it right away. If I break down, I'm just pushed over to the other side till another man takes my place. The only thing they have on their mind is to keep that line running.

I'll do the best I can. I believe in an eight-hour pay for an eight- 16 hour day. But I will not try to outreach my limits. If I can't cut it, I just don't do it. I've been there three years and I keep my nose pretty clean. I never cussed anybody or anything like that. But I've had some real brushes with foremen.

What happened was my job was overloaded. I got cut and it got 17 infected. I got blood poisoning. The drill broke. I took it to the foreman's desk. I says, "Change this as soon as you can." We were running specials for XL hoods. I told him I wasn't a repair man. That's how the conflict began. I says, "If you want, take me to the Green House." Which is a superintendent's office — disciplinary station. This is when he says, "Guys like you I'd like to see in the parking lot."

One foreman I know, he's about the youngest out here, he has t' idea: I'm it and if you don't like it, you know what you can do. Anyt' this other foreman says, he usually overrides. Even in some cas' foremen don't get along. They're pretty hard to live with, even w' other.

Oh yeah, the foreman's got somebody knuckling down c ting the screws to him. But a foreman is still free to go to t' go get a cup of coffee. He doesn't face the penalties. Wh in there, I kind of envied foremen. Now, I wouldn't ' job. I wouldn't give 'em the time of the day.

When a man becomes a foreman, he has to f' ing human, as far as feelings are concerned. You s' to death. So what, buddy? That line's gotta ke' that. To me, if a man gets hurt, first thing ' attention.

About the blood poisoning. It came f'

bin' against me. It caused quite a bit of pain. I went down to the medics. They said it was a boil. Got to my doctor that night. He said blood poisoning. Running fever and all this. Now I've smartened up.

22   They have a department of medics. It's basically first aid. There's no doctor on our shift, just two or three nurses, that's it. They've got a door with a sign on it that says Lab. Another door with a sign on it: Major Surgery. But my own personal opinion, I'm afraid of 'em. I'm afraid if I were to get hurt, I'd get nothin' but back talk. I got hit square in the chest one day with a bar from a rack and it cut me down this side. They didn't take x-rays or nothing. Sent me back on the job. I missed three and a half days two weeks ago. I had bronchitis. They told me I was all right. I didn't have a fever. I went home and my doctor told me I couldn't go back to work for two weeks. I really needed the money, so I had to go back the next day. I woke up still sick, so I took off the rest of the week.

23   I pulled a muscle on my neck, straining. This gun, when you grab this thing from the ceiling, cable, weight, I mean you're pulling everything. Your neck, your shoulders, and your back. I'm very surprised more accidents don't happen. You have to lean over, at the same time holding down the gun. This whole edge here is sharp. I go through a shirt every two weeks, it just goes right through. My coveralls catch on fire. I've had gloves catch on fire. (Indicates arm.) See them little holes? That's what sparks do. I've got burns across here from last night.

24   I know I could find better places to work. But where could I get the money I'm making? Let's face it, $4.32 an hour. That's real good money now. Funny thing is, I don't mind working at body construction. To a great degree, I enjoy it. I love using my hands — more than I do my mind. I love to be able to put things together and see something in the long run. I'll be the first to admit I've got the easiest job on the line. But I'm against this thing where I'm being held back. I'll work like a dog until I get what I want. The job I really want is utility.

25   It's where I can stand and say I can do any job in this department, and nobody has to worry about me. As it is now, out of say, sixty jobs, I can do almost half of 'em. I want to get away from standing in one spot. Utility can do a different job every day. Instead of working right there for eight hours I could work over there for eight, I could work the other place for eight. Every day it would change. I would be around more people. I go out on my lunch break and work on the fork truck for a half-hour — to get the experience. As soon as I got it down pretty good, the foreman in charge says he'll take me. I don't want the other s to see me. When I hit that fork lift, you just stop your thinking

and you concentrate. Something right there in front of you, not in the past, not in the future. This is real healthy.

I don't eat lunch at work. I may grab a candy bar, that's enough. 26 I wouldn't be able to hold it down. The tension your body is put under by the speed of the line . . . When you hit them brakes, you just can't stop. There's a certain momentum that carries you forward. I could hold the food, but it wouldn't set right.

Proud of my work? How can I feel pride in a job where I call a 27 foreman's attention to a mistake, a bad piece of equipment, and he'll ignore it. Pretty soon you get the idea they don't care. You keep doing this and finally you're titled a troublemaker. So you just go about your work. You *have* to have pride. So you throw it off to something else. And that's my stamp collection.

I'd break both my legs to get into social work. I see all over so many 28 kids really gettin' a raw deal. I think I'd go into juvenile. I tell kids on the line, "Man, go out there and get that college." Because it's too late for me now.

When you go into Ford, first thing they try to do is break your spirit. 29 I seen them bring a tall guy where they needed a short guy. I seen them bring a short guy where you have to stand on two guys' backs to do something. Last night, they brought a fifty-eight-year-old man to do the job I was on. That man's my father's age. I know damn well my father couldn't do it. To me, this is humanely wrong. A job should be a job, not a death sentence.

The younger worker, when he gets uptight, he talks back. But you 30 take an old fellow, he's got a year, two years, maybe three years to go. If it was me, I wouldn't say a word, I wouldn't care what they did. 'Cause, baby, for another two years I can stick it out. I can't blame this man. I respect him because he had enough will power to stick it out for thirty years.

It's gonna change. There's a trend. We're getting younger and 31 younger men. We got this new Thirty and Out. Thirty years seniority and out. The whole idea is to give a man more time, more time to slow down and live. While he's still in his fifties, he can settle down in a camper and go out and fish. I've sat down and thought about it. I've got twenty-seven years to go. (Laughs.) That's why I don't go around causin' trouble or lookin' for a cause.

The only time I get involved is when it affects me or it affects a 32 man on the line in a condition that could be me. I don't believe in lost causes, but when it all happened . . . (He pauses, appears bewildered.)

The foreman was riding the guy. The guy either told him to go 33 away or pushed him, grabbed him . . . You can't blame the guy — Jim Grayson. I don't want nobody stickin' their finger in my face. I'd've probably hit him beside the head. The whole thing was: Damn it, it's about time we took a stand. Let's stick up for the guy. We stopped the line. (He pauses, grins.) Ford lost about twenty units. I'd figure about five grand a unit — whattaya got? (Laughs.)

34   I said, "Let's all go home." When the line's down like that, you can go up to one man and say, "You gonna work?" If he says no, they can fire him. See what I mean? But if nobody was there, who the hell were they gonna walk up to and say, "Are you gonna work?" Man, there woulda been nobody there! If it were up to me, we'd gone home.

35   Jim Grayson, the guy I work next to, he's colored. Absolutely. That's the first time I've seen unity on that line. Now it's happened once, it'll happen again. Because everybody just sat down. Believe you me. (Laughs.) It stopped at eight and it didn't start till twenty after eight. Everybody and his brother were down there. It was really nice to see, it really was.

_____ **CONSIDERATIONS** _____

1. Terkel is famous for his ability to catch the voice of the people he interviews. Study the language of Phil Stallings and list some of the features of his voice.

2. In addition to diction, what removes this selection from the category of "essay"?

3. How does Stallings indicate his opinion that the company puts a higher value on its machines than on its men?

4. Does Stallings agree with what Caroline Bird says in her essay on the value of college (pages 79–89)?

5. What occurrence on the line, described toward the end of the interview, reveals Stallings's social consciousness?

6. Interview someone you find interesting. Try to shape the material from the interview into something with a point.

Lewis Thomas (b. 1913) received his M.D. from Harvard Medical School in 1937, and since 1973 has headed the Memorial Sloan-Kettering Cancer Center in New York City. In 1971 he began to contribute meticulous essays to the New England Journal of Medicine, *since collected in* The Lives of a Cell *(1974) and* Late Night Thoughts on Listening to Mahler's Ninth Symphony *(1983). He has also written a memoir of his life as a doctor,* The Youngest Science *(1983) in which he reprints a poem that he published as a young man in* The Atlantic Monthly.

71

LEWIS THOMAS
The Iks

The small tribe of Iks, formerly nomadic hunters and gatherers in the mountain valleys of northern Uganda, have become celebrities, literary symbols for the ultimate fate of disheartened, heartless mankind at large. Two disastrously conclusive things happened to them: the government decided to have a national park, so they were compelled by law to give up hunting in the valleys and become farmers on poor hillside soil, and then they were visited for two years by an anthropologist who detested them and wrote a book about them.

The message of the book is that the Iks have transformed themselves into an irreversibly disagreeable collection of unattached, brutish creatures, totally selfish and loveless, in response to the dismantling of their traditional culture. Moreover, this is what the rest

of us are like in our inner selves, and we will all turn into Iks when
the structure of our society comes all unhinged.

3   The argument rests, of course, on certain assumptions about the
core of human beings, and is necessarily speculative. You have to agree
in advance that man is fundamentally a bad lot, out for himself alone,
displaying such graces as affection and compassion only as learned
habits. If you take this view, the story of the Iks can be used to confirm
it. These people seem to be living together, clustered in small, dense
villages, but they are really solitary, unrelated individuals with no evident use for each other. They talk, but only to make ill-tempered
demands and cold refusals. They share nothing. They never sing. They
turn the children out to forage as soon as they can walk, and desert the
elders to starve whenever they can, and the foraging children snatch
food from the mouths of the helpless elders. It is a mean society.

4   They breed without love or even casual regard. They defecate on
each other's doorsteps. They watch their neighbors for signs of misfortune, and only then do they laugh. In the book they do a lot of laughing,
having so much bad luck. Several times they even laughed at the anthropologist, who found this especially repellent (one senses, between
the lines, that the scholar is not himself the world's luckiest man).
Worse, they took him into the family, snatched his food, defecated on
his doorstep, and hooted dislike at him. They gave him two bad years.

5   It is a depressing book. If, as he suggests, there is only Ikness at
the center of each of us, our sole hope for hanging on to the name of
humanity will be in endlessly mending the structure of our society, and
it is changing so quickly and completely that we may never find the
threads in time. Meanwhile, left to ourselves alone, solitary, we will
become the same joyless, zestless, untouching lone animals.

6   But this may be too narrow a view. For one thing, the Iks are extraordinary. They are absolutely astonishing, in fact. The anthropologist
has never seen people like them anywhere, nor have I. You'd think, if
they were simply examples of the common essence of mankind, they'd
seem more recognizable. Instead, they are bizarre, anomalous. I have
known my share of peculiar, difficult, nervous, grabby people, but I've
never encountered any genuinely, consistently detestable human beings
in all my life. The Iks sound more like abnormalities, maladies.

7   I cannot accept it. I do not believe that the Iks are representative
of isolated, revealed man, unobscured by social habits. I believe their
behavior is something extra, something laid on. This unremitting, compulsive repellence is a kind of complicated ritual. They must have
learned to act this way; they copied it, somehow.

I have a theory, then. The Iks have gone crazy.   8

The solitary Ik, isolated in the ruins of an exploded culture, has   9
built a new defense for himself. If you live in an unworkable society
you can make up one of your own, and this is what the Iks have done.
Each Ik has become a group, a one-man tribe on its own, a constituency.

Now everything falls into place. This is why they do seem, after   10
all, vaguely familiar to all of us. We've seen them before. This is precisely
the way groups of one size or another, ranging from committees to nations, behave. It is, of course, this aspect of humanity that has lagged
behind the rest of evolution, and this is why the Ik seems so primitive.
In his absolute selfishness, his incapacity to give anything away, no matter what, he is a successful committee. When he stands at the door of
his hut, shouting insults at his neighbors in a loud harangue, he is city
addressing another city.

Cities have all the Ik characteristics. They defecate on doorsteps,   11
in rivers and lakes, their own or anyone else's. They leave rubbish. They
detest all neighboring cities, give nothing away. They even build institutions for deserting elders out of sight.

Nations are the most Iklike of all. No wonder the Iks seem famil-   12
iar. For total greed, rapacity, heartlessness, and irresponsibility there
is nothing to match a nation. Nations, by law, are solitary, self-centered,
withdrawn into themselves. There is no such thing as affection between
nations, and certainly no nation ever loved another. They bawl insults
from their doorsteps, defecate into whole oceans, snatch all the food,
survive by detestation, take joy in the bad luck of others, celebrate the
death of others, live for the death of others.

That's it, and I shall stop worrying about the book. It does not sig-   13
nify that man is a sparse, inhuman thing at his center. He's all right.
It only says what we've always known and never had enough time to
worry about, that we haven't yet learned how to stay human when
assembled in masses. The Ik, in his despair, is acting out this failure,
and perhaps we should pay closer attention. Nations have themselves
become too frightening to think about, but we might learn some things
by watching these people.

_____ **CONSIDERATIONS** _____

1. A True/False question: Does Lewis Thomas believe that the Iks represent our inner selves? Why might a hurried reader, who relies upon understanding an essay by scanning the first paragraphs, be likely to come up with the

wrong answer to the question posed? Explain your answer to this last question by examining Thomas's organization.

2. What sentence in Paragraph 6 suggests that there are no such people as the Iks? How could you confirm or refute such a possibility?

3. Many writers have described our contemporary world as a fragmented society that has lost its old values and not yet found new ones. Is this what Thomas means, in Paragraph 9, by "an exploded culture"? As you look about your world, do you see any signs of such fragmentation or explosion? Explain.

4. Whether or not the Iks are real, how does Thomas use them to make his final point in the closing paragraph?

5. In Paragraph 4, Thomas hints that the anthropologist's account of the Iks' culture might have been distorted by their unfriendly treatment of him. Is it possible to give an unbiased description of a person or group that you despise? Would the same challenge apply to describing a movie or a book or a course of study you dislike?

Henry David Thoreau (1817–1862) is one of the greatest American writers, and Walden *one of the great American books. Thoreau attended Concord Academy, in the Massachusetts town where he was born and lived. Then he went to Harvard and completed his formal education, which was extensive in mathematics, literature, Greek, Latin, and French — and included smatterings of Spanish and Italian and some of the literature of India and China. He and his brother founded a school that lasted four years, and then he was a private tutor to a family. He also worked for his father, manufacturing pencils. But mostly Thoreau walked, meditated, observed nature, and wrote.*

A friend of Ralph Waldo Emerson's, Thoreau was influenced by the older man, and by Transcendentalism — a doctrine that recognized the unity of man and nature. For Thoreau, an idea required testing by life itself; it never remained merely mental. In his daily work on his journals, and in the books he carved from them — A Week on the Concord and Merrimack Rivers *(1849) as well as* Walden *(1854) — he observed the detail of daily life, human and natural, and he speculated on the universal laws he could derive from this observation.*

"To know it by experience, and be able to give a true account of it" *— these words could be carved on Thoreau's gravestone.* "To give a true account" *he became a great writer, a master of observation.*

Thoreau was our greatest observer of nature, but his observations were not limited to fish and elm trees. He was ardently opposed to slavery and disgusted with fellow Northerners who accepted enforcement of the Fugitive Slave Act. Two entries from his journal, on two successive days, respond to one dreadful occasion involving the case of Anthony Burns. When a mob tried to free the fugitive slave, the government called out the militia to ensure that the trial was held. Burns was returned to the South although his identity, as an escaped slave, was doubtful. Never again was the Fugitive Slave Act enforced in Massachusetts.

413

72

HENRY DAVID THOREAU
June 16, 1854

1   The effect of a good government is to make life more valuable,
— of a bad government, to make it less valuable. We can afford that
railroad and all merely material stock should depreciate, for that only
compels us to live more simply and economically; but suppose the value
of life itself should be depreciated. Every man in New England capable
of the sentiment of patriotism must have lived the last three weeks with
the sense of having suffered a vast, indefinite loss. I had never respected
this government, but I had foolishly thought that I might manage to
live here, attending to my private affairs, and forget it. For my part, my
old and worthiest pursuits have lost I cannot say how much of their
attraction, and I feel that my investment in life here is worth many per
cent. less since Massachusetts last deliberately and forcibly restored an
innocent man, Anthony Burns, to slavery. I dwelt before in the illusion
that my life passed somewhere only *between* heaven and hell, but now
I cannot persuade myself that I do not dwell wholly within hell. The
sight of that political organization called Massachusetts is to me morally
covered with scoriæ and volcanic cinders, such as Milton imagined. If
there is any hell more unprincipled than our rulers and our people, I
feel curious to visit it. Life itself being worthless, all things with it, that
feed it, are worthless. Suppose you have a small library, with pictures
to adorn the walls, — a garden laid out around, — and contemplate scientific and literary pursuits, etc., etc., and discover suddenly that your villa,
with all its contents, is located in hell, and that the justice of the peace
is one of the devil's angels, has a cloven foot and forked tail, — do not
these things suddenly lose their value in your eyes? Are you not disposed
to sell at a great sacrifice?

2   I feel that, to some extent, the State has fatally interfered with my
just and proper business. It has not merely interrupted me in my passage

through Court Street on errands of trade, but it has, to some extent, interrupted me and every man on his onward and upward path, on which he had trusted soon to leave Court Street far behind. I have found that hollow which I had relied on for solid.

I am surprised to see men going about their business as if nothing   3
had happened, and say to myself, "Unfortunates! they have not heard the news;" that the man whom I just met on horseback should be so earnest to overtake his newly bought cows running away, — since all property is insecure, and if they do not run away again, they may be taken away from him when he gets them. Fool! does he not know that his seed-corn is worth less this year, — that all beneficent harvests fail as he approaches the empire of hell? No prudent man will build a stone house under these circumstances, or engage in any peaceful enterprise which it requires a long time to accomplish. Art is as long as ever, but life is more interrupted and less available for a man's proper pursuits. It is time we had done referring to our ancestors. We have used up all our inherited freedom, like the young bird the albumen in the egg. It is not an era of repose. If we would save our lives, we must fight for them.

The discovery is what manner of men your countrymen are. They   4
steadily worship mammon — and on the seventh day curse God with a tintamarre from one end of the *Union* to the other. I heard the other day of a meek and sleek devil of a Bishop Somebody, who commended the law and order with which Burns was given up. I would like before I sit down to a table to inquire if there is one in the company who styles himself or is styled Bishop, and he or I should go out of it. I would have such a man wear his bishop's hat and his clerical bib and tucker, that we may know him.

Why will men be such fools as [to] trust to lawyers for a *moral*   5
reform? I do not believe that there is a judge in this country prepared to decide by the principle that a law is immoral and therefore of no force. They put themselves, or rather are by character, exactly on a level with the marine who discharges his musket in any direction in which he is ordered. They are just as much tools, and as little men.

——— **CONSIDERATIONS** ———————————————————

1. In expressing disgust over the Fugitive Slave Act at work in his own state of Massachusetts, Thoreau distinguishes between a high material standard of living and a high valuing to life itself. Thus, he would be willing to dispense with railroads and other creature comforts if the value of life could

be preserved. Do you hold similar feelings? Are you willing to trade civil liberties for comforts and conveniences? Is such a trade necessary?

2. To show how the court decisions about Anthony Burns have changed
his life, Thoreau makes use of allusion — a literary device — when he refers
to Milton's description of hell. If that allusion does not elicit the dramatic effect
Thoreau intends, turn to "Book 1" of Milton's *Paradise Lost*. In your next essay,
try to employ an allusion — not necessarily to Milton — to strengthen a point.

3. How does Thoreau use his knowledge of natural history to make credible his statement that "We have used up all our inherited freedom"?

73

HENRY DAVID THOREAU
June 17, 1854

The judges and lawyers, and all men of expediency, consider not whether the Fugitive Slave Law is right, but whether it is what they call constitutional. They try the merits of the case by a very low and incompetent standard. Pray, is virtue constitutional, or vice? Is equity constitutional, or iniquity? It is as impertinent, in important moral and vital questions like this, to ask whether a law is constitutional or not, as to ask whether it is profitable or not. They persist in being the servants of man, and the worst of men, rather than the servants of God. Sir, the question is not whether you or your grandfather, seventy years ago, entered into an agreement to serve the devil, and that service is not accordingly now due; but whether you will not now, for once and at last, serve God, — in spite of your own past recreancy or that of your ancestors, — and obey that eternal and only just Constitution which he, and not any Jefferson or Adams, has written in your being. Is the Constitution a thing to live by? or die by? No, as long as we are alive we forget it, and when we die we have done with it. At most it is only to swear by. While they are hurrying off Christ to the cross, the ruler decides that he cannot *constitutionally* interfere to save him. The Christians, now and always, are they who obey the higher law, who discover it to be according to their constitution to interfere. They at least cut off the ears of the police; the others pocket the thirty pieces of silver. This was meaner than to crucify Christ, for he could better take care of himself.

CONSIDERATIONS

1. Thoreau groups judges and lawyers into a class he calls "men of expediency." Look up that last word and explain why a man of principle detests those who make their decisions on the basis of expediency.

417

2. Thoreau questions the wisdom and morality of arguing about a law's constitutionality. Would he have raised the same question had he observed the number of times in recent years that constitutional arguments have been the means of preserving civil liberties?

3. What higher law does Thoreau prefer over Massachusetts law? Why might appeals to that higher law be likely to produce more arguments than it could resolve?

4. In his widely reprinted essay, "On the Duty of Civil Disobedience," Thoreau announces that he is a party of one and that "any man more right than his neighbors constitutes a majority of one." Lewis Thomas (pages 409–412) describes the "Iks" in similar terms: "Each Ik has become a group, a one-man tribe on its own, a constituency." Is this the kind of "party of one" Thoreau has in mind? Explain.

The elm tree is fast disappearing. Here Thoreau writes about elms, about vision, about observation — about love of the natural world.

74

HENRY DAVID THOREAU
October 12, 1857

I see a very distant mountain house in a direction a little to the   1
west of Carlisle, and two elms in the horizon on the right of it. Measuring carefully on the map of the county, I think it must be the Baptist Church in North Tewksbury, within a small fraction of fourteen miles from me. I think that this is the greatest distance at which I have seen an elm without a glass. There is another elm in the horizon nearly north, but not so far. It looks very much larger than it is. Perhaps it looms a little. The elm, I think, can be distinguished further than any other tree, and, however faintly seen in the distant horizon, its little dark dome, which the thickness of my nail will conceal, just rising above the line of the horizon, apparently not so big as a prominence on an orange, it suggests ever the same quiet rural and domestic life passing beneath it. It is the vignette to an unseen idyllic poem. Though that little prominence appears so dark there, I know that it is now a rich brownish-yellow canopy of rustling leaves, whose harvest-time is already come, sending down its showers from time to time. Homestead telegraphs to homestead through these distant elms seen from the hilltops. I fancy I hear the house-dog's bark and lowing of the cows asking admittance to their yard beneath it. The tea-table is spread; the master and mistress and the hired men now have just sat down in their shirt-sleeves. Some are so lifted up in the horizon that they seem like portions of the earth detached and floating off by themselves into space.

Their dark masses against the sky can be seen as far, at least, as a white spire, though it may be taller. Some of these trees, seen through a glass, are not so large . . . .

2   This was what those scamps did in California. The trees were so grand and venerable that they could not afford to let them grow a hair's breadth bigger, or live a moment longer to reproach themselves. They were so big that they resolved they should never be bigger. They were so venerable that they cut them right down. It was not for sake of the wood; it was only because they were very grand and venerable.

_____ CONSIDERATIONS _____

1. Many readers think of Thoreau as a naturalist, belly-down on the shores of Walden Pond, staring intently at a tiny frog. This excerpt shows a different side. Working from your study of the October 12 journal item, how would you describe what he is doing? How does it affect the conventional view of him?

2. Why, according to Thoreau, did the Californians cut down their giant trees? Who might be more inclined to agree with him: loggers or environmentalists?

3. What have the elms — and Thoreau's way of seeing them — to do with his sense of place?

4. Thoreau's fierce insistence on personal freedom and responsibility is well known. For example, he chose to go to jail rather than to pay an unjust tax. Is his principle of freedom irreconcilable with the daydreaming he does in this excerpt? Explain.

These passages come from his journal, the disciplined daily writing from which Thoreau shaped his finished books. Here he writes about the bream — a small, silvery, flattish freshwater fish — not so much by describing it as by recounting his reaction to it and by ruminating on the relationship between people and the natural world.

75

HENRY DAVID THOREAU
November 30, 1858

I cannot but see still in my mind's eye those little striped breams 1
poised in Walden's glaucous water. They balance all the rest of the world in my estimation at present, for this is the bream that I have just found, and for the time I neglect all its brethren and am ready to kill the fatted calf on its account. For more than two centuries have men fished here and have not distinguished this permanent settler of the township. It is not like a new bird, a transient visitor that may not be seen again for years, but there it dwells and has dwelt permanently, who can tell how long? When my eyes first rested on Walden the striped bream was poised in it, though I did not see it, and when Tahatawan paddled his canoe there. How wild it makes the pond and the township to find a new fish in it! America renews her youth here. But in my account of this bream I cannot go a hair's breadth beyond the mere statement that it exists, — the miracle of its existence, my contemporary and neighbor, yet so different from me! I can only poise my thought there by its side and try to think like a bream for a moment. I can only think of precious jewels, of music, poetry, beauty, and the mystery of life. I only see the

bream in its orbit, as I see a star, but I care not to measure its distance or weight. The bream, appreciated, floats in the pond as the centre of the system, another image of God. Its life no man can explain more than he can his own. I want you to perceive the mystery of the bream. I have a contemporary in Walden. It has fins where I have legs and arms. I have a friend among the fishes, at least a new acquaintance. Its character will interest me, I trust, not its clothes and anatomy. I do not want it to eat. Acquaintance with it is to make my life more rich and eventful. It is as if a poet or an anchorite had moved into the town, whom I can see from time to time and think of yet oftener. Perhaps there are a thousand of these striped bream which no one had thought of in that pond, — not their mere impressions in stone, but in the full tide of the bream life.

2   Though science may sometimes compare herself to a child picking up pebbles on the seashore, that is a rare mood with her; ordinarily her practical belief is that it is only a few pebbles which are *not* known, weighed and measured. A new species of fish signifies hardly more than a new name. See what is contributed in the scientific reports. One counts the fin-rays, another measures the intestines, a third daguerreotypes a scale, etc., etc.; otherwise there's nothing to be said. As if all but this were done, and these were very rich and generous contributions to science. Her votaries may be seen wandering along the shore of the ocean of truth, with their backs to that ocean, ready to seize on the shells which are cast up. You would say that the scientific bodies were terribly put to it for objects and subjects. A dead specimen of an animal, if it is only preserved in alcohol, is just as good for science as a living one preserved in its native element.

3   What is the amount of my discovery to me? It is not that I have got one in a bottle, that it has got a name in a book, but that I have a little fishy friend in the pond. How was it when the youth first discovered fishes? Was it the number of their fin-rays or their arrangement, or the place of the fish in some system that made the boy dream of them? Is it these things that interest mankind in the fish, the inhabitant of the water? No, but a faint recognition of a living contemporary, a provoking mystery. One boy thinks of fishes and goes a-fishing from the same motive that his brother searches the poets for rare lines. It is the poetry of fishes which is their chief use; their flesh is their lowest use. The beauty of the fish, that is what it is best worth the while to measure. Its place in our systems is of comparatively little importance. Generally the boy loses some of his perception and his interest in the fish; he degenerates into a fisherman or an ichthyologist.

_____ CONSIDERATIONS _____

1. Thoreau's excitement in describing the bream was generated by his discovery of a species living unnoticed in Walden Pond. But why, according to him, can he do no more than say that it exists? Why is that statement sufficient?

2. What kind of truth — scientific, philosophic, economic, aesthetic — can you find in Thoreau's statement that the bream "is the center of the system, another image of God"? Look carefully at his sentence in Paragraph 1. Why pay particular attention to the word "appreciated," which is set off by commas?

3. What does Thoreau's excitement over discovering the bream have in common with Wendell Berry's "A Native Hill" (pages 63–74)?

4. Why, in his closing statement, does Thoreau consider both the fisherman and the ichthyologist deplorable?

5. "Mystery" is an important word in Thoreau's essay. What is there about the way scientists work that limits their appreciation of the mystery of creation? Is it the same sort of "mystery" that figures so importantly in John Berger's "Her Secrets" (pages 57–62)?

James Thurber (1894–1961) was born in Columbus, Ohio, the scene of many of his funniest stories. He graduated from Ohio State University, and after a period as a newspaper man in Paris, began to work for The New Yorker. *For years his comic writing and his cartoons — drawings of sausage-shaped dogs and of men and women forever at battle — were fixtures of that magazine. His collection of essays, short stories, and cartoons include* The Owl in the Attic and Other Perplexities *(1931),* The Seal in the Bedroom and Other Predicaments *(1932),* My Life and Hard Times *(1933),* Men, Women, and Dogs *(1943), and* Alarms and Diversions *(1957). He also wrote an account of life on* The New Yorker *staff,* The Years with Ross *(1959).* Selected Letters of James Thurber *appeared in 1981.*

An elegant stylist, Thurber was always fussy about language. "Which" is an example not only of his fascination with language — which became obsessive at times — but also of his humor.

76

JAMES THURBER
Which

1   The relative pronoun "which" can cause more trouble than any other word, if recklessly used. Foolhardy persons sometimes get lost in which-clauses and are never heard of again. My distinguished contemporary, Fowler, cites several tragic cases, of which the following is one: "It was rumoured that Beaconsfield intended opening the Conference with a speech in French, his pronounciation of which language leaving everything to be desired . . ." That's as much as Mr. Fowler quotes

because, at his age, he was afraid to go any farther. The young man who originally got into that sentence was never found. His fate, however, was not as terrible as that of another adventurer who became involved in a remarkable which-mire. Fowler has followed his devious course as far as he safely could on foot: "Surely what applies to games should also apply to racing, the leaders of which being the very people from whom an example might well be looked for . . ." Not even Henry James could have successfully emerged from a sentence with "which," "whom," and "being" in it. The safest way to avoid such things is to follow in the path of the American author, Ernest Hemingway. In his youth he was trapped in a which-clause one time and barely escaped with his mind. He was going along on solid ground until he got into this: "It was the one thing of which, being very much afraid — for whom has not been warned to fear such things — he . . ." Being a young and powerfully built man, Hemingway was able to fight his way back to where he had started, and begin again. This time he skirted the treacherous morass in this way: "He was afraid of one thing. This was the one thing. He had been warned to fear such things. Everybody has been warned to fear such things." Today Hemingway is alive and well, and many happy writers are following along the trail he blazed.

What most people don't realize is that one "which" leads to another. 2
Trying to cross a paragraph by leaping from "which" to "which" is like Eliza crossing the ice. The danger is in missing a "which" and falling in. A case in point is this: "He went up to a pew which was in the gallery, which brought him under a colored window which he loved and always quieted his spirit." The writer, worn out, missed the last "which" — the one that should come just before "always" in that sentence. But supposing he had got it in! We would have: "He went up to a pew which was in the gallery, which brought him under a colored window which he loved and which always quieted his spirit." Your inveterate whicher in this way gives the effect of tweeting like a bird or walking with a crutch, and is not welcome in the best company.

It is well to remember that one "which" leads to two and that two 3
"whiches" multiply like rabbits. You should never start out with the idea that you can get by with one "which." Suddenly they are all around you. Take a sentence like this: "It imposes a problem which we either solve, or perish." On a hot night, or after a hard day's work, a man often lets himself get by with a monstrosity like that, but suppose he dictates that sentence bright and early in the morning. It comes to him typed out by his stenographer and he instantly senses that something is the matter with it. He tries to reconstruct the sentence, still clinging to the

"which," and gets something like this: "It imposes a problem which we either solve, or which, failing to solve, we must perish on account of." He goes to the water-cooler, gets a drink, sharpens his pencil, and grimly tries again. "It imposes a problem which we either solve or which we don't solve . . ." He begins once more: "It imposes a problem which we either solve, or which we do not solve, and from which . . ." The more times he does it the more "whiches" he gets. The way out is simple: "We must either solve this problem, or perish." Never monkey with "which." Nothing except getting tangled up in a typewriter ribbon is worse.

_____ CONSIDERATIONS _____

1. James Thurber concentrates on one word from an important class of function words. These relative pronouns often complicate life for the writer wishing to write clear sentences more complex than "I see Spot. Spot is a dog. Spot sees me." What other words belong to this class? Do you find any of them tripping you up in your sentences?

2. A grammar lesson may seem a peculiar place to find humor, but humor is Thurber's habit, whatever his subject. How does he make his treatment of the relative pronoun "which" entertaining?

3. Compare Fowler's book with an American version such as Wilson Follett's *Modern American Usage*. This could lead you into a study of the concept of usage as the ultimate authority in establishing conventions of grammar, spelling, definition, and punctuation.

4. "One 'which' leads to another" is a play on the old saying, "One drink leads to another." Consider how changing one word can revive a thought that George Orwell would call a hackneyed phrase. See how it is done by substituting a key word in several familiar sayings.

5. The two writers Thurber mentions, Henry James and Ernest Hemingway, are not idly chosen. Why not?

John Updike (b. 1932) grew up in Pennsylvania and went to Harvard, where he edited the humor magazine, the Lampoon. *On a fellowship year at Oxford, Updike sold a poem to* The New Yorker *and began his long relationship with that magazine. First he worked on the staff of* The New Yorker, *contributing to "The Talk of the Town." When he quit to free-lance, he continued to write stories, poems, reviews, and articles for the magazine.* The Poorhouse Fair *(1959), his first novel, appeared in the same year as his first collection of stories,* The Same Door, *from which we take "Ace in the Hole." This story appears to be the seed of his second novel,* Rabbit, Run *(1960) — also about an ex-basketball star with a deteriorating marriage.*

Updike has published stories, novels, poems, and three miscellaneous collections, Assorted Prose *(1965),* Picked-up Pieces *(1975), and* Hugging the Shore *(1983). Among his best-known novels are* The Centaur *(1963) and* The Witches of Eastwick *(1984), which was made into a film in 1987. In "Ace in the Hole," Updike writes with his usual precision and finish, and with a final image that illuminates everything that has gone before it, gilding the dross of the present with a recollected gold.*

77

JOHN UPDIKE
Ace in the Hole

1   No sooner did his car touch the boulevard heading home than Ace flicked on the radio. He needed the radio, especially today. In the seconds before the tubes warmed up, he said aloud, doing it just to hear a human voice, "Jesus. She'll pop her lid." His voice, though familiar, irked him; it sounded thin and scratchy, as if the bones in his head were picking up static. In a deeper register Ace added, "She'll murder me." Then the radio came on, warm and strong, so he stopped worrying. The Five Kings were doing "Blueberry Hill"; to hear them made Ace feel so sure inside that from the pack pinched between the car roof and sun shield he plucked a cigarette, hung it on his lower lip, snapped a match across the rusty place on the dash, held the flame in the instinctive spot near the tip of his nose, dragged, and blew out the match, all in time to the music. He rolled down the window and snapped the match so it spun end-over-end into the gutter. "Two points," he said, and cocked the cigarette toward the roof of the car, sucked powerfully, and exhaled two plumes through his nostrils. He was beginning to feel like himself, Ace Anderson, for the first time that whole day, a bad day. He beat time on the accelerator. The car jerked crazily. "On Blueberry Hill," he sang, "my heart stood still. The wind in the wil-low tree" — he braked for a red light — "played love's suh-*weet* melodee —"

2   "Go, Dad, bust your lungs!" a kid's voice blared. The kid was riding in a '52 Pontiac that had pulled up beside Ace at the light. The profile of the driver, another kid, was dark over his shoulder.

3   Ace looked over at him and smiled slowly, just letting one side of his mouth lift a little. "Shove it," he said, good-naturedly, across the

428

little gap of years that separated them. He knew how they felt, young and mean and shy.

But the kid, who looked Greek, lifted his thick upper lip and spat 4 out the window. The spit gleamed on the asphalt like a half-dollar.

"Now isn't that pretty?" Ace said, keeping one eye on the light. 5 "You miserable wop. You are *mis*erable." While the kid was trying to think of some smart comeback, the light changed. Ace dug out so hard he smelled burned rubber. In his rear-view mirror he saw the Pontiac lurch forward a few yards, then stop dead, right in the middle of the intersection.

The idea of them stalling their fat tin Pontiac kept him in a good 6 humor all the way home. He decided to stop at his mother's place and pick up the baby, instead of waiting for Evey to do it. His mother must have seen him drive up. She came out on the porch holding a plastic spoon and smelling of cake.

"You're out early," she told him. 7

"Friedman fired me," Ace told her. 8

"Good for you," his mother said. "I always said he never treated 9 you right." She brought a cigarette out of her apron pocket and tucked it deep into one corner of her mouth, the way she did when something pleased her.

Ace lighted it for her. "Friedman was O.K. personally," he said. "He 10 just wanted too much for his money. I didn't mind working Saturdays, but until eleven, twelve Friday nights was too much. Everybody has a right to some leisure."

"Well, I don't dare think what Evey will say, but I, for one, thank 11 dear God you had the brains to get out of it. I always said that job had no future to it — no future of any kind, Freddy."

"I guess," Ace admitted. "But I wanted to keep at it, for the family's 12 sake."

"Now, I know I shouldn't be saying this, but any time Evey — this 13 is just between us — any time Evey thinks she can do better, there's room for you *and* Bonnie right in your father's house." She pinched her lips together. He could almost hear the old lady think, *There, I've said it.*

"Look, Mom, Evey tries awfully hard, and anyway you know she 14 can't work that way. Not that *that* — I mean, she's a realist, too . . ." He let the rest of the thought fade as he watched a kid across the street dribbling a basketball around a telephone pole that had a backboard and net nailed on it.

"Evey's a wonderful girl of her own kind. But I've always said, and 15 your father agrees, Roman Catholics ought to marry among themselves.

Now I know I've said it before, but when they get out in the greater world —"

16   "*No*, Mom."

17   She frowned, smoothed herself, and said, "Your name was in the paper today."

18   Ace chose to let that go by. He kept watching the kid with the basketball. It was funny how, though the whole point was to get the ball up into the air, kids grabbed it by the sides and squeezed. Kids just didn't think.

19   "Did you hear?" his mother asked.

20   "Sure, but so what?" Ace said. His mother's lower lip was coming at him, so he changed the subject. "I guess I'll take Bonnie."

21   His mother went into the house and brought back his daughter, wrapped in a blue blanket. The baby looked dopey. "She fussed all day," his mother complained. "I said to your father, 'Bonnie is a dear little girl, but without a doubt she's her mother's daughter.' You were the best-natured boy."

22   "Well I *had* everything," Ace said with an impatience that made his mother blink. He nicely dropped his cigarette into a brown flower-pot on the edge of the porch and took his daughter into his arms. She was getting heavier, solid. When he reached the end of the cement walk, his mother was still on the porch, waving to him. He was so close he could see the fat around her elbow jiggle, and he only lived a half block up the street, yet here she was, waving to him as if he was going to Japan.

23   At the door of his car, it seemed stupid to him to drive the measly half block home. His old coach, Bob Behn, used to say never to ride where you could walk. Cars were the death of legs. Ace left the ignition keys in his pocket and ran along the pavement with Bonnie laughing and bouncing at his chest. He slammed the door of his landlady's house open and shut, pounded up the two flights of stairs, and was panting so hard when he reached the door of his apartment that it took him a couple of seconds to fit the key into the lock.

24   The run must have tuned Bonnie up. As soon as he lowered her into the crib, she began to shout and wave her arms. He didn't want to play with her. He tossed some blocks and a rattle into the crib and walked into the bathroom, where he turned on the hot water and began to comb his hair. Holding the comb under the faucet before every stroke, he combed his hair forward. It was so long, one strand curled under his nose and touched his lips. He whipped the whole mass back with a single pull. He tucked in the tufts around his ears, and ran the comb straight back on both sides of his head. With his fingers he felt for the little ridge at the back where the two sides met. It was there, as it should have

been. Finally, he mussed the hair in front enough for one little lock to droop over his forehead, like Alan Ladd. It made the temple seem lower than it was. Every day, his hairline looked higher. He had observed all around him how blond men went bald first. He remembered reading somewhere, though, that baldness shows virility.

On his way to the kitchen he flipped the left-hand knob of the   25
television. Bonnie was always quieter with the set on. Ace didn't see how she could understand much of it, but it seemed to mean something to her. He found a can of beer in the refrigerator behind some brownish lettuce and those hot dogs Evey never got around to cooking. She'd be home any time. The clock said 5:12. She'd pop her lid.

Ace didn't see what he could do but try and reason with her. "Evey,"   26
he'd say, "you ought to thank God I got out of it. It had no future to it at all." He hoped she wouldn't get too mad, because when she was mad he wondered if he should have married her, and doubting that made him feel crowded. It was bad enough, his mother always crowding him. He punched the two triangles in the top of the beer can, the little triangle first, and then the big one, the one he drank from. He hoped Evey wouldn't say anything that couldn't be forgotten. What women didn't seem to realize was that there were things you knew but shouldn't say.

He felt sorry he had called the kid in the car a wop.   27

Ace balanced the beer on a corner where two rails of the crib met   28
and looked under the chairs for the morning paper. He had trouble find-ing his name, because it was at the bottom of a column on an inside sports page, in a small article about the county basketball statistics:

> "Dusty" Tremwick, Grosvenor Park's sure-fingered center, cop-ped the individual scoring honors with a season's grand (and we do mean grand) total of 376 points. This is within eighteen points of the all-time record of 394 racked up in the 1949–1950 season by Olinger High's Fred Anderson.

Ace angrily sailed the paper into an armchair. Now it was Fred   29
Anderson; it used to be Ace. He hated being called Fred, especially in print, but then the sportswriters were all office boys anyway, Behn used to say.

"Do not just ask for shoe polish," a man on television said, "but   30
ask for *Emu Shoe Gloss,* the *only* polish that absolutely *guarantees* to make your shoes look shinier than new." Ace turned the sound off, so that the man moved his mouth like a fish blowing bubbles. Right away, Bonnie howled, so Ace turned it up loud enough to drown her out and went into the kitchen, without knowing what he wanted there. He wasn't hungry; his stomach was tight. It used to be like that when he

walked to the gymnasium alone in the dark before a game and could see the people from town, kids and parents, crowding in at the lighted doors. But once he was inside, the locker room would be bright and hot, and the other guys would be there, laughing it up and towel-slapping, and the tight feeling would leave. Now there were whole days when it didn't leave.

31   A key scratched at the door lock. Ace decided to stay in the kitchen. Let *her* find *him*. Her heels clicked on the floor for a step or two; then the television set went off. Bonnie began to cry. "Shut up, honey," Evey said. There was a silence.

32   "I'm home," Ace called.

33   "No kidding. I thought Bonnie got the beer by herself."

34   Ace laughed. She was in a sarcastic mood, thinking she was Lauren Bacall. That was all right, just so she kept funny. Still smiling, Ace eased into the living room and got hit with, "What are *you* smirking about? Another question: What's the idea running up the street with Bonnie like she was a football?"

35   "You saw that?"

36   "Your mother told me."

37   "You saw her?"

38   "Of course I saw her. I dropped by to pick up Bonnie. What the hell do you think? — I read her tiny mind?"

39   "Take it easy," Ace said, wondering if Mom had told her about Friedman.

40   "Take it easy? Don't coach *me*. Another question: Why's the car out in front of her place? You give the car to her?"

41   "Look, I parked it there to pick up Bonnie, and I thought I'd leave it there."

42   "Why?"

43   "Whaddeya mean, why? I just did. I just thought I'd walk. It's not that far, you know."

44   "No, I don't know. If you'd been on your feet all day long a block would look like one hell of a long way."

45   "Okay. I'm sorry."

46   She hung up her coat and stepped out of her shoes and walked around the room picking up things. She stuck the newspaper in the wastebasket.

47   Ace said, "My name was in the paper today."

48   "They spell it right?" She shoved the paper deep into the basket with her foot. There was no doubt; she knew about Friedman.

"They called me Fred." 49

"Isn't that your name? What *is* your name anyway? Hero J. Great?" 50

There wasn't any answer, so Ace didn't try any. He sat down on 51
the sofa, lighted a cigarette, and waited.

Evey picked up Bonnie. "Poor thing stinks. What does your mother 52
do, scrub out the toilet with her?"

"Can't you take it easy? I know you're tired." 53

"You should. I'm always tired." 54

Evey and Bonnie went into the bathroom; when they came out, 55
Bonnie was clean and Evey was calm. Evey sat down in an easy chair
beside Ace and rested her stocking feet on his knees. "Hit me," she said,
twiddling her fingers for the cigarette.

The baby crawled up to her chair and tried to stand, to see what 56
he gave her. Leaning over close to Bonnie's nose, Evey grinned, smoke
leaking through her teeth, and said, "Only for grownups, honey."

"Eve," Ace began, "there was no future in that job. Working all 57
Saturday, and then Friday nights on top of it."

"I know. Your mother told *me* all that, too. All I want from you 58
is what happened."

She was going to take it like a sport, then. He tried to remember 59
how it *did* happen. "It wasn't my fault," he said. "Friedman told me to
back this '51 Chevvy into the line that faces Church Street. He just
bought it from an old guy this morning who said it only had thirteen
thousand on it. So in I jump and start her up. There was a knock in
the engine like a machine gun. I almost told Friedman he'd bought a
squirrel, but you know I cut that smart stuff out ever since Palotta laid
me off."

"You told me that story. What happens in this one?" 60

"Look, Eve. I *am* telling ya. Do you want me to go out to a movie 61
or something?"

"Suit yourself." 62

"So I jump in the Chevvy and snap it back in line, and there was 63
a kind of scrape and thump. I get out and look and Friedman's running
over, his arms going like *this*" — Ace whirled his own arms and
laughed — "and here was the whole back fender of a '49 Merc mashed
in. Just looked like somebody took a planer and shaved off the bulge,
you know, there at the back." He tried to show her with his hands. "The
Chevvy, though, didn't have a dent. It even gained some paint. But *Friedman*, to *hear* him — Boy, they can rave when their pocketbook's hit.
He said" — Ace laughed again — "never mind."

Evey said, "You're proud of yourself." 64

65   "No, listen. I'm not happy about it. But there wasn't a thing I could *do*. It wasn't my driving at all. I looked over on the other side, and there was just two or three inches between the Chevvy and a Buick. *Nobody* could have gotten into that hole. Even if it had hair on it." He thought this was pretty good.

66   She didn't. "You could have looked."

67   "There just wasn't the *space*. Friedman said stick it in; I stuck it in."

68   "But you could have looked and moved the other cars to make more room."

69   "I guess that would have been the smart thing."

70   "I guess, too. Now what?"

71   "What do you mean?"

72   "I mean now what? Are you going to give up? Go back to the Army? Your mother? Be a basketball pro? What?"

73   "You know I'm not tall enough. Anybody under six-six they don't want."

74   "Is that so? Six-six? Well, please listen to this, Mr. Six-Foot-Five-and-a-Half: I'm fed up. I'm ready as Christ to let you run." She stabbed her cigarette into an ashtray on the arm of the chair so hard the ashtray jumped to the floor. Evey flushed and shut up.

75   What Ace hated most in their arguments was these silences after Evey had said something so ugly she wanted to take it back. "Better ask the priest first," he murmured.

76   She sat right up. "If there's one thing I don't want to hear about from you it's priests. You let the priests to me. You don't know a damn thing about it. Not a damn thing."

77   "Hey, look at Bonnie," he said, trying to make a fresh start with his tone.

78   Evey didn't hear him. "If you think," she went on, "if for one rotten moment you think, Mr. Fred, that the be-all and end-all of my life is you and your hot-shot stunts —"

79   "Look, Mother," Ace pleaded, pointing at Bonnie. The baby had picked up the ashtray and put it on her head for a hat and was waiting for praise.

80   Evey glanced down sharply at the child. "Cute," she said. "Cute as her daddy."

81   The ashtray slid from Bonnie's head and she patted where it had been and looked around puzzled.

82   "Yeah, but watch," Ace said. "Watch her hands. They're really terrific hands."

83   "You're nuts," Evey said.

"No, honest. Bonnie's great. She's a natural. Get the rattle for her. 84
Never mind, I'll get it." In two steps, Ace was at Bonnie's crib, picking
the rattle out of the mess of blocks and plastic rings and beanbags. He
extended the rattle toward his daughter, shaking it delicately. Made wary
by this burst of attention, Bonnie reached with both hands; like two
separate animals they approached from opposite sides and touched the
smooth rattle simultaneously. A smile bubbled up on her face. Ace
tugged weakly. She held on, and then tugged back. "She's a natural," Ace
said, "and it won't do her any good because she's a girl. Baby, we got
to have a boy."

"I'm not your baby," Evey said, closing her eyes. 85

Saying "Baby" over and over again, Ace backed up to the radio and, 86
without turning around, switched on the volume knob. In the moment
before the tubes warmed up, Evey had time to say, "Wise up, Freddy.
What shall we do?"

The radio came in on something slow: dinner music. Ace picked 87
Bonnie up and set her in the crib. "Shall we dance?" he asked his wife,
bowing.

"I want to talk." 88

"Baby. It's the cocktail hour." 89

"This is getting us no place," she said, rising from her chair, though. 90

"Fred Junior. I can see him now," he said, seeing nothing. 91

"We will have no Juniors." 92

In her crib, Bonnie whimpered at the sight of her mother being 93
seized. Ace fitted his hand into the natural place on Evey's back and
she shuffled stiffly into his lead. When, with a sudden injection of sax-
ophones, the tempo quickened, he spun her out carefully, keeping the
beat with his shoulders. Her hair brushed his lips as she minced in, then
swung away, to the end of his arm; he could feel her toes dig into the
carpet. He flipped his own hair back from his eyes. The music ate
through his skin and mixed with the nerves and small veins; he seemed
to be great again, and all the other kids were around them, in a ring,
clapping time.

_____ CONSIDERATIONS _____

1. Updike often uses minute physical observations. Do you find any of
these in "Ace in the Hole"? How do they contribute to the story's effect?

2. How old is Ace? What information in the story prompts you to make
a guess? What kind of age do you mean — chronological, mental, emotional?
How important is his age to the story?

3. What are Ace's *real* interests: wife, child, job, future career? How does Updike help you discriminate between Ace's casual and lasting interests?

4. Which is most important to Ace — the past, the present, or the future? Cite evidence. Of what thematic significance is this question?

5. If you were a marriage counselor, would you have any advice for this young couple? Would you say that their marriage is in trouble? What are the chances that they would even consider consulting a marriage counselor? For your answers use the story itself.

6. What importance has play had in Ace's life? What particulars in the story reveal his attitude toward play, sport, games, fun, diversions, recreation?

7. Compare the reactions of Ace's mother and his wife to losing the job. How do their different attitudes toward this event reveal important things about Ace's life at this time?

Gore Vidal (b. 1925) entered the army after graduating from Phillips Exeter Academy and never attended college. He published his first novel the year he turned twenty-one. Since then, he has run for Congress and lived in Europe. Vidal's writing includes plays, essays, and chiefly novels, including Julian *(1964),* Myra Breckinridge *(1968),* Burr *(1973),* Kalki *(1979), and* Lincoln *(1984).*

78

GORE VIDAL
Drugs

It is possible to stop most drug addiction in the United States   1
within a very short time. Simply make all drugs available and sell them at cost. Label each drug with a precise description of what effect — good and bad — the drug will have on the taker. This will require heroic honesty. Don't say that marijuana is addictive or dangerous when it is neither, as millions of people know   unlike "speed," which kills most unpleasantly, or heroin, which is addictive and difficult to kick.

For the record, I have tried — once — almost every drug and liked   2
none, disproving the popular Fu Manchu theory that a single whiff of opium will enslave the mind. Nevertheless many drugs are bad for certain people to take and they should be told why in a sensible way.

Along with exhortation and warning, it might be good for our   3
citizens to recall (or learn for the first time) that the United States was the creation of men who believed that each man has the right to do what he wants with his own life as long as he does not interfere with his neighbor's pursuit of happiness (that his neighbor's idea of happiness is persecuting others does confuse matters a bit).

4   This is a startling notion to the current generation of Americans. They reflect a system of public education which has made the Bill of Rights, literally, unacceptable to a majority of high school graduates (see the annual Purdue reports) who now form the "silent majority" — a phrase which that underestimated wit Richard Nixon took from Homer who used it to describe the dead.

5   Now one can hear the warning rumble begin: if everyone is allowed to take drugs everyone will and the GNP will decrease, the Commies will stop us from making everyone free, and we shall end up a race of Zombies, passively murmuring "groovie" to one another. Alarming thought. Yet it seems most unlikely that any reasonably sane person will become a drug addict if he knows in advance what addiction is going to be like.

6   Is everyone reasonably sane? No. Some people will always become drug addicts just as some people will always become alcoholics, and it is just too bad. Every man, however, has the power (and should have the legal right) to kill himself if he chooses. But since most men don't, they won't be mainliners either. Nevertheless, forbidding people things they like or think they might enjoy only makes them want those things all the more. This psychological insight is, for some mysterious reason, perennially denied our governors.

7   It is a lucky thing for the American moralist that our country has always existed in a kind of time-vacuum: we have no public memory of anything that happened before last Tuesday. No one in Washington today recalls what happened during the years alcohol was forbidden to the people by a Congress that thought it had a divine mission to stamp out Demon Rum — launching, in the process, the greatest crime wave in the country's history, causing thousands of deaths from bad alcohol, and creating a general (and persisting) contempt among the citizenry for the laws of the United States.

8   The same thing is happening today. But the government has learned nothing from past attempts at prohibition, not to mention repression.

9   Last year when the supply of Mexican marijuana was slightly curtailed by the Feds, the pushers got the kids hooked on heroin and deaths increased dramatically, particularly in New York. Whose fault? Evil men like the Mafiosi? Permissive Dr. Spock? Wild-eyed Dr. Leary? No.

10   The Government of the United States was responsible for those deaths. The bureaucratic machine has a vested interest in playing cops and robbers. Both the Bureau of Narcotics and the Mafia want strong

laws against the sale and use of drugs because if drugs are sold at cost there would be no money in it for anyone.

If there was no money in it for the Mafia, there would be no friendly   11
playground pushers, and addicts would not commit crimes to pay for the next fix. Finally, if there was no money in it, the Bureau of Narcotics would wither away, something they are not about to do without a struggle.

Will anything sensible be done? Of course not. The American peo-   12
ple are as devoted to the idea of sin and its punishment as they are to making money — and fighting drugs is nearly as big a business as pushing them. Since the combination of sin and money is irresistible (particularly to the professional politician), the situation will only grow worse.

—— CONSIDERATIONS ——————————————————

1. One mark of the experienced arguer is the ability to anticipate and thus neutralize his opponent's rebuttal. Where does Vidal do this? How effective is his attempt?

2. Vidal's argument (Paragraphs 10, 11, and 12) that "the bureaucratic machine has a vested interest in playing cops and robbers" rests on his implication that lawmen are at least as interested in preserving their jobs as they are in preserving law and order. Does he present any evidence to support this argument? What kind of evidence could he offer? How could you support a counterargument?

3. Vidal contends that every man "should have the legal right to kill himself." How far would he (or you) extend that "right"? To all varieties of suicide, for instance?

4. Refresh your memory of the Bill of Rights — where do you find it? — and explain why Vidal says it has become "unacceptable to a majority of high school graduates."

5. Is the slang term "groovie" — usually spelled "groovy" — still current? Linguists often study slang because it changes faster than standard language. For the same reason, geneticists study fruit flies because the quick turnover of generations allows them to investigate principles of genetics within a brief period of time. In what way(s) do changes in slang parallel changes in English in general?

6. Given Vidal's belief in freedom of the individual, how do you think he would approach the question of gun control?

7. Write a rebuttal to Vidal's argument, using current statistics and trends in drug abuse.

*Alice Walker (b. 1944) grew up in Georgia and went to Sarah
Lawrence College in New York City. She first published as a
poet, with* Once *and* Revolutionary Petunias, *and has added
collections of short stories, a biography of Langston Hughes,
and novels — most notably* The Color Purple.

She collected her essays as In Search of Our Mothers'
Gardens, *from which we take this article originally published
in 1970. Elsewhere in* A Writer's Reader *you will find the white
Southern writers, William Faulkner and Flannery O'Connor,
whom Alice Walker mentions in this essay.*

79

ALICE WALKER

The Black Writer and the Southern Experience

1   My mother tells of an incident that happened to her in the thirties during the Depression. She and my father lived in a small Georgia
town and had half a dozen children. They were sharecroppers, and food,
especially flour, was almost impossible to obtain. To get flour, which
was distributed by the Red Cross, one had to submit vouchers signed
by a local official. On the day my mother was to go into town for flour
she received a large box of clothes from one of my aunts who was living in the North. The clothes were in good condition, though well worn,
and my mother needed a dress, so she immediately put on one of those
from the box and wore it into town. When she reached the distribution

center and presented her voucher she was confronted by a white woman who looked her up and down with marked anger and envy.

"What'd you come up here for?" the woman asked.   2

"For some flour," said my mother, presenting her voucher.   3

"Humph," said the woman, looking at her more closely and with   4
unconcealed fury. "Anybody dressed up as good as you don't need to come here *begging* for food."

"I ain't begging," said my mother; "the government is giving away   5
flour to those that need it, and I need it. I wouldn't be here if I didn't. And these clothes I'm wearing was given to me." But the woman had already turned to the next person in line, saying over her shoulder to the white man who was behind the counter with her, "The *gall* of niggers coming in here dressed better than me!" This thought seemed to make her angrier still, and my mother, pulling three of her small children behind her and crying from humiliation, walked sadly back into the street.

"What did you and Daddy do for flour that winter?" I asked my   6
mother.

"Well," she said, "Aunt Mandy Aikens lived down the road from   7
us and she got plenty of flour. We had a good stand of corn so we had plenty of meal. Aunt Mandy would swap me a bucket of flour for a bucket of meal. We got by all right."

Then she added thoughtfully, "And that old woman that turned   8
me off so short got down so bad in the end that she was walking on *two* sticks." And I knew she was thinking, though she never said it: Here I am today, my eight children healthy and grown and three of them in college and me with hardly a sick day for years. Ain't Jesus wonderful?

In this small story is revealed the condition and strength of a peo-   9
ple. Outcasts to be used and humiliated by the larger society, the Southern black sharecropper and poor farmer clung to his own kind and to a religion that had been given to pacify him as a slave but which he soon transformed into an antidote against bitterness. Depending on one another, because they had nothing and no one else, the sharecroppers often managed to come through "all right." And when I listen to my mother tell and retell this story I find that the white woman's vindictiveness is less important than Aunt Mandy's resourceful generosity or my mother's ready stand of corn. For their lives were not about that pitiful example of Southern womanhood, but about themselves.

What the black Southern writer inherits as a natural right is a sense 10
of *community*. Something simple but surprisingly hard, especially these days, to come by. My mother, who is a walking history of our com-

munity, tells me that when each of her children was born the midwife accepted as payment such home-grown or homemade items as a pig, a quilt, jars of canned fruits and vegetables. But there was never any question that the midwife would come when she was needed, whatever the eventual payment for her services. I consider this each time I hear of a hospital that refuses to admit a woman in labor unless she can hand over a substantial sum of money, cash.

11   Nor am I nostalgic, as a French philosopher once wrote, for lost poverty. I am nostalgic for the solidarity and sharing a modest existence can sometimes bring. We knew, I suppose, that we were poor. Somebody knew; perhaps the landowner who grudgingly paid my father three hundred dollars a year for twelve months' labor. But we never considered ourselves to be poor, unless, of course, we were deliberately humiliated. And because we never believed we were poor, and therefore worthless, we could depend on one another without shame. And always there were the Burial Societies, the Sick-and-Shut-in Societies, that sprang up out of spontaneous need. And no one seemed terribly upset that black sharecroppers were ignored by white insurance companies. It went without saying, in my mother's day, that birth and death required assistance from the community, and that the magnitude of these events was lost on outsiders.

12   As a college student I came to reject the Christianity of my parents, and it took me years to realize that though they had been force-fed a white man's palliative, in the form of religion, they had made it into something at once simple and noble. True, even today, they can never successfully picture a God who is not white, and that is a major cruelty, but their lives testify to a greater comprehension of the teachings of Jesus than the lives of people who sincerely believe a God *must* have a color and that there can be such a phenomenon as a "white" church.

13   The richness of the black writer's experience in the South can be remarkable, though some people might not think so. Once, while in college, I told a white middle-aged Northerner that I hoped to be a poet. In the nicest possible language, which still made me as mad as I've ever been, he suggested that a "farmer's daughter" might not be the stuff of which poets are made. On one level, of course, he had a point. A shack with only a dozen or so books is an unlikely place to discover a young Keats. But it is narrow thinking, indeed, to believe that a Keats is the only kind of poet one would want to grow up to be. One wants to write poetry that is understood by one's people, not by the Queen of England. Of course, should she be able to profit by it too, so much the better,

but since that is not likely, catering to her tastes would be a waste of time.

For the black Southern writer, coming straight out of the country, 14
as Wright did — Natchez and Jackson are still not as citified as they like to think they are — there is the world of comparisons; between town and country, between the ugly crowding and griminess of the cities and the spacious cleanliness (which actually seems impossible to dirty) of the country. A country person finds the city confining, like a too tight dress. And always, in one's memory, there remain all the rituals of one's growing up: the warmth and vividness of Sunday worship (never mind that you never quite believed) in a little church hidden from the road, and houses set so far back into the woods that at night it is impossible for strangers to find them. The daily dramas that evolve in such a private world are pure gold. But this view of a strictly private and hidden existence, with its triumphs, failures, grotesqueries, is not nearly as valuable to the socially conscious black Southern writer as his double vision is. For not only is he in a position to see his own world, and its close community ("Homecomings" on First Sundays, barbecues to raise money to send to Africa — one of the smaller ironies — the simplicity and eerie calm of a black funeral, where the beloved one is buried way in the middle of a wood with nothing to mark the spot but perhaps a wooden cross already coming apart), but also he is capable of knowing, with remarkably silent accuracy, the people who make up the larger world that surrounds and suppresses his own.

It is a credit to a writer like Ernest J. Gaines, a black writer who 15
writes mainly about the people he grew up with in rural Louisiana, that he can write about whites and blacks exactly as he sees them and *knows* them, instead of writing of one group as a vast malignant lump and of the others as a conglomerate of perfect virtues.

In large measure, black Southern writers owe their clarity of vi- 16
sion to parents who refused to diminish themselves as human beings by succumbing to racism. Our parents seemed to know that an extreme negative emotion held against other human beings for reasons they do not control can be blinding. Blindness about other human beings, especially for a writer, is equivalent to death. Because of this blindness, which is, above all, racial, the works of many Southern writers have died. Much that we read today is fast expiring.

My own slight attachment to William Faulkner was rudely bro- 17
ken by realizing, after reading statements he made in *Faulkner in the University*, that he believed whites superior morally to blacks; that

whites had a duty (which at their convenience they would assume) to "bring blacks along" politically, since blacks, in Faulkner's opinion, were "not ready" yet to function properly in a democratic society. He also thought that a black man's intelligence is directly related to the amount of white blood he has.

18   For the black person coming of age in the sixties, where Martin Luther King stands against the murderers of Goodman, Chaney, and Schwerner, there appears no basis for such assumptions. Nor was there any in Garvey's day, or in Du Bois's or in Douglass's or in Nat Turner's. Nor at any other period in our history, from the very founding of the country; for it was hardly incumbent upon slaves to be slaves and saints too. Unlike Tolstoy, Faulkner was not prepared to struggle to change the structure of the society he was born in. One might concede that in his fiction he did seek to examine the reasons for its decay, but unfortunately, as I have learned while trying to teach Faulkner to black students, it is not possible, from so short a range, to separate the man from his works.

19   One reads Faulkner knowing that his "colored" people had to come through "Mr. William's" back door, and one feels uneasy, and finally enraged that Faulkner did not burn the whole house down. When the provincial mind starts out *and continues* on a narrow and unprotesting course, "genius" itself must run on a track.

20   Flannery O'Connor at least had the conviction that "reality" is at best superficial and that the puzzle of humanity is less easy to solve than that of race. But Miss O'Connor was not so much of Georgia, as in it. The majority of Southern writers have been too confined by prevailing social customs to probe deeply into mysteries that the Citizens Councils insist must never be revealed.

21   Perhaps my Northern brothers will not believe me when I say there is a great deal of positive material I can draw from my "underprivileged" background. But they have never lived, as I have, at the end of a long road in a house that was faced by the edge of the world on one side and nobody for miles on the other. They have never experienced the magnificent quiet of a summer day when the heat is intense and one is so very thirsty, as one moves across the dusty cotton fields, that one learns forever that water is the essence of all life. In the cities it cannot be so clear to one that he is a creature of the earth, feeling the soil between the toes, smelling the dust thrown up by the rain, loving the earth so much that one longs to taste it and sometimes does.

22   Nor do I intend to romanticize the Southern black country life. I can recall that I hated it, generally. The hard work in the fields, the

shabby houses, the evil greedy men who worked my father to death and almost broke the courage of that strong woman, my mother. No, I am simply saying that Southern black writers, like most writers, have a heritage of love and hate, but that they also have enormous richness and beauty to draw from. And, having been placed, as Camus says, "halfway between misery and the sun," they, too, know that "though all is not well under the sun, history is not everything."

No one could wish for a more advantageous heritage than that be-   23
queathed to the black writer in the South: a compassion for the earth, a trust in humanity beyond our knowledge of evil, and an abiding love of justice. We inherit a great responsibility as well, for we must give voice to centuries not only of silent bitterness and hate but also of neighborly kindness and sustaining love.

———— **CONSIDERATIONS** ————————————————————

1. In Paragraph 15, Alice Walker pays tribute to another black novelist, Ernest J. Gaines, for refusing to make his characters into stereotypes of the white villain and the black martyr. She has trouble acknowledging the achievements of another, more famous Southern novelist, William Faulkner. Why? Carefully read Paragraph 18 for the answer.

2. Read Eudora Welty's short story, "A Worn Path" (pages 446–454), and speculate on what Walker might say about Welty's understanding of the black Southern experience.

3. Is Walker sentimental in expressing the values of her poverty-stricken childhood? Find specific statements or phrases to support your answer. Compare her tone with E. B. White's in "Once More to the Lake" (pages 461–468) or Sue Shellenbarger's in "Selling Off the Family Farm" (pages 373–378).

4. "But Miss O'Connor was not so much of Georgia, as in it," writes Walker, in expressing her reservation about Flannery O'Connor's contribution. Why does she distinguish between "of Georgia" and "in it"?

5. Walker mentions several ironies in connection with the black experience in the American South. Isolate a few of these and try explaining the nature and appeal of irony in a writer's work.

6. How does the story in Paragraphs 1 through 8 help make Walker's conclusions in Paragraph 23 credible?

7. Compare Walker's comments with those of two other important black writers: Ralph Ellison (pages 153–160) and James Baldwin (pages 51–56).

Eudora Welty (b. 1909) lives in her native Jackson, Mississippi, where she continues to write, deliberately and slowly, her perfect stories and novels. A Curtain of Green *(1941) was her first volume of collected stories. Her novels include* Losing Battles *(1970) and* The Optimist's Daughter *(1972), which won her a Pulitzer Prize. In 1980* The Collected Stories of Eudora Welty *was published, and in 1984, a reminiscence,* One Writer's Beginnings.

Here is one of her stories, followed by a useful essay she wrote about it years later, which appears in her book The Eye of the Story *(1978), and a passage of reminiscence from* One Writer's Beginnings.*

80

EUDORA WELTY
A Worn Path

1   It was December — a bright frozen day in the early morning. Far out in the country there was an old Negro woman with her head tied in a red rag, coming along a path through the pinewoods. Her name was Phoenix Jackson. She was very old and small and she walked slowly in the dark pine shadows, moving a little from side to side in her steps, with the balanced heaviness and lightness of a pendulum in a grandfather clock. She carried a thin, small cane made from an umbrella, and with this she kept tapping the frozen earth in front of her. This made a grave and persistent noise in the still air, that seemed meditative, like the chirping of a solitary little bird.

She wore a dark striped dress reaching down to her shoetops, and an equally long apron of bleached sugar sacks, with a full pocket; all neat and tidy, but every time she took a step she might have fallen over her shoelaces, which dragged from her unlaced shoes. She looked straight ahead. Her eyes were blue with age. Her skin had a pattern all its own of numberless branching wrinkles and as though a whole little tree stood in the middle of her forehead, but a golden color ran underneath, and the two knobs of her cheeks were illuminated by a yellow burning under the dark. Under the red rag her hair came down on her neck in the frailest of ringlets, still black, and with an odor like copper. 2

Now and then there was a quivering in the thicket. Old Phoenix said, "Out of my way, all you foxes, owls, beetles, jack rabbits, coons, and wild animals! . . . Keep out from under these feet, little bobwhites. . . . Keep the big wild hogs out of my path. Don't let none of those come running in my direction. I got a long way." Under her small black-freckled hand her cane, limber as a buggy whip, would switch at the brush as if to rouse up any hiding things. 3

On she went. The woods were deep and still. The sun made the pine needles almost too bright to look at, up where the wind rocked. The cones dropped as light as feathers. Down in the hollow was the mourning dove — it was not too late for him. 4

The path ran up a hill. "Seem like there is chains about my feet, time I get this far," she said, in the voice of argument old people keep to use with themselves. "Something always take a hold on this hill — pleads I should stay." 5

After she got to the top she turned and gave a full, severe look behind her where she had come. "Up through pines," she said at length. "Now down through oaks." 6

Her eyes opened their widest and she started down gently. But before she got to the bottom of the hill a bush caught her dress. 7

Her fingers were busy and intent, but her skirts were full and long, so that before she could pull them free in one place they were caught in another. It was not possible to allow the dress to tear. "I in the thorny bush," she said. "Thorns, you doing your appointed work. Never want to let folks past — no sir. Old eyes thought you was a pretty little *green* bush." 8

Finally, trembling all over, she stood free, and after a moment dared to stoop for her cane. 9

"Sun so high!" she cried, leaning back and looking, while the thick tears went over her eyes. "The time getting all gone here." 10

11   At the foot of this hill was a place where a log was laid across the creek.

12   "Now comes the trial," said Phoenix.

13   Putting her right foot out, she mounted the log and shut her eyes. Lifting her skirt, leveling her cane fiercely before her, like a festival figure in some parade, she began to march across. Then she opened her eyes and she was safe on the other side.

14   "I wasn't as old as I thought," she said.

15   But she sat down to rest. She spread her skirts on the bank around her and folded her hands over her knees. Up above her was a tree in a pearly cloud of mistletoe. She did not dare to close her eyes, and when a little boy brought her a little plate with a slice of marble-cake on it she spoke to him. "That would be acceptable," she said. But when she went to take it there was just her own hand in the air.

16   So she left that tree, and had to go through a barbed-wire fence. There she had to creep and crawl, spreading her knees and stretching her fingers like a baby trying to climb the steps. But she talked loudly to herself: she could not let her dress be torn now, so late in the day, and she could not pay for having her arm or leg sawed off if she got caught fast where she was.

17   At last she was safe through the fence and risen up out in the clearing. Big dead trees, like black men with one arm, were standing in the purple stalks of the withered cotton field. There sat a buzzard.

18   "Who you watching?"

19   In the furrow she made her way along.

20   "Glad this not the season for bulls," she said, looking sideways, "and the good Lord made his snakes to curl up and sleep in the winter. A pleasure I don't see no two-headed snake coming around that tree, where it come once. It took a while to get by him, back in the summer."

21   She passed through the old cotton and went into a field of dead corn. It whispered and shook, and was taller than her head. "Through the maze now," she said, for there was no path.

22   Then there was something tall, black, and skinny there, moving before her.

23   At first she took it for a man. It could have been a man dancing in the field. But she stood still and listened, and it did not make a sound. It was as silent as a ghost.

24   "Ghost," she said sharply, "who be you the ghost of? For I have heard of nary death close by."

25   But there was no answer, only the ragged dancing in the wind.

She shut her eyes, reached out her hand, and touched a sleeve. She   26
found a coat and inside that an emptiness, cold as ice.

"You scarecrow," she said. Her face lighted. "I ought to be shut up   27
for good," she said with laughter. "My senses is gone. I too old. I the
oldest people I ever know. Dance, old scarecrow," she said, "while I dancing with you."

She kicked her foot over the furrow, and with mouth drawn down   28
shook her head once or twice in a little strutting way. Some husks blew
down and whirled in streamers about her skirts.

Then she went on, parting her way from side to side with the cane,   29
through the whispering field. At last she came to the end, to a wagon
track, where the silver grass blew between the red ruts. The quail were
walking around like pullets, seeming all dainty and unseen.

"Walk pretty," she said. "This the easy place. This the easy going."   30

She followed the track, swaying through the quiet bare fields,   31
through the little strings of trees silver in their dead leaves, past cabins
silver from weather, with the doors and windows boarded shut, all like
old women under a spell sitting there. "I walking in their sleep," she
said, nodding her head vigorously.

In a ravine she went where a spring was silently flowing through   32
a hollow log. Old Phoenix bent and drank. "Sweetgum makes the water
sweet," she said, and drank more. "Nobody knows who made this well,
for it was here when I was born."

The track crossed a swampy part where the moss hung as white   33
as lace from every limb. "Sleep on, alligators, and blow your bubbles."
Then the track went into the road.

Deep, deep the road went down between the high green-colored   34
banks. Overhead the live-oaks met, and it was as dark as a cave.

A black dog with a lolling tongue came up out of the weeds by   35
the ditch. She was meditating, and not ready, and when he came at her
she only hit him a little with her cane. Over she went in the ditch, like
a little puff of milk-weed.

Down there, her senses drifted away. A dream visited her, and she   36
reached her hand up, but nothing reached down and gave her a pull.
So she lay there and presently went to talking. "Old woman," she said
to herself, "that black dog come up out of the weeds to stall you off,
and now there he sitting on his fine tail, smiling at you."

A white man finally came along and found her — a hunter, a young   37
man, with his dog on a chain.

"Well, Granny!" he laughed. "What are you doing there?"   38

39   "Lying on my back like a June-bug waiting to be turned over, mister," she said, reaching up her hand.

40   He lifted her up, gave her a swing in the air, and set her down, "Anything broken, Granny?"

41   "No sir, them old dead weeds is springy enough," said Phoenix, when she had got her breath. "I thank you for your trouble."

42   "Where do you live, Granny?" he asked, while the two dogs were growling at each other.

43   "Away back yonder, sir, behind that ridge. You can't even see it from here."

44   "On your way home?"

45   "No, sir, I going to town."

46   "Why that's too far! That's as far as I walk when I come out myself, and I get something for my trouble." He patted the stuffed bag he carried, and there hung down a little closed claw. It was one of the bobwhites, with its beak hooked bitterly to show it was dead. "Now you go on home, Granny!"

47   "I bound to go to town, mister," said Phoenix. "The time come around."

48   He have another laugh, filling the whole landscape. "I know you colored people! Wouldn't miss going to town to see Santa Claus!"

49   But something held Old Phoenix very still. The deep lines in her face went into a fierce and different radiation. Without warning she had seen with her own eyes a flashing nickel fall out of the man's pocket on to the ground.

50   "How old are you, Granny?" he was saying.

51   "There is no telling, mister," she said, "no telling."

52   Then she gave a little cry and clapped her hands, and said, "Git on away from here, dog! Look! Look at that dog!" She laughed as if in admiration. "He ain't scared of nobody. He a big black dog." She whispered, "Sick him!"

53   "Watch me get rid of that cur," said the man. "Sick him, Pete! Sick him!"

54   Phoenix heard the dogs fighting and heard the man running and throwing sticks. She even heard a gunshot. But she was slowly bending forward by that time, further and further forward, the lids stretched down over her eyes, as if she were doing this in her sleep. Her chin was lowered almost to her knees. The yellow palm of her hand came out from the fold of her apron. Her fingers slid down and along the ground under the piece of money with the grace and care they would have in lifting an egg from under a sitting hen. Then she slowly straightened

up, she stood erect, and the nickel was in her apron pocket. A bird flew by. Her lips moved. "God watching me the whole time. I come to stealing."

The man came back, and his own dog panted about them. "Well, 55 I scared him off that time," he said, and then he laughed and lifted his gun and pointed it at Phoenix.

She stood straight and faced him. 56

"Doesn't the gun scare you?" he said, still pointing it. 57

"No, sir, I seen plenty go off closer by, in my day, and for less what 58 I done," she said, holding utterly still.

He smiled, and shouldered the gun. "Well, Granny," he said, "you 59 must be a hundred years old, and scared of nothing. I'd give you a dime if I had any money with me. But you take my advice and stay home, and nothing will happen to you."

"I bound to go on my way, mister," said Phoenix. She inclined her 60 head in the red rag. Then they went in different directions, but she could hear the gun shooting again and again over the hill.

She walked on. The shadows hung from the oak trees to the road 61 like curtains. Then she smelled wood-smoke, and smelled the river, and she saw a steeple and the cabins on their steep steps. Dozens of little black children whirled around her. There ahead was Natchez shining. Bells were ringing. She walked on.

In the paved city it was Christmas time. There were red and green 62 electric lights strung and crisscrossed everywhere, and all turned on in the daytime. Old Phoenix would have been lost if she had not distrusted her eyesight and depended on her feet to know where to take her.

She paused quietly on the sidewalk, where people were passing by. 63 A lady came along in the crowd, carrying an armful of red-, green-, and silver-wrapped presents; she gave off perfume like the red roses in hot summer, and Phoenix stopped her.

"Please, missy, will you lace up my shoe?" She held up her foot. 64

"What do you want, Grandma?" 65

"See my shoe," said Phoenix. "Do all right for out in the country, 66 but wouldn't look right to go in a big building."

"Stand still then, Grandma," said the lady. She put her packages 67 down carefully on the sidewalk beside her and laced and tied both shoes tightly.

"Can't lace 'em with a cane," said Phoenix. "Thank you, missy. I 68 doesn't mind asking a nice lady to tie up my shoe when I gets out on the street."

Moving slowly and from side to side, she went into the stone 69 building and into a tower of steps, where she walked up and around and around until her feet knew to stop.

70   She entered a door, and there she saw nailed up on the wall the document that had been stamped with the gold seal and framed in the gold frame which matched the dream that was hung up in her head.

71   "Here I be," she said. There was a fixed and ceremonial stiffness over her body.

72   "A charity case, I suppose," said an attendant who sat at the desk before her.

73   But Phoenix only looked above her head. There was sweat on her face; the wrinkles shone like a bright net.

74   "Speak up, Grandma," the woman said. "What's your name? We must have your history, you know. Have you been here before? What seems to be the trouble with you?"

75   Old Phoenix only gave a twitch to her face as if a fly were bothering her.

76   "Are you deaf?" cried the attendant.

77   But then the nurse came in.

78   "Oh, that's just old Aunt Phoenix," she said. "She doesn't come for herself — she has a little grandson. She makes these trips just as regular as clockwork. She lives away back off the Old Natchez Trace." She bent down. "Well, Aunt Phoenix, why don't you just take a seat? We won't keep you standing after your long trip." She pointed.

79   The old woman sat down, bolt upright in the chair.

80   "Now, how is the boy?" asked the nurse.

81   Old Phoenix did not speak.

82   "I said, how is the boy?"

83   But Phoenix only waited and stared straight ahead, her face very solemn and withdrawn into rigidity.

84   "Is his throat any better?" asked the nurse. "Aunt Phoenix, don't you hear me? Is your grandson's throat any better since the last time you came for the medicine?"

85   With her hand on her knees, the old woman waited, silent, erect, and motionless, just as if she were in armor.

86   "You mustn't take up our time this way, Aunt Phoenix," the nurse said. "Tell us quickly about your grandson, and get it over. He isn't dead, is he?"

87   At last there came a flicker and then a flame of comprehension across her face, and she spoke.

88   "My grandson. It was my memory had left me. There I sat and forgot why I made my long trip."

89   "Forgot?" The nurse frowned. "After you came so far?"

Then Phoenix was like an old woman begging a dignified   90
forgiveness for waking up frightened in the night. "I never did go to
school — I was too old at the Surrender," she said in a soft voice. "I'm
an old woman without an education. It was my memory fail me. My
little grandson, he is just the same, and I forgot it in the coming."

"Throat never heals, does it?" said the nurse, speaking in a loud,   91
sure voice to Old Phoenix. By now she had a card with something written on it, a little list. "Yes. Swallowed lye. When was it — January —
two — three years ago —"

Phoenix spoke unasked now. "No, missy, he not dead, he just the   92
same. Every little while his throat begin to close up again, and he not
able to swallow. He not get his breath. He not able to help himself. So
the time come around, and I go on another trip for soothing medicine."

"All right. The doctor said as long as you came to get it you could   93
have it," said the nurse. "But it's an obstinate case."

"My little grandson, he sit up there in the house all wrapped up,   94
waiting by himself," Phoenix went on. "We is the only two left in the
world. He suffer and it don't seem to put him back at all. He got a sweet
look. He going to last. He wear a little patch quilt and peep out, holding
his mouth open like a little bird. I remembers so plain now. I not going
to forget him again, no, the whole enduring time. I could tell him from
all the others in creation."

"All right." The nurse was trying to hush her now. She brought   95
her a bottle of medicine. "Charity," she said, making a check mark in
a book.

Old Phoenix held the bottle close to her eyes and then carefully   96
put it into her pocket.

"I thank you," she said.   97

"It's Christmas time, Grandma," said the attendant. "Could I give   98
you a few pennies out of my purse?"

"Five pennies is a nickel," said Phoenix stiffly.   99

"Here's a nickel," said the attendant.   100

Phoenix rose carefully and held out her hand. She received the   101
nickel and then fished the other nickel out of her pocket and laid it
beside the new one. She stared at her palm closely, with her head on
one side.

Then she gave a tap with her cane on the floor.   102

"This is what come to me to do," she said. "I going to the store   103
and buy my child a little windmill they sells, made out of paper. He
going to find it hard to believe there such a thing in the world. I'll march
myself back where he waiting, holding it straight up in this hand."

She lifted her free hand, gave a little nod, turned round, and walked   104 out of the doctor's office. Then her slow step began on the stairs, going down.

—— CONSIDERATIONS ——————————————————

1. Some features of Old Phoenix's long journey might bring to mind Everyman's difficult travel through life. Do specific passages suggest that Old Phoenix's journey is symbolic or archetypal?

2. Would you say that Old Phoenix is senile, or is she in excellent control of her thoughts? What evidence can you find for your answer?

3. Is the grandson alive or dead? After you answer this question, read Welty's own comments on the story in the next selection.

4. Who was the little boy with the slice of marble-cake? Why does he appear and disappear so abruptly?

5. Eudora Welty makes no comment in the story on Old Phoenix's encounter with the white man. Do the details of that encounter reveal anything about relations between whites and blacks?

6. What do you learn of Old Phoenix's sense of morality, sense of humor, and feeling of personal worth?

81

EUDORA WELTY
The Point of the Story

A story writer is more than happy to be read by students; the fact   1
that these serious readers think and feel something in response to his
work he finds life-giving. At the same time he may not always be able
to reply to their specific questions in kind. I wondered if it might clarify
something, for both the questioners and myself, if I set down a general
reply to the question that comes to me most often in the mail, from
both students and their teachers, after some classroom discussion. The
unrivaled favorite is this: "Is Phoenix Jackson's grandson really *dead?*"
It refers to a short story I wrote years ago called "A Worn Path," which
tells of a day's journey an old woman makes on foot from deep in the
country into town and into a doctor's office on behalf of her little grandson; he is at home, periodically ill, and periodically she comes for his
medicine; they give it to her as usual, she receives it and starts the
journey back.

I had not meant to mystify readers by withholding any fact; it is   2
not a writer's business to tease. The story is told through Phoenix's mind
as she undertakes her errand. As the author at one with the character
as I tell it, I must assume that the boy is alive. As the reader, you are
free to think as you like, of course: the story invites you to believe that
no matter what happens, Phoenix for as long as she is able to walk and
can hold to her purpose will make her journey. The *possibility* that she
would keep on even if he were dead is there in her devotion and its single-
minded, single-track errand. Certainly the *artistic* truth, which should
be good enough for the fact, lies in Phoenix's own answer to that question. When the nurse asks, "He isn't dead, is he?" she speaks for herself:
"He still the same. He going to last."

3   The grandchild is the incentive. But it is the journey, the going of the errand, that is the story, and the question is not whether the grandchild is in reality alive or dead. It doesn't affect the outcome of the story or its meaning from start to finish. But it is not the question itself that has struck me as much as the idea, almost without exception implied in the asking, that for Phoenix's grandson to be dead would somehow make the story "better."

4   It's *all right*, I want to say to the students who write to me, for things to be what they appear to be, and for words to mean what they say. It's all right, too, for words and appearances to mean more than one thing — ambiguity is a fact of life. A fiction writer's responsibility covers not only what he presents as the facts of a given story but what he chooses to stir up as their implications; in the end, these implications, too, become facts, in the larger, fictional sense. But it is not all right, not in good faith, for things not to mean what they say.

5   The grandson's plight was real and it made the truth of the story, which is the story of an errand of love carried out. If the child no longer lived, the truth would persist in the "wornness" of the path. But his being dead can't increase the truth of the story, can't affect it one way or the other. I think I signal this, because the end of the story has been reached before old Phoenix gets home again: she simply starts back. To the question "Is the grandson really dead?" I could reply that it doesn't make any difference. I could also say that I did not make him up in order to let him play a trick on Phoenix. But my best answer would be: "Phoenix is alive."

6   The origin of a story is sometimes a trustworthy clue to the author — or can provide him with the clue — to its key image; maybe in this case it will do the same for the reader. One day I saw a solitary old woman like Phoenix. She was walking; I saw her, at middle distance, in a winter country landscape, and watched her slowly make her way across my line of vision. That sight of her made me write the story. I invented an errand for her, but that only seemed a living part of the figure she was herself; what errand other than for someone else could be making her go? And her going was the first thing, her persisting in her landscape was the real thing, and the first and the real were what I wanted and worked to keep. I brought her up close enough, by imagination, to describe her face, make her present to the eyes, but the full-length figure moving across the winter fields was the indelible one and the image to keep, and the perspective extending into the vanishing distance the true one to hold in mind.

7   I invented for my character as I wrote, some passing adventures — some dreams and harassments and a small triumph or two, some jolts

to her pride, some flights of fancy to console her, one or two encounters to scare her, a moment that gave her cause to feel ashamed, a moment to dance and preen — for it had to be a journey, and all these things belonged to that, parts of life's uncertainty.

A narrative line is in its deeper sense, of course, the tracing out 8 of a meaning, and the real continuity of a story lies in this probing forward. The real dramatic force of a story depends on the strength of the emotion that has set it going. The emotional value is the measure of the reach of the story. What gives any such content to "A Worn Path" is not its circumstances but its subject: the deep-grained habit of love.

What I hoped would come clear was that in the whole surround 9 of this story, the world it threads through, the only certain thing at all is the worn path. The habit of love cuts through confusion and stumbles or contrives its way out of difficulty, it remembers the way even when it forgets, for a dumbfounded moment, its reason for being. The path is the thing that matters.

Her victory — old Phoenix's — is when she sees the diploma in 10 the doctor's office, when she finds "nailed up on the wall the document that had been stamped with the gold seal and framed in the gold frame, which matched the dream that was hung up in her head." The return with the medicine is just a matter of retracing her own footsteps. It is the part of the journey, and of the story, that can now go without saying.

In the matter of function, old Phoenix's way might even do as a 11 sort of parallel to your way of work if you are a writer of stories. The way to get there is the all-important, all-absorbing problem, and this problem is your reason for undertaking this story. Your only guide, too, is your sureness about your subject, about what this subject is. Like Phoenix, you work all your life to find your way, through all the obstructions and the false appearances and the upsets you may have brought on yourself, to reach a meaning — using inventions of your imagination, perhaps helped out by your dreams and bits of good luck. And finally too, like Phoenix, you have to assume that what you are working in aid of is life, not death.

But you would make the trip anyway — wouldn't you? — just on 12 hope.

—— CONSIDERATIONS ——

1. Welty says that Old Phoenix's return trip is "the part of the journey, and of the story, that can now go without saying." If you were writing this story would you choose a different place to end it? Would you follow Old Phoenix all the way back into the hills? Would you show the grandson? Why?

2. How does Welty feel about writers who intentionally mystify their readers?

3. Does "A Worn Path" illustrate what Welty means when she says, "A narrative line is in its deeper sense . . . the tracing out of a meaning"?

4. In Paragraph 4, Welty touches on the "factuality" of a work of fiction. This introduces a fascinating (if maddening) question: what is the difference between fiction and nonfiction?

5. Another Southern writer, William Faulkner, wrote a short novel, *As I Lay Dying*, that can be read as a fuller version of "A Worn Path." It too is based on "an errand of love," as Welty puts it. Read the novel and discuss its parallels with Welty's story.

6. What do you think of Welty's response to the question about her story? Does it help you understand and appreciate the story? Does it avoid the initial question?

82

EUDORA WELTY
The Baby Question

It was when my mother came out onto the sleeping porch to tell
me goodnight that her trial came. The sudden silence in the double bed
meant my younger brothers had both keeled over in sleep, and I in the
single bed at my end of the porch would be lying electrified, waiting
for this to be the night when she'd tell me what she'd promised for so
long. Just as she bent to kiss me I grabbed her and asked: "Where do
babies come from?"

My poor mother! But something saved her every time. Almost any
night I put the baby question to her, suddenly, as if the whole outdoors
exploded, Professor Holt would start to sing. The Holts lived next door;
he taught penmanship (the Palmer Method), typing, bookkeeping and
shorthand at the high school. His excitable voice traveled out of their
diningroom windows across the two driveways between our houses, and
up to our upstairs sleeping porch. His wife, usually so quiet and gentle,
was his uncannily spirited accompanist at the piano. "High-ho! Come
to the Fair!" he'd sing, unless he sang "Oho ye oho ye, who's bound for
the ferry, the briar's in bud and the sun's going down!"

"Dear, this isn't a very good time for you to hear Mother, is it?"

She couldn't get started. As soon as she'd whisper something, Professor Holt galloped into the chorus, "And 'tis but a penny to
Twickenham town!" "Isn't that enough?" she'd ask me. She'd told me
that the mother and the father had to both *want* the baby. This couldn't
be enough. I knew she was not trying to fib to me, for she never did
fib, but also I could not help but know she was not really *telling* me.
And more than that, I was afraid of what I was going to hear next. This
was partly because she wanted to tell me in the dark. I thought *she* might

459

be afraid. In something like childish hopelessness I thought she probably *couldn't* tell, just as she *couldn't* lie.

5   On the night we came the closest to having it over with, she started to tell me without being asked, and I ruined it by yelling, "Mother, look at the lightning bugs!"

6   In those days, the dark was dark. And all the dark out there was filled with the soft, near lights of lightning bugs. They were everywhere, flashing on the slow, horizontal move, on the upswings, rising and subsiding in the soundless dark. Lightning bugs signaled and answered back without a stop, from down below all the way to the top of our sycamore tree. My mother just gave me a businesslike kiss and went on back to Daddy in their room at the front of the house. Distracted by lightning bugs, I had missed my chance. The fact is she never did tell me.

7   I doubt that any child I knew ever was told by her mother any more than I was about babies. In fact, I doubt that her own mother ever told her any more than she told me, though there were five brothers who were born after Mother, one after the other, and she was taking care of babies all her childhood.

_____ CONSIDERATIONS _____

1. Welty's account could open up a serious discussion of the controversial matter of sex education. Have you had or heard of an experience in sex education that might be useful for an essay on the subject? Why is the subject so controversial?

2. How does Eudora Welty, the writer, avoid making her mother's failure appear more serious than it was?

3. In Welty's case, how does the child herself complicate her mother's task?

4. What in Welty's account reminds us that she is primarily a storyteller, not a psychologist?

E. B. White (1899–1985) was born in Mount Vernon, New York, graduated from Cornell in 1921, and joined the staff of The New Yorker *in 1926. For many years, he wrote the brief essay which led off that magazine's "The Talk of the Town" and edited other "Talk" segments. In 1929, White collaborated with James Thurber on a book called* Is Sex Necessary? *and from time to time he published collections of essays and poems, most of them taken from* The New Yorker *and Harper's. Some of his best-known collections are* One Man's Meat *(1942),* The Second Tree from the Corner *(1953), and* The Points of My Compass *(1962). He is also the author of children's books, most notably* Stuart Little *(1945) and* Charlotte's Web *(1952), and the celebrated book on prose,* The Elements of Style *(with William Strunk, Jr., 1959).*

In 1937, White retired from The New Yorker *and moved to a farm in Maine, where he continued to write those minimal, devastating comments attached to the proofhacks and other errors printed at the ends of* The New Yorker's *columns. There he continued his slow, consistent writing of superb prose. In recent years, the collected* Letters of E. B. White *(1976), and* Essays of E. B. White *(1977), and* Poems and Sketches of E. B. White *(1981), have reconfirmed this country's infatuation with the versatile author. A special citation from the Pulitzer Prize Committee in 1978 celebrated the publication of White's letters.*

83

E. B. WHITE

Once More to the Lake

1   One summer, along about 1904, my father rented a camp on a lake in Maine and took us all there for the month of August. We all got ringworm from some kittens and had to rub Pond's Extract on our arms and legs night and morning, and my father rolled over in a canoe with all his clothes on; but outside of that the vacation was a success and from then on none of us ever thought there was any place in the world like that lake in Maine. We returned summer after summer — always on August 1st for one month. I have since become a salt-water man, but sometimes in summer there are days when the restlessness of the tides and the fearful cold of the sea water and the incessant wind that blows across the afternoon and into the evening make me wish for the placidity of a lake in the woods. A few weeks ago this feeling got so strong I bought myself a couple of bass hooks and a spinner and returned to the lake where we used to go, for a week's fishing and to revisit old haunts.

2   I took along my son, who had never had any fresh water up his nose and who had seen lily pads only from train windows. On the journey over to the lake I began to wonder what it would be like. I wondered how time would have marred this unique, this holy spot — the coves and streams, the hills that the sun set behind, the camps and the paths behind the camps. I was sure that the tarred road would have found it out and I wondered in what other ways it would be desolated. It is strange how much you can remember about places like that once you allow your mind to return into the grooves that lead back. You remember one thing, and that suddenly reminds you of another thing. I guess I remembered clearest of all the early mornings, when the lake

From *Essays of E. B. White.* Copyright 1941, 1969 by E. B. White. Reprinted by permission of Harper & Row, Publishers, Inc.

was cool and motionless, remembered how the bedroom smelled of the lumber it was made of and of the wet woods whose scent entered through the screen. The partitions in the camp were thin and did not extend clear to the top of the rooms, and as I was always the first up I would dress softly so as not to wake the others, and sneak out into the sweet outdoors and start out in the canoe, keeping close along the shore in the long shadows of the pines. I remembered being very careful never to rub my paddle against the gunwale for fear of disturbing the stillness of the cathedral.

The lake had never been what you would call a wild lake. There were cottages sprinkled around the shores, and it was in farming country although the shores of the lake were quite heavily wooded. Some of the cottages were owned by nearby farmers, and you would live at the shore and eat your meals at the farmhouse. That's what our family did. But although it wasn't wild, it was a fairly large and undisturbed lake and there were places in it which, to a child at least, seemed infinitely remote and primeval. 3

I was right about the tar: it led to within half a mile of the shore. But when I got back there, with my boy, and we settled into a camp near a farmhouse and into the kind of summertime I had known, I could tell that it was going to be pretty much the same as it had been before — I knew it, lying in bed the first morning, smelling the bedroom, and hearing the boy sneak quietly out and go off along the shore in a boat. I began to sustain the illusion that he was I, and therefore, by simple transposition, that I was my father. This sensation persisted, kept cropping up all the time we were there. It was not an entirely new feeling, but in this setting it grew much stronger. I seemed to be living a dual existence. I would be in the middle of some simple act, I would be picking up a bait box or laying down a table fork, or I would be saying something, and suddenly it would be not I but my father who was saying the words or making the gesture. It gave me a creepy sensation. 4

We went fishing the first morning. I felt the same damp moss covering the worms in the bait can, and saw the dragonfly alight on the tip of my rod as it hovered a few inches from the surface of the water. It was the arrival of this fly that convinced me beyond any doubt that everything was as it always had been, that the years were a mirage and there had been no years. The small waves were the same, chucking the rowboat under the chin as we fished at anchor, and the boat was the same boat, the same color green and the ribs broken in the same places, and under the floor-boards the same fresh-water leavings and débris — the dead hellgrammite, the wisps of moss, the rusty discarded fishhook, 5 the dried blood from yesterday's catch. We stared silently at the tips of our rods, at the dragonflies that came and went. I lowered the tip of mine into the water, tentatively, pensively dislodging the fly, which darted two feet away, poised, darted two feet back, and came to rest again a little farther up the rod. There had been no years between the ducking of this dragonfly and the other one — the one that was part of memory. I looked at the boy, who was silently watching his fly, and it was my hands that held his rod, my eyes watching. I felt dizzy and didn't know which rod I was at the end of.

6   We caught two bass, hauling them in briskly as though they were mackerel, pulling them over the side of the boat in a businesslike manner without any landing net, and stunning them with a blow on the back of the head. When we got back for a swim before lunch, the lake was exactly where we had left it, the same number of inches from the dock, and there was only the merest suggestion of a breeze. This seemed an utterly enchanted sea, this lake you could leave to its own devices for a few hours and come back to, and find that it had not stirred, this constant and trustworthy body of water. In the shallows, the dark, water-soaked sticks and twigs, smooth and old, were undulating in clusters on the bottom against the clean ribbed sand, and the track of the mussel was plain. A school of minnows swam by, each minnow with its small individual shadow, doubling the attendance, so clear and sharp in the sunlight. Some of the other campers were in swimming, along the shore, one of them with a cake of soap, and the water felt thin and clear and unsubstantial. Over the years there had been this person with the cake of soap, this cultist, and here he was. There had been no years.

7   Up to the farmhouse to dinner through the teeming, dusty field, the road under our sneakers was only a two-track road. The middle track was missing, the one with the marks of the hooves and splotches of dried, flaky manure. There had always been three tracks to choose from in choosing which track to walk in; now the choice was narrowed down to two. For a moment I missed terribly the middle alternative. But the way led past the tennis court, and something about the way it lay there in the sun reassured me; the tape had loosened along the backline, the alleys were green with plantains and other weeds, and the net (installed in June and removed in September) sagged in the dry noon, and the whole place steamed with midday heat and hunger and emptiness. There was a choice of pie for dessert, and one was blueberry and one was apple, and the waitresses were the same country girls, there having been no passage of time, only the illusion of it as in a dropped curtain — the waitresses were still fifteen; their hair had been washed, that was the

only difference — they had been to the movies and seen the pretty girls with the clean hair.

Summertime, oh summertime, pattern of life indelible, the fadeproof lake, the woods unshatterable, the pasture with the sweetfern and the juniper forever and ever, summer without end; this was the background, and the life along the shore was the design, the cottages with their innocent and tranquil design, their tiny docks with the flagpole and the American flag floating against the white clouds in the blue sky, the little paths over the roots of the trees leading from camp to camp and the paths leading back to the outhouses and the can of lime for sprinkling, and at the souvenir counters at the store the miniature birch-bark canoes and the post cards that showed things looking a little better than they looked. This was the American family at play, escaping the city heat, wondering whether the newcomers in the camp at the head of the cove were "common" or "nice," wondering whether it was true that the people who drove up for Sunday dinner at the farmhouse were turned away because there wasn't enough chicken. 8

It seemed to me, as I kept remembering all this, that those times and those summers had been infinitely precious and worth saving. There had been jollity and peace and goodness. The arriving (at the beginning of August) had been so big a business in itself, at the railway station the farm wagon drawn up, the first smell of the pine-laden air, the first glimpse of the smiling farmer, and the great importance of the trunks and your father's enormous authority in such matters, and the feel of the wagon under you for the long ten-mile haul, and at the top of the last long hill catching the first view of the lake after eleven months of not seeing this cherished body of water. The shouts and cries of the other campers when they saw you, and the trunks to be unpacked, to give up their rich burden. (Arriving was less exciting nowadays, when you sneaked up in your car and parked it under a tree near the camp and took out the bags and in five minutes it was all over, no fuss, no loud wonderful fuss about trunks.) 9

Peace and goodness and jollity. The only thing that was wrong now, really, was the sound of the place, an unfamiliar nervous sound of the outboard motors. This was the note that jarred, the one thing that would sometimes break the illusion and set the years moving. In those other summertimes all motors were inboard; and when they were at a little distance, the noise they made was a sedative, an ingredient of summer sleep. They were one-cylinder and two-cylinder engines, and some were make-and-break and some were jump-spark, but they all made a sleepy sound across the lake. The one-lungers throbbed and fluttered, and the 10 twin-cylinder ones purred and purred and that was a quiet sound too. But now the campers all had outboards. In the daytime, in the hot mornings, these motors made a petulant, irritable sound; at night, in the still evening when the afterglow lit the water, they whined about one's ears like mosquitoes. My boy loved our rented outboard, and his great desire was to achieve singlehanded mastery over it, and authority, and he soon learned the trick of choking it a little (but not too much), and the adjustment of the needle valve. Watching him I would remember the things you could do with the old one-cylinder engine with the heavy flywheel, how you could have it eating out of your hand if you got really close to it spiritually. Motor boats in those days didn't have clutches, and you would make a landing by shutting off the motor at the proper time and coasting in with a dead rudder. But there was a way of reversing them, if you learned the trick, by cutting the switch and putting it on again exactly on the final dying revolution of the flywheel, so that it would kick back against compression and begin reversing. Approaching a dock in a strong following breeze, it was difficult to slow up sufficiently by the ordinary coasting method, and if a boy felt he had complete mastery over his motor, he was tempted to keep it running beyond its time and then reverse it a few feet from the dock. It took a cool nerve, because if you threw the switch a twentieth of a second too soon you could catch the flywheel when it still had speed enough to go up past center, and the boat would leap ahead, charging bull-fashion at the dock.

11   We had a good week at the camp. The bass were biting well and the sun shone endlessly, day after day. We would be tired at night and lie down in the accumulated heat of the little bedrooms after the long hot day and the breeze would stir almost imperceptibly outside and the smell of the swamp drift in through the rusty screens. Sleep would come easily and in the morning the red squirrel would be on the roof, tapping out his gay routine. I kept remembering everything, lying in bed in the mornings — the small steamboat that had a long rounded stern like the lip of a Ubangi, and how quietly she ran on the moonlight sails, when the older boys played their mandolins and the girls sang and we ate doughnuts dipped in sugar, and how sweet the music was on the water in the shining light, and what it had felt like to think about girls then. After breakfast we would go up to the store and the things were in the same place — the minnows in a bottle, the plugs and spinners disarranged and pawed over by the youngsters from the boys' camp, the fig newtons and the Beeman's gum. Outside, the road was tarred and cars stood in front of the store. Inside, all was just as it had always been, except there was more Coca-Cola and not so much Moxie and root beer

and birch beer and sarsaparilla. We would walk out with a bottle of pop apiece and sometimes the pop would backfire up our noses and hurt. We explored the streams, quietly, where the turtles slid off the sunny logs and dug their way into the soft bottom; and we lay on the town wharf and fed worms to the tame bass. Everywhere we went I had trouble making out which was I, the one walking at my side, the one walking in my pants.

One afternoon while we were there at that lake a thunderstorm   12
came up. It was like the revival of an old melodrama that I had seen long ago with childish awe. The second-act climax of the drama of the electrical disturbance over a lake in America had not changed in any important respect. This was the big scene, still the big scene. The whole thing was so familiar, the first feeling of oppression and heat and a general air around camp of not wanting to go very far away. In midafternoon (it was all the same) a curious darkening of the sky, and a lull in everything that had made life tick; and then the way the boats suddenly swung the other way at their moorings with the coming of a breeze out of the new quarter, and the premonitory rumble. Then the kettle drum, then the snare, then the bass drum and cymbals, then crackling light against the dark, and the gods grinning and licking their chops in the hills. Afterward the calm, the rain steadily rustling in the calm lake, the return of light and hope and spirits, and the campers running out in joy and relief to go swimming in the rain, their bright cries perpetuating the deathless joke about how they were getting simply drenched, and the children screaming with delight at the new sensation of bathing in the rain, and the joke about getting drenched linking the generations in a strong indestructible chain. And the comedian who waded in carrying an umbrella.

When the others went swimming my son said he was going in too.   13
He pulled his dripping trunks from the line where thay had hung all through the shower, and wrung them out. Languidly, and with no thought of going in, I watched him, his hard little body, skinny and bare, saw him wince slightly as he pulled up around his vitals the small, soggy, icy garment. As he buckled the swollen belt suddenly my groin felt the chill of death.

_____ CONSIDERATIONS _____

1. A master of the personal essay, E. B. White transforms an exercise in memory into something universal, timeless, and profound. Study Paragraph 4 to see how.

2. White rejuvenates bits and pieces of language that have become worn and lackluster through repetition. Can you find an example of this technique in Paragraph 2?

3. White notes many changes at the old summer place, but he is more moved by the sameness. Locate examples of his feeling of sameness and consider how these examples contribute to his themes.

4. The author expresses a predictable dislike of outboard motors on the otherwise quiet lake. Does he avoid stereotype when he writes about motors elsewhere in this essay?

5. What device does White use in his description of the thunderstorm in Paragraph 12?

6. How is the last sentence of the essay a surprise? How has White prepared us for it?

When E. B. White reprinted a few brief essays from The New
Yorker's *"Talk of the Town," he called them editorials, and we
follow him. He also mentioned that he signed his name to
them "hesitantly, for it is questionable whether anyone can
properly assume authorship of material which is published
anonymously." Yet when we read them they do not seem
anonymous; White's singular prose style announces itself.*

84

E. B. WHITE
The Wild Flag

April 19, 1943

    The time is at hand to revive the discussion of companionate mar-   1
riage, for it is now apparent that the passion of nations will shortly lead
to some sort of connubial relationship, either a companionate one (as
in the past) or a lawful one (which would be something new). If you
observe closely the courtship among nations, if you read each morning
the many protestations of affection and the lively plans for consumma-
tion, you will find signs that the drift is still toward an illicit arrangement based on love, respect, and a strong foreign policy. Countries
appear to be on the verge of making new and solemn compacts with
each other, of renewing old pledges. If it is to be this and no more, we
predict that they will lie together in rapture for a while and then bust
up as usual. The companionate idea is appealing to nations because it
is familiar, because it demands little, and because it is exciting to the
blood. The mention of a license and the thought of relinquishing
something of one's independence come hard to the sovereign ear and

mind. Even at this woebegone time it seems questionable whether the grim institution of marriage will be embraced by the world's states, which have always practiced free love and are used to its excesses and its tragic violence.

2   Our advice to the nations who call themselves united is to go out and buy rings. If there is to be love-in-bloom at the war's end, we should prefer to see it legal this time, if only for a change. The history of the modern world is the story of nations having affairs with each other. These affairs have been based on caprice and on ambition; they have been oiled with diplomacy and intrigue and have been unsanctified by law, there having been no law covering the rights and obligations of the contracting parties. The result has been chaotic and there still is no law. We are informed, almost hourly, that a new world order is in the making, yet most of the talk is of policy and almost none of the talk is of law.

3   America and China are in love. England and Russia are seen frequently together in public. France, Norway, the Netherlands, Greece, Poland, Czechoslovakia — each is groping for the other's hand in the darkness of the newsreel. What is going to come of this romantic and wonderful condition — a few stolen kisses, a key to an apartment somewhere, a renewal of individual vows and general irresponsibility? Considering how eager the nations are to lie down with each other, it seems to us time for a brief notice to be inserted in the world's paper, inviting interested parties to a preliminary meeting, a sociable if you want, to talk over the whole situation and perhaps even discuss the end of policy and laxity in their love life and the beginning of law and of force. The notice should be carefully worded and should be at least as honest as those wistful little ads which the lovelorn and the lonely place in the classified columns. It should conclude with that desperate yet somehow very hopeful phrase 'Object, matrimony.'

_____ CONSIDERATIONS _____

1. One of E. B. White's techniques is to mix different dictions in the same piece. In Paragraph 1, for example, he uses general and abstract words, such as "companionate marriage," "connubial relationship," "protestations of affection." But there is one phrase in the same paragraph that brings us down to earth with a refreshing thump. Find it and comment on its utility in this passage.

2. White's entire editorial is an exercise in analogy, or the extended metaphor. Sort out the essential parts of the metaphor — the vehicle and the tenor — to see how consistently he maintains that figurative device. Then try your hand at the same technique with a substantial paragraph on a topic of your own choice.

You might get ideas for topics by looking into the *Letters of E. B. White,* edited by Dorothy Lobrano Guth (Harper & Row, 1976).

   3. Despite his characteristic playfulness with language, White's editorial is distinctly an argumentative essay. State his thesis in literal terms. What institution has been formed to further that thesis since White's editorial appeared?

   4. White has a knack for using commonplace detail to help us understand something far more important. Study the phrase in Paragraph 3, ". . . each is groping for the other's hand in the darkness of the newsreel." Why "groping"? Why "darkness"? Why "newsreel"?

George F. Will (b. 1941) was born in Illinois and graduated from Princeton University. He has taught politics — at Michigan State University, the University of Illinois, and the University of Toronto — and worked as an aid to a Senator. His newspaper columns on politics, originally printed in the Washington Post, *are syndicated nationwide, and have been collected into three books:* The Pursuit of Happiness and Other Sobering Thoughts *(1979),* The Pursuit of Virtue and Other Tory Notions *(1982), and* The Morning After *(1986), from which we take this column. A witty conservative, artful and allusive in his prose style, Will has received the ultimate accolade; Gary Trudeau's "Doonesbury" strip has satirized him.*

Well known for his eloquent tributes to baseball, this political columnist does indeed write about lighter things than politics — as well as the darker sides of lighter things.

85

GEORGE F. WILL
Exploring the Racer's Edge

1   It has been said that someone who cheats in an amateur contest is a cheat, whereas a professional who cheats to feed his family is a competitor. Piffle. All sports should conform to the International Olympic Committee's ban on "the use by a competing athlete of any substance foreign to the body or of any physiological substance taken in abnormal quantity or taken by an abnormal route of entry into the body, with the sole intention of increasing in an artificial and an unfair manner his performance in competition." But even this careful language con-

tains crucial ambiguities — "foreign to the body," "abnormal quantity," "an artificial and unfair manner." Define "fair" and you are home free. Let's start at the fringe of the subject and nibble in.

Seven U.S. Olympic cyclists, including four medal winners, prac- 2 ticed "blood doping." They received infusions of blood from relatives or others with the same blood type, in an attempt — it is not clear this works — to increase their red-cell count and accelerate the transfer of oxygen to muscles during endurance events. An eighth cyclist had a rein-fusion of his own blood that had been drawn several weeks earlier. Was his blood (or any blood) "foreign to the body?" Clearly blood doping in-volves an abnormal quantity of blood entering the body through an ab-normal route to increase performance in an artificial (and therefore unfair?) manner.

Steroids can enhance muscle mass. They also can kill you, if they 3 do not just decrease sexual capacity, injure your liver and heart, and do sundry other damages. Some people say: It's the athlete's body, he can mess it up as he pleases — besides, sports often involve injuries. But it is one thing to injure yourself in exertion, another to injure yourself with chemicals in pursuit of the ultimate competitive "edge." And it is surely unfair to force your opponent to choose between similarly risking harm and competing at a disadvantage.

It is said that the improper pursuit of edge derives from valuing 4 winning too much. Actually, it derives from misunderstanding why win-ning is properly valued.

There is a broad gray area of difficult judgments. For example, what, 5 precisely, is the moral difference between eating energy-giving glucose pills and taking a steroid that increases muscle mass? What is the difference between taking vitamins — or, for that matter, eating spin-ach — in "abnormal quantities" and taking a drug that deadens the pain of an injured foot or (watch it — we are crossing some kind of line here) a drug that increases aggressiveness?

The science of sports medicine is no longer just about the preven- 6 tion or treatment of injuries. It uses kinesiology and biomechanics and computer analysis of movement — high-tech stuff that would make even Gary Hart's head swim — to improve performance. Just as the launching of Sputnik I aroused American interest in science education, minds were concentrated on sports medicine by another embarrassment — the 1976 Montreal Olympics, where East Germany won more gold medals than the United States. (Of course the phrase "East German amateur athlete" is as much an oxymoron as "married bachelor," and some of those East German, er, ladies probably had interesting concoctions of hormones.)

7   As sports medicine and related technologies become more sophisticated, there is anxiety about the integrity of sport. This anxiety is an intuition in search of clarifying criteria. When sprinters began using starting blocks (remember in *Chariots of Fire* each runner carried a trowel to dig toeholds in the track at the starting line) the new equipment was available to all competitors and improved performances without altering the performers. When pole vaulters abandoned stiff bamboo and metal poles in favor of flexible fiberglass poles that fling vaulters skyward, the competition remained essentially the same, although at a previously undreamed-of plateau of achievement. Perhaps we are getting close to the key that unlocks the puzzle: Techniques and technologies are unobjectionable when they improve performance without devaluing it. Proper athletics are activities all of us can attempt. The use of certain exotic drugs or techniques alters the character of an activity and devalues it by making it exotic — no longer a shared activity.

8   We should listen to the promptings of our intuitions about appropriate language. It is one thing to be intense, even obsessive about training, including nutrition. It is different to pursue edge by means of chemical technologies — drugs — that we instinctively speak of as "unnatural" manipulations of the body. Intense training should involve enhancing powers by means of measures or materials that are part of the body's normal functioning, rather than by radical interventions in the body. Interventions are radical when they are designed not just to enhance normal functioning but to cause the body to behave abnormally — not unusually well but unnaturally well.

9   Illegitimate technologies are subverting the integrity of a sport when we feel inclined to speak of "the body," not "the athlete," performing well. Technologies can blur the sense of the self-involved. We admire people who run fast, not bodies that are made fast by chemical boosters. Some athletes probably are nagged by thoughts like: "My weight-lifting achievement is not mine, it belongs to my medicine cabinet."

10   The ancient Greeks, who invented the Olympics and political philosophy, believed that sport was a religious and civic — in a word, moral — undertaking. Sport, they said, is morally serious because a noble aim of life is appreciation of worthy things, such as beauty and bravery. By using their bodies beautifully, athletes teach our souls to appreciate beauty. By competing bravely, athletes make bravery vivid and exemplary.

11   Sport is competition to demonstrate excellence in admired activities. The excellence is most praiseworthy when the activity demands

virtues of the spirit — of character — as well as physical prowess. Admirable athletic attainments involve mental mastery of pain and exhaustion — the triumph of character, not chemistry, over adversity. We want sport to reward true grit, not sophisticated science. We do not want a child to ask an athlete, "Can I get the autograph of your pharmacist?"

___ CONSIDERATIONS _____

1. To understand Will's parenthetical statement at the end of Paragraph 6, look up "oxymoron." Find examples of that literary device and explain how it works.

2. Will mentions and deplores methods some athletes have used to gain the "competitive edge." Could these methods be labeled "hi-tech"? Might it follow that Will also would deplore advanced technology in other competitive fields: automobile manufacture, the work of popular musicians, photography, food preparation, the media? If Will were with Frank Conroy (see "A Yo-Yo Going Down," pages 119–126) in the yo-yo contest, would he find it unfair if a boy showed up with a synthetic string that would not become snared or tangled?

3. In Paragraph 4, Will overturns a common remark about winning in order to point the reader to his major concerns. How does this help him reveal his anxieties about the "integrity of sport"?

4. Will quotes the International Olympic Committee's ban in Paragraph 1 and then points out certain ambiguities. Do you agree that these phrases are ambiguous? Why are we to understand ambiguity as a fault? Why is it so difficult to avoid ambiguous language? Is ambiguity ever useful? Reread Eudora Welty's comments on ambiguity in "The Point of the Story" (pages 455–458).

5. Some of Will's argument presupposes our accepting that sports are "a shared activity." To what extent are America's most popular sports — football, baseball, basketball — "shared activities"? Shared with whom?

6. Admitting the difficulty of pinning down our "anxieties" and doubts about some athletic achievements, Will falls back on "intuition" and on the ideals that motivated athletes in ancient Greece. Are these ideas effective in his argument?

7. If you read the title of Will's essay aloud, you may be amused and surprised. Is the word play merely clever or does it add to the essay? Look again at Consideration 4.

Virginia Woolf (1882–1941) is best known as a novelist. The
Voyage Out appeared in 1915, followed by Night and Day
(1919), Jacob's Room (1922), Mrs. Dalloway (1925), To The
Lighthouse (1927), Orlando (1928), The Waves (1931), The Years
(1937), and Between the Acts, published shortly after her death.
Daughter of Sir Leslie Stephen, Victorian critic and essayist
who edited the Dictionary of National Biography, she was
educated at home, and began her literary career as a critic for
the Times Literary Supplement. She wrote essays regularly until her death; four volumes of her Collected Essays appeared in
the United States in 1967. More recently, her publishers have
issued six volumes of her collected letters, and her diary is being published.

With her sister Vanessa, a painter, her husband Leonard
Woolf, an editor and writer, and Vanessa's husband Clive Bell,
an art critic, Woolf lived at the center of the Bloomsbury group
— artists and intellectuals who gathered informally to talk and
to amuse each other, and whose unconventional ideas and
habits, when they were known, shocked the stolid British
public. John Maynard Keynes, the economist, was a member of
the varied group, which also included the biographer Lytton
Strachey, the novelist E. M. Forster, and eventually the expatriate American poet, T. S. Eliot. With her husband, Virginia
Woolf founded The Hogarth Press, a small firm dedicated to
publishing superior works. Among its authors were Eliot and
Woolf herself.

Virginia Woolf, a recent biography by her nephew Quentin
Bell, gives an intimate picture of the whole group. Of all the
Bloomsbury people, Woolf was perhaps the most talented.
Through most of her life, she struggled against recurring mental
illness, which brought intense depression and suicidal im-
pulses. When she was fifty-nine she drowned herself in the
River Ouse. The following famous passage from A Room of
One's Own (1929) presents a feminist argument by means of a
memorable supposition.

86

VIRGINIA WOOLF

If Shakespeare Had Had a Sister

It is a perennial puzzle why no woman wrote a word of that extraordinary [Elizabethan] literature when every other man, it seemed, was capable of song or sonnet. What were the conditions in which women lived, I asked myself; for fiction, imaginative work that is, is not dropped like a pebble upon the ground, as science may be; fiction is like a spider's web, attached ever so lightly perhaps, but still attached to life at all four corners. Often the attachment is scarcely perceptible; Shakespeare's plays, for instance, seem to hang there complete by themselves. But when the web is pulled askew, hooked up at the edge, torn in the middle, one remembers that these webs are not spun in midair by incorporeal creatures, but are the work of suffering human beings, and are attached to grossly material things, like health and money and the house we live in. . . .

But what I find . . . is that nothing is known about women before the eighteenth century. I have no model in my mind to turn about this way and that. Here am I asking why women did not write poetry in the Elizabethan age, and I am not sure how they were educated; whether they were taught to write; whether they had sitting-rooms to themselves; how many women had children before they were twenty-one; what, in short, they did from eight in the morning till eight at night. They had no money, evidently; according to Professor Trevelyan they were married whether they liked it or not before they were out of the nursery, at fifteen or sixteen very likely. It would have been extremely odd, even upon this showing, had one of them suddenly written the plays of Shakespeare, I concluded, and I thought of that old gentleman, who is dead now, but was a bishop, I think, who declared that it was impossible for any woman, past, present, or to come, to have the genius of Shakespeare. He wrote to the papers about it. He also told a lady who applied to him for information that cats do not as a matter of fact go to heaven, though they have, he added, souls of a sort. How much thinking those old gentleman used to save one! How the borders of ignorance shrank back at their approach! Cats do not go to heaven. Women cannot write the plays of Shakespeare.

3   Be that as it may, I could not help thinking, as I looked at the works of Shakespeare on the shelf, that the bishop was right at least in this; it would have been impossible, completely and entirely, for any woman to have written the plays of Shakespeare in the age of Shakespeare. Let me imagine, since facts are so hard to come by, what would have happened had Shakespeare had a wonderfully gifted sister, called Judith, let us say. Shakespeare himself went, very probably — his mother was an heiress — to the grammar school, where he may have learnt Latin — Ovid, Virgil and Horace — and the elements of grammar and logic. He was, it is well known, a wild boy who poached rabbits, perhaps shot a deer, and had, rather sooner than he should have done, to marry a woman in the neighbourhood, who bore him a child rather quicker than was right. That escapade sent him to seek his fortune in London. He had, it seemed, a taste for the theatre; he began by holding horses at the stage door. Very soon he got work in the theatre, became a successful actor, and lived at the hub of the universe, meeting everybody, knowing everybody, practising his art on the boards, exercising his wits in the streets, and even getting access to the palace of the queen. Meanwhile his extraordinarily gifted sister, let us suppose, remained at home. She was as adventurous, as imaginative, as agog to see the world as he was. But she was not sent to school. She had no chance of learning grammar and logic, let alone of reading Horace and Virgil. She picked up a book now and then, one of her brother's perhaps, and read a few pages. But then her parents came in and told her to mend the stockings or mind the stew and not moon about with books and papers. They would have spoken sharply but kindly, for they were substantial people who knew the conditions of life for a woman and loved their daughter — indeed, more likely than not she was the apple of her father's eye. Perhaps she scribbled some pages up in an apple loft on the sly, but was careful to hide them or set fire to them. Soon, however, before she was out of her teens, she was to be betrothed to the son of a neighbouring wool-stapler. She cried out that marriage was hateful to her, and for that she was severely beaten by her father. Then he ceased to scold her. He begged her instead not to hurt him, not to shame him in this matter of her mar-

riage. He would give her a chain of beads or a fine petticoat, he said; and there were tears in his eyes. How could she disobey him? How could she break his heart? The force of her own gift alone drove her to it. She made up a small parcel of her belongings, let herself down by a rope one summer's night and took the road to London. She was not seventeen. The birds that sang in the hedge were not more musical than she was. She had the quickest fancy, a gift like her brother's, for the tune of words. Like him, she had a taste for the theatre. She stood at the stage door; she wanted to act, she said. Men laughed in her face. The manager — a fat, loose-lipped man — guffawed. He bellowed something about poodles dancing and women acting — no woman, he said, could possibly be an actress. He hinted — you can imagine what. She could get no training in her craft. Could she even seek her dinner in a tavern or roam the streets at midnight? Yet her genius was for fiction and lusted to feed abundantly upon the lives of men and women and the study of their ways. At last — for she was very young, oddly like Shakespeare the poet in her face, with the same grey eyes and rounded brows — at last Nick Greene the actor-manager took pity on her; she found herself with child by that gentleman and so — who shall measure the heat and violence of the poet's heart when caught and tangled in a woman's body? — killed herself one winter's night and lies buried at some cross-roads where the omnibuses now stop outside the Elephant and Castle.

That, more or less, is how the story would run, I think, if a woman   4
in Shakespeare's day had had Shakespeare's genius. But for my part, I agree with the deceased bishop, if such he was — it is unthinkable that any woman in Shakespeare's day should have had Shakespeare's genius. For genius like Shakespeare's is not born among labouring, uneducated, servile people. It was not born in England among the Saxons and the Britons. It is not born today among the working classes. How, then, could it have been born among women whose work began, according to Professor Trevelyan, almost before they were out of the nursery, who were forced to it by their parents and held to it by all the power of law and custom?

_____ **CONSIDERATIONS** _____

1. In Paragraph 3, Woolf develops at length an imaginary sister of Shakespeare. Why does the writer call that sister Judith rather than Priscilla or Elizabeth or Megan? A quick look at Shakespeare's biography will give you the answer and alert you to a mischievous side of Woolf.

2. At the end of Paragraph 2, Woolf says, "How the borders of ignorance shrank back at their approach!" Is this a straight statement, or does she mean

something other than what the words say? Study the differences among the following terms, which often are used mistakenly as synonyms: sarcasm, satire, irony, wit, humor, cynicism, invective, the sardonic.

3. Woolf's essay consists of four paragraphs, one of which accounts for more than half of the composition. Can you find a justification for this disproportionately long paragraph?

4. Concoct an imaginary biograpy, with a purpose, like Woolf's account of Judith: for example, Mozart's daughter, Napoleon's father, the brother of Jesus Christ, the Queen of Luxembourg, Tolstoi's nephew or niece.

5. ". . . for fiction . . . is not dropped like a pebble upon the ground, as science may be . . ." (Paragraph 1). In what sense is science dropped like a pebble upon the ground? What is the point of this odd comparison?

6. If you were to invite three authors from this book to an informal discussion of Woolf's essay, whom would you select? Why? Make your selections on the basis of some relationship between their ideas and hers. What sort of outcome would you expect from such a conversation? Write a page of this dialogue.

7. Woolf wrote in the informal idiom of an educated Englishwoman of the 1920s; there are a number of differences between her language and ours. Circle a half dozen such differences and contrast British English with American English.

Richard Wright (1908–1960) was born on a plantation in Natchez, Mississippi. A restless and unruly child, he left home at fifteen and supported himself doing unskilled work, gradually improving his employment until he became a clerk in a post office. In this essay from his autobiography Black Boy *(1944) he writes about an occasion that transformed his life. By chance he became obsessed with the notion of reading H. L. Mencken, the iconoclastic editor and essayist. He schemed and plotted to borrow Mencken's books from the library, and when he succeeded, his career as a writer began.*

Determined to be a successful writer, Richard Wright worked on the Federal Writers' Project, wrote for the New Masses, *and finally won a prize from* Story *magazine for a short novel called* Uncle Tom's Children. *The following year, he was awarded a Guggenheim Fellowship, and in 1940 he published his novel* Native Son, *which has become an American classic. In 1946 he emigrated to Paris, where he lived until his death. His later novels include* The Outsider *(1953) and* The Long Dream *(1958). In 1977, his publisher issued the second half of* Black Boy, *entitled* American Hunger.

87

RICHARD WRIGHT
The Library Card

One morning I arrived early at work and went into the bank lobby   1
where the Negro porter was mopping. I stood at a counter and picked
up the Memphis *Commercial Appeal* and began my free reading of the
press. I came finally to the editorial page and saw an article dealing with
one H. L. Mencken. I knew by hearsay that he was the editor of the

American Mercury, but aside from that I knew nothing about him. The article was a furious denunciation of Mencken, concluding with one, hot, short sentence: Mencken is a fool.

2   I wondered what on earth this Mencken had done to call down upon him the scorn of the South. The only people I had ever heard denounced in the South were Negroes, and this man was not a Negro. Then what ideas did Mencken hold that made a newspaper like the *Commercial Appeal* castigate him publicly? Undoubtedly he must be advocating ideas that the South did not like. Were there, then, people other than Negroes who criticized the South? I knew that during the Civil War the South had hated northern whites, but I had not encountered such hate during my life. Knowing no more of Mencken than I did at that moment, I felt a vague sympathy for him. Had not the South, which had assigned me the role of a non-man, cast at him its hardest words?

3   Now, how could I find out about this Mencken? There was a huge library near the riverfront, but I knew that Negroes were not allowed to patronize its shelves any more than they were the parks and playgrounds of the city. I had gone into the library several times to get books for the white men on the job. Which of them would now help me to get books? And how could I read them without causing concern to the white men with whom I worked? I had so far been successful in hiding my thoughts and feelings from them, but I knew that I would create hostility if I went about the business of reading in a clumsy way.

4   I weighed the personalities of the men on the job. There was Don, a Jew; but I distrusted him. His position was not much better than mine and I knew that he was uneasy and insecure; he had always treated me in an offhand, bantering way that barely concealed his contempt. I was afraid to ask him to help me get books; his frantic desire to demonstrate a racial solidarity with the whites against Negroes might make him betray me.

5   Then how about the boss? No, he was a Baptist and I had the suspicion that he would not be quite able to comprehend why a black boy would want to read Mencken. There were other white men on the job whose attitudes showed clearly that they were Kluxers or sympathizers, and they were out of the question.

6   There remained only one man whose attitude did not fit into an anti-Negro category, for I had heard the white men refer to him as a "Pope lover." He was an Irish Catholic and was hated by the white Southerners. I knew that he read books, because I had got him volumes from the library several times. Since he, too, was an object of hatred,

I felt that he might refuse me but would hardly betray me. I hesitated, weighing and balancing the imponderable realities.

One morning I paused before the Catholic fellow's desk. 7

"I want to ask you a favor," I whispered to him. 8

"What is it?" 9

"I want to read. I can't get books from the library. I wonder if you'd let me use your card?" 10

He looked at me suspiciously. 11

"My card is full most of the time," he said. 12

"I see," I said and waited, posing my question silently. 13

"You're not trying to get me into trouble, are you, boy?" he asked, staring at me. 14

"Oh, no, sir." 15

"What book do you want?" 16

"A book by H. L. Mencken." 17

"Which one?" 18

"I don't know. Has he written more than one?" 19

"He has written several." 20

"I didn't know that." 21

"What makes you want to read Mencken?" 22

"Oh, I just saw his name in the newspaper," I said. 23

"It's good of you to want to read," he said. "But you ought to read the right things." 24

I said nothing. Would he want to supervise my reading? 25

"Let me think," he said. "I'll figure out something." 26

I turned from him and he called me back. He stared at me quizzically. 27

"Richard, don't mention this to the other white men," he said. 28

"I understand," I said. "I won't say a word." 29

A few days later he called me to him. 30

"I've got a card in my wife's name," he said. "Here's mine." 31

"Thank you, sir." 32

"Do you think you can manage it?" 33

"I'll manage fine," I said. 34

"If they suspect you, you'll get in trouble," he said. 35

"I'll write the same kind of notes to the library that you wrote when you sent me for books," I told him. "I'll sign your name." 36

He laughed. 37

"Go ahead. Let me see what you get," he said. 38

That afternoon I addressed myself to forging a note. Now, what 39 were the names of books written by H. L. Mencken? I did not know any of them. I finally wrote what I thought would be a foolproof note: *Dear Madam: Will you please let this nigger boy —* I used the word "nigger" to make the librarian feel that I could not possibly be the author of the note — *have some books by H. L. Mencken?* I forged the white man's name.

40   I entered the library as I had always done when on errands for whites, but I felt that I would somehow slip up and betray myself. I doffed my hat, stood a respectful distance from the desk, looked as unbookish as possible, and waited for the white patrons to be taken care of. When the desk was clear of people, I still waited. The white librarian looked at me.

41   "What do you want, boy?"

42   As though I did not possess the power of speech, I stepped forward and simply handed her the forged note, not parting my lips.

43   "What books by Mencken does he want?" she asked.

44   "I don't know, ma'am," I said, avoiding her eyes.

45   "Who gave you this card?"

46   "Mr. Falk," I said.

47   "Where is he?"

48   "He's at work, at the M——— Optical Company," I said. "I've been in here for him before."

49   "I remember," the woman said. "But he never wrote notes like this."

50   Oh, God, she's suspicious. Perhaps she would not let me have the books? If she had turned her back at that moment, I would have ducked out the door and never gone back. Then I thought of a bold idea.

51   "You can call him up, ma'am," I said, my heart pounding.

52   "You're not using these books, are you?" she asked pointedly.

53   "Oh, no, ma'am. I can't read."

54   "I don't know what he wants by Mencken," she said under her breath.

55   I knew now that I had won; she was thinking of other things and the race question had gone out of her mind. She went to the shelves. Once or twice she looked over her shoulder at me, as though she was still doubtful. Finally she came forward with two books in her hand.

56   "I'm sending him two books," she said. "But tell Mr. Falk to come in next time, or send me the names of the books he wants. I don't know what he wants to read."

57   I said nothing. She stamped the card and handed me the books. Not daring to glance at them, I went out of the library, fearing that the woman would call me back for further questioning. A block away from

the library I opened one of the books and read a title: *A Book of Prefaces.*
I was nearing my nineteenth birthday and I did not know how to pronounce the word "preface." I thumbed the pages and saw strange words
and strange names. I shook my head, disappointed. I looked at the other
book; it was called *Prejudices.* I knew what that word meant; I had heard
it all my life. And right off I was on guard against Mencken's books.
Why would a man want to call a book *Prejudices?* The word was so
stained with all my memories of racial hate that I could not conceive
of anybody using it for a title. Perhaps I had made a mistake about Mencken? A man who had prejudices must be wrong.

When I showed the books to Mr. Falk, he looked at me and frowned.   58

"That librarian might telephone you," I warned him.   59

"That's all right," he said. "But when you're through reading those   60
books, I want you to tell me what you get out of them."

That night in my rented room, while letting the hot water run over   61
my can of pork and beans in the sink, I opened *A Book of Prefaces* and
began to read. I was jarred and shocked by the style, the clear, clean
sweeping sentences. Why did he write like that? And how did one write
like that? I pictured the man as a raging demon, slashing with his pen,
consumed with hate, denouncing everything American, extolling
everything European or German, laughing at the weaknesses of people,
mocking God, authority. What was this? I stood up, trying to realize
what reality lay behind the meaning of the words . . . Yes, this man was
fighting, fighting with words. He was using words as a weapon, using
them as one would use a club. Could words be weapons? Well, yes, for
here they were. Then, maybe, perhaps, I could use them as a weapon?
No. It frightened me. I read on and what amazed me was not what he
said, but how on earth anybody had the courage to say it.

Occasionally I glanced up to reassure myself that I was alone in   62
the room. Who were these men about whom Mencken was talking so
passionately? Who was Anatole France? Joseph Conrad? Sinclair Lewis,
Sherwood Anderson, Dostoevski, George Moore, Gustave Flaubert,
Maupassant, Tolstoy, Frank Harris, Mark Twain, Thomas Hardy, Arnold
Bennett, Stephen Crane, Zola, Norris, Gorky, Bergson, Ibsen, Balzac,
Bernard Shaw, Dumas, Poe, Thomas Mann, O. Henry, Dreiser, H. G.
Wells, Gogol, T. S. Eliot, Gide, Baudelaire, Edgar Lee Masters, Stendhal,
Turgenev, Huneker, Nietzsche, and scores of others? Were these men
real? Did they exist or had they existed? And how did one pronounce
their names?

I ran across many words whose meanings I did not know, and I   63
either looked them up in a dictionary or, before I had a chance to do

that, encountered the word in a context that made its meaning clear. But what strange world was this? I concluded the book with the conviction that I had somehow overlooked something terribly important in life. I had once tried to write, had once reveled in feeling, had let my crude imagination roam, but the impulse to dream had been slowly beaten out of me by experience. Now it surged up again and I hungered for books, new ways of looking and seeing. It was not a matter of believing or disbelieving what I read, but of feeling something new, of being affected by something that made the look of the world different.

64   As dawn broke I ate my pork and beans, feeling dopey, sleepy. I went to work, but the mood of the book would not die; it lingered, coloring everything I saw, heard, did. I now felt that I knew what the white men were feeling. Merely because I had read a book that had spoken of how they lived and thought, I identified myself with that book. I felt vaguely guilty. Would I, filled with bookish notions, act in a manner that would make the whites dislike me?

65   I forged more notes and my trips to the library became frequent. Reading grew into a passion. My first serious novel was Sinclair Lewis's *Main Street*. It made me see my boss, Mr. Gerald, and identify him as an American type. I would smile when I saw him lugging his golf bags into the office. I had always felt a vast distance separating me from the boss, and now I felt closer to him, though still distant. I felt now that I knew him, that I could feel the very limits of his narrow life. And this had happened because I had read a novel about a mythical man called George F. Babbitt.

66   The plots and stories in the novels did not interest me so much as the point of view revealed. I gave myself over to each novel without reserve, without trying to criticize it; it was enough for me to see and feel something different. And for me, everything was something different. Reading was like a drug, a dope. The novels created moods in which I lived for days. But I could not conquer my sense of guilt, my feeling that the white men around me knew that I was changing, that I had begun to regard them differently.

67   Whenever I brought a book to the job, I wrapped it in newspaper — a habit that was to persist for years in other cities and under other circumstances. But some of the white men pried into my packages when I was absent and they questioned me.

68   "Boy, what are you reading those books for?"

69   "Oh, I don't know, sir."

70   "That's deep stuff you're reading, boy."

71   "I'm just killing time, sir."

"You'll addle your brains if you don't watch out."   72

I read Dreiser's *Jennie Gerhardt* and *Sister Carrie* and they revived   73
in me a vivid sense of my mother's suffering; I was overwhelmed. I grew
silent, wondering about the life around me. It would have been impossible for me to have told anyone what I derived from these novels, for
it was nothing less than a sense of life itself. All my life had shaped
me for the realism, the naturalism of the modern novel, and I could not
read enough of them.

Steeped in new moods and ideas, I bought a ream of paper and tried   74
to write; but nothing would come, or what did come was flat beyond
telling. I discovered that more than desire and feeling were necessary
to write and I dropped the idea. Yet I still wondered how it was possible
to know people sufficiently to write about them? Could I ever learn
about life and people? To me, with my vast ignorance, my Jim Crow
station in life, it seemed a task impossible of achievement. I now knew
what being a Negro meant. I could endure the hunger. I had learned to
live with hate. But to feel that there were feelings denied me, that the
very breadth of life itself was beyond my reach, that more than anything
else hurt, wounded me. I had a new hunger.

In buoying me up, reading also cast me down, made me see what   75
was possible, what I had missed. My tension returned, new, terrible,
bitter, surging, almost too great to be contained. I no longer *felt* that
the world about me was hostile, killing; I *knew* it. A million times I
asked myself what I could do to save myself, and there were no answers.
I seemed forever condemned, ringed by walls.

I did not discuss my reading with Mr. Falk, who had lent me his   76
library card; it would have meant talking about myself and that would
have been too painful. I smiled each day, fighting desperately to maintain my old behavior, to keep my disposition seemingly sunny. But some
of the white men discerned that I had begun to brood.

"Wake up there, boy!" Mr. Olin said one day.   77

"Sir!" I answered for the lack of a better word.   78

"You act like you've stolen something," he said.   79

I laughed in the way I knew he expected me to laugh, but I resolved   80
to be more conscious of myself, to watch my every act, to guard and
hide the new knowledge that was dawning within me.

If I went north, would it be possible for me to build a new life then?   81
But how could a man build a life upon vague, unformed yearnings? I
wanted to write and I did not even know the English language. I bought
English grammars and found them dull. I felt that I was getting a better
sense of the language from novels than from grammars. I read hard,

discarding a writer as soon as I felt that I had grasped his point of view. At night the printed page stood before my eyes in sleep.

82   Mrs. Moss, my landlady, asked me one Sunday morning:

83   "Son, what is this you keep on reading?"

84   "Oh, nothing. Just novels."

85   "What you get out of 'em?"

86   "I'm just killing time," I said.

87   "I hope you know your own mind," she said in a tone which implied that she doubted if I had a mind.

88   I knew of no Negroes who read the books I liked and I wondered if any Negroes ever thought of them. I knew that there were Negro doctors, lawyers, newspapermen, but I never saw any of them. When I read a Negro newspaper I never caught the faintest echo of my preoccupation in its pages. I felt trapped and occasionally, for a few days, I would stop reading. But a vague hunger would come over me for books, books that opened up new avenues of feeling and seeing, and again I would forge another note to the white librarian. Again I would read and wonder as only the naïve and unlettered can read and wonder, feeling that I carried a secret, criminal burden about with me each day.

89   That winter my mother and brother came and we set up housekeeping, buying furniture on the installment plan, being cheated and yet knowing no way to avoid it. I began to eat warm food and to my surprise found that regular meals enabled me to read faster. I may have lived through many illnesses and survived them, never suspecting that I was ill. My brother obtained a job and we began to save toward the trip north, plotting our time, setting tentative dates for departure. I told none of the white men on the job that I was planning to go north; I knew that the moment they felt I was thinking of the North they would change toward me. It would have made them feel that I did not like the life I was living, and because my life was completely conditioned by what they said or did, it would have been tantamount to challenging them.

90   I could calculate my chances for life in the South as a Negro fairly clearly now.

91   I could fight the southern whites by organizing with other Negroes, as my grandfather had done. But I knew that I could never win that way; there were many whites and there were but few blacks. They were strong and we were weak. Outright black rebellion could never win. If I fought openly I would die and I did not want to die. News of lynchings were frequent.

92   I could submit and live the life of a genial slave, but that was impossible. All my life had shaped me to live by my own feelings, and

thoughts. I could make up to Bess and marry her and inherit the house. But that, too, would be the life of a slave; if I did that, I would crush to death something within me, and I would hate myself as much as I knew the whites already hated those who had submitted. Neither could I ever willingly present myself to be kicked, as Shorty had done. I would rather have died than do that.

I could drain off my restlessness by fighting with Shorty and Harrison. I had seen many Negroes solve the problem of being black by transferring their hatred of themselves to others with a black skin and fighting them. I would have to be cold to do that, and I was not cold and I could never be. 93

I could, of course, forget what I had read, thrust the whites out of my mind, forget them; and find release from anxiety and longing in sex and alcohol. But the memory of how my father had conducted himself made that course repugnant. If I did not want others to violate my life, how could I voluntarily violate it myself? 94

I had no hope whatever of being a professional man. Not only had I been so conditioned that I did not desire it, but the fulfillment of such an ambition was beyond my capabilities. Well-to-do Negroes lived in a world that was almost as alien to me as the world inhabited by whites. 95

What, then, was there? I held my life in my mind, in my consciousness each day, feeling at times that I would stumble and drop it, spill it forever. My reading had created a vast sense of distance between me and the world in which I lived and tried to make a living, and that sense of distance was increasing each day. My days and nights were one long, quiet, continuously contained dream of terror, tension, and anxiety. I wondered how long I could bear it. 96

_____ CONSIDERATIONS _____

1. How do you heat a can of beans if you don't have a hot plate or a stove? How is Wright's answer to this question an autobiographical fact that might affect your appreciation of his essay?

2. In Paragraph 65, Wright says of himself, "Reading grew into a passion." You don't have to look too far in the lives of other writers to find similar statements about reading. Reread the first paragraph of the Preface to this book, and think about the importance of reading to your prospects of improving as a writer. See also Ralph Ellison's "On Becoming a Writer" (pages 153–160).

3. Compare what Wright had to endure to use the public library with your own introduction to the same institution. How do you account for the motivation Wright needed to break the barriers between him and freedom to read?

4. The word Wright uses throughout to refer to his own race is no longer widely accepted. Why? What other words have been used at other times in American history? What difference does a name make?

5. Notice how Wright uses dialogue in this essay. How do you decide when to use dialogue? What are its purposes?

6. The authors mentioned by Wright in his essay would make a formidable reading program for anyone. If you were to lay out such a program for yourself, what titles would you include? Why?

A Rhetorical Index

The various writing patterns—argument and persuasion, description, exposition, and narration—are amply illustrated in the many essays, stories, journal entries, and poems in *A Writer's Reader*. If any classification of writing according to type is suspect—because good writers inevitably merge the types—this index offers one plausible arrangement. Anyone looking for models or examples for study and imitation may well begin here.

A word about subcategories: We index two sorts of argument—formal and implicit—because some selections are obvious attempts to defend a stated proposition, often in high style, whereas others argue indirectly, informally, or diffusely, but persuasively nonetheless. Under "Description" we index not only whole selections, but also sections within selections that primarily describe persons, places, or miscellaneous phenomena. We call "Expository" selections those that clearly show the various rhetorical patterns of development: example, classification, cause and effect, comparison and contrast, process analysis, and definition. Again, both whole selections and separate paragraphs are listed. "Narration" categorizes memoirs, essays, stories, and nonfiction nonautobiographical narratives.

We have starred short selections (under 1,200 words). Numbers in parentheses refer to paragraph numbers within selections. At the end, we list the non-essay materials in the *Reader*—journal entries, short stories, poems, and drama.

ARGUMENT AND PERSUASION

Formal, Overt
ABBEY, *Science with a Human Face*, 1–7
ATWOOD, *Pornography*, 40–46
BIRD, *Where College Fails Us*, 79–89

DESCRIPTION

EXPOSITION

Analogy (see Comparison, Contrast, Analogy)

Cause and Effect

Classification and Division

NARRATION

JOURNALS, DIARIES, NOTEBOOKS, SHORT TAKES

SHORT STORIES

POEMS

DRAMA

A Thematic Index

BIOGRAPHY, AUTOBIOGRAPHY, TRUE STORIES

CHILDHOOD, GROWING UP, RITES OF PASSAGE

CONTESTS, STRUGGLES, WINS AND LOSSES

EDUCATION, THE GETTING OF WISDOM

EPIPHANY, IMAGINATION, VISION

FAMILIES, PARENTS AND OFFSPRING

FREEDOM AND RESTRAINT, OPPRESSORS AND OPPRESSED

HEROES, LEADERS, PERFORMERS

HISTORY, THE POWER OF THE PAST

HUMOR, WIT, SATIRE

THE IMPORTANCE OF PLACE, "ROOTS"

NATURE, ENVIRONMENT, WONDERS OF CREATION

PLAY, GAMES, SPORTING LIFE

REBELS AND CONFORMISTS

RELIGION, GOD, FAITH, SPIRITUAL LIFE

SCIENTIFIC INQUIRY AND DISCOVERY

THE SOCIAL FABRIC, GOVERNMENT, FAMILY OF MAN

WORKING

WRITING, LANGUAGE, RHETORIC, AND STYLE

To the Student

Part of our job as educational publishers is to try to improve the textbooks we publish. Thus, when revising we take into account the experience of both instructors and students with the previous edition. At some time in the future your instructor will be asked to comment extensively on *A Writer's Reader*, Fifth Edition, but right now we want to hear from you. After all, although your instructor assigned this book, you are the one for whom it is intended (and the one who paid for it).

Please help us by completing this questionnaire and returning it to College Division, Scott, Foresman/Little, Brown, 34 Beacon Street, Boston, MA 02108.

School _____ Course Title _____

Instructor's Name _____

Other Books Assigned _____

Tell us about the readings.

	KEEP	DROP	DID NOT READ
ABBEY, *Science with a Human Face*	____	____	____
ADAMS, *Winter and Summer*	____	____	____
AGEE, *Knoxville, Summer 1915*	____	____	____
ALLEN, *Death Knocks*	____	____	____
ANGELOU, *Mr. Red Leg*	____	____	____
ASHER, *On the Road with the College Applicant*	____	____	____

	KEEP	DROP	DID NOT READ
ATWOOD, *Pornography*	___	___	___
BACON, *The Sphinx*	___	___	___
BALDWIN, *Autobiographical Notes*	___	___	___
BERGER, *Her Secrets*	___	___	___
BERRY, *A Native Hill*	___	___	___
BIERCE, *Some Devil's Definitions*	___	___	___
BIRD, *Where College Fails Us*	___	___	___
BLOUNT, *How to Raise Your Boys to Play Pro Ball*	___	___	___
BRESLIN, *Dies the Victim, Dies the City*	___	___	___
CATTON, *Grant and Lee . . .*	___	___	___
CHENEY, *Students of Success*	___	___	___
CONNELL, *A Brief Essay on the Subject of Celebrity with Numerous Digressions and Particular Attention to the Actress, Rita Hayworth*	___	___	___
CONROY, *A Yo-Yo Going Down*	___	___	___
DICKINSON, *There's a certain Slant of light*	___	___	___
DIDION, *On Keeping a Notebook*	___	___	___
DILLARD, *Strangers to Darkness*	___	___	___
DILLARD, *Sojourner*	___	___	___
DOUGLASS, *Plantation Life*	___	___	___
EISELEY, *More Thoughts on Wilderness*	___	___	___
ELLISON, *On Becoming a Writer*	___	___	___
EPHRON, *A Few Words about Breasts*	___	___	___
FAULKNER, *A Rose for Emily*	___	___	___
FROST, *Design*	___	___	___
FROST, *In White*	___	___	___
FROST, *The Figure a Poem Makes*	___	___	___
GANSBERG, *38 Who Saw Murder . . .*	___	___	___
GOULD, *The Politics of Census*	___	___	___
HELLMAN, *Runaway*	___	___	___
HEMINGWAY, *Hills Like White Elephants*	___	___	___
HOAGLAND, *What I Think, What I Am*	___	___	___
HUGHES, *Salvation*	___	___	___
HUGHES, *Two Poems*	___	___	___
JEFFERSON, *The Declarations . . .*	___	___	___

	KEEP	DROP	DID NOT READ
KNIGHT, *The Idea of Ancestry*	____	____	____
LAKOFF, *You Are What You Say*	____	____	____
LINCOLN, *The Gettysburg Address*	____	____	____
LOPEZ, *The Stone Horse*	____	____	____
MACHIAVELLI, *How a Prince Should Keep His Word*	____	____	____
MARKHAM, *He Was a Good Lion*	____	____	____
MARVELL, *To His Coy Mistress*	____	____	____
OATES, *On Boxing*	____	____	____
O'CONNOR, *The Total Effect and the Eighth Grade*	____	____	____
O'CONNOR, *A Good Man Is Hard to Find*	____	____	____
O'CONNOR, *From Flannery O'Connor's Letters*	____	____	____
ORWELL, *Politics and the English Language*	____	____	____
ORWELL, *Shooting an Elephant*	____	____	____
ORWELL, *A Hanging*	____	____	____
PERÉNYI, *Partly Cloudy*	____	____	____
PLATH, *Journal Entries . . .*	____	____	____
PLATH, *The Bee Meeting*	____	____	____
QUAMMEN, *The Big Goodbye*	____	____	____
RAYMO, *Dinosaurs and Creationists*	____	____	____
RETTIE, *"But A Watch in the Night"*	____	____	____
RILKE, *On Love*	____	____	____
SAGAN, *Nuclear Winter*	____	____	____
SHELLENBARGER, *Selling Off the Family Farm*	____	____	____
SILKO, *Slim Man Canyon*	____	____	____
SHAKESPEARE, *That time of year . . .*	____	____	____
SHARP, *Under the Hood*	____	____	____
SMITH, *The New Abolitionism*	____	____	____
STAFFORD, *A Way of Writing*	____	____	____
STAFFORD, *Traveling Through the Dark*	____	____	____
SWIFT, *A Modest Proposal*	____	____	____
TERKEL, *Phil Stallings, Spot Welder*	____	____	____
THOMAS, *The Iks*	____	____	____
THOREAU, *June 16, 1854*	____	____	____

	KEEP	DROP	DID NOT READ
THOREAU, *June 17, 1854*	_____	_____	_____
THOREAU, *October 12, 1857*	_____	_____	_____
THOREAU, *November 30, 1858*	_____	_____	_____
THURBER, *Which*	_____	_____	_____
UPDIKE, *Ace in the Hole*	_____	_____	_____
VIDAL, *Drugs*	_____	_____	_____
WALKER, *The Black Writer and the Southern Experience*	_____	_____	_____
WELTY, *A Worn Path*	_____	_____	_____
WELTY, *The Point of the Story*	_____	_____	_____
WELTY, *The Baby Question*	_____	_____	_____
WHITE, *Once More to the Lake*	_____	_____	_____
WHITE, *Editorial*	_____	_____	_____
WILL, *Exploring the Racer's Edge*	_____	_____	_____
WOOLF, *If Shakespeare Had Had a Sister*	_____	_____	_____
WRIGHT, *The Library Card*	_____	_____	_____

Did you use the Rhetorical and Thematic Indexes? _____

How might they be improved? _____

_____

_____

Were the Introductions and Considerations that accompany each selec-

tion helpful? _____ How might they be improved? _____

_____

_____

Should we add more stories and poems? _____

Please add any further comments or suggestions. _____

_____

Date _____ Your Name _____

Mailing Address